THE ART OF CEREMONY

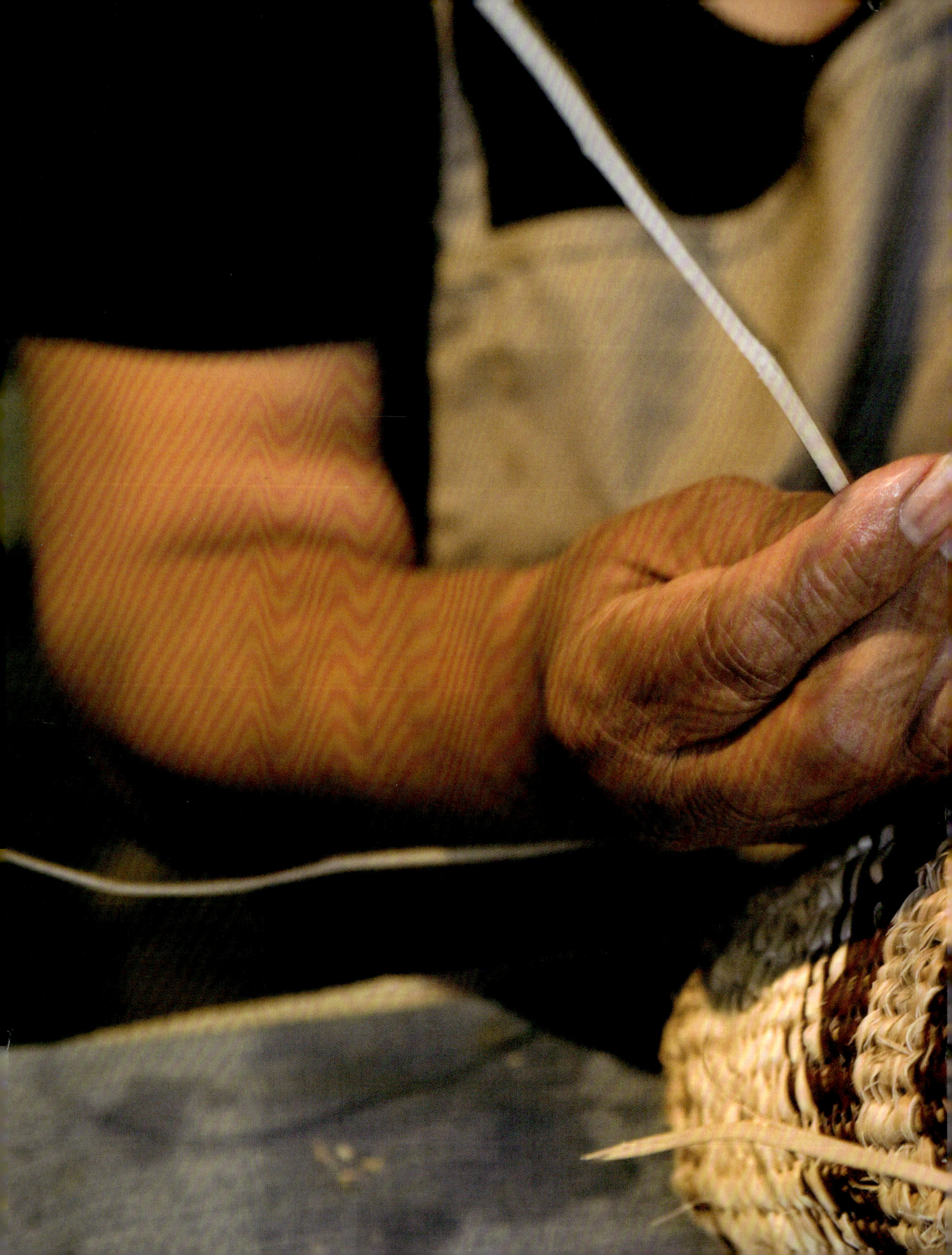

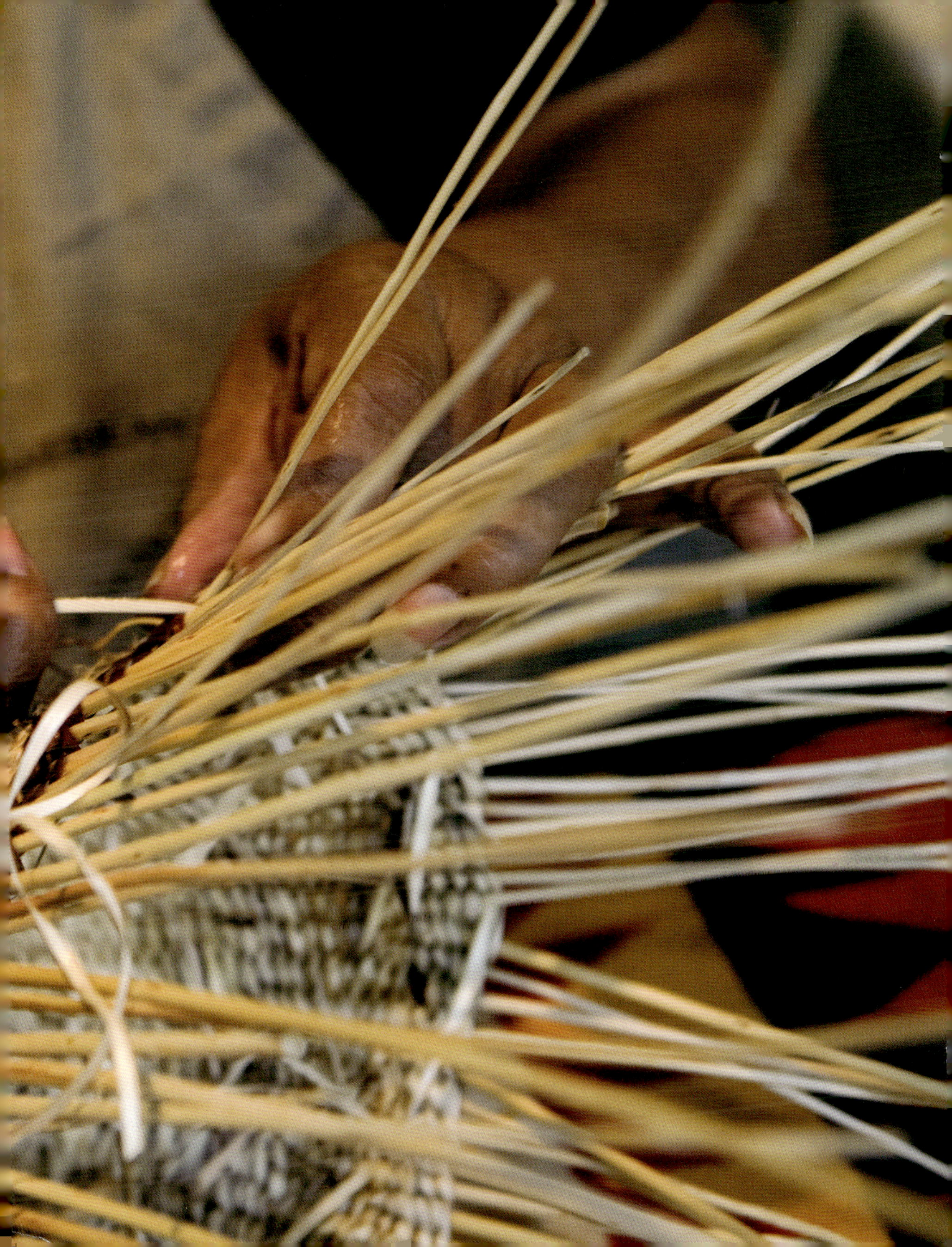

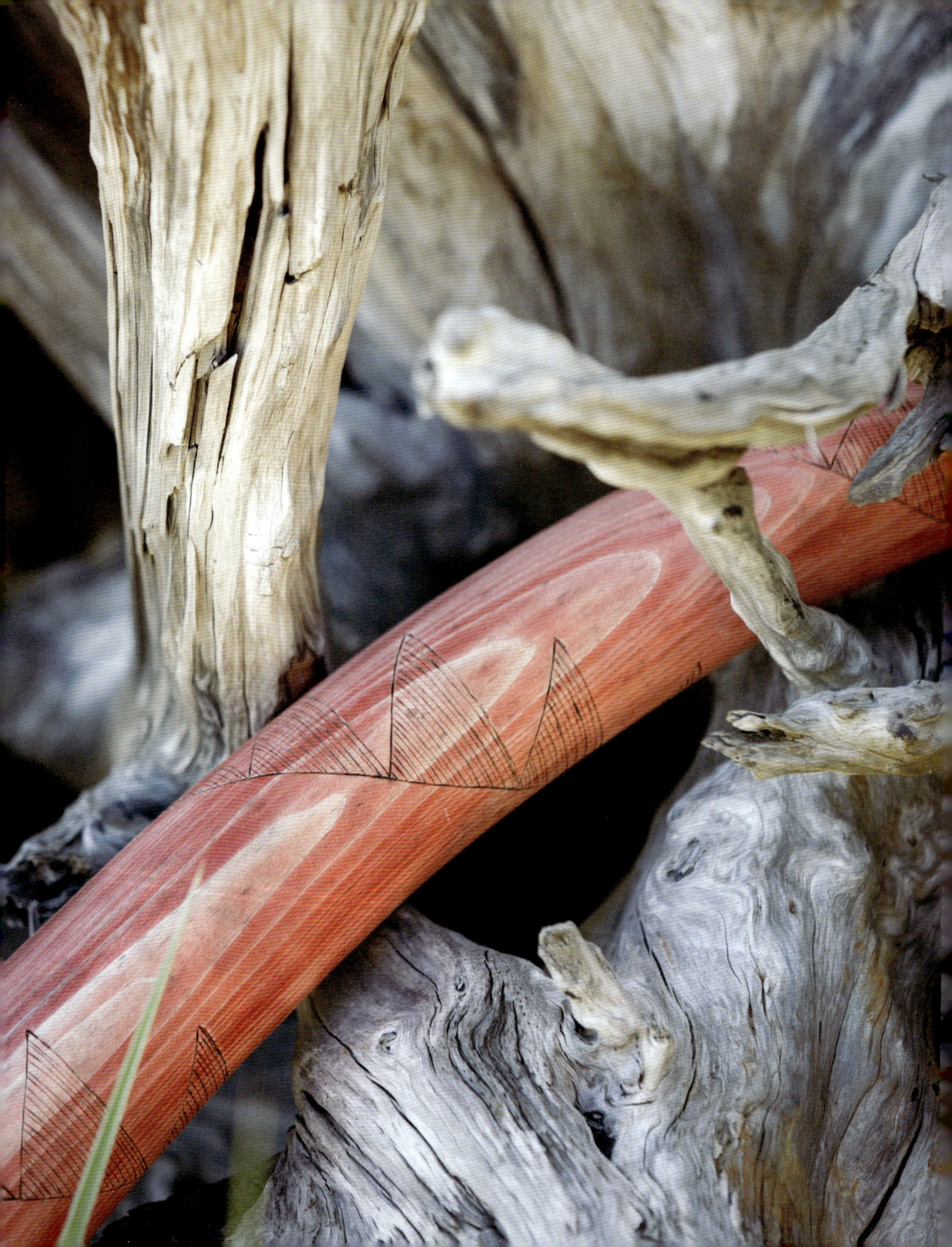

THE ART of CEREMONY

Voices of Renewal from Indigenous Oregon

REBECCA J. DOBKINS

Foreword by Alfred "Bud" Lane III

Afterword by Roberta "Bobbie" Conner

University of Washington Press · *Seattle*

JACOB LAWRENCE SERIES ON AMERICAN ARTISTS
The Art of Ceremony was supported by a grant from the Jacob Lawrence Endowment, established through the generosity of Jacob Lawrence, Gwendolyn Knight, and other donors.

A HELEN MARIE RYAN WYMAN BOOK
Helen Marie Ryan Wyman was intelligent, curious, and gregarious; she took great stock in books and reading, and books abounded in her life. The Wyman family is proud to sponsor this book in Native American and Indigenous studies in her name.

The Art of Ceremony was made possible in part by a generous gift from Suzanne Ragen, in memory of Brooks Ragen.

This book was also supported by grants from the Hugh and Jane Ferguson Foundation and the Tulalip Tribes Charitable Fund, which provides the opportunity for a sustainable and healthy community for all.

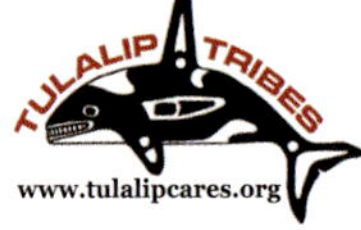

Portions of the introduction are adapted from Rebecca Dobkins, "Life Stories for New Generations: The Living Art of Oregon Tribal Regalia," in *Oregon Historical Quarterly* (September 2009): 420–39.

Design by M. Wright

Composed in Warnock Pro, typeface designed by Robert Slimbach

26   25   24   23   22   5   4   3   2   1

Printed and bound in China

UNIVERSITY OF WASHINGTON PRESS
uwapress.uw.edu

Library of Congress Cataloging-in-Publication Data

Names: Dobkins, Rebecca J., author, photographer.
Title: The art of ceremony : voices of renewal from Indigenous Oregon / Rebecca J. Dobkins.
Description: Seattle : University of Washington Press, [2022] | Includes bibliographical references and index.
Identifiers: LCCN 2021056895 (print) | LCCN 2021056896 (ebook) | ISBN 9780295750309 (hardcover: alk. paper) | ISBN 9780295750668 (paperback) | ISBN 9780295750316 (ebook)
Subjects: LCSH: Indians of North America—Oregon—Rites and ceremonies. | Indians of North America—Oregon—Social life and customs.
Classification: LCC E78.O6 D63 2022 (print) | LCC E78.O6 (ebook) | DDC 979.004/97—dc23/eng/20220103
LC record available at https://lccn.loc.gov/2021056895
LC ebook record available at https://lccn.loc.gov/2021056896
⊗ This paper meets the requirements of ANSI/NISO Z39.48-1992 (Permanence of Paper).

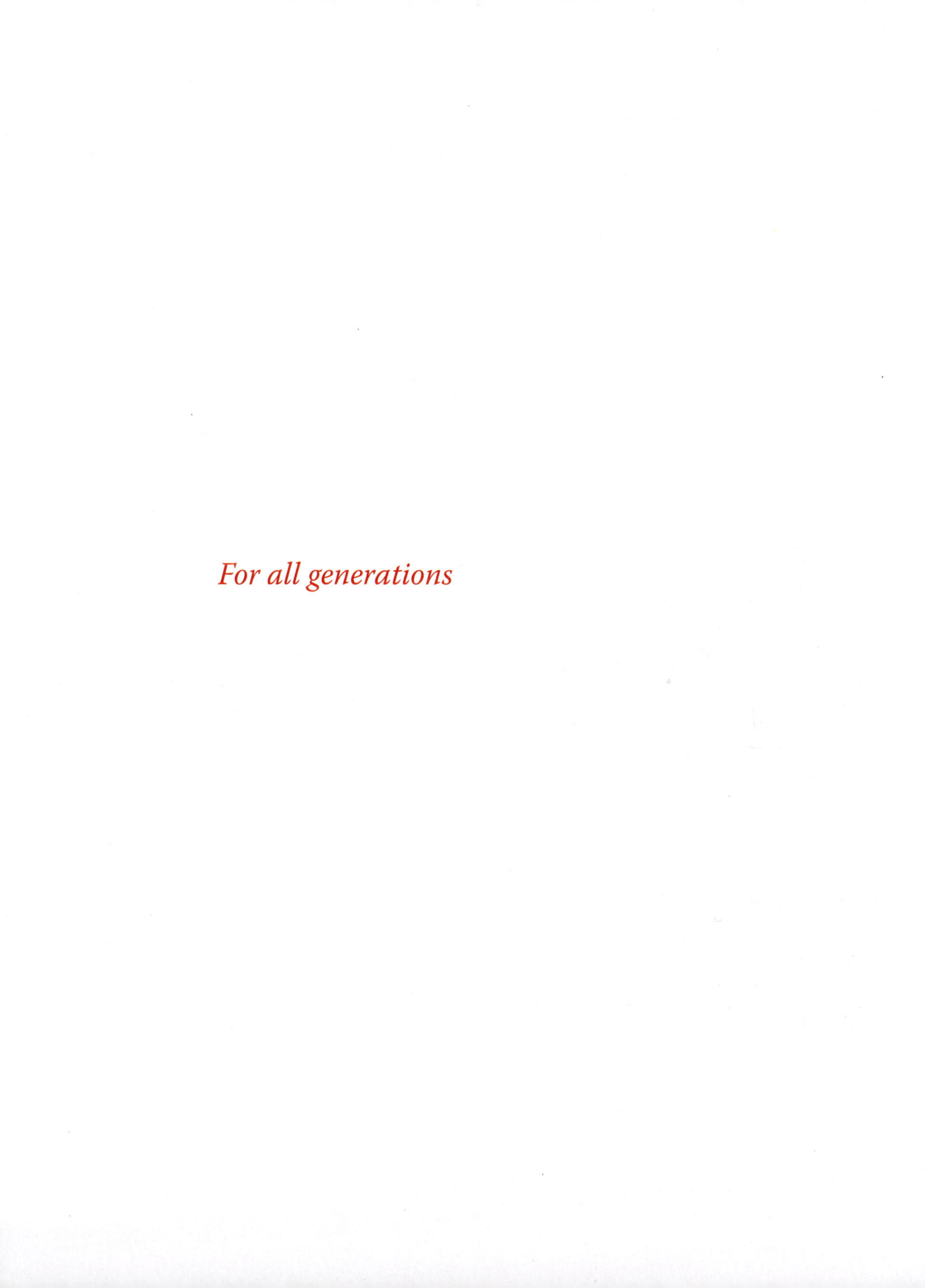

For all generations

CONTENTS

FOREWORD

Alfred "Bud" Lane III

Vice Chair, Confederated Tribes of Siletz Indians

I first crossed paths with Rebecca Dobkins in 1997. She had just joined the faculty at Willamette University in Salem, Oregon, and wanted to meet Native artists in the area. She called me to make arrangements and came out to Siletz (about eighty miles from Salem). We had a really nice visit and discussed the Siletz Tribe's culture and the arts. I had no idea that short visit would lead to collaborations and events that would change our lives.

The Art of Ceremony: Voices of Renewal from Indigenous Oregon is a beautifully written and illustrated examination of the regalia of the first peoples in Oregon and the ceremonies in which it functions. Dobkins does a wonderful job in portraying each ceremony through the lens of the practitioners and participants. It is extremely rare for an academic to gain such unfettered access. It shows the level of trust that Native peoples in Oregon have in her and her approach to Native arts and other issues.

The concept for *The Art of Ceremony* grew out of an earlier exhibit at Willamette's Hallie Ford Museum of Art. Dobkins was a central figure in *The Eternal Thread*, an exhibit from New Zealand featuring a wide array of Māori arts. *The Eternal Thread* opened in 2005, and Dobkins had traveled to New Zealand the prior year to plan with Toi Māori (the National Māori Arts Organization) its venue at the Hallie Ford. Those plans included the participation of the Tribes in Oregon with the different teams of Māori artists that came to the Northwest for each venue. It was from that participation and interaction that the seed for the exhibition *The Art of Ceremony: Regalia of Native Oregon* was planted. The only art exhibit I am aware of that featured some of the ceremonies and works from all of the nine federally recognized Tribes in Oregon, *The Art of Ceremony*, opened at the Hallie Ford Museum of Art and began its journey on September 27, 2008. It went on to Pendleton, Oregon (Tamástslikt Cultural Institute), Warm Springs, Oregon (The Museum at Warm Springs), and ended at the Oregon Historical Society in Portland.

In this book Dobkins tells the story of ceremony and traditions through the tribal voice. Our oral histories tell us that our peoples have been here since the beginning of time. Our ceremonies are our way of thanking the Creator for creating our world and us. Dobkins has worked for many years with the Native peoples in Oregon and beyond, and she has earned our trust and friendship. *The Art of Ceremony: Voices of Renewal from Indigenous Oregon* contains much about us, a rare view into the ceremonial life of Native Oregon.

ACKNOWLEDGMENTS

This book represents the extraordinary efforts of many individuals
and organizations over many years. As explained in the introduction,
its foundation was an exhibition titled *The Art of Ceremony: Regalia
of Native Oregon* that originated at the Hallie Ford Museum of Art at
Willamette University in 2008. I appreciate the many people who gave
generously of their time and knowledge to make both the exhibition
and the book *The Art of Ceremony: Voices of Renewal from Indigenous
Oregon* a success. Some of those named below have passed since this
project began and I wish especially to acknowledge their contributions.
My hope is that this book will honor their work and lives. I apologize for
any omissions or errors, and I am ultimately responsible for the interpretations presented here.

I thank all the community curators associated with each of the nine
federally recognized Tribes in Oregon who served as key advisers to
the exhibition and book project: the late Minerva Teeman Soucie,
Diane Teeman (Burns Paiute); Jesse Beers, Margaret Corvi, Courtney
Krossman, Sue Perry Olson, David Petrie (Confederated Tribes of
Coos, Lower Umpqua, and Siuslaw Indians); Denni Hockema, Brenda
Meade, Lyman Meade (Coquille Indian Tribe); Louis LaChance, Rhonda
Richardson, Michael Rondeau, Sherri Shaffer (Cow Creek Band of
Umpqua Tribe of Indians); Tony Johnson (Chinook Nation); Bobby

Mercier, members of the Grand Ronde and Chinook Canoe Families, Lindy Trolan (Confederated Tribes of the Grand Ronde Community of Oregon); Perry Chocktoot, Gerald Skelton (Klamath Tribes); Robert Kentta, Alfred "Bud" Lane III, Alfred "Buddy" Lane IV, Alissa Lane, Cheryl Lane (Confederated Tribes of Siletz Indians); Roberta "Bobbie" Conner, Dallas Dick, Randall Melton, Malissa Minthorn-Winks, Susan Sheoships, Marjorie Waheneka (Tamástslikt Cultural Institute, Confederated Tribes of the Umatilla Indian Reservation); and Carol Leone, Natalie Moody, atwai Evaline Patt, Rosalind Sampson, Elizabeth Woody (The Museum at Warm Springs, Confederated Tribes of Warm Springs). I am deeply grateful to Alfred "Bud" Lane III for his friendship and guidance over the years and for writing the foreword. I'm profoundly thankful to Roberta "Bobbie" Conner for writing the afterword and for her brilliant intellect, whose imprint is all over this book. The staff of the Office of Indian Education in the Oregon Department of Education, April Campbell, Ramona Halcomb, Trinity Minihan, and Deleana Otherbull, graciously read through the entire manuscript and generously contributed a Reflection. I am so appreciative of the work all these remarkable people do every day.

In addition, I thank the following individuals and families who contributed their knowledge by participating in interviews and other conversations that informed this book: Doug Barrett, Brenda Brainard, Courtney Krossman, Patricia Whereat Phillips, Ashley Russell, John Schaefer, Sara Siestreem, Don "Doc" Slyter (Confederated Tribes of Coos, Lower Umpqua, and Siuslaw Indians); Anne Burnette Niblett, the late Don Ivy, Shirod Younker (Coquille Indian Tribe); the late Del "Red Hawk" Ansures, Elaine Davis, Larry Davis, Elizabeth (Beth) Gipson, Cindy Delay Grizzle, Mary Dumont Howren, the late Charles "Chuck" Jackson, Clara Young Keller, the late Clementine Young Rice, Michael Rondeau, Sherry Shaffer, the late Ralph Young (Cow Creek Band of Umpqua Indians); Kathryn Harrison, Cristina Lara, Lisa Leno, Bob Tom (Confederated Tribes of the Grand Ronde Community of Oregon); Don Gentry, Jeff Mitchell, Taylor R. Tupper (Klamath Tribes); Dee Pigsley (Confederated Tribes of Siletz Indians); John Bevis, Phillip Cash Cash, Atway Alphonse Halfmoon, Linda Jones, Les Minthorn, Toby Patrick, Lona Pond, Dr. Ronald Pond, Marjorie Waheneka, Ramona Yeager (Confederated Tribes of the Umatilla Indian Reservation); and Rosalind

(Rosie) Johnson, Rayann Katchia Satanus, Brigette McConville (Confederated Tribes of the Warm Springs Reservation). I also thank Donna Fields (Cow Creek Band of Umpqua Indians) and Bridgett Wheeler (Coquille Indian Tribe) for their help in getting the book to its final stages.

I thank all the artists who created the regalia as well as the individuals and families who generously loaned their most precious treasures for the exhibition, thus inspiring so many people: Duane Alderman, Steve Allely, Victor Bates, John Bevis, Gladys Bolton, Jenn Branting, Kitzen Branting, Laura Bremner, Heather Butler, Lillie Butler, Reggie Butler Sr., Reggie Butler Jr., Perry Chocktoot, Joan Deroko, Cindy Elbert, Frank Gist Jr., the Grand Ronde and Chinook Canoe Families, Betty and Eric Hawley and the family of Agnes Benning Hawley, Phillip and Clara Hawks, Margie Houston, the Tony and Mechele Johnson family, Robert Kentta, Brian Krehbiel, Louis LaChance, Alfred "Bud" Lane III, Alissa Lane, Kelly Laura, Molly Leno, Carol Lindhorse, Nan MacDoald, Jackie Many Hides, Bradley Marshall, Deborah McConnell, Brenda Meade, Lyman Meade, Sarah Meade, Bobby Mercier, Les Minthorn, Mavis Oard, Sue Perry Olson, Red Man, Arlissa Rhoan, Mitzi Shoemake, Gerald D. Skelton, the late Minerva Soucie, Crystal Szczepanski, Courtney Terry, and Vi Wasamundt.

I thank all those who shared their artistic practice with the public and with one another during the exhibition's tenure and thus contributed to conversations about regalia-making and the art of ceremony, including many of those already named as well as the following: Sara Barton, Judy Berg, Beth Coahran, Amelia Colwash, Gloria Doughty, the late Connie Graves, Merle Kirk, Roberta Kirk, Karen Nisson, Olivia Wallulatum, and Fred Wallulatum.

I give thanks to the individuals and families who have donated objects to The Museum at Warm Springs that were included in the original *Art of Ceremony* exhibition: Susan Coronado, Harrison Davis, Larry Dick, Pauline Hoptowit, Geraldine Jim, Catherine Katchia, Ursula Little, Adeline Miller, Harry Miller, Marena Miller, Robert Miller, Art Mitchell, Bernice Mitchell, Elfrieda Mitchell, Rose Mitchell, Robert Ogle, Arlita Rhoan, Beatrice Scott, Wilma Scott, Norma Smith, Ada Sooksoit, Eileen Spino, the Brian Stovall Collection, Phyllis Strong, Davis Stwyer, Pat Tanewasha, Yvonne Tapedo, Emma Telakish, Loretta Tewee, Caroline Tohet, Ina Tohet, Grant Waheneka, Virgil Windyboy, and Josie Wolfe.

I also thank the individuals and families who have donated objects to the Tamástslikt Cultural Institute that were included in the exhibition: B. F. Bowman, Les Minthorn, William and Vivian Minthorn, and Malissa Minthorn.

The photographs in this book are an enormous part of its power. In particular, Frank Miller, who was Willamette University's staff photographer from 2002 to 2020, was an essential part of this effort over many years. I am tremendously grateful to him and to all the photographers who have contributed work: Michelle Alaimo, Joel Davis, Micah Fischer, Dave Fullerton, the late Don Ivy, Jonathon Ivy, Alissa Lane, Douglas Manger, Toby McClary, Peter Murphy, Anne Burnette Niblett, Dale Peterson, Rhonda Richardson, Ashley Russell, John Schaefer, Sara Siestreem, Christopher Tanner, Taylor R. Tupper, and Patrice Hall Walters.

The staff of the Hallie Ford Museum of Art at Willamette University has been foundational to this entire project, and I cannot express my thanks enough for the teamwork and camaraderie we share. I especially thank director John Olbrantz, who never hesitated to say "yes" to almost anything. In addition, my gratitude goes to Jonathan Bucci, the late David Andersen (who we lost far too early in 2017), Elizabeth Garrison, Leslie Whitaker, and all the students who worked on phases of this project over the years, especially Stephanie Brown, Rachael Lew, Madelyn Malone, Rachel Mayer, and Emily Schmierer. Conservator Tom Fuller played an essential role in caring for much of the regalia that was included in and photographed for the exhibition.

The University of Washington Press staff has been beyond patient and supportive of this entire endeavor. Larin McLaughlin, Neecole Bostick, and Joeth Zucco were vital guides and cheerleaders in the final phases of the book. Regan Huff, formerly of UW Press, was the first editor with whom I worked, and I doubt I would have felt able to even begin such an ambitious project if it were not for her encouragement. Copy editors Nick Allison and Sigrid Asmus played crucial roles as manuscript wranglers, over a period of years, and I am so grateful for their support. Many thanks also to copy editor Amy Smith Bell, indexer Chris Dodge, and book designer M. Wright for bringing this work to light. In addition, I thank the anonymous readers who reviewed the book while in manuscript form; their care and professional engagement with this work improved it significantly.

The preparation of this book was supported by a Cultural Development Grant from the Oregon Cultural Trust in 2015–2016 and, from Willamette University, a grant from the Center for the Study of Religion, Law, and Democracy in 2012–2013 and sabbatical leaves in 2015 and 2019. An Earle A. Chiles Award in 2012, given by the High Desert Museum, offered resources that launched this book's early stages. The 2008 exhibition from which this project grew was supported by the National Endowment for the Arts American Masterpieces grant, awarded by the Oregon Arts Commission, and additional funds came from an endowment gift to the Hallie Ford Museum of Art by the Confederated Tribes of Grand Ronde through their Spirit Mountain Community Fund, and by grants from the Siletz Tribal Charitable Fund, the city of Salem's Transient Occupancy Tax funds, the Oregon Arts Commission, the William and Flora Hewlett Foundation, and a Millicent C. McIntosh Fellowship from the Woodrow Wilson Foundation.

Finally, at the core, is my family, born and chosen, including those who have passed but who live through memory. I am grateful every day for the gift of my late parents R. E. and Betty Brooke Dobkins, my late brother Brooke Dobkins, sisters Susan and Louise Dobkins and Eve Ash and their families, my son Elijah Dobkins, and for Francesca Freccero. Close colleagues at Willamette have been more support than they will ever know, especially my "sabbatical gang" of Jade Aguilar, Jonneke Koomen, and Courtney Stevens, and my extended family of Vincent Pham, Yaejoon Kwon, Jovin Pham-Kwon, and Omari Weekes. Carol Murdock arrived just at the perfect time, in the final laps. The members of the Native American Advisory Council at Willamette as well as the family of scholars associated with the Native American Art Studies Association have been vital to my intellectual and personal well-being over the past several decades. The "Fellowship of the Rim"—the whanau (*family*) of artists and cultural workers involved in the Pacific Rim international Indigenous exchanges—deserve rich thanks for all the ways they have made the world a more beautiful place. I give special thanks to Lillian Pitt and Darcy Nicholas for connecting so many of us and to the late Waana Davis for her visionary leadership. To all, my deepest gratitude.

NOTE TO READER

Indigenous language words are presented in roman (regular) font followed by an English translation. This choice centers the Indigenous term for the concept or artwork and presents the English term as the foreign translation of the original meaning. When an Indigenous term is used as a title for an artwork or object, as in *Stank'iya*, the canoe of the Grand Ronde Canoe Family, it is capitalized and italicized in the same way an English-language title is. Following current conventions in tribal press and correspondence, the word "Tribe" is capitalized and the singular or plural may be used when referring to a specific tribe or confederation of tribes, dependent upon local usage. When reference is made collectively to the nine federally recognized Tribes in Oregon, "Tribes" is capitalized.

THE ART OF CEREMONY

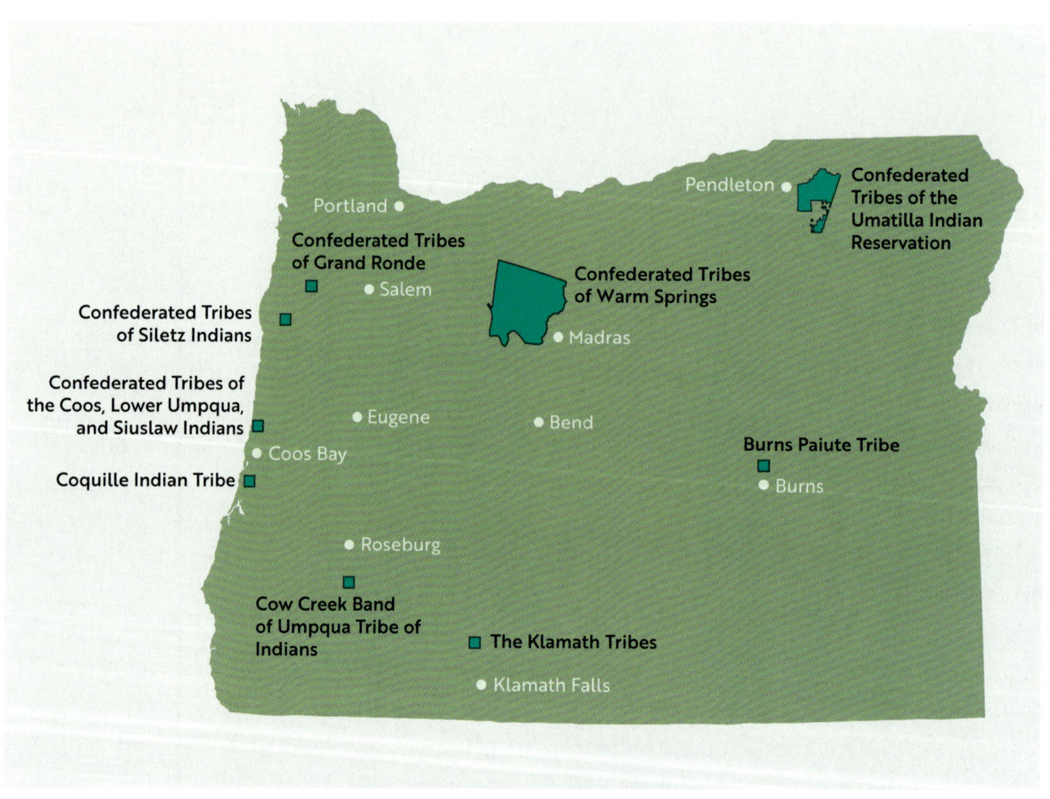

Federally recognized tribes and reservations in Oregon, 2022. Locations are approximate; for detailed land base and ancestral territory information, see the website of each tribe or tribal confederation. Based on a map by Brady Smith, courtesy of Willamette University Office of Marketing and Communication.

INTRODUCTION

"Everything emanates from our relationship with the earth," said Bobbie Conner in a June 2014 conversation at Willamette University about how the research for this book would proceed. Conner, a member of the Confederated Tribes of the Umatilla Indian Reservation and director of its Tamástslikt Cultural Institute, went on to say that the art of ceremony means "doing things beautifully, doing things in a beautiful manner." Whether that beauty is in the "ceremony itself or the things you wear," these things are made beautiful "out of respect for the life that has been taken." In every instance, making ceremony and its associated regalia involves a life being given or shared—the life of a being, whether plant (for firewood, weaving fibers, medicinal use), animal (for hides and fur, shell decorations, feathers), earth (rocks for the sweat lodge, the foundation for the dance house), or water (present or implied in all ceremonies). As Conner emphasized: "It's out of respect for the life that you've taken that you should make it well." The relationship among people, land, and the beings Conner referred to is lived now, not in a historical vacuum, and has been transformed by the dramatic alterations wrought by Euro-American settlement. In the aftershocks of these changes, members of the tribes indigenous to what is now Oregon continue in the twenty-first century to make ceremony in a "beautiful manner."

The conversations and images gathered for this book offer perspectives on the art of ceremony from members of the nine federally recognized Tribes in Oregon. The word *ceremony* is an imprecise term for a whole range of practices that range from more private, everyday actions to relatively public occasions where the whole community is called to be present. The resulting portraits are rich yet necessarily selective and partial; none of the chapters can possibly communicate the complexity of this subject. This book aims to communicate the fact that ceremony and the efforts to continue and renew it involve the complex work of art, language, performance, kinship, environmental relations, and even legal and political strategizing. The individuals who participated in the conversations reflect on this work and, in doing so, contribute to that work. I hope, in turn, that these reflections and contributions will be received as invaluable offerings by the book's intended audience, which is first and foremost the tribal communities where these conversations originated. With this priority in mind, this text centers the voices of knowledge bearers and knowledge learners and in doing so benefits all potential audiences, including other Indigenous communities, a general public readership that can gain from listening to Indigenous perspectives, and academic practitioners engaged in community-based participatory research and collaborative museology, both in tribal and nontribal settings.

The book has its origins in the exhibition *The Art of Ceremony: Regalia of Native Oregon*, organized in 2008 by the Hallie Ford Museum of Art at Willamette University, which featured historic and contemporary regalia drawn from—and selected by—the nine federally recognized tribal communities in Oregon. As the museum's curator of Native American art and a professor of anthropology, I served as organizing curator and collaborated with curatorial representatives from each tribe. While the idea for the exhibition had been circulating since 2006, the catalyst for its timing was the award to the project of a National Endowment for the Arts American Masterpieces Project grant by the Oregon Cultural Trust in 2008. Consonant with the grant program theme, *The Art of Ceremony* presented tribal regalia as masterworks of American art. The award of the grant had significance beyond the exhibition, moreover, as it in essence recognized decades of work on the part of tribes in Oregon to assert their sovereignty, their continuing presence, and their centrality to America's story. These efforts are part of a larger global story of Indigenous rights and cultural resurgence in the twenty-first century.

From *The Eternal Thread* to *The Art of Ceremony*

Indigenous peoples from opposite sides of the Pacific Rim gathered on the Willamette University campus on September 23, 2005, to celebrate the opening at the Hallie Ford Museum of Art of *Toi Māori: The Eternal Thread*, an exhibition of contemporary and customary Māori weaving that included ceremonial feather cloaks and other prized garments.[1] A Procession of Nations welcomed representatives of the Māori of New Zealand (or Aotearoa, the "land of the long white cloud," in the Māori language) to the ancestral homeland of the tribes of what is now called the Willamette Valley. The Māori delegation requested permission to enter the territory of their Indigenous hosts; representatives of the land's Native nations granted that permission with songs and prayers of respect and welcome. One tribal leader from western Oregon commented that this occasion marked the first time in modern history that a "foreign" nation had asked permission to enter their territory. The events contrasted sharply with the actions of Jason Lee and his fellow Methodist missionaries who had entered these homelands in the 1830s, more than 170 years earlier, and founded a mission boarding school, the Indian Manual Labor Training School, which eventually metamorphosed into Willamette University.[2]

The Māori and their taonga, or cultural treasures, were arriving at the Hallie Ford Museum because of both individual and collective historical forces. In an immediate sense the visit was set in motion through the friendship of Warm Springs artist Lillian Pitt of Oregon and Māori artist Darcy Nicholas of New Zealand, who had met in the 1980s in New Mexico when Nicholas was a Fulbright scholar in the United States studying Native American art. That meeting can be understood to have been part of a larger process of international Indigenous exchange and alliance-building that has produced wide-ranging effects in the past several decades—from the local staging of artist gatherings to the creation of the global United Nations Declaration on the Rights of Indigenous Peoples.[3] As a point within that stream of events,

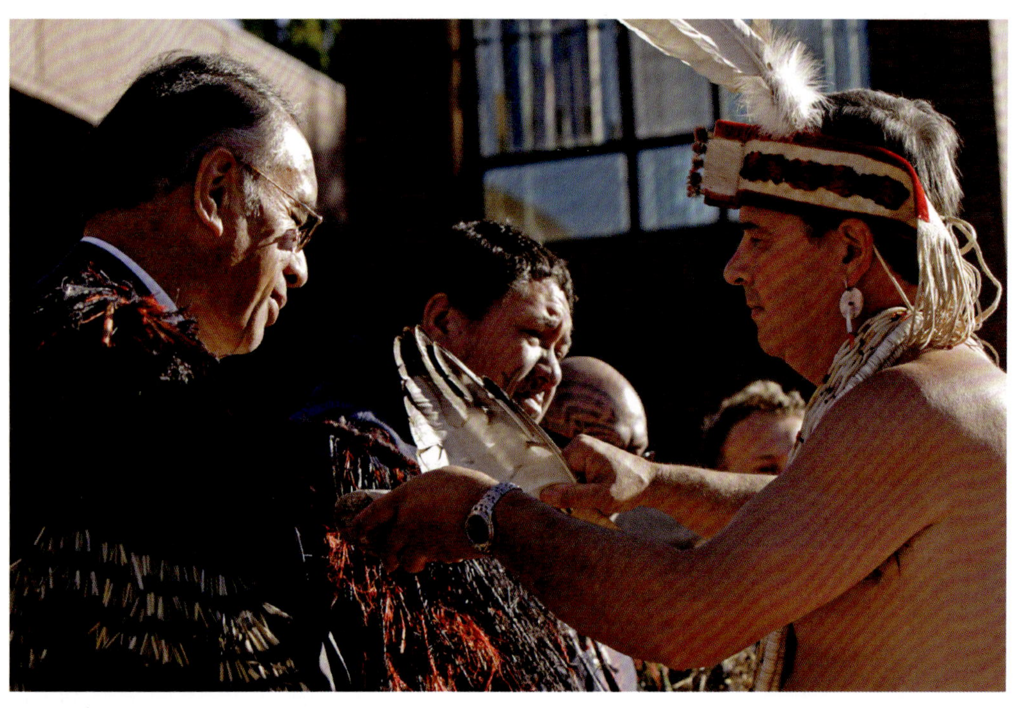

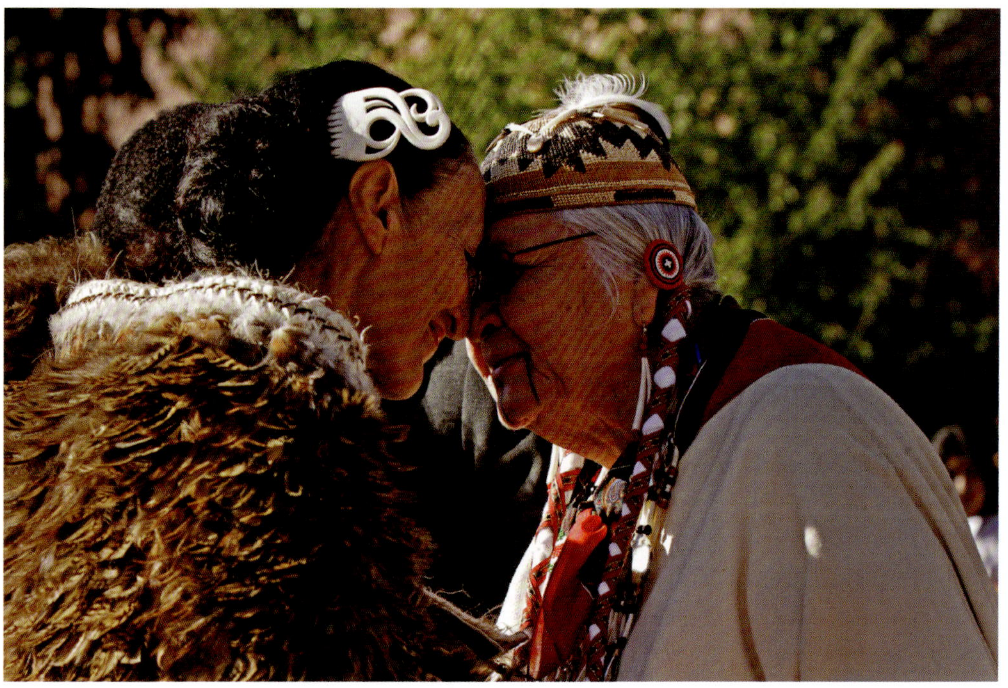

the meeting between Pitt and Nicholas produced a deep and enduring friendship that has rippled out to include hundreds of Indigenous artists and non-Indigenous supporters in a series of exchanges and gatherings in both New Zealand and North America. The arrival of *The Eternal Thread* in the United States was one of the most ambitious manifestations of these relationships.

In late 2003, Pitt called me, urging the Hallie Ford Museum to consider hosting *The Eternal Thread* in 2005. She had been in touch with Nicholas, who, as the director of the Pataka Museum of Arts and Culture in New Zealand, organized the exhibition with weavers of Toi Māori, the national Māori arts organization. Nicholas sought North American venues for *The Eternal Thread* and specifically wished to identify Northwest museums to build upon the preexisting relationships the Māori had with Northwest Indigenous artists such as Pitt, Rick Bartow, and Joe Feddersen, as well as with institutions such as the Longhouse at The Evergreen State College in Olympia, Washington. The Burke Museum at the University of Washington, in Seattle, and The Museum at Warm Springs, in Oregon, had already been secured as venues, but Toi Māori and Nicholas sought one more location. In 2003–4, Pitt had worked with me and other museum staff when we hosted *Lillian Pitt: Spirits Keep Whistling Me Home* at the Hallie Ford, and she thought we were the kind of venue that Nicholas was seeking, one that could facilitate visits among the Māori, local tribal communities, and the public. So Pitt began to work, simultaneously engaging both with us at the Hallie Ford and in convincing Nicholas that we were up to the responsibility of hosting.

By December 2003, Pitt's intercessions had cemented the partnership. In February 2004, I flew to New Zealand for the premiere of *The Eternal Thread* at the Pataka Museum in Porirua City. Staying at a seaside wharenui, a communal meeting house similar to a Northwest Coast longhouse, I woke each morning alongside sixty or so Māori weavers and supporters who had assembled for a hui, or cultural gathering, in celebration of the exhibition opening. My task was to prepare for the Hallie Ford's borrowing of *The Eternal Thread*. I met artists at work and learned more about the kakahu (*feather cloaks*) and the kete (*baskets*) at the heart of the exhibition, as well as the cutting-edge installations influenced by customary weaving techniques and materials.

What was the context for these treasures? How did they arise from the land, the history, and the contemporary lives of Māori people? What was the significance of the metaphor of "an eternal thread" and what did it convey about the connection Māori have to their ancestors, to other Indigenous peoples, and to the future? These questions would resonate far beyond my time in New Zealand, and in coming years they were recast in the Oregon context in the *Art of Ceremony* project that has resulted in this book.

My Māori hosts emphasized that my primary responsibility once back home was to facilitate connections between them and the Indigenous peoples of Oregon. One of Toi Māori's requirements for our borrowing of the exhibition was that the Hallie Ford Museum of Art coordinate cultural exchanges between Māori and Northwest Native American weavers and artists. As soon as I returned home from New Zealand in March 2004, I traveled to the Grand Ronde, Siletz, and Warm Springs communities to talk about *The Eternal Thread* and to brainstorm about all the possibilities presented by the impending project. By September 2005 these tribes had developed a full itinerary of experiences for their Māori guests; in the years since, several tribes in Oregon have hosted more exchanges involving Māori artists, ranging from visits of weavers and carvers to paddlers on canoe journeys.

How did *The Art of Ceremony* grow out of these international Indigenous connections? Members of the Native communities who hosted the Māori during *The Eternal Thread* project were inspired by the open sharing of ceremonial regalia and brought out their own as part of the process of exchange. This willingness to share with the public departs from the understandable self-protectiveness of tribal communities, who have good reason to avoid revealing traditional knowledge to a broader society that alternatively exploits and misrepresents Native cultures. *The Eternal Thread* provided a success story—an example of an Indigenous people communicating the symbolism and skill behind their art forms without compromising the integrity and privacy of spiritual practices.

When *The Eternal Thread* completed its final US stop at The Museum at Warm Springs, Natalie Moody, then curator at the museum, raised the idea of developing a contemporary regalia exhibition from tribes in Oregon. Bud Lane of Siletz, who had also been closely involved with *The Eternal Thread* while it was in Oregon and in October 2005 had

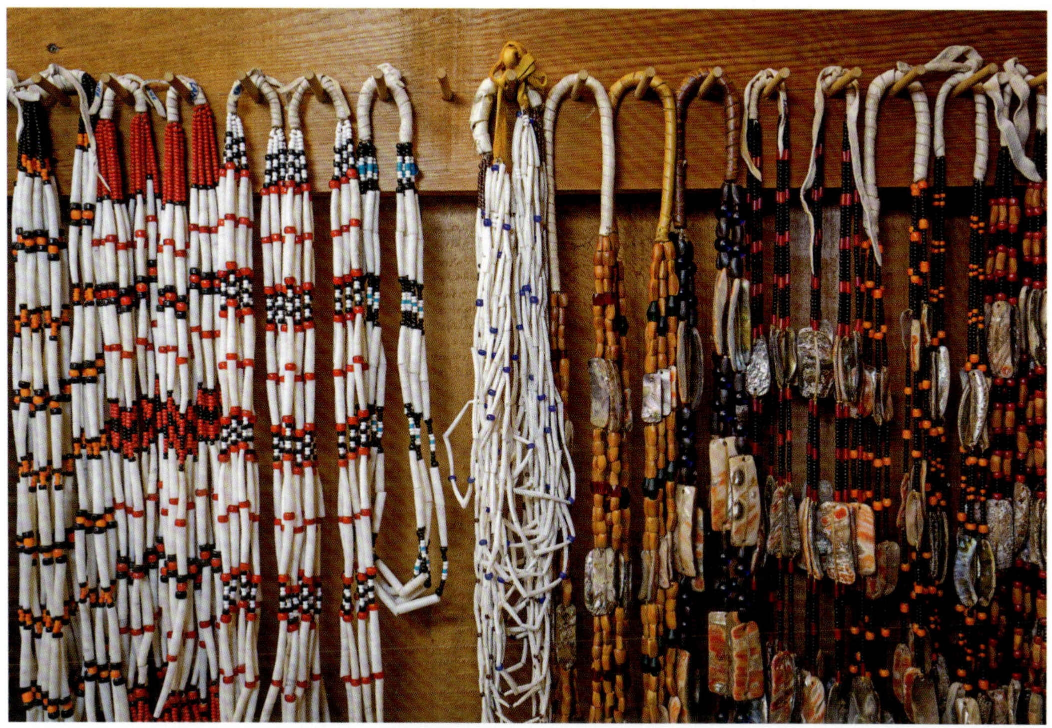

traveled to a weavers' gathering in New Zealand, also suggested the idea. The three of us extended the discussion to other tribes' traditional artists and museum and cultural resources department personnel, working on the assumption that such a project was years away, perhaps to come to fruition around 2010. But in early 2007 the Hallie Ford Museum of Art learned of a grant competition sponsored by the Oregon Arts Commission for funding from the National Endowment for the Arts (NEA) American Masterpieces Project.[4] Although the museum was at first told by the Oregon Arts Commission that the American Masterpieces grant category was intended to support canonical American masterworks by individual master artists (historically conceptualized as solitary geniuses, the majority of whom had been white and male in US history), not "traditional" arts such as tribal regalia, we went ahead and applied, making the case that tribal regalia was the very essence of *American master work*.[5] Regalia embodies the American homeland and its flora and fauna, it arises from Indigenous artistry developed over millennia, and it is continually influenced by emerging

Dentalium and bead necklaces at the Confederated Tribes of Siletz Indians dance house dressing room, ready to be used in ceremony, 2015. Photograph by Frank Miller Courtesy of Frank Miller and Willamette University.

ideas and materials as well as by customary knowledge. When the Oregon Arts Commission eventually notified us that they were awarding the 2008 NEA American Masterpieces grant to *The Art of Ceremony*, it was a vindication of what tribal members already understood: objects of regalia are of course American masterpieces, and the ceremonies in which they are used are themselves beautiful art forms.

There was one hitch. To award the NEA American Masterpieces grant, the Oregon Arts Commission required that we open *The Art of Ceremony* in calendar year 2008. It was already June 2007—the project was still in a conceptual stage, and opening a major exhibition featuring the contemporary regalia of all nine federally recognized Tribes in just a year's time seemed beyond impossible.[6] But John Olbrantz, the director of the Hallie Ford Museum of Art, believed it was feasible and was willing to set aside other exhibition projects to make it happen. When I asked the tribal community curators about the accelerated timing, they all agreed it was vital to move forward with the imprimatur of the NEA American Masterpieces grant and that they would work as quickly as required. So, collectively, we set to work.

All those involved conceptualized this project as a collaboration between the museum and the Tribes, although the term *collaboration*

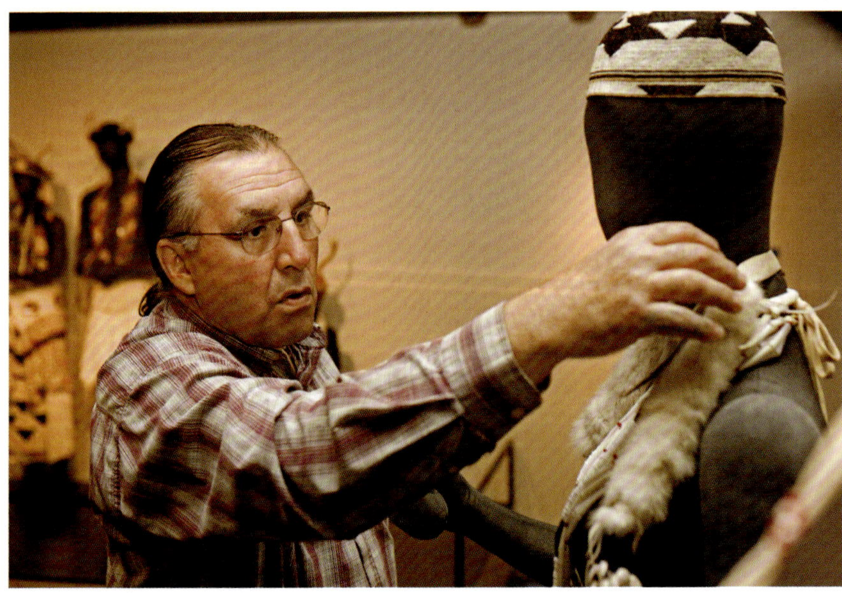

Louis LaChance (Cow Creek Band of Umpqua Indians) installing regalia for *The Art of Ceremony* exhibition, 2008. Photograph by Frank Miller. Courtesy of Frank Miller and Willamette University.

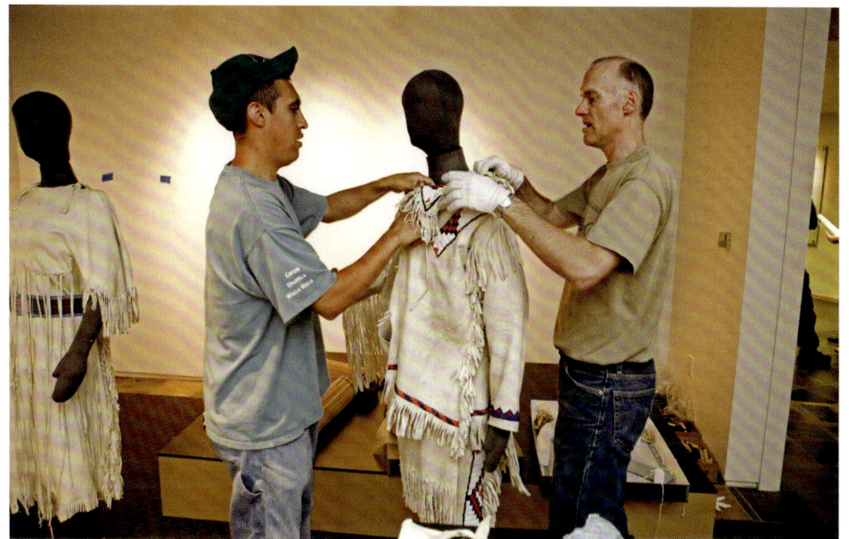

Randall Melton (Seminole), collections curator at Tamástslikt Cultural Institute, and David Andersen, Hallie Ford Museum of Art exhibition designer, installing regalia for *The Art of Ceremony* exhibition, 2008. Photograph by Frank Miller. Courtesy of Frank Miller and Willamette University.

can gloss over what are very complex relationships inside as well as outside a tribal community.[7] For the exhibition (and ultimately for this book) the museum staff and I worked with tribal representatives who ranged from tribal museum personnel to cultural resources department staff. A background common among the representatives was that each held an official position of responsibility for supporting his or her community's cultural life and interpreting it to the public, though none claimed to speak for all tribal members. Given all the possible interpretations of *ceremony* that any given community could have, I relied on each tribal representative to decide upon a focus for the exhibition and to make curatorial choices in ways that met standards of cultural protocol in that community.

As the coordinating curator for the project, I traveled around Oregon, meeting with the community curators to talk about the types of ceremonies they wished to represent and the masterworks that would best illuminate them. Many of the selections, particularly those from communities without tribal museums at the time, came directly from individual and family collections. After an intensive year of work in 2007–8 by members of all nine Tribes, including the commissioning and making of new art objects as well as the restoration of historical heirlooms, *The Art of Ceremony* opened at the Hallie Ford Museum of

Art at Willamette University on September 27, 2008. Representatives of the nine federally recognized Tribes gathered for a Procession of Nations to open the exhibition ceremonially and later celebrated with a meal of traditional foods such as salmon, root vegetables, and huckleberries, followed by storytelling, singing, and dancing. The exhibit traveled in 2009 to the Tamástslikt Cultural Institute at the Confederated Tribes of the Umatilla Indian Reservation, to The Museum at Warm Springs on the Confederated Tribes of Warm Springs Reservation, and finally to the Oregon Historical Society in Portland.

The conversations convened for this book in the years since *The Art of Ceremony* have taken a turn away from an exhibition's inescapable focus on objects. For peoples whose philosophies and religions are land-based, ceremony is about renewing and building the relationships

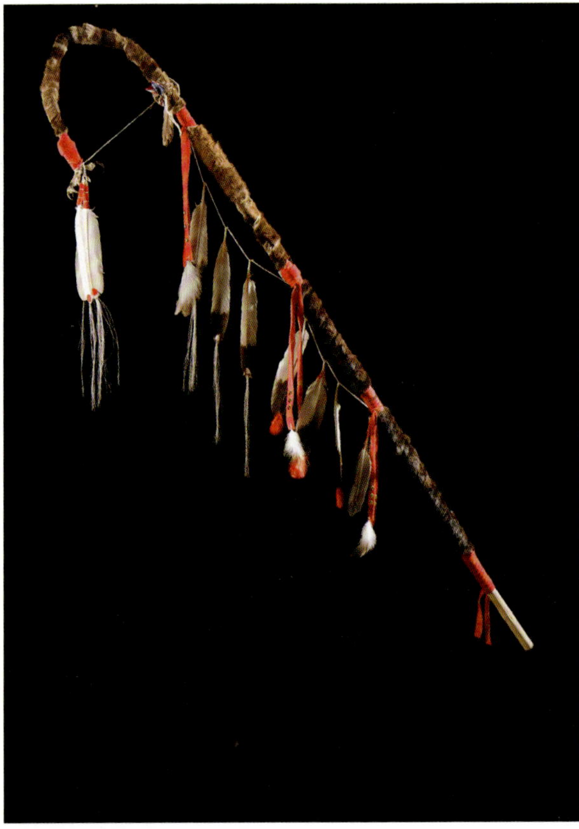

Eagle feather staff, by John Bevis (Umatilla), 2008. Wood, eagle feathers, deer hide. Commissioned for *The Art of Ceremony*. Collection of the Tamástslikt Cultural Institute, Pendleton, Oregon. Photograph by Frank Miller. Courtesy of Frank Miller and Willamette University.

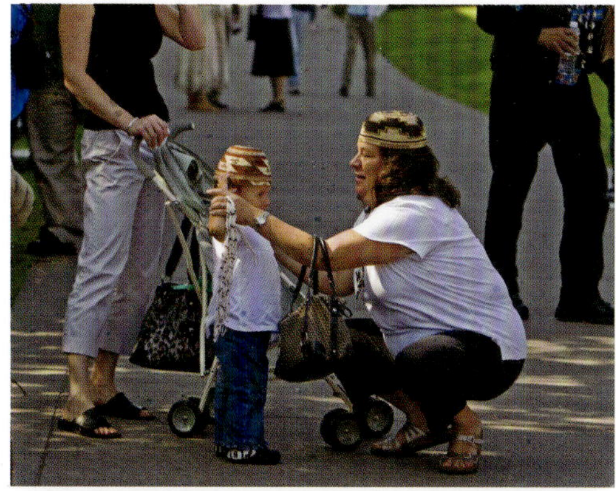

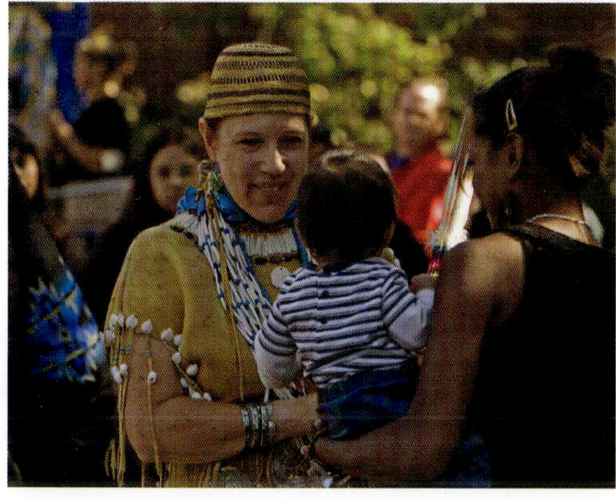

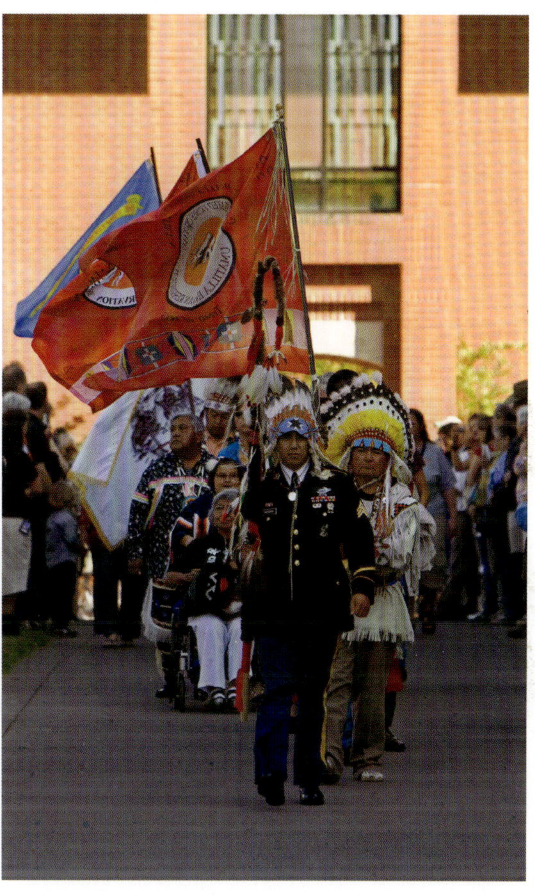

Cheryl Lane (Siletz) adjusting dentalium necklaces for her granddaughter Halli Lane (Siletz), at the opening events for *The Art of Ceremony*, September 27, 2008. Photograph by Frank Miller. Courtesy of Frank Miller and Willamette University.

Procession of Nations for *The Art of Ceremony*, led by Eric Sheoships (Umatilla) and Les Minthorn (Umatilla), September 27, 2008. Sheoships carries an eagle staff commissioned for the occasion (see facing page). Photograph by Frank Miller. Courtesy of Frank Miller and Willamette University.

Brenda Brainard (Confederated Tribes of Coos, Lower Umpqua, and Siuslaw Indians) with fellow tribal member Ramil Beers in the arms of his mother, Maree Beers, September 27, 2008. Photograph by Frank Miller. Courtesy of Frank Miller and Willamette University.

between people, the Creator, and creation—the land and its beings. So while ceremony may involve spectacular regalia, as in the Nee Dosh (Feather Dances) of western Oregon or in Plateau traditional weddings, it may also employ the simplest of tools, as for example a plastic bucket for harvesting huckleberries or a rounded river rock that holds heat for a sweat. Such ceremonies are at their heart about the work of renewal, work that reflects constant change at the same time that it draws upon deep relationships going back millennia. That work is what is discussed in the chapters that follow.

Talking about Ceremony: How This Book Came to Be

At each of the four venues of *The Art of Ceremony* exhibition, regalia makers came together for public programs, dialoguing with visitors and one another about their work. Many non-Indigenous visitors' remarks revealed how little is taught or understood about the historical experiences of tribes in what is now Oregon, especially about the rapid destruction of Native life and society precipitated by white settlement in the early 1800s, the crushing effects of removal to reservations in the mid-1800s, the systematic erosion of language and social organization through the boarding schools, the massive loss of once communally held lands through allotment policies, and the erasure of identity and livelihood brought about by the baldly named Termination Act of 1954, which severed the federal-tribal government-to-government relationship of dozens of tribes in western and southern Oregon. Furthermore, many visitors had little knowledge of contemporary tribal communities and the ways they have responded to these onslaughts and are engaged in contemporary nation-building. Audiences sometimes had difficulty taking in the fact that much of the regalia on view had been made since 2000, even though one of the key points of the exhibit was that the concept of "masterpiece" was not time-bound and that newer pieces were no less "traditional" or "authentic" than older work.[8]

These responses point to the difficulty much of the public has in conceptualizing Native Americans as being of the present instead of only the past. In Oregon specifically, few book-length publications dealing with the history and contemporary life of all the federally recognized Tribes in the state are available, other than the very important *The First*

Oregonians, originally published by the Oregon Council for the Humanities in 1991 and reissued as a second edition in 2007, and Stephen Dow Beckham's edited volume of historical documents, *Oregon Indians: Voices from Two Centuries*, published in 2006.[9] While the Hallie Ford Museum of Art had produced a sixteen-page publication in association with *The Art of Ceremony* exhibition, many of the tribal collaborators and I felt something extending beyond the exhibition's life was sorely needed. The idea for this book was sown.

The book's research methodology was modeled on the exhibition's collaborative process, described earlier. As the project moved from exhibition to book, I spoke with each tribal representative to identify the specific focus for that tribe's chapter, the processes through which participants were to be identified for conversations, the questions and topics that would be included in the conversations, and how they would be conducted and recorded. Today most tribes in the United States, including those in Oregon, have protocols through which proposed research is reviewed, tribal input and direction are incorporated, and final products are vetted. I conducted research for this book under conditions set by each tribe or representative of the tribe. Those conditions varied; for example, in the tribes with museums the project was understood to be part of a previous museum-based collaboration and thus was guided and reviewed by museum staff. In some others the tribal council required a research permit application, with review conducted by council members or their designees.[10] All those interviewed for the project gave permission to be recorded and to have their words and names used in the book. Everyone involved (including those in "official" positions) repeatedly emphasized they were not speaking for all members of their communities but were offering perspectives based upon their own lived experiences.

Between 2014 and 2017, supported by grants and a sabbatical leave from Willamette University and a project grant from the Oregon Cultural Trust (OCT), I traveled to tribal communities to record conversations and attend ceremonies; specific circumstances of the research in each community are presented toward the beginning of each chapter. The transcribed conversations became the basis for the contours of each chapter, which I shaped according to my sense of the core elements of what tribal members articulated, a subjective process given the inherent difficulty of representing others' lived experiences. After drafting each chapter, I sent it to the tribal representative, who reviewed it, circulated to the participants and other readers, and returned it to me with suggestions, which I incorporated. I am deeply grateful for the investment in both the exhibition and book project by so many people, who are thanked by name in the acknowledgments.

The illustrations for the book were created and chosen through a variety of processes. Both the collaborators and I felt images were crucial in communicating respect for and illustrating concepts of ceremony, yet we were also wary of violating community sensibilities about what should and shouldn't be depicted. As with the text, tribal representatives participated in selecting images to illustrate their respective chapters and approved all final selections. Another concern, more difficult to address, was that the book portray Native people as living fully contemporary lives. This objective is easy to assert and nearly impossible to achieve, given that the general public views almost any image of American Indians through a distorting and objectifying lens. Moreover, the portrayal of Native Americans in photography is exceptionally fraught, most famously in the work of Edward S. Curtis, whose early twentieth-century images romanticized American Indians and created a sense of nostalgia for what he and others felt was a "vanishing race." Many Native American photographers have critiqued Curtis's habit of staging his subjects in order to freeze-frame them in a timeless aboriginal past and, in so doing, failing to portray the contemporaneity of Native lives at the time. But Curtis is just one of the clearest examples of this distortion; as scholar Pauline Turner Strong has argued in *American Indians and the American Imaginary*, the othering of Native people permeates their representation in "an ever-widening set of cultural domains" and continues to be extraordinarily persistent.[11]

So, knowing how important yet difficult it is to dislodge the straitjacket of ahistorical representation that paralyzes images of American Indians, this book enters this territory, hoping to contribute more nuanced visual narratives. While photographers working with the Hallie Ford Museum of Art had taken a large number of photographs at the time of *The Art of Ceremony* exhibition, of both participants and artwork, I knew that to tell a more holistic story the book would need additional photographs of the processes involved in preparing

and conducting ceremony.[12] Again, as with the text, the goal was to
be selective rather than encyclopedic, with the aim of communicating
some core themes. Each tribal representative and I discussed the images
to be included and how and whether new photography should (and
could) be coordinated. In some instances, existing photographs were
identified by tribal representatives for inclusion. A 2015 project grant
from the Oregon Cultural Trust supported some new photography
to document elements of the featured ceremonies and related processes.
In the end, technological, logistical, and time constraints limited the
universe of choices for each chapter, but within these limits tribal representatives had a key role in approving the final selections.

The book's chapters are organized alphabetically by tribe, following
the precedent of *The Art of Ceremony* exhibition booklet as well as
The First Oregonians. Each chapter presents information about the
circumstances of research in that community, including information
about that tribe's original *Art of Ceremony* exhibition contribution.
Although it is impossible to adequately portray even a fraction of any
tribe's complex history, each chapter offers a brief historical sketch to
contextualize the ceremonial practice being described.

Intertwined themes consistently weave in and out of the conversations that inform this book. As Bobbie Conner's remarks in the
opening paragraph of this introduction suggest, ceremony has its basis
in the place-based cosmologies of Indigenous peoples. Ceremony is
conducted at specific locations within tribal homelands, regalia and
resources used for ceremony have their origins in the land, and ceremony itself references creation as known from a particular place. Place
is not merely landscape but a living community of plants, animals, and
geological features tied to the lives of people of past, current, and future
generations. As just one illustration, the Klamath Tribes' Return of the
C'waam Ceremony is held on the banks of the Sprague River at the site
of a fishing camp used for generations by tribal members. A few miles
away is a ridge where in the myth-age, Creator first made the c'waam
(*sucker fish*), to feed the people in a time of famine. But the c'waam are
now endangered as a result of more than a hundred years of habitat
degradation from dams and agricultural development in the region. The
ceremony, honoring the fish and giving thanks for their sacrifice, once
marked the beginning of the spring catch. Today, respect and gratitude

remain central to the ceremony, although now the focus is not on harvest but on hope for the future restoration of the c'waam. The chapter contextualizes the ceremony in the ecological history that has resulted in this shift.

Many chapters include references to political forces that constrain the making of ceremony and regalia, including federal policies of removal and post-reservation restrictions on movement that interrupted people's access to land-based knowledge. Overt repression of religious practices by Indian agents on reservations in western Oregon at end of the nineteenth century directly impacted knowledge transmission, although did not entirely destroy it. For instance, even though dance houses were ordered burned to the ground on the Siletz reservation, dances continued in private homes in the early twentieth century. Later in the century, the recollections of elders about these events helped inform subsequent generations as they reestablished the Feather Dance, or Nee Dosh.

Individuals in several communities said that although there has been great destruction, they wish to focus upon the constructive forces that contribute to the renewal of ceremonial life. Many tribal members spoke of the ways they work to protect and restore the relationships between their people and their ancestral lands. At Burns Paiute, tribal members have worked to steward the lands now known as the Malheur National Wildlife Refuge (NWR), whose nearly two hundred thousand acres have been home to their people for millennia, in order to protect culturally important sites so that members can continue to practice what they understand as the core of their spiritual life—the ability to visit and care for locations of the ancestors and to gather foods and plants in "everyday ceremony." In the aftermath of the illegal 2016 occupation of the headquarters of the Malheur NWR by white militia members, who called for the end of federal control of the lands, the Paiute have worked with federal authorities to heal the disturbed land and ancestral sites. Across the state the Confederated Tribes of Coos, Lower Umpqua, and Siuslaw Indians have taken the innovative step of joining their Cultural and Natural Resources Departments into one program, in recognition of the inseparability of cultural and environmental knowledge and property and as a central dimension of their nation-building process in the twenty-first century.

The 1970s marked the beginning of restoration of previously terminated tribes in western Oregon and the political strengthening of
tribes east of the Cascades that had not been legally terminated but
had suffered economically and socially in the same period. Since that
time, increasing exercise of self-governance, as well as the passage of the
federal 1988 Indian Gaming Regulatory Act, have facilitated the development of new economic opportunities in many of the state's tribal
communities. Although every tribal economy differs, all tribes have
sought to improve health, education, employment, and housing for their
citizens. As these basic needs are increasingly being addressed, many
tribes have also been able to devote new resources to cultural work.
Among the initiatives at Grand Ronde, for example, are Chinuk Wawa
language instruction programs for preschool through adult, resources
for canoe carving, and a hand-split cedar plankhouse that was a decade
in the making. At Coquille, tribal members talk about the ways they
have infused the philosophy of the potlatch throughout many initiatives,
as part of the Tribe's post-restoration nation-building process, in order
to share their abundance.

Making regalia and making ceremony entail accessing customary
knowledge; every conversation touched upon how such knowledge
is based in tribal homelands and their natural resources. Talk about
traditional weddings at Warm Springs, for example, turned to the role
of tule mats, made from the bulrush or tule reed, as an essential part of
the ceremony, the place on which the bride and groom come together
to make their vows. Ideally, the mat is purpose-made for each couple;
this requires that knowledge about harvesting and processing tule and
mat-making techniques be perpetuated, even if only among a small
number of tribal members. Harvest—of tule or of the many traditional
foods featured at weddings and other occasions, at Warm Springs and
in other tribal communities—requires not only knowing where and
when to go, but having access to sites for gathering, whether on the
reservation or on off-reservation ceded lands. Even some of the rocks
favored for use in sweat lodges at Umatilla, chosen for their ability to
hold heat because of their volcanic origins, can be understood as being
"harvested" at particular streambeds on the slopes of Mount Hood.

One way tribes protect the practice of this knowledge—or make
possible its reanimation if it has been interrupted—is through the

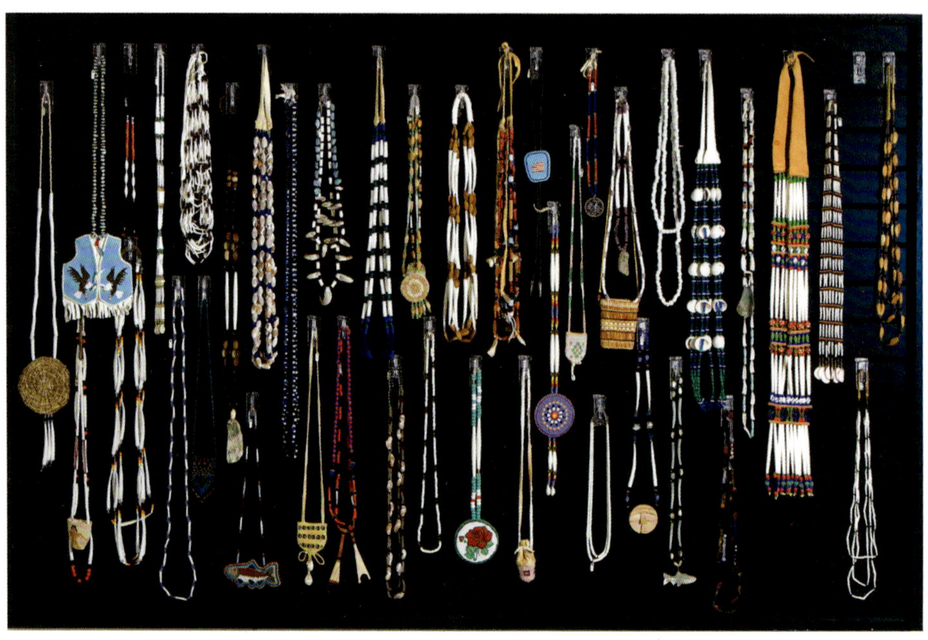

exercise of tribal sovereignty. On the most fundamental level, sovereignty is the inherent authority of a nation to self-govern. Under federal law tribal sovereignty has been recognized through treaties, executive orders, court decisions, and laws, although its exercise is limited by the position of the tribes as "domestic dependent nations" within the US nation-state. Tribes persistently push against these limits and are increasingly effective in finding ways their sovereignty can be exercised for the purpose of protecting and nurturing ancestral lands, and the natural resources upon them, that were ceded during the treaty-making era. This exercise may take place with the benefit of a formal agreement between a tribe and a public-lands management agency, as for example the Siletz have done with the Willamette National Forest to protect habitat for beargrass, used for weaving and regalia-making. The Cow Creek Band of Umpqua Tribe of Indians worked with the US Forest Service to establish increased protection of huckleberry fields where tribal members have been gathering since time beyond memory. But whether or not done with the benefit of formal agreements, the act of tending and harvesting traditional ecological resources used for cultural practices is an exercise of sovereignty that nurtures tribal relationships with place.[13]

The disruptions of recent centuries mean that great variation is found in knowledge about and practice of ceremonies within tribal communities, yet every tribe in Oregon is engaged in efforts to strengthen its members' relationships with their homelands. These relationships are ultimately the basis of ceremonial practice and are what motivated many individuals to become part of this project to document the creativity of what is being done now. The conversations and images in this book are evidence of that work, the art of ceremony.

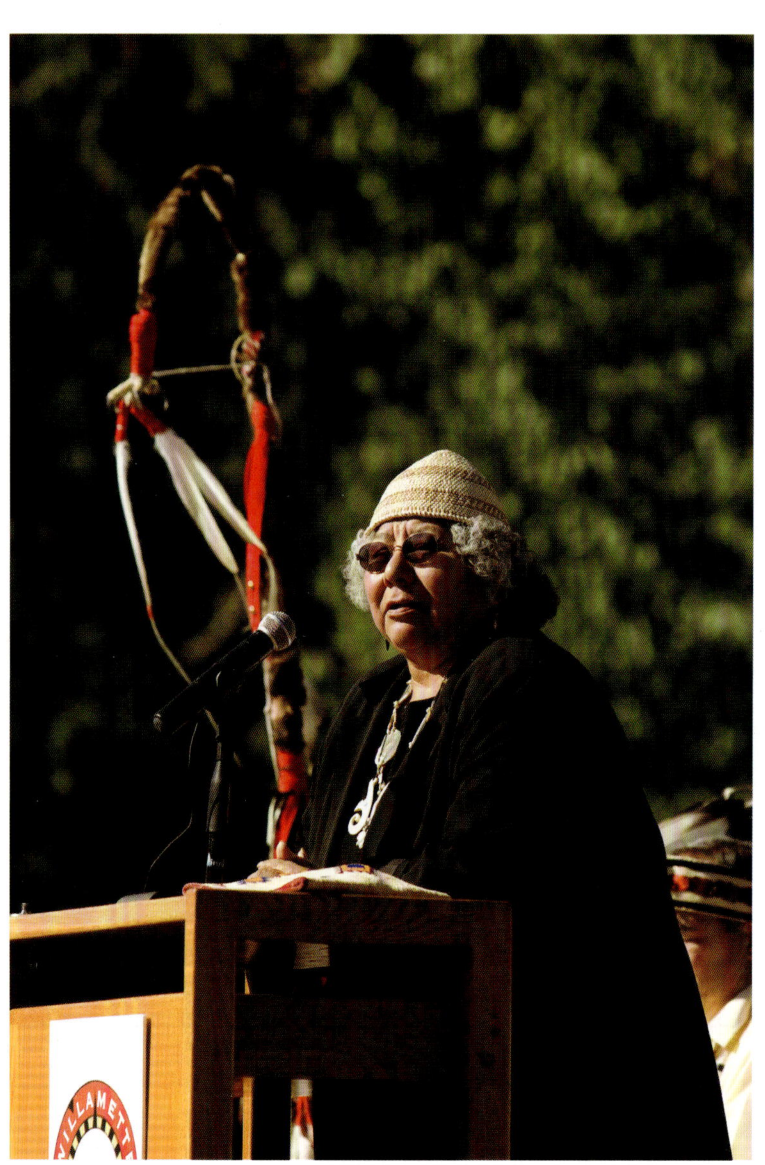

CHAPTER 1

THE PEOPLE ARE THE LAND AND THE LAND IS THE PEOPLE

The Burns Paiute Tribe

Minerva Teeman Soucie (1945–2012), Burns Paiute weaver, educator, and former Tribal Council chair, was a key partner in the development of *The Art of Ceremony* exhibition project. Minerva represented the Burns Paiute community in the gatherings associated with *Toi Māori: The Eternal Thread* at the Hallie Ford Museum of Art in 2005, later hosted Māori weavers in Burns, and even traveled to New Zealand with her granddaughter Kristeny Soucie for the events surrounding the return of *The Eternal Thread* to the Christchurch Art Gallery in February 2007.

I first met Minerva around 1997 as the inaugural exhibits for the Hallie Ford Museum of Art were being prepared. I was seeking to learn more about the Paiute basketry in the museum's collection and had been told she was a committed weaver and culture bearer for her tribal community.[1] We got to know one another over the years, and when it came time to host *Toi Māori: The Eternal Thread* in 2005, Minerva enthusiastically joined in, frequently driving hours to Salem from eastern Oregon and back. Later, as the Burns Paiute community curator for *The Art of Ceremony*, Minerva thought carefully about

facing page: Minerva Teeman Soucie speaking at *The Art of Ceremony* opening events at Willamette University, September 27, 2008. Photograph by Frank Miller. Courtesy of Frank Miller and Willamette University.

the selections for the exhibition. She wanted first and foremost to represent the relationship that the Burns Paiute people had with their land
as well as to communicate how knowledge and learning were passed on
from generation to generation. To do this, she chose invaluable family
heirlooms from her own and other families' collections for the exhibition. While Minerva passed away far too early in 2012, the principles
underlying her curatorial choices made a lasting imprint on *The Art of
Ceremony* exhibition project and ultimately this book.

Most Burns Paiute tribal members are descendants of the Wadatika
band of Northern Paiute, the people indigenous to the Great Basin
region, which extends through present-day Oregon, Nevada, California,
and Idaho. Their name translates literally to the "wada-eaters," in reference to the wada or seepweed (*Suaeda depressa*) plant once found in
abundance around Malheur and Harney Lakes, and whose seeds were
harvested and processed by the Northern Paiute into nutrient-rich food.

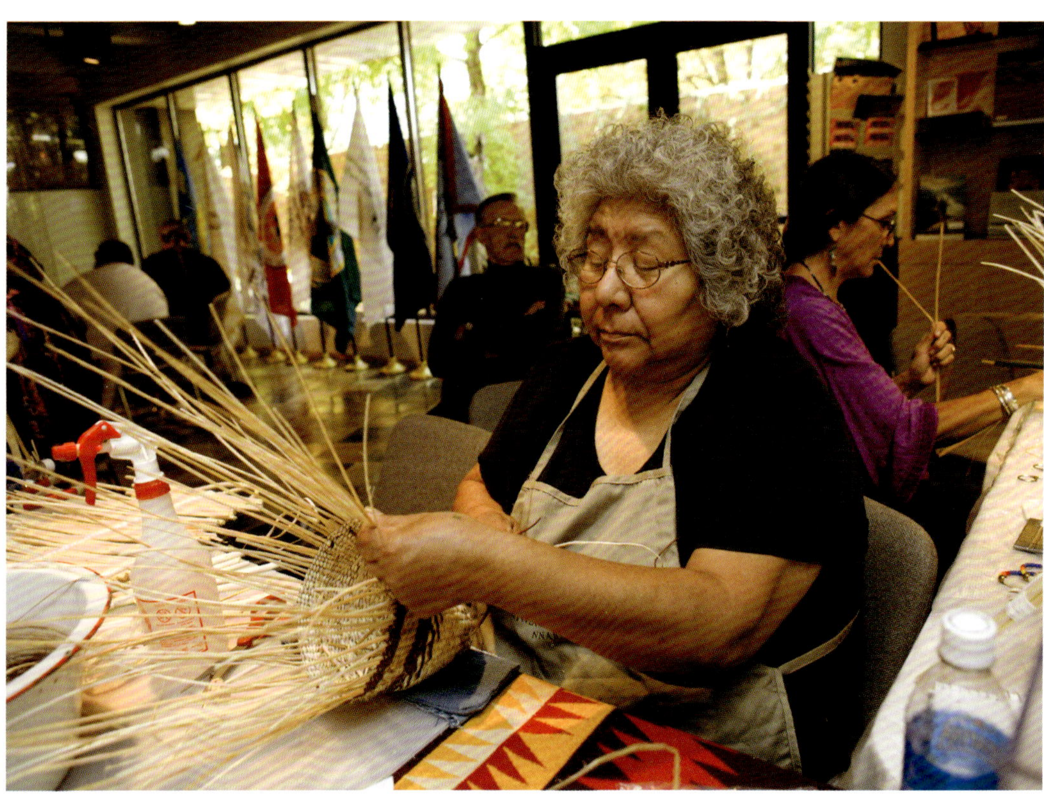

As their very name suggests, the Wadatika were—and are—inseparable from their high desert ecosystem. The Wadatika are what they eat; they are the land. Their aboriginal territory extended over 5,250 square miles; their relatively remote location ("remote" from the perspective of settler-colonists) initially meant colonization was delayed in comparison to other parts of Oregon. As the Burns Paiute tribal website states, "Our history is both tragic and inspiring to living tribal members. We are the last truly free people in Oregon. Our ancestors resisted encroachment of settlers, refused to cede any of our lands, and fought to preserve our traditional life ways."[2] While the Wadatika did negotiate a Treaty of Peace and Friendship with federal agents in 1868, which would have reserved a homeland, it was never ratified by the US Senate. The Wadatika never ceded their ancestral territory.

In 1872, President Ulysses S. Grant signed an executive order establishing the Malheur Indian Reservation, an area of nearly 1.8 million acres. By 1875 several hundred Paiute and Bannock Indians were reported to be living there by the federal Indian agent.[3] Yet Euro-American settlers were fast encroaching, eager to use reservation lands for their cattle herds. Conditions at the Malheur Reservation worsened, as it became more difficult to carry out the seasonal round of gathering and hunting, and conflict grew with the incoming white ranchers. In the broader region, tensions between encroaching settlers and Indigenous peoples were building, with grave impact upon the Burns Paiute. The so-called Bannock War of 1878 in southwestern Idaho and northeastern Oregon between white settlers and Bannock Indians who were fighting to retain their ancestral territories had repercussions at the Malheur Reservation. All Paiute were blamed for the "war" and those at the Malheur Reservation were forcibly marched in the winter of 1878–79 to Fort Simcoe on the Yakama Reservation or to Fort Vancouver, Washington. After the Malheur Reservation was "emptied," it was dissolved by President Chester Arthur by executive orders in 1882 and 1883, thereby placing the lands in the public domain and opening them for white settlement and ranching. Released from their captivity in Washington State in 1883, the Paiute were given the option to return to their homelands; those who did return in the 1880s to the Harney basin area found themselves landless, although some established a small tribal encampment on the outskirts of Burns.[4]

In 1908 about 190,000 acres of the original Malheur Indian Reservation lands became the basis of the Malheur National Wildlife Refuge.[5] It was not until 1972—fully one hundred years after the original establishment of the Malheur Indian Reservation—that the Burns Paiute were successful in establishing a tiny reservation of 770 acres. Although this was only a fraction of their ancestral lands, the tribe began the process of building a community with housing, a gathering center, and eventually a health clinic. Today there are just over four hundred members of the Burns Paiute Tribe, half of whom are under eighteen years old; through the persistent efforts of tribal government, the land base has grown to nearly 14,000 acres.

Familial Relations

In 2017, I returned to Burns to visit with Diane L. Teeman, culture and heritage director for the Burns Paiute Tribe, to discuss the aims of this chapter. Teeman, who is a tribal member as well as a doctoral student in archaeology at the University of Nevada–Reno, shared several of her writings with me. In a chapter published in the *Handbook of Landscape Archaeology* (2008), she has written that Northern Paiute people's relationship with their homelands must be understood as "familial."[6] Stressing that this relationship is much richer and more complex than what the ethnographic literature has labeled as a "simple" subsistence relationship between a people and an ecosystem, Teeman explains: "The people are the land and the land is the people."[7]

Teeman goes on to elaborate two of the many bases underlying this cosmology. One is that, in the worldview of Great Basin cultures, there was once a time when all peoples and other beings of the land could communicate with one another. Since that time, Teeman writes, "it has been carried down from generation to generation so that we are today, as Great Basin peoples, related to the other animals who share our landscape."[8] These kin relationships, shaped by reciprocity and egalitarianism, extend not just to fauna but also to flora and geographic locations. A second tenet of the familial relationship with the land is that "the landscape is the keeper of our history."[9] It is worth quoting Teeman at length here:

The acts and events occurring on the landscape become part
of it. A component of the people who were part of those acts
and events is forever intermingled with those places; in effect,
an action on a landscape is also an action on not only prior acts
and events but also [on] the people who were involved in those
activities. Moreover, the actual physical remains of the ancestors
of Indigenous Great Basin peoples are intermingled with the soil
of the landscapes of our homelands. *Because of this fact, we are
the landscape from which we came and will each some day return.*
Our success at protection of important places is vital to this cycle
of individual life and death, and the health and well being of our
communities depends on our ability to actively participate in a
healthy relationship with our lands.[10]

The complex biocultural system built from the principle that "we are
the landscape" has immense implications for understanding the ceremonial as well as everyday objects that Northern Paiute people have
crafted from and with the landscape.

A fundamental element of the Great Basin worldview for the groups
who are Numic language speakers (a branch of the broader Uto-Aztecan
language family of western North America) is the concept of Puha
(*power*). In a volume titled *Collaborative Archaeology at Stewart Indian
School*, coedited by Teeman, the concept of Puha is explained as
representing "the life force that resides in all things and connects past,
present, and future; it constitutes the fabric of the universe."[11] The
past is not somehow separate from the present; the past is alive in the
present. Thus objects made or touched by ancestors provide living
connections between the present and the past, and in fact collapse any
distinction between those temporal realms. Whether a cultural object
is in the household of a living Paiute family or is found in situ in a landscape by an archaeologist, it is alive, sentient, and is of the present
as much as it is of the past, no matter how ancient its manufacture.[12]
With these principles in mind, we can now turn to the objects of regalia
Minerva Soucie so carefully selected for *The Art of Ceremony*, and
through them, learn something not only about human familial relations
but about familial land-people relations.

Family/Heirlooms: Rabbit Robes, Rose Beadwork, and Willow Cradleboards

As discussed in the introduction, one of the core arguments for the award of a National Endowment for the Arts American Masterpieces Project grant in 2007 for *The Art of Ceremony* exhibition project was that tribal regalia should be understood as the very essence of American masterwork. Regalia embodies Indigenous American landscapes and the creatures therein, and arises from Indigenous knowledge that developed in familial relationships with all living beings and features of tribal homelands.

One such masterpiece for the Paiute is the kamme wigya (*rabbit robe*). The kamme wigya in the exhibition was loaned by the family of Agnes Benning Hawley and was featured in a drawing on the front cover of *The First Oregonians*.[13] It is believed to have been made around 1900 and is one of the few older robes to still be in the possession of a Burns Paiute family—in part, as Minerva wrote at the time of the exhibition, "because of the tradition of burying ancestors with their robes." Minerva further explained the importance of the rabbit blankets (as they were also called in English) to Paiute survival in the winter: "Surviving the cold high desert nights for Paiute people required that each member own a rabbit blanket to keep them warm. Each blanket required a hundred or more rabbit pelts. The pelts were first processed and twisted and then assembled with very strong dogbane (*Apocynum cannabinum*) cordage." The twisting of the pelts created hollow tubes of rabbit fur (hide side in) that, when stitched together, create an insulated blanket with warming properties similar to those of a down comforter.

Rabbits were one of the few fur-bearing creatures available to the Paiute in the high desert and were highly valued both as a food source and for clothing. In the Paiute worldview rabbits were also relatives from back in the myth-age, when animals were people and everyone spoke the same language.[14] Great Basin peoples hunted rabbits through drives, a hunting technique with a spiritual dimension. The Paiute concept of Puha, introduced earlier, illuminates this dimension: in driving rabbits into concentrated spaces, Paiute "encourage[d] power to concentrate"; some of that power was "transferred from the slain creatures to human beneficiaries, provided the former were treated with respect."[15]

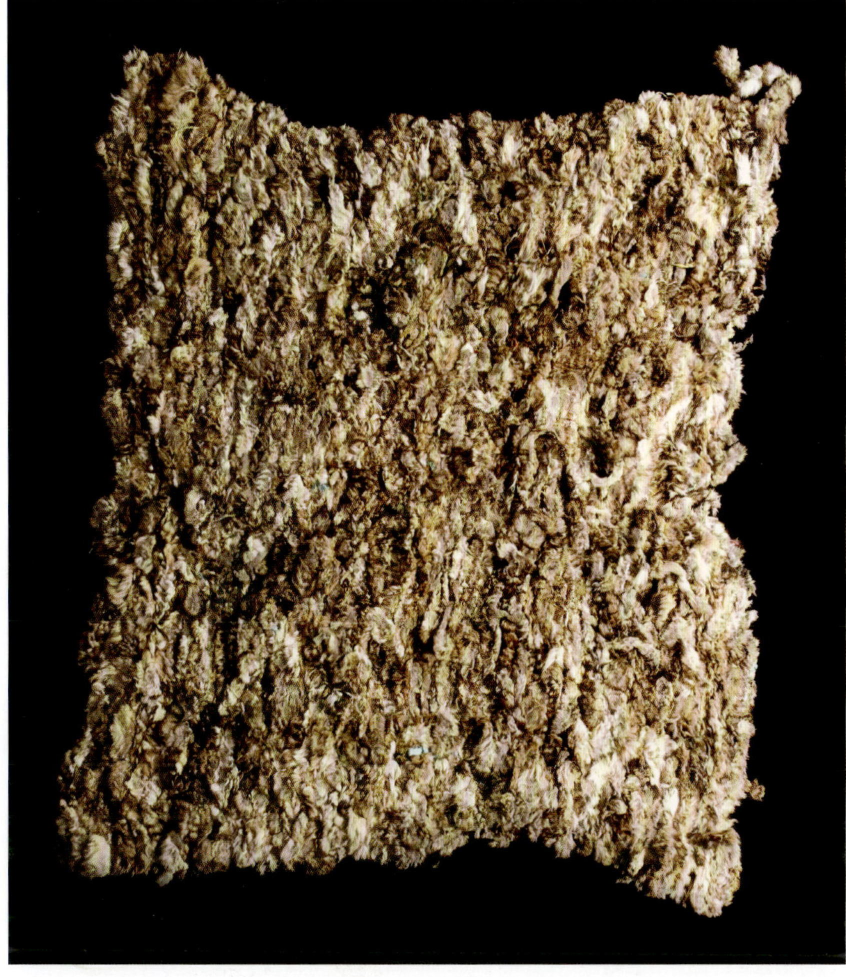

Kamme wigya (*rabbit robe*), ca. 1900. Rabbit pelts, cotton cloth. Collection of the family of Agnes Benning Hawley. Photograph by Frank Miller. Courtesy of Frank Miller and Willamette University.

Rabbit robes resulting from such hunts were thus imbued with power transferred through the animals' sacrifice.

But the disruptions of the past 150 years to both land and culture mean that rabbit robes simply can't be made as they once were. Minerva made the point that few such blankets are made in contemporary times because of the drastic changes in jackrabbit habitat and populations: "Today, it is difficult to make one of these blankets due to the scarcity of jack rabbits in Harney County. In the last fifty years the rabbit population has dwindled so much that it is difficult to get even 10–20 hides in the winter, when the thick fur is preferred. Rabbit bounties in the fifties and other means of eradication have left few rabbits for the Paiutes to process into blankets."[16] Degradation from agriculture, ranching, drought, and other factors contribute to the decline in rabbit robe making—robes can't be made if jackrabbits aren't thriving. In other words, if the ecosystem isn't hospitable for jackrabbits, it isn't hospitable for the generational transfer of Paiute technological and cultural knowledge either. The potential for restoration of jackrabbit habitat in the Great Basin is thus deeply entwined with the future well-being of Paiute peoples.

In her selection of objects, Minerva emphasized the intergenerational kin relationships manifested in those objects, as well as the stories of the things themselves.[17] Combining these emphases upon intergenerational kin relations, the biographies of the things themselves, and the concept of Puha or life force, we can understand how Minerva's selections and interpretations offer insights into the Paiute understanding of the web of interconnections between landscape, creatures, and resources, the people and ancestors who made and used them, and the generations who will use them in the future.

To illustrate the importance of intergenerational relationships and the ways regalia manifests creativity and continuity of traditions across the life cycle, Minerva focused on women's and girl's outfits for *The Art of Ceremony*. To represent a young girl, Minerva chose a girl's buckskin dress, a tsua'a nah-kwi, made in 1973 by her mother Bernice Beers Teeman, who tanned and processed the deer hide. The dress was made for Minerva's daughter, Charisse Soucie, to wear for dancing and in parades. Bernice sewed the dress in the Paiute fashion, using a welt seam in her stitching (a type of ridged seam, a technique associated with Paiute hidework).[18] As both Charisse and the dress "grew up," Minerva added beadwork and lengthened the dress by adding fringe at the bottom. In the Teeman Soucie family's next generation the dress was worn by Charisse's daughter, Kristeny Soucie, until she outgrew it. It remains in the family, ready for future generations.

Another part of the outfit was a maggo (*beaded handbag*), made in the 1920s by an unknown Paiute artist and given to Minerva by her mother, Bernice, when Charisse began dancing as a little girl. Minerva extended the functional life of the bag by sewing in a new liner and repairing the stitching. Minerva handed it down to Charisse, hoping

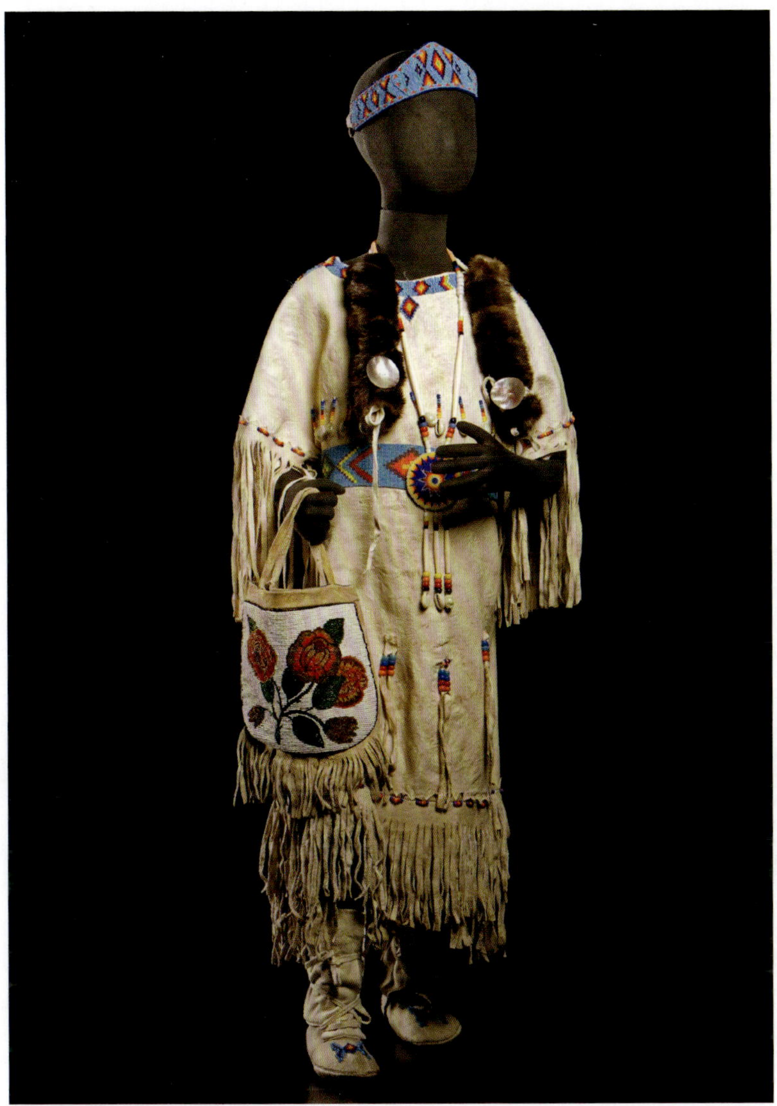

Girl's outfit. Beaded girl's crown, 1975. Minerva Teeman Soucie. Cut-glass beads, deer hide. Tsua'a nah-kwi (*girl's buckskin dress*), 1973. Bernice Beers Teeman and Minerva Teeman Soucie. Deer hide, glass beads, shell. Maggo (*floral-beaded handbag*), 1920s. Paiute artist. Deer hide, glass beads, silk lining. Abalone hair ties, 1990. Minerva Teeman Soucie. Abalone, deer hide. Nah –ti (*loom-beaded belt*), 1978. Chinook or Klamath artist. Glass beads. Otter ties, 1995. Artist undocumented, gifted to Kristeny Soucie by Jim Soucie. Otter skin with buckskin ties. Girl's necklace, 1975. Artist undocumented, gifted to Minerva Teeman Soucie by Betty Teeman Hawley. Buckskin, beads, and shells. Tsua'a Moko (*girl's beaded moccasins*), 1973. Minerva Teeman Soucie. Deer hide, glass beads. Collection of Minerva Teeman Soucie family. Photograph by Frank Miller. Courtesy of Frank Miller and Willamette University.

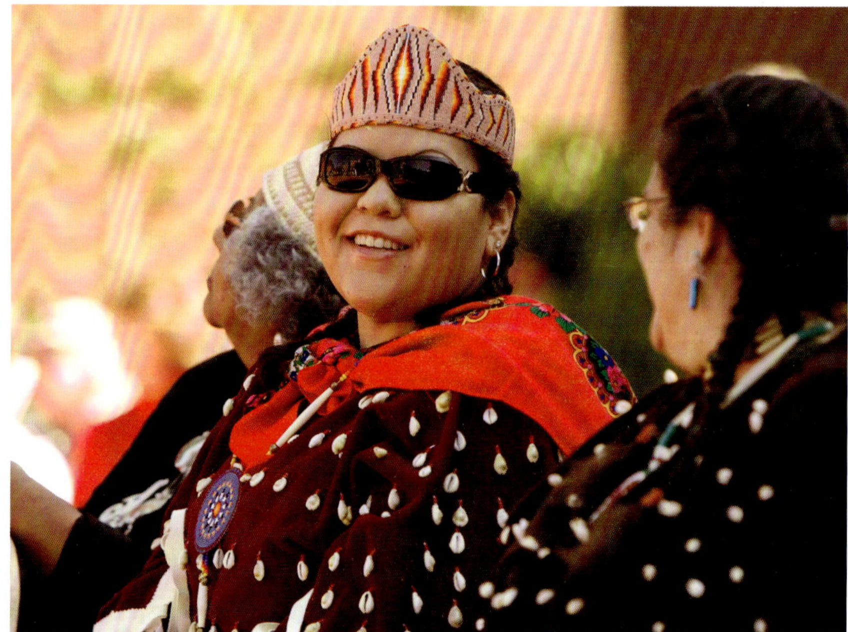

she would pass it down to *her* granddaughter someday. As her daughter, Charisse, grew up, Minerva made three gradually larger pairs of tsua'a moko (*beaded moccasins*). They provide tangible evidence of the transmission of knowledge across generations: Minerva learned how to process and tan deer hides and to bead from her mother, who had been taught by *her* mother, Mable Smoke Jim Beers, and her aunt, Marion Smoke Jim Louie, twin sisters.

The woman's outfit Minerva assembled for the exhibition was built around a remarkable Paiute dress, owa' suh / nah kwi, worn by Ramona Charles in the 1940s as a wedding dress when she married Doyle Charles, a Paiute man from Burns, Oregon. The dress is beaded across the top with seed beads and has handmade copper tins hanging down that create a jingle sound when the wearer is moving. Eventually the family traded the dress to Mavis Oard, who owned and operated a service station and a trading post and gallery in tiny Buchanan, Oregon (still owned by the Oard family).[19] Paiute families in need of cash or supplies have brought items to trade or sell to the Oards for decades; as a result, Oard's Gallery and Museum has the largest single collection of Paiute cradleboards and other handmade items in Harney County.

Although Ramona Charles's wedding dress was given a monetary value and alienated from its maker and wearer's possession when it was transferred to Oard's Gallery and Museum, from Minerva's (and a more general Paiute) perspective, the dress never stopped being a member of the Charles family or the broader "family" of ancestral knowledge. Because of her long-standing relationship with Mavis Oard, Minerva was able to borrow the Ramona Charles wedding dress for *The Art of Ceremony*.

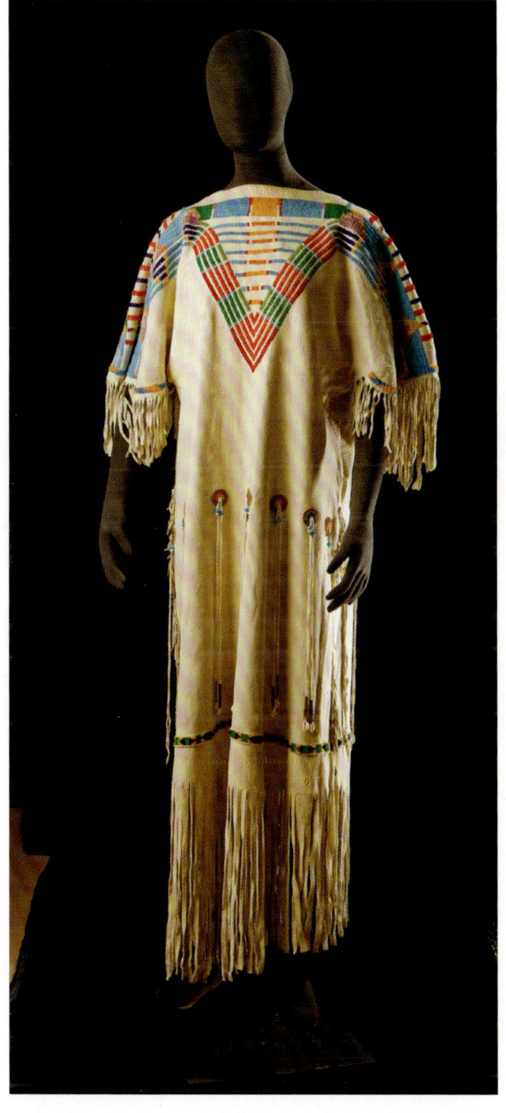

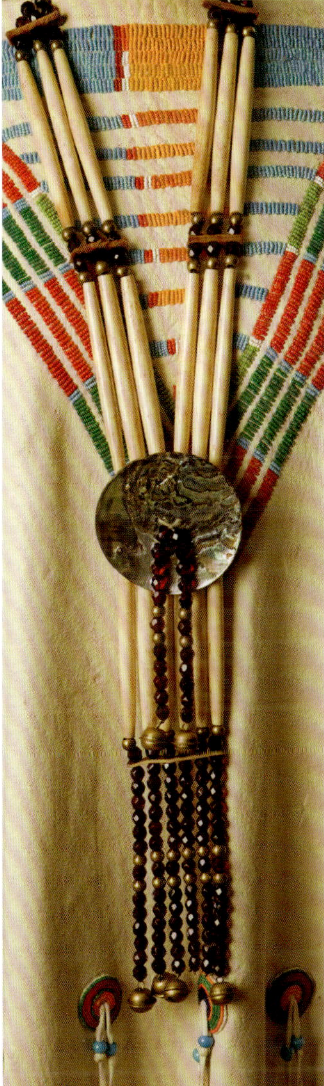

left:
Qwa' suh / nah kwi (Paiute *wedding dress*), 1940s. Attributed to Ramona Charles and family. Deer hide, glass beads, copper jingles. Worn by Ramona Charles at her marriage to Doyle Charles. Traded to Oard's Gallery and Museum, Buchanan, Oregon. Photograph by Frank Miller. Courtesy of Frank Miller and Willamette University.

right:
Brass and bone necklace, 1950s. Paiute artist. Bone pipe beads, brass bells, faceted glass beads, shell. Gift from Bernice Teeman to granddaughter Charisse Soucie. Photograph by Frank Miller. Courtesy of Frank Miller and Willamette University.

The remainder of the outfit was drawn from Minerva's family heirlooms, and although they have biographies associated with specific individuals, they are also more broadly representative of the people-land relationships at the heart of this conversation. A brass and bone necklace once owned by Minerva's mother, Bernice, graced the outfit. More than just a necklace, it represents a lifetime of traditional root digging by Bernice Teeman and the social relations surrounding the practice. Root digging was and is a social and familial experience, not just an isolated "subsistence" practice. After collecting roots, Bernice loved to offer them in trade to other Indian women. Minerva theorized that she may have acquired this brass and bone necklace during one of these bartering times, probably during the 1950s. Bernice eventually gave it to her granddaughter, Charisse Soucie, and in an extension of its trajectory as a valued item exchanged between women, the necklace has since been worn by several Paiute girls when they needed a necklace to wear with their buckskin dresses.

The woman's outfit also featured a bag made by Minerva Soucie in 1963, when she was an eighteen-year-old newlywed living in Portland, Oregon; it took a whole year to make because when Minerva ran out of beads she had to write her mother in Bend, who sent strands through the mail. The bag is beaded with a rose design; the wild rose is a plant of great significance to Great Basin peoples and considered a symbol of life. Parts of the wild rose plant were and are used for food, to make tea, as a dressing for wounds, and to make arrow shafts. The rose protects people from spiritual harm; rose flowers or water are given to those in mourning and to infants for protection and for resilience.[20]

Minerva included a pair of high-top beaded deer-hide moccasins to finish the outfit; they were made for her by a Shoshone-Bannock woman from Fort Hall, Idaho, in 1960, when she was only a teenager. Later in her life, Minerva wore them on special occasions, such as when she was tribal chair of the Burns Paiute Tribe in the 1980s and was involved with various conferences. Even later, Minerva's granddaughter Kristeny wore them when she first started learning how to fancy dance. Their inclusion in the outfit suggests how valued they had become over a lifetime, as a result of being associated with significant occasions for the wearer.

Minerva was one of the foremost weavers among the Burns Paiute, and taught youth, adults, and anyone who wanted to learn about basketry plants and techniques. She frequently made women's hats and wore them for public and ceremonial occasions. The tso-tuh-ah (*hat*) that she chose for *The Art of Ceremony* was made in 2005 from cedar bark and beargrass. Such hats were needed by Paiute women as a shield from the hot sun and to cushion the forehead when carrying a burden basket; a strap would be attached to the basket and laid on the hat, rather than directly on the forehead. Minerva also included a willow burden basket, ku-du /wo-no, made by Jennie Dick (Paiute) in 1995 and gifted to Minerva. Burden baskets were made from willow withes and twined with split willow. The willow is gathered in the fall after the first frost, stripped and sorted by size, then put away to season for a year. Paiute people believe that the willows are strong during autumn and will make sturdy baskets. Burden baskets were made to carry items in the old days from camp to camp, like a suitcase would be used today to move between households. Women carried the baskets on their backs, filled with clothing, food, and rabbit robes. The basket was suspended from a woven strap, or tumpline, that went across the hat-covered forehead to balance the basket.

Perhaps the most powerfully symbolic and generative object in the exhibition was a hu-pe (Paiute *cradleboard*) that Minerva had made in 1995 from willow sticks, deer hide, beads, and shells. Generally, a small newborn cradle was made first, then after thirty days a new, larger one was made. Babies were snugly swaddled in cradleboards for the first months of their lives and carried to be with their mothers and caregivers throughout the activities of the day, secure and included. New mothers were taught how to make the cradleboards by their grandmothers, aunties, or mothers. When she was twenty years old, Minerva was shown how to make a cradleboard by her mother: first scrape a deer hide, then tan it and fit it on a willow frame, and finally create the shade or hood. The Burns Paiute community, like others, has experienced a resurgence in cradleboard making in recent decades; Minerva was part of this renewal, as was elder Rena Adams Beers, who began making cradleboards later in life, and continued making them almost up to her passing at age ninety-nine in 2018.[21]

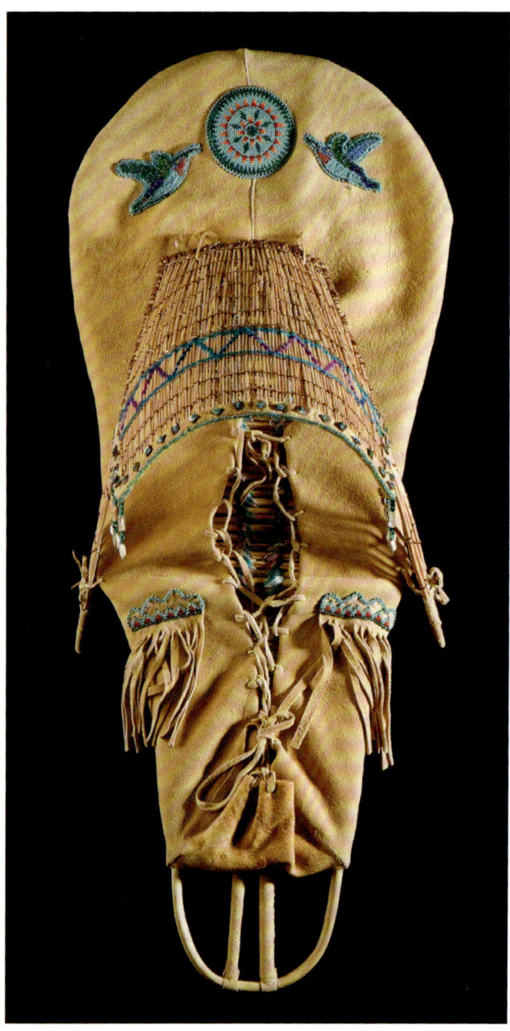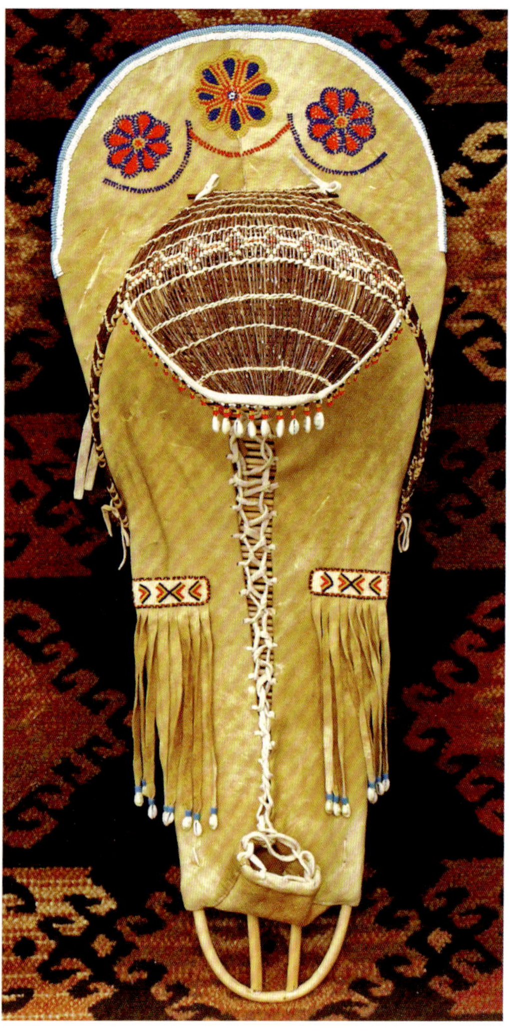

Hu-pe (Paiute *cradleboard*), 1995. Minerva Teeman Soucie. Willow, deer hide, beads, shells. Photograph by Frank Miller. Courtesy of Frank Miller and Willamette University.

Cradleboard with floral design, made prior to 2014. Rena Adams Beers. Photograph by Douglas Manger. Courtesy of the Oregon Folklife Network.

facing page:
Rena Adams Beers, at her home in Burns, Oregon, 2014. Photograph by Douglas Manger. Courtesy of the Oregon Folklife Network.

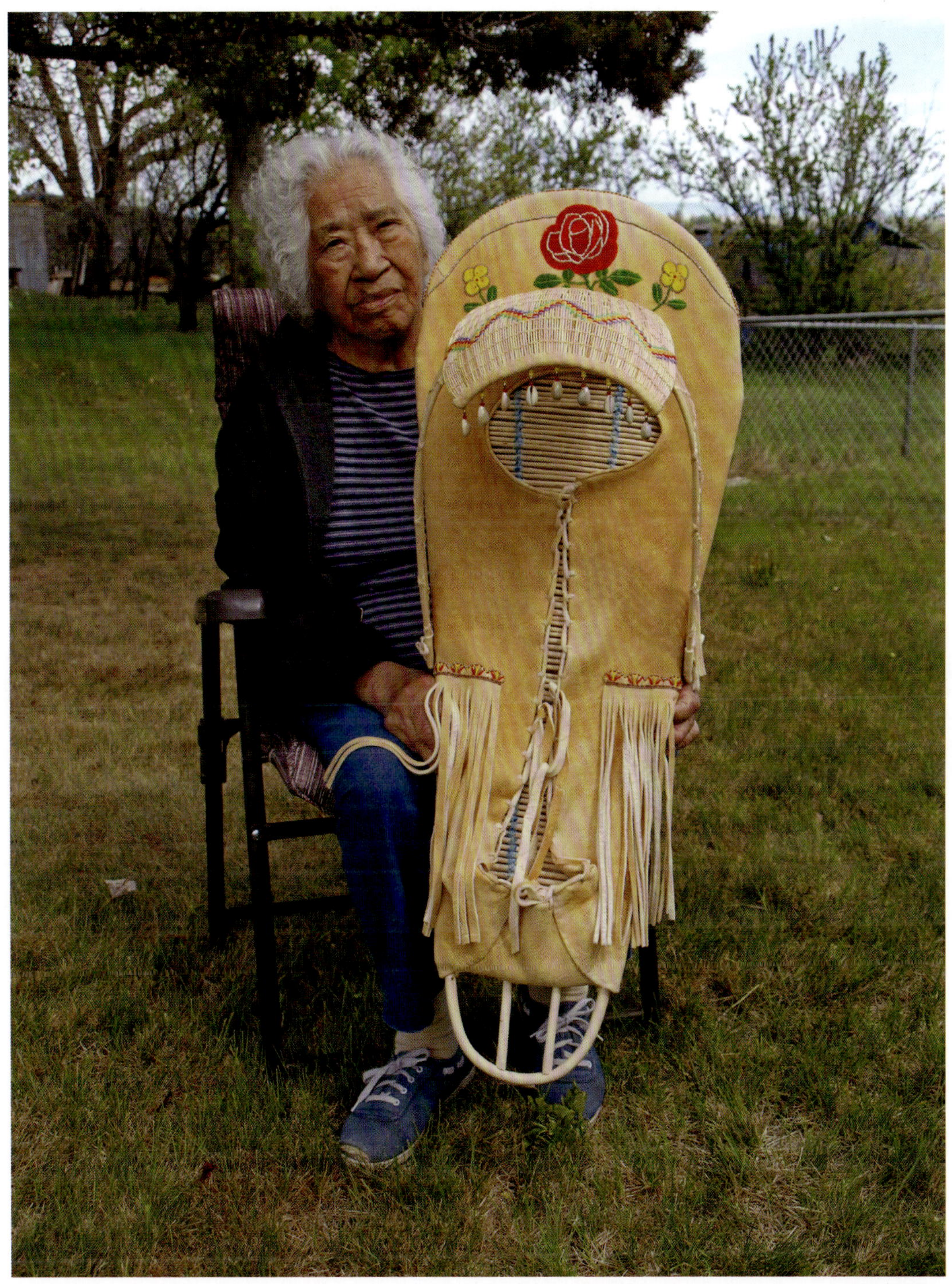

Nurturing the Family: Protecting Cultural and Natural Resources

In the weekly *Tu'Kwa Hone Newsletter* of the Burns Paiute Tribe, one can get a sense of the multifaceted ways that the Tribe is seeking to support its members.[22] While fewer than about 150 tribal citizens live on or near the Burns Paiute Reservation, the Tribe has an active after-school and summer youth program, a language program, health services, and regalia-making classes. In addition, the Tribe's Departments of Natural Resources and Cultural and Heritage are charged with protecting the Tribe's cultural and natural resources. In 2006 the Burns Paiute Tribe crafted an official Aboriginal Territorial Protection Policy, which spells out the Tribe's approach to the protections of cultural and natural resources on its vast ancestral territory. The introduction to the thirteen-page document explains the urgency behind the Tribe's concern for its homelands: "The resources found within this ancestral territory sustained the Wadatika, and provided for their material, spiritual, and medicinal needs. Today, the Tribe's prehistoric, historic, and contemporary cultural materials—including plant resources, medicines, fish, and wildlife—are on the decline throughout the Tribe's traditional territory. This decline places the preservation and maintenance of the Tribe's culture in jeopardy."[23]

The Tribe's Natural Resources Department actively seeks to protect and enhance fish and wildlife and traditional land uses. As opportunities have arisen and resources allow, the Tribe has acquired properties that the department works with diligently to mitigate prior degradation and restore native plant and animal life. The Tribe collaborates with other state and federal agencies in efforts to restore native salmonid populations (bull trout and redband trout) to the Malheur River basin; incremental success in recent years has been a source of hope, especially for tribal youth.[24]

Many thousands of acres of original Northern Paiute territory are today under the control of federal land management agencies, such as the Bureau of Land Management, the US Forest Service, and the US Fish and Wildlife Service. With great patience and persistence, the Burns Paiute Tribe has worked for decades to build constructive relationships with these agencies, with the goal of protecting their

never-ceded ancestral lands. One such federal property, the Malheur
National Wildlife Refuge, came to wide public attention in early 2016,
when an armed group of mostly white men led by Nevada rancher
Ammon Bundy took over the refuge's headquarters and illegally occupied it for forty-one days. These occupiers, or militia as they came to be
known, demanded that the refuge be "given back" to private "ranchers,
loggers, and miners," employing an anti–federal government argument
that completely disregarded Indigenous history and sovereignty.[25] The
militia denigrated the Burns Paiute relationship with the land, with one
leader, Ryan Bundy, saying that the Paiute "lost" their claim to the land
and that the "current culture is the most important," with the implication being that the current culture *is* white settler culture and excludes
contemporary Native Americans.[26]

The Northern Paiute, however, consider the area to be the very heart
of their land and crucial home of their namesake, the wada plant. Diane
Teeman explained to me why "heart" is meant as more than a metaphor:

> [The refuge] was one of the primary wada collecting areas in the
> fall. That food source . . . at one time was plentiful enough and
> important enough that that's how we got our name, even though
> [now] it's not really available and when it is available it's really not
> very accessible to us. . . . Then, just the sheer number of people
> who are still [buried] there makes it . . . of the highest importance
> to the community. . . . Its importance isn't just about its location.
> Really all of the blood vessels [the waterways in and out] have
> been impacted so heavily over the last 150 years that it's in critical
> condition.[27]

During the 2016 occupation of the refuge and its headquarters,
militia members handled tribal artifacts and records with extreme
disrespect and built roads and dug latrines in areas of great cultural
sensitivity, proximate to burials.[28] For their part, Burns Paiute tribal
members showed tremendous restraint in the face of this onslaught,
even while they decried the occupation. Then tribal chair Charlotte
Rodrique called for the federal government to fulfill its trust relationship to safeguard tribal rights and ancestral property; at the same time,
tribal members prayed for peace and chose not to engage in direct
physical confrontation with the militia.[29] But to tribal members, it was

incredibly ironic that while the militia occupied the refuge, the FBI and other federal agencies stopped the Burns Paiute from going in to protect their resources and carry out their responsibilities to the land while the authorities chose not to go in to halt the destruction by the militia. After the occupation was over, the Burns Paiute were eventually able to go back onto the refuge and, with US Fish and Wildlife Service financial support, mitigate the damage to the degree physically possible.[30] Although today the Malheur National Wildlife Refuge outwardly appears restored, the occupation brought spiritual disruption that will take time to heal.

What Has Come Before and What Will Become in the Future

The worldview of the Wadatika, as articulated by Diane Teeman, has tremendous implications: "As Indigenous people of the Northern Great Basin, we are taught that living Wadatika people have a moral imperative to protect our ancestors, our lands, and our way of life. We are charged with protecting what has come before for what will become in the future."[31] Events and lives from the past are part of the present, and careful respect for "what has come before" is essential to the future well-being of all creation. As Diane told me in our 2017 conversation, "People have been born, lived, and died everywhere on this landscape, and their essences are still there regardless of whether their body is completely returned to dust or not. But even the dust is part of [those] physical beings, that's everywhere."[32] The moral responsibility to protect the ancestors extends to the protection of all living things: "Everything has a right to be, and so we need to try and make sure that they're treated fairly. . . . When we're interacting with other things in the landscape, you don't take too many . . . but there's also this responsibility as being part of the family. If there's someone else that's encroaching or bothering [living] things to try and speak for them and protect."[33]

One of the most poignant efforts of the Burns Paiute Tribe is its work to restore tribal language.[34] Many Wadatika elders held on to their language well into the twentieth century, due to their own strength as well as their relative isolation from English-dominant urban society, and several fluent speakers are alive today. The Tribe has an active language program that encourages everyone from youth to elders to learn vocabulary and conversational fundamentals. The importance of this goes beyond interpersonal human relationships, however. Strengthening the language and having it heard on the landscape contributes to the health of the land and the people's relationship to the land. I asked Diane how encouraging the use of the Paiute language is important to the people's relationship with the land. She answered with a story:

> I was thinking about that last night, in terms of how you, when you hear the geese flying over seasonally and the mourning doves and the other animals that we have here, and how that our language is not on the landscape right now in the way that it was before. And just wondering to myself how that might be affecting everything, like the ecosystem and the traditional way of things interacting. It was on my way, actually, to the language meeting last night so I didn't have a lot of time to dwell on that issue, but it's definitely something that has been taken away from the natural system. Not just for us but for everything on the landscape. So, I think that's important for us to focus on, trying to reincorporate it back in somehow. . . . I'm not a fluent speaker so I can't attest to this through experience but through what people have told me. . . . if you talk about something in the language that is foreign to the system, the meaning is not being expressed in the way that it should be or could be. So, you're missing out on some of the nuance of the meaning when you're speaking in a different language that's not part of that familial relationship.[35]

So, to restore language is to restore the familial relationship to the land. There is no question that this is an exceedingly daunting task, in the face of the ongoing economic and social challenges faced in general by Burns Paiute tribal members. Nevertheless, the Tribe offers biweekly language classes and game nights and in 2019 hosted its first annual "Wadatika Language Bowl," a friendly competition with age-cohort teams, from children to teens to adults to elders.

Since 2016, the Burns Paiute Tribe has been developing a systematic, twenty-first-century approach to the preservation and teaching of Wadatika Yaduan (Yaduan translates as *language*). In addition to regular community gatherings and games, tribal language technicians have

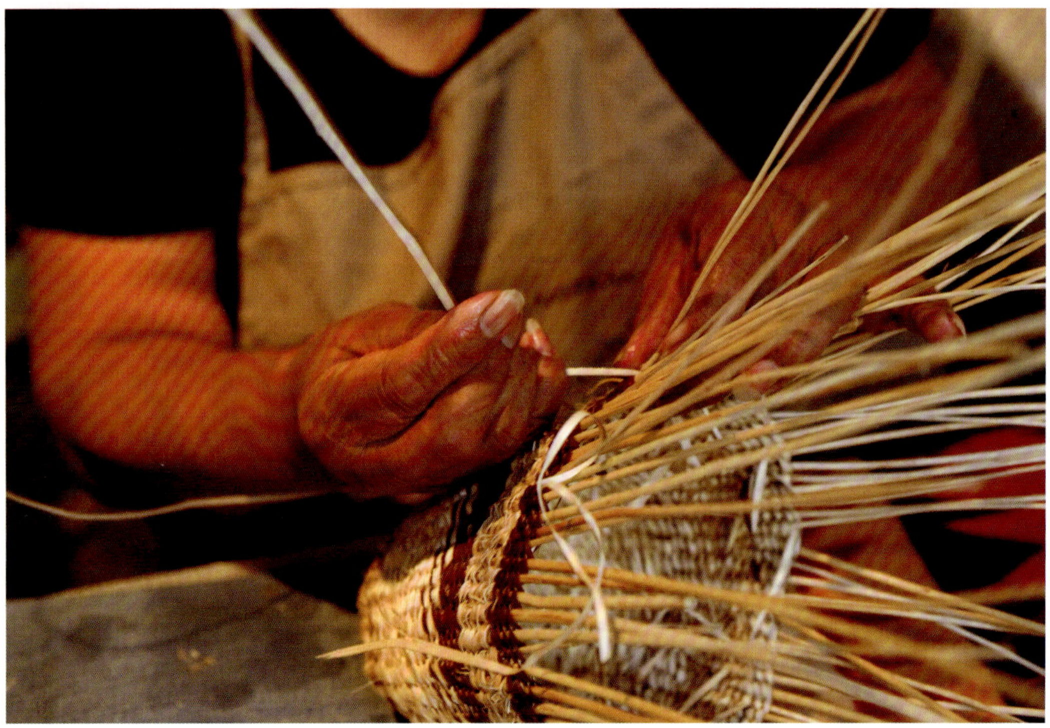

Minerva Teeman Soucie, weaving with willow sticks, September 28, 2008. Hallie Ford Museum of Art, opening program for *The Art of Ceremony.* Photograph by Frank Miller. Courtesy of Frank Miller and Willamette University.

recorded thousands of Northern Paiute words and phrases and will be developing a Wadatika Yaduan app that can be downloaded onto tablets and phones, so that conversational Paiute is just a touch away. The goal of the program is to have "the whole community interacting and expressing our Wadatika Yaduan freely, lively, and vigorously: as it once was."[36] With hope, Wadatika will be heard upon the land with increasing frequency, contributing to its healing and the restoration of family relations.

CHAPTER 2

RESTORING CONNECTIONS WITH THE LAND

The Confederated Tribes of the Coos, Lower Umpqua, and Siuslaw Indians

Sue Perry Olson, of Lower Umpqua heritage through her father's side of the family, was born in 1938. Her life story has been shaped by the Confederated Tribes of the Coos, Lower Umpqua, and Siuslaw (CTCLUSI) Indians' collective history of displacement, termination, restoration, and renewal, and in turn she has helped shape this history. The ancestral homelands of the Tribes were over 1.6 million acres along the southwestern and central coast of present-day Oregon, stretching from the Siuslaw River watershed in the north to the Umpqua River and Coos Bay to the south, ending at a pole that once stood north of Bandon, and extending inland along the crest of the Coast Range.[1] While Olson's childhood family of origin moved inland from the Tribes' ancestral homelands to near Eugene in the Willamette Valley, in adulthood Olson has worked on the effort to restore the CTCLUSI. After the confederation's hard-won 1984 restoration, the Tribes have been continuously engaged in nation-building. In this crucial historical period, Olson served on tribal committees and as an elected member of the Tribal Council.[2]

Alongside these contributions, Olson has strengthened her community through regalia-making. In 2007–8, as preparations for *The Art of Ceremony* were under way, Olson was identified by David Petrie (Hanis Coos), then the director of the CTCLUSI Culture Department, as being one of the community's most active regalia-makers. In the late twentieth century, when few other members of the CTCLUSI were in a position to make regalia, Olson researched museum and photographic collections to learn more about her people's artistic traditions. Through a process of trial and error, she taught herself how to make beaded collars, inspired particularly by photographs of Annie Miner Peterson (Miluk Coos). *The Art of Ceremony* featured a full set of women's regalia created by Olson, including a buckskin dress, a shawl, and a stunning cap made of dentalia (*Antalis pretiosum*), the shells of several species of mollusks that are found almost exclusively along the coast of what is now Vancouver Island, British Columbia.

For dentalium caps, as with the beaded collars, Olson took inspiration from her research of museum collections to reanimate these treasures' construction. As she wrote in *The Art of Ceremony* exhibition publication: "Our tribal ancestors wore a type of basket hat made of spruce roots or cedar bark and other coastal plants. Documentation

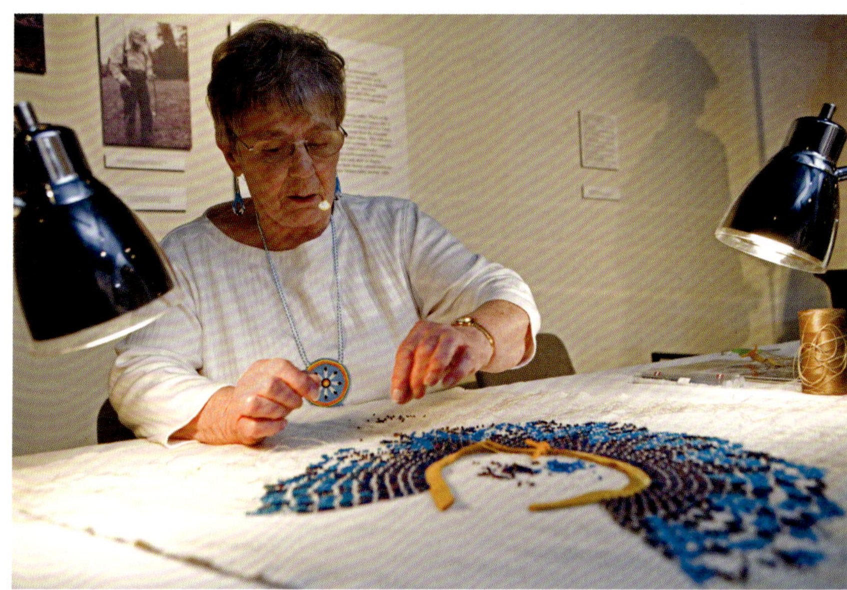

Sue Perry Olson at the Hallie Ford Museum of Art, September 28, 2008. Photograph by Frank Miller. Courtesy of Frank Miller and Willamette University.

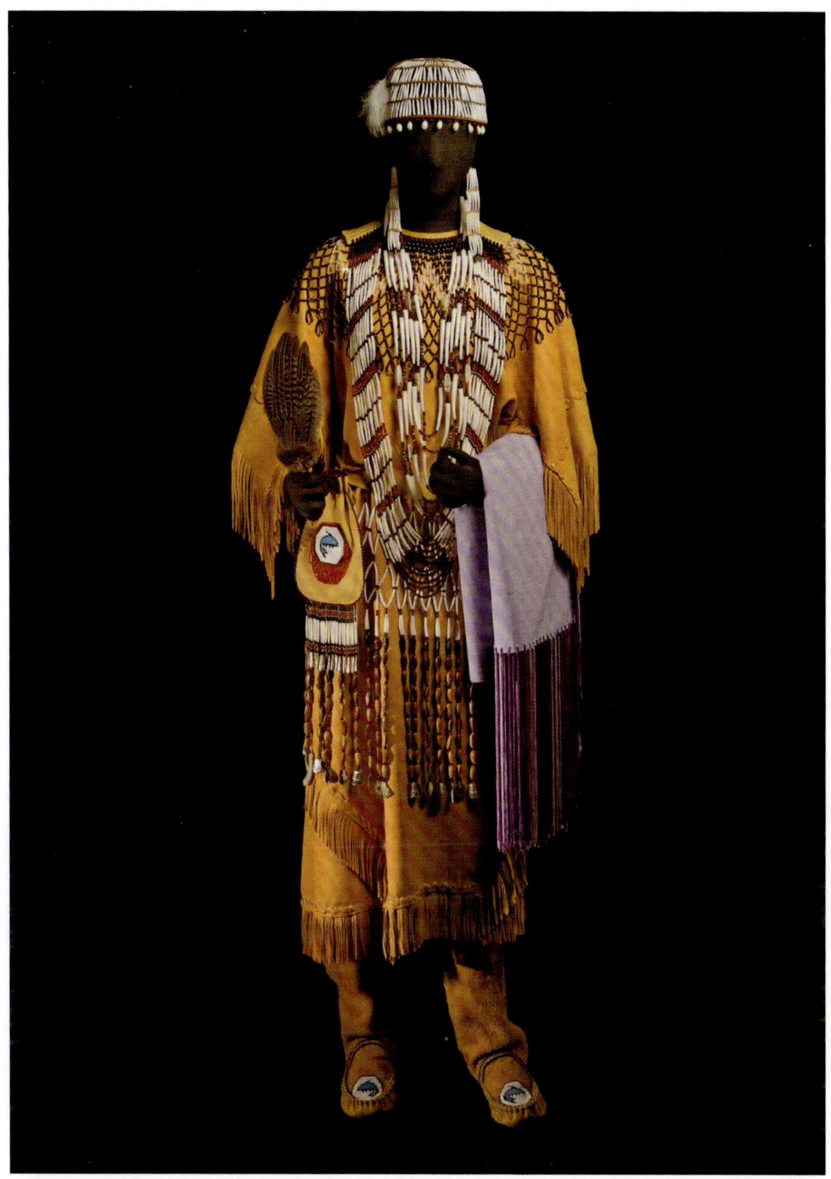

Sue Perry Olson's regalia, as displayed in *The Art of Ceremony*. Buckskin dress, 2002. Pine nut apron, 1999. Deer hide, dentalia, glass beads, pine nuts, cowrie shells, thimbles, Chinese coins, abalone. Earrings, 1995. Deer hide, dentalia, abalone, glass beads. Multiple-strand necklace, 1998. Dentalia, glass beads, metal beads, carved bone. Necklace, 1995. Dentalia, glass beads, deer hide. Salmon design pouch, 1998. Deerskin, glass beads, hair bones, tin cones. Shawl, 1995. Cotton, polyester fringe. All by Sue Perry Olson. Grouse feather fan, 2001. Artist undocumented. Grouse feathers, deer hide. Moccasins, 2001. Carol Lindhorse. Deer hide uppers and elk hide soles; glass seed beads. Collection of Sue Perry Olson. Photograph by Frank Miller. Courtesy of Frank Miller and Willamette University. For cap, see next page.

shows that some very wealthy girls wore 'white eagle head' hats made of buckskin strips and small dentalium shells. The dentalium strands were so many and fitted together so snugly that the girl's head was perfectly covered in white, just like a bald eagle's head. It took several months for me to teach myself to create this type of head covering. It is with pride and honor for our ancestors that I wear a dentalium hat as part of my regalia."[3] Dentalia, harvested from northern waters and traded to more southerly and inland tribes, have been highly valued for millennia by Indigenous peoples throughout western North America. Whether in strands or incorporated into regalia, dentalia represent wealth and status, not only in material terms but also in spiritual dimensions. Wealth comes in part from the good one does for the community.

By this measure, Olson is herself a treasure, as she has shared her knowledge generously with her community, helping to spur renewed interest in beaded collars, which many tribal members can now make for themselves and their family members. The collars have become one of many symbols of renewal for the CTCLUSI. Tribal member Patricia Whereat Phillips (Miluk Coos), author of *Ethnobotany of the Coos, Lower Umpqua, and Siuslaw Indians*, pointed out to me that the collars' method of construction—a netting stitch—is kin to the techniques used to weave fiber cordage into fishing nets, here and the world over.[4]

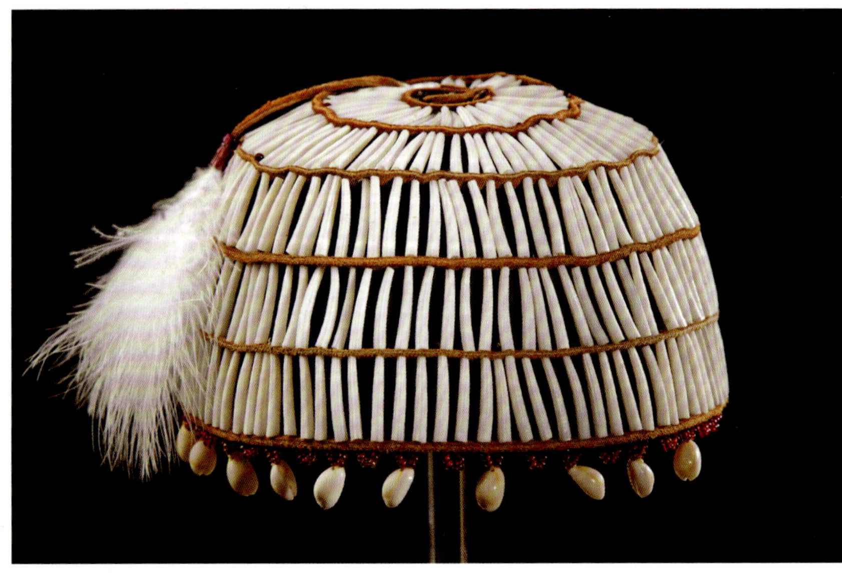

Dentalium cap, 2002. Sue Perry Olson. Dentalia, deer hide, glass beads, cowrie shells. Collection of the artist. Photograph by Frank Miller. Courtesy of Frank Miller and Willamette University.

With this in mind, the netted collars can be understood to symbolize a connection among people, artistry, and resources—a connection that leads to the next dimension of the CTCLUSI's story of renewal.

First, though, to fully understand the challenges facing the Coos, Lower Umpqua, and Siuslaw peoples, it is critical to have an overview of their histories.[5] These three Tribes are four neighboring bands: to the south, the Hanis Coos and Miluk Coos, who spoke two related but distinct languages, and to the north, the Lower Umpqua (Quuiich) and Siuslaw (Sha'yuushtl'a), who spoke Siuslawan (Sha'yuushtl'a wa'as).[6] Although there were distinctions among these locally sovereign groups, all relied on an abundance of coastal, riverine, and forest resources. By the early 1800s, European explorers and fur trappers had entered the Tribes' homelands, bringing smallpox and measles, with catastrophic effects on the Indigenous population. After the boundaries of the US portion of the Oregon Country were negotiated with Britain in 1846, more settlers flooded in, disrupting Indigenous lifeways. In 1855 the three Tribes negotiated a treaty with the United States that would have ceded ancestral lands in exchange for compensation and protection by the federal government. However, Congress essentially ignored the treaty, and the Senate never brought it to a vote for ratification. This meant that the Tribes' ancestral lands were taken without compensation with the devastating consequence of leaving the Tribes in legal limbo and exceptionally vulnerable.

As settler-Indian relations became more violent in Oregon, many tribal members were forcibly removed from Coos Bay north to Fort Umpqua in 1856 (although some tribal women were allowed to stay in their Coos Bay homelands if they were married to white settlers; these women included Jane Jordan and Jane Talbot, from whom many tribal members today are descended). Then in 1859 another forced removal occurred, to a reserve at the Alsea Sub-agency of the Great Coast Reservation on the Yachats River, where an extraordinary number of people, probably half, died from the horrible conditions. Yet less than a generation later, in 1875, due to the closure of the Alsea Sub-agency, the people were ordered to move to the northern Siletz Reservation. Some did move, but many did not and with great effort returned to their homelands, lands where their relatives and distant ancestors were laid to rest and which held their hunting and gathering locations. Although this land had been transformed, it was still home. Coos, Lower Umpqua, and Siuslaw people did their best to survive, often intermarrying with whites or finding other ways to adjust to the new settler society.

Although they were without formal recognition as a tribal confederation, and under tremendous pressure to assimilate, many tribal members quietly maintained relationships with their lands through resource tending, harvest practices, and related ceremonies. As they had for millennia prior to colonization, tribal members practiced Indigenous self-governance by continuing to meet, gather, and converse about matters of concern. In 1916, recognizing that an elected council was advantageous for dealing with the federal government, the Tribes organized a contemporary government structure. Between 1916 and 1941 the Tribes pursued land claims with the federal government, an effort that demonstrated a commitment to its membership and way of life. The federal authorities wrongfully denied the land claims and the Tribes were never compensated for the lands they lost in the nineteenth century.

In 1941 the Bureau of Indian Affairs took into trust a small parcel of 6.1 acres in the Empire area of Coos Bay for the Tribes and built a Tribal Hall, where the council regularly met throughout the twentieth century and which is still in use today. In the 1940s and 1950s the US federal government promoted tribal termination, a policy strongly opposed by the Confederated Tribes, who were still seeking recognition. Despite their objection, the Coos, Lower Umpqua, and Siuslaw Tribes were included in the 1954 Western Oregon Termination Act. After three decades of tremendous effort on the part of many tribal members and families, the Tribes were legally restored by Congress in 1984. However, a land base was not restored at the same time, thus compromising the Tribes' efforts toward self-sufficiency. Though in the decades since 1984 the CTCLUSI acquired modest parcels of land, it took until 2018 for Congress to rectify the situation with the passage of the Western Oregon Tribal Fairness Act, which transfers nearly 15,000 acres of federal land into trust for the Tribes.[7] The following accounts need to be understood against this backdrop. One of the core elements of this story is the key role that the relationship with natural resources and the generation and transmission of related knowledge have played in the community, despite the violence of displacement and interruption.

Clamming as Ceremony

When I reached out to the CTCLUSI Culture Department in 2015 to discuss how we might approach the development of this chapter, I became acquainted with Jesse Beers (Siuslaw), who became its director in 2013. Jesse, born in 1982, is part of a generation of younger leaders who are actively working to renew and strengthen the tribal community's land-coast-resources relationships. Beers grew up inland, within Siuslaw homelands near Indian Creek; after college, he was a committee member on the CTCLUSI Child Protection Team and then became staff for the Tribes. It was he who suggested that clam digging be featured as an example of the connection between tribal members and their homelands and traditional resources—of the living art of ceremony.

At Jesse's invitation, Willamette University photographer Frank Miller and I attended a CTCLUSI clam-dig outing on a Saturday morning under silvery skies in Coos Bay in April 2016. We assembled first at the Tribal Hall; Jesse and his wife and two children were joined by a handful of other tribal members. Together, we drove to the boat launch and with Doug Barrett (Siuslaw), the skipper, readied the Tribes' canoe

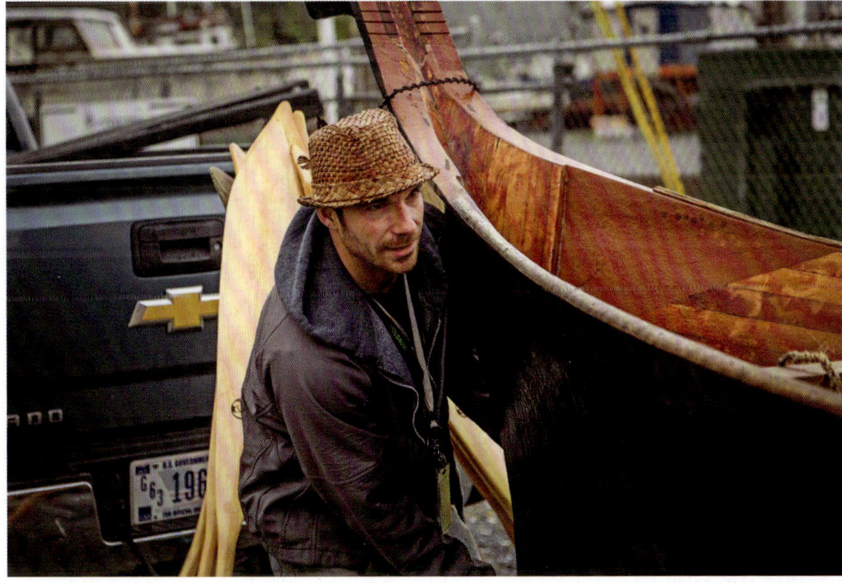

Jesse Beers, Coos Bay, Oregon, 2016. Photograph by Frank Miller. Courtesy of Frank Miller and Willamette University.

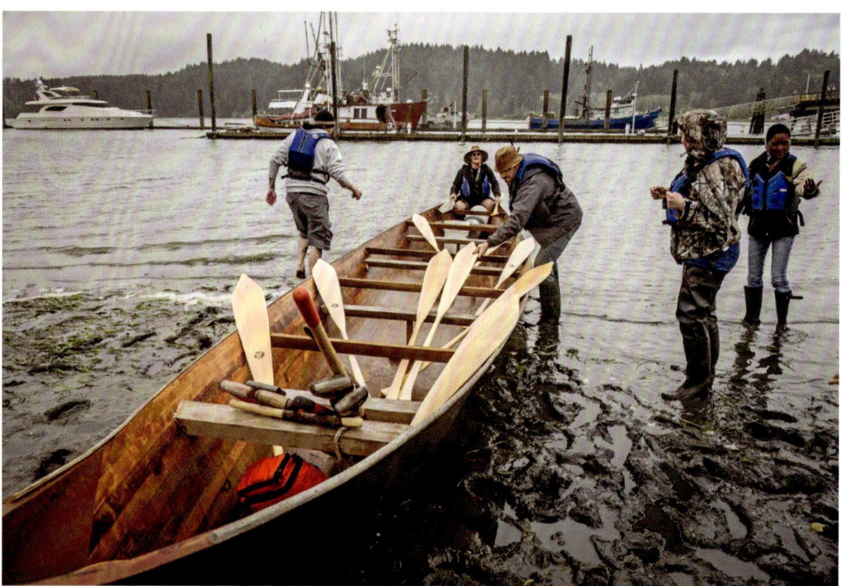

Coos, Lower Umpqua, and Siuslaw tribal members preparing canoe for launch, Coos Bay, Oregon, 2016. Photograph by Frank Miller. Courtesy of Frank Miller and Willamette University.

to be launched. After placing the canoe in the water, Jesse and Doug led the group in smudging the canoe and ourselves in sage smoke, and together we prayed for a good day, giving thanks to the Creator.

We paddled out to the clam-dig site, which at low tide was a spit of sand below a bluff where an ancient village once thrived. In the shadow of the ancestral village, the group fanned out to dig for clams. Members of the Tribes' Brainard family were already there on the shore, beginning to fill their buckets. John Schaefer, a water protection specialist and biologist for the CTCLUSI as well as a tribal member of Hanis Coos background, had joined us, having motored the Tribes' water-quality monitoring boat (used this day as a backup safety boat for the canoe) parallel to the canoe. John did his best to help me spot the presence of clams from the surface; he had extraordinary ability, gained through decades of experience, to look at the sand and know where the clams were by interpreting surface holes and bubbles. To me it was a foreign language; to him, it was a native tongue. The variety of species was amazing: gapers, Empires, horsenecks, butter clams, Martha Washingtons.

After a couple hours of clamming, we paddled back to the dock, Doug guiding us on how to paddle, at what pace and direction, when to put paddles up and catch the wind. On the trip out, Doug had spoken

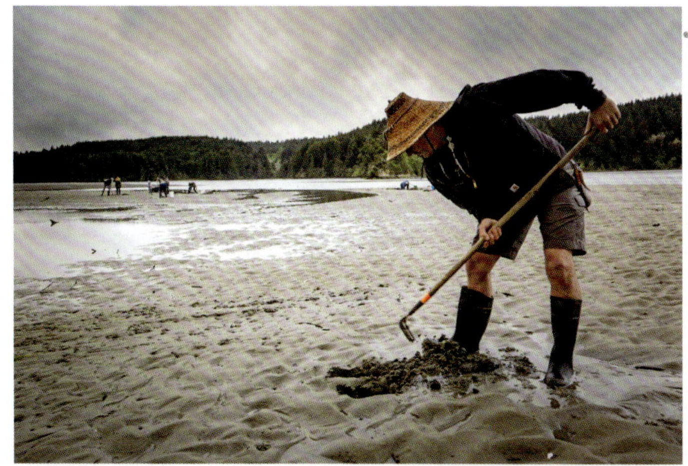

Doug Barrett, Confederated Tribes of Coos, Lower Umpqua, and Siuslaw Indians canoe family skipper, digging for clams, Coos Bay, Oregon, 2016. Photograph by Frank Miller. Courtesy of Frank Miller and Willamette University.

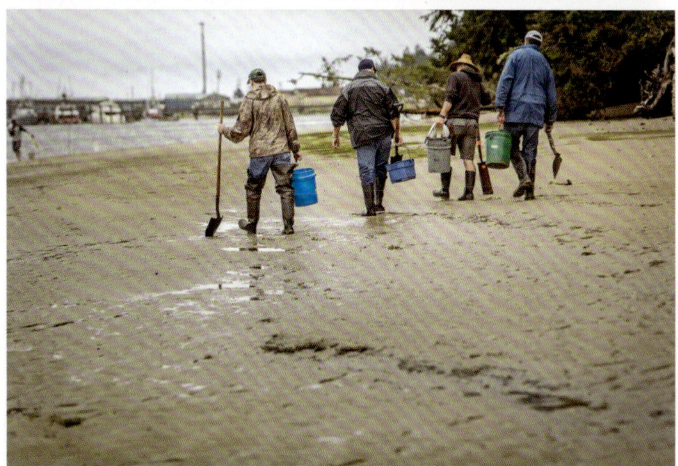

Clamming group returning to canoe, Coos Bay, Oregon, 2016. Photograph by Frank Miller. Courtesy of Frank Miller and Willamette University.

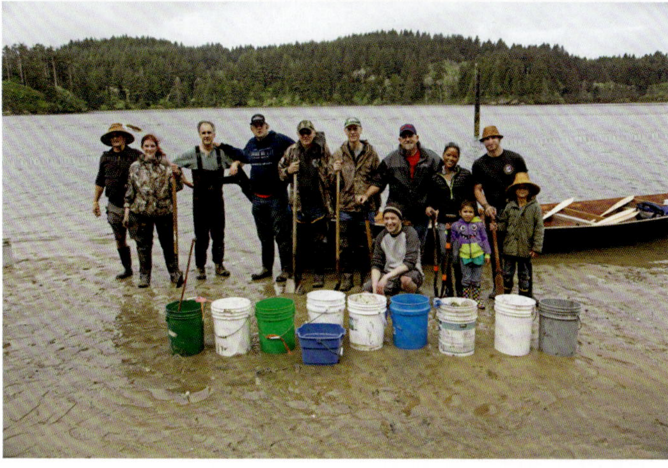

Clamming party, Coos Bay, Oregon, 2016. Left to right, back row: Doug Barrett, KayLynn Vaughan, John Schaefer, Andrew Brainard, Roy Brainard, Warren T. Brainard, Bill Logans (non-tribal member), Maree Beers, Jesse Beers. Front row: Scott Slyter, Zhade Beers, Ramil Beers. Photograph by Frank Miller. Courtesy of Frank Miller and Willamette University.

of how the canoe brings well-being for those who paddle; this message of the canoe and its restorative properties is one widespread in the Pacific Northwest, where tribal canoe families have been formed in many communities (see chapter 5, "Canoe Family, Dig Deep: The Confederated Tribes of Grand Ronde," for further discussion of the tribal Canoe Journey movement). We unloaded the clams at the dock, and paddled the canoe back to shore. With the help of the Brainards, the canoe was pulled in and loaded on the trailer; the whole community went back to the Tribal Hall and, after lunch, began cleaning the shellfish. Everyone worked, teaching techniques as needed to novices like me and leaning over outdoor sinks, shared hoses, knives, and buckets. By afternoon's end, buckets of clams were ready to take home to family members and deliver to elders.

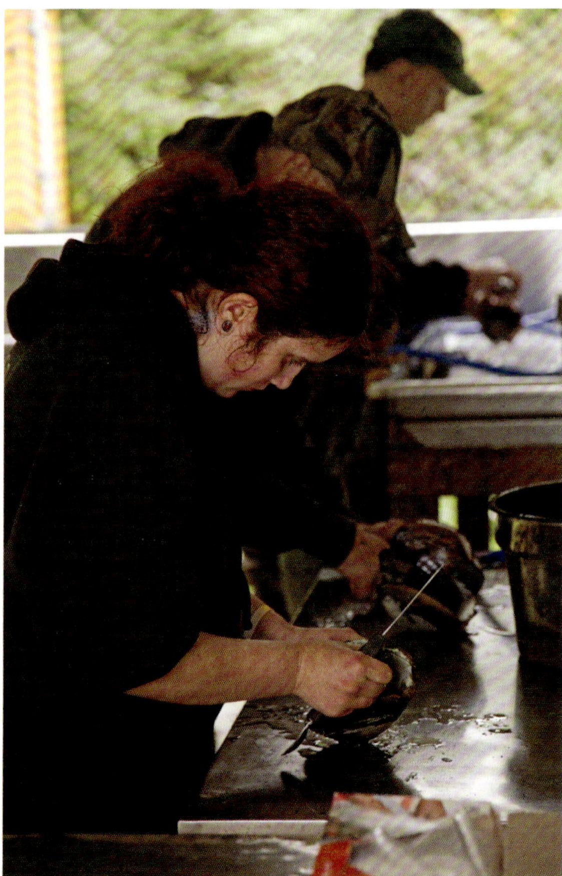

KayLynn Vaughan (Hanis Coos), cleaning clams. Confederated Tribes of Coos, Lower Umpqua, and Siuslaw Indians Community Center, 2016. Photograph by Frank Miller. Courtesy of Frank Miller and Willamette University.

To continue the dialogue about the renewal of land-people relationships, I returned to Coos Bay in summer 2017 to interview tribal
members at the Department of Natural Resources and Culture over
the course of a few days.[8] At the CTCLUSI these two departments have
been combined since 2016, embodying the approach that "culture" is
not independent of "nature." In our conversation Jesse reflected on how
the experience of clam digging offered continuity with tribal ancestors
and a way of being a tribal member today. He said:

> It's something that we get to do that we do just like our ancestors.
> . . . It's communal. When you think about it in relation to arts of
> ceremony, it's not just going out and clam digging. There's bless-
> ing of yourself and your tools before you go. You have to prepare
> yourself for getting into the canoe. To me, it makes it more of a
> sacred thing. It allows you to put in some extra work, sweat; those
> aren't bad things, those are good things. To be able to get out
> there and canoe to a spot that for the Coos people is a traditional
> village site. So you're going to a spot that your ancestors dug clam.
> It's just amazing to me.

Margaret Corvi (Hanis Coos), then-director of natural resources
for the CTCLUSI, born in 1977, vividly remembered clam digging from
childhood, going out with family and getting muddy. When she became
a mother, it was so essential to Margaret that her son have this experience that she took him out on the clam flats before he was two months
old. She said:

> I took him out [on the clam flats] before I went back to work. I
> carried him out there in a pack on me, changed his diaper out
> there because it's way too far to try to go back. It was so import-
> ant for me to have him out there already and know what that was
> about. I think it's very important for me to convey how that's part
> of who we are: We dig clams, we eat clams. I want to pass that on.
> That's a reflection of how significant that is in my childhood, in
> growing up. I retained the importance of fish and shellfish; that
> was already in me. My parents and grandparents and everybody
> was like, "Yes, these are your resources."

Ashley Russell (Miluk Coos), who was born in 1986, grew up away from Coos Bay yet strongly recalls going out first-foods gathering when she visited her father and his family: clam digging, crabbing, mushroom picking, fishing. As a young adult, with an environmental science degree from Oregon State University, she returned to the Tribes in 2014 and began working in water-quality protection. She's come to understand just how impacted traditional shellfish resources have been by pollutants and toxins, and is reluctant to go clamming or crabbing as a result. It is painfully ironic that just at the time younger generations are returning to learn about their ancestral resources, tribal scientists are documenting just how polluted some of these resources are. Ashley expressed hope that as her fellow tribal members continue to harvest despite these environmental impacts, the broader public will recognize Indigenous history and presence: "We were here. And [we are here] to reestablish our culture and our ties to the land and be good stewards of those lands. Hopefully that will rub off on the rest of the community!"

In addition to these tribal staff members in Natural Resources and Culture, I spoke with Hanis Coos elder Don "Doc" Slyter, born in 1951, who has served on the Tribal Council many times and was elected Tribal Chief in 2020 for a ten-year term. Doc's mother, Carolyn Slyter (also Hanis Coos), was one of the many tribal members who worked tirelessly for restoration in 1984. Doc emphasized the ways that clamming and other experiences, such as the annual salmon ceremony in August, create a context to "get the community back so you can have those talks," time to share knowledge as well as values, especially with younger tribal members. He described four qualities—courage, patience, endurance, and alertness—that are developed through shared community practices. These qualities, along with gratitude, enhance one's ability to be an effective and responsible harvester of resources: "It is up to us to give thanks for [all of creation]. Everybody likes to be thanked. I think we tend to have that tendency more to take everything for granted. That is where that alertness comes in. They say the Creator hid special things out in plain sight. You're not going to see them unless you use that alertness. Ceremony to give thanks for what you receive is a really important thing to do. It makes you a part of what is around you."[9] The practice of clamming in community with other tribal members is one way this becoming takes place.

Weaving Ancestral Ties

Basket weaving is another dimension of community life that brings tribal members into relationship with natural resources and the transfer of customary knowledge. Weaving, like food harvesting, begins with being in right relationship with the source materials. As Jesse Beers explained:

> All the gathering of materials is very similar, whether you're eating it, whether you're giving it to somebody else to utilize to make a basket, or using it for medicine, or whatever you're using it for. There's always some sort of ceremony that goes into it, there's always some kind of trade that's happening, whether it be tobacco or sage to smudge or, if you don't have something, a little bit of hair or something. You're giving of yourself, you're giving of something you have for something. That really comes down to just showing that you are thankful for that thing. That plant or tree or clam is giving a part or a whole of itself to you. Whether you look at it like that or not, it's happening. So, in our minds and hearts, we just want to make sure that we're seen as being thankful for those things because that's what our traditions teach us.

One of many punishing consequences of colonization was the rupture of weaving traditions, including cultural knowledge of plant harvesting, processing, and weaving technologies. In the past few decades, CTCLUSI tribal members of various generations have reengaged with these traditions. Brenda Brainard (Miluk Coos), born in 1956, a mere forty-eight days before final termination, began taking weaving classes in the 1990s and immediately "fell in love" with it. The smell and feel of cedar, she said, have an affecting impact upon her. When she went home and told her parents as much, her father "dragged out all of our family baskets that had been in storage." Brenda recalled:

> These baskets had been passed down from my great-grandmother to my grandfather, when he passed away to his wife, my grandmother, and then my grandmother gave them to my father. So, there were all these Coos tribal baskets. I was just euphoric, touching them, holding them. I could feel my ancestors in those

works of art. Basketry deepened my tie to my tribal culture and I was drawn to the baskets and immersed myself into what constitutes a Coos/Southern Coast basket: What is basketry according to my Tribe's style and culture; what materials did we use; how did we use them; when did we use them; what they were used for and what they were not used for. Then, I just started working with a lot of different teachers from the West Coast tribes all the way from Northern California up the Coast into Washington. There were some people and teachers that really knew a lot about the baskets from the southwestern Oregon Coast. I was able to take my baskets to them and they were able to tell me very specific nuances about them that made them from our Tribe.

Initially Brenda focused more on gathering and processing the materials than on basket making. An elder from Washington State insisted that Brenda learn to weave so she could teach others. This precious elder told her: "You need to be a teacher." So Brenda learned to weave so that she could teach. In the years since that time, she has inspired many other tribal members to take up the practice, which for some becomes a way of life.

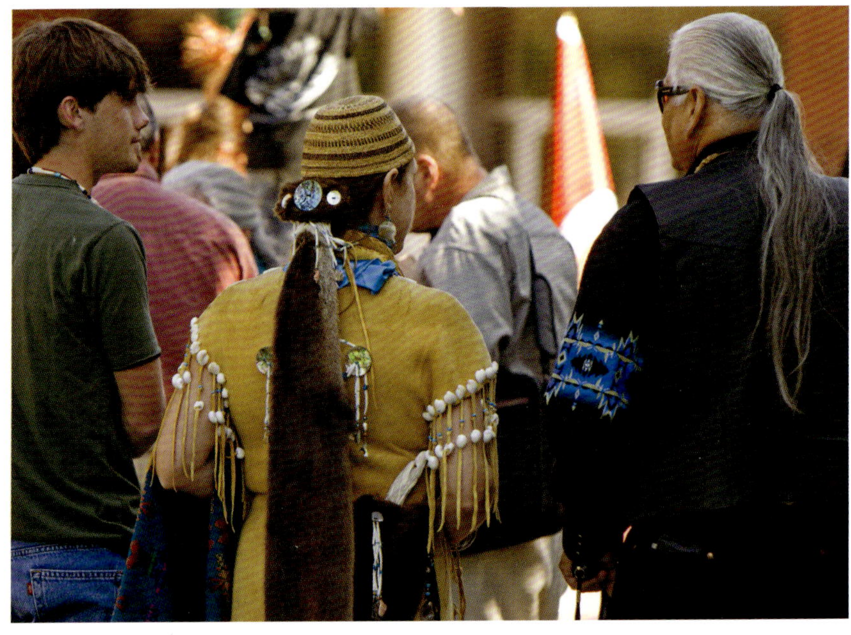

At opening ceremonies for *The Art of Ceremony*, Willamette University, September 27, 2008. Left to right: Mark Petrie, Brenda Brainard, and Joe Brainard. Photograph by Frank Miller. Courtesy of Frank Miller and Willamette University.

Weaving reinforces social bonds and in that way builds a sense of community for tribal members who participate. As Patricia Whereat Phillips, who was born in 1969, explained, weaving "tends to be social." She said:

> You have a small group of people getting together to collect something and [have] a class. It's getting out in nature and reconnecting with the plants and the land. Plants also have a spirit, so they're not treated like inanimate objects. They are living things. A lot of tribes teach that the plants want to have a relationship with people, going back thousands of years, these relationships with people digging and aerating the soil, which helps the plants in the long run. We're all working together with plants to create a thriving plant community, which in turn benefits some of the animals. There's complex cultural and ecological relationships there. And language ties into it, because people want to learn the original names of plants for that particular region and then carry on this ancient tradition of basketry. We can look at these samples from the past that are amazing, [yet] it creates a whole new level of understanding to go out into the wild and gather the plants and season them and learn how to put these different materials together and create something. At the same time, both very new and very old!

Taking inspiration from Brenda and Patricia and other tribal members, younger generations born in the 1970s and after are taking up weaving. In 2015 contemporary fine artist Sara Siestreem (Hanis Coos, born in 1976) began a "field to studio" weaving program for tribal members that focused on every stage involved in the art form—from identifying and collecting source materials on ancestral lands, to processing the gathered fibers, to creating baskets themselves.[10] These experiences not only taught skills but also created a community of practitioners who generated deeper ties with one another and with the lands upon which they gathered. In summer 2016, Sara worked with the University of Oregon Museum of Natural and Cultural History to organize *Continuum*, an exhibit of work made by her and the tribal members who were involved in the weaving program, alongside selections from that museum's collection of Coos Bay baskets, which had provided important inspiration to Sara. In an artist statement composed in 2018 for an exhibition project at the Pacific Northwest College of Art in Portland, Sara reflected upon how vital it is that her community reanimate its weaving and regalia-making practices, especially for rising generations:

> The genocide that arrived in my tribal community in the 1850s was almost complete. Our cultural lifeways have been hibernating since that time. My generation did not have the privilege of growing up wearing [regalia] items, speaking our language, practicing our traditional arts, or living the seasonal round. We are working to bring these traditions back but the wounds are still pretty active in places.
>
> Part of the colonial agenda was to alienate us from our traditions, to infect us with identity crisis through forced assimilation, so that in and through our pain and confusion we will be complicit in the death of our culture. Part of wanting to provide our tribal youth with the finery of our culture from an early age is to help them identify with all parts of themselves. I want them to be able to connect all the parts of their life and represent this way of being with ease and celebration. My goal is that our youth grow up feeling proud and beautiful in their skin and cultural effects, to know who we are, to feel the love of our ancestors, and be able to help shoulder our responsibility to our community and the next generations with our support and guidance. I want to silence the oppressor's voice, inside and outside of us, and replace it with the ones who have always been with us and who put us here to begin with.[11]

This desire—to reanimate traditions and for youth to "grow up feeling proud and beautiful" and "feel the love of our ancestors"—was echoed in the words of the weavers I spoke with in 2017 who had participated in the workshops with Sara. These weavers included Margaret Corvi, Ashley Russell, and Courtney Krossman, all of whom are or have been staff of the Department of Natural Resources and Culture and have a strong investment in learning to weave.

Margaret emphasized the importance of learning together with others. At the time of our 2017 interview, given the demands of her job as natural resources director and her role as a mother, she had not yet had time to weave many baskets. However, the practice of weaving, she said, has been "a very spiritual experience for me." Margaret worked on one basket made of spruce root over the course of a year, and when it was finished, she felt it was "one of the most beautiful things I've made in a long time. . . . I did a lot of it with other people and it represents conversations you have, it represents connections that you have to the place wherever the plant came from. It was really just a huge celebration of my ancestors."

Water-quality protection expert Ashley Russell spoke of how learning to gather materials and to weave offers her a connection with the land and with her ancestors in a way she did not have as a child growing up away from Coos Bay. After her return to Coos Bay to work for the CTCLUSI, Ashley learned to gather spruce roots, initially from fellow

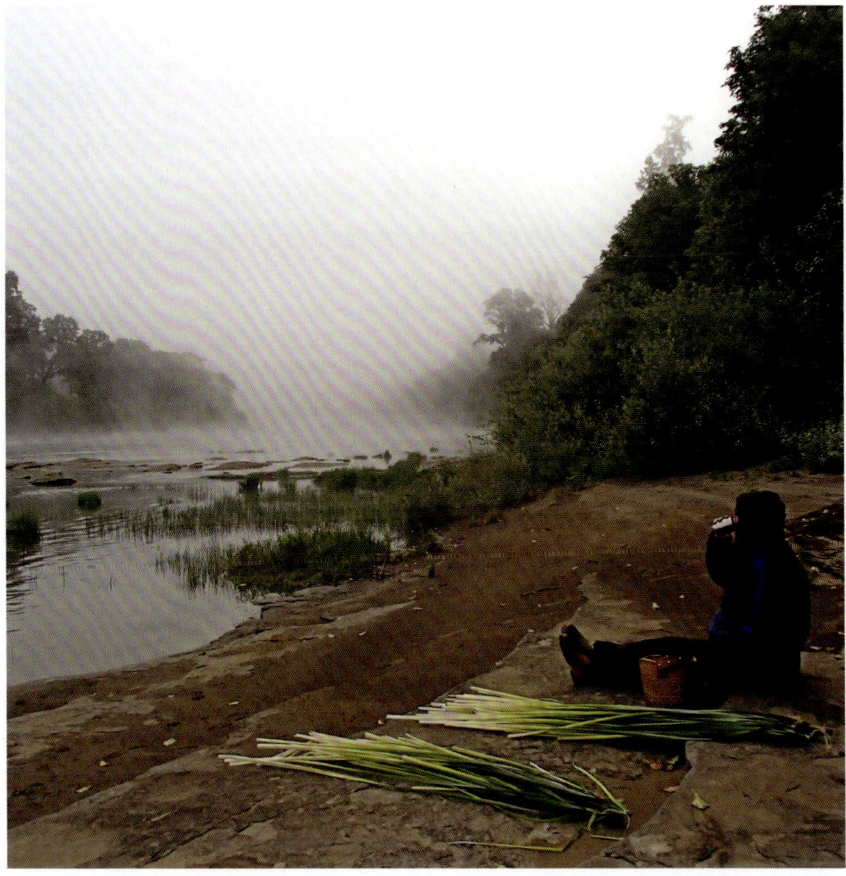

Amanda Craig (Hanis Coos), harvesting tule, 2016. Photograph by Sara Siestreem (Hanis Coos).

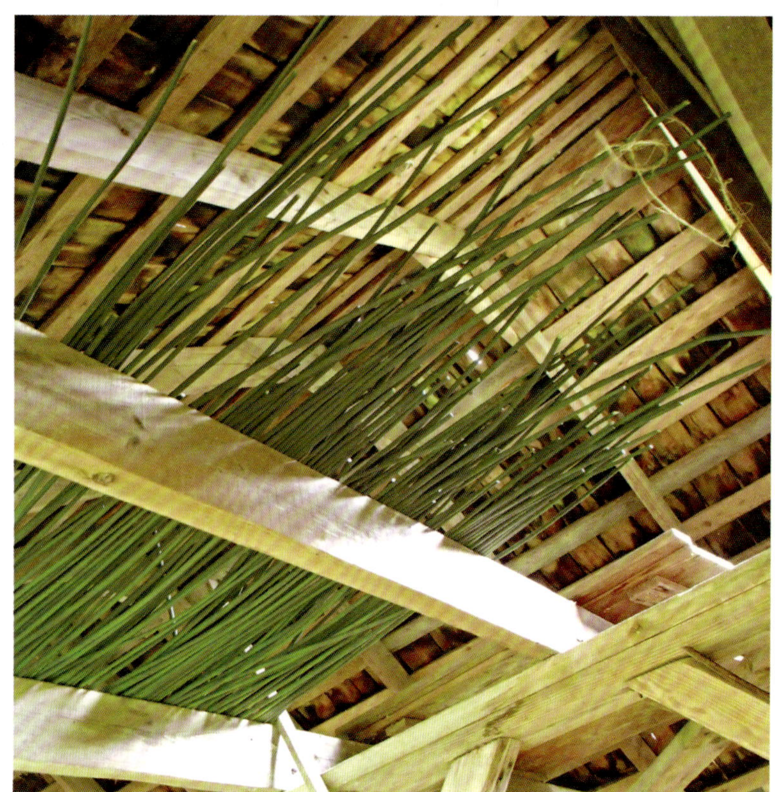

Tule drying after weavers' harvest, 2016. Photograph by Sara Siestreem (Hanis Coos).

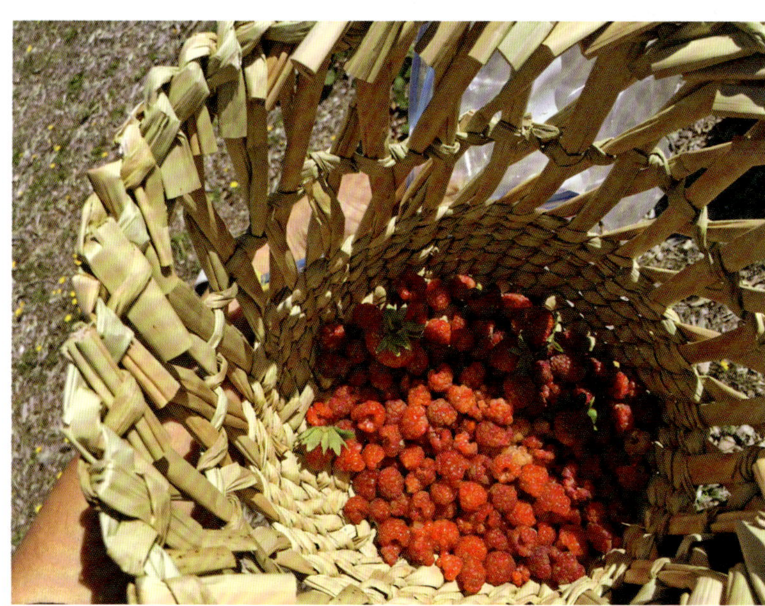

Tule basket made by Ashley Russell, with raspberries and strawberries gathered from tribal community garden, 2015. Photograph by Ashley Russell. Courtesy of the Confederated Tribes of Coos, Lower Umpqua, and Siuslaw Indians.

tribal member Enna Helms. She joined the annual cedar bark pull sponsored by the Tribes, and she apprenticed to Sara Siestreem in the weaving workshop program. When gathering, Ashley takes her children along with her and stresses to them the importance of being a good steward of resources. She explains to them that the process of gathering is ceremonial: "You speak to the tree and it speaks to you. You have to actually have a conversation. It's reciprocal; you're taking from that tree so you're asking for permission, saying, 'Hey I want to do this with you, making a beautiful basket or this is what I plan on doing.' Then paying for it."

Ashley described making an offering of locally cultivated tobacco, or some other kind of offering that had taken effort to produce, in reciprocity for the years of effort the plants invest to be ready to harvest. She feels that the ancestors are almost calling out to her, when she is on the land, saying, "'Hurry up! I've got all this information I want to unload on you. Where you been? I'm glad you're ready now.'" Ashley explained: "I feel as a descendant it's a responsibility in order to bring back those traditions, bring back the culture. Otherwise my ancestors, they suffered and died for nothing. It's really, really strong. Pressure's on." This kind of pressure may be daunting, but it is also tremendously motivating: Ashley not only is a weaver and conservation scientist, she is also renowned as a fine singer, who studies archival recordings of songs and creates new ones to share with her community.

Courtney Krossman (Miluk Coos), born in 1994, works in Cultural Resource Protection for the Tribes. She emphasizes that weaving materials are both natural *and* cultural resources. Courtney considers watching out for these resources, the "weaving gardens that have been there for thousands of years," central to her job. She studied archaeology and Native American Studies at University of Oregon and returned to work for the CTCLUSI as an intern in natural resources in 2015. Since then, she has become involved in Canoe Journeys, skippering a women's canoe, and played an important role in interviewing tribal elders and community members about traditional cultural resources. So far, Courtney has done more gathering than actual weaving but feels that weaving is "something we should be doing, we've always been doing. As soon as I wove my first basket, I was just hooked." She's particularly excited that tribal members are making baskets to be used for things like clamming. "We want to use them," she says, "we don't want them to sit on a shelf."

This idea is reinforced by Brenda Brainard, who stresses that utilitarian baskets were made every day, used up and made again, and "they should be just as precious to our people as more intricate, decorative baskets." She gave the example of children's duck-egg collecting pouches, woven simply from tule reeds. These were purposefully small in part to teach "that you don't take many eggs from one nest." Brenda stresses that it is important to know not "only this is how you make the basket, but this is how this basket was used and this is why you made the basket this way." Knowing and practicing such traditions, to Brenda, is "a way of remaining who you are and what you are." Brenda illustrated this with a profound example. She once came across a cedar tree near Florence whose bark had been peeled perhaps a hundred years earlier by another gatherer.

In response, Brenda said, "I just sat down. I was almost crying. To think my ancestors did this, years ago before I ever stepped foot on this land. I think they would be happy with me, I think they would be pleased with what I'm doing. My heart aches for what my ancestors went through. I am so incredibly blessed to be who I am and what I am and that I am able to have this, albeit somewhat tenuous, tie to my ancestors. I have baskets that they touched, and I'm going to touch the same materials. It's ancient but it's really today." This encounter—between Brenda and the cedar tree and its evidence of an earlier gatherer's hand—encapsulates why tribal members' continuing connections with their ancestral lands are so crucial. Protecting and enhancing those connections is seen by the CTCLUSI as essential work today.

Remaining Place-Based People

In recounting early twentieth-century efforts of the Coos, Lower Umpqua, and Siuslaw to seek redress for the taking of their lands, historian David Beck describes how tribal members testified for land-claims hearings about the places where they and their ancestors had lived, gathered, hunted, and fished, often using Native languages to name the locations.[12] As Beck asserts, it is "now commonly accepted that place names and resource usage both play significant roles in defining aboriginal territory."[13] Protecting those places and resources is one of the foremost priorities of the CTCLUSI today, and informed the Tribes' decision to unify its Department of Natural Resources and Culture into an integrated unit. This responsibility to protect is exceptionally challenging in the case of the CTCLUSI because, with its history of dispossession, the confederation has had little direct control over tribal homelands. The restoration of lands under the Western Oregon Tribal Fairness Act of 2018, an act the CTCLUSI had advocated for years, is but a recent occurrence and represents only a tiny fraction of aboriginal homelands. To steward ancestral lands and perpetuate their cultural identity, tribal staff and representatives constantly navigate the complex workings of local, county, state, and federal agencies to locate possible entry points for input.[14]

One path the CTCLUSI has taken to protect its traditional practices and resources, way of life, and cultural heritage and places was to propose a Traditional Cultural Property Historic District to the Oregon State Historic Preservation Office in 2018 for nomination to the National Register of Historic Places.[15] The proposed district is called Q'alya ta Kukwis shichdii me, Coosan for Jordan Cove and Coos Bay, which is translated to English as *to place like a necklace and the Bay of the Coos People*. According to the National Park Service (NPS), a Traditional Cultural Property (TCP) is a property "eligible for inclusion in the National Register because of its association with cultural practices or beliefs of a living community that (a) are rooted in that community's history, and (b) are important in maintaining the continuing cultural identity of the community."[16] One of the benefits of National Register TCP status is that it recognizes the traditional place-based practices and beliefs of the Coos people. It affords documentation and protection of a location and its physical resources and requires a review process for any federal or federally assisted projects that are proposed for the property, including consulting with the affected community.[17] A National Register–eligible TCP involves an extensive process of documentation, public comment, and vetting by a State Historic Preservation Office, which is the body that must forward the proposal to the National Park Service for a final determination of eligibility.

Examples of TCPs in other parts of the United States include Nantucket Sound in Massachusetts, associated with two Wampanoag tribes, and Kuchamaa (Tecate Peak) in California, associated with the Kumeyaay Nation. The Nantucket Sound TCP (approved for inclusion

by the National Park Service in 2010) has particular resonance with
the Coos Bay TCP proposal, because part of the timing of the original
2009 nomination by the Massachusetts State Historic Preservation
Office and the Wampanoag was related to development pressures posed
upon the Sound by a large-scale wind turbine development (known as
the Cape Wind Energy Project). The Wampanoag were concerned that
their input be officially included regarding any development that could
potentially transform their relationship with Nantucket Sound.[18] In the
case of the Q'alya ta Kukwis shichdii me TCP nomination, made in early
2019, the timing was urgent given that the potential impacts associated
with the then pending Jordan Cove Energy Project, which proposed the
construction of a massive liquefied natural gas (LNG) export terminal in Coos Bay and a connecting pipeline across southern Oregon.[19]
Jordan Cove is a location within Coos Bay that bears the name of the
nineteenth-century Euro-American settler James T. Jordan and his wife
Jane, a Hanis Coos woman, from whom many tribal members descend.
Potential impacts of the proposed Jordan Cove Energy Project included
destruction and degradation of places associated with cultural practices
and beliefs as well as burial sites.

The proposed TCP district, Q'alya ta Kukwis shichdii me, a twenty-
six-square-mile area tracing the horseshoe-shaped estuary of Coos
Bay, has been historically associated with the Coos people since time
immemorial. In keeping with the requirements of a TCP designation,
the area is recognized by the CTCLUSI as being central to the ongoing
maintenance of the cultural identity of the community and its future
generations. CTCLUSI chief Warren Brainard (Miluk Coos) has said
that the TCP proposal is a natural outcome of the tribal government's
fundamental understanding of its reason for being: "Our efforts are a
response to the Tribal Constitution, which states that the Tribal Government is established to perpetuate our unique tribal identify and to
promote and protect that identity. The resources we seek to protect
through this listing are central to the Coos Tribe's identity."[20]

Margaret Corvi, who coordinated the submission of the proposal
as then-director of the Department of Natural Resources and Culture,
explained that the research to develop the required documentation
was built upon "the shoulders of giants." By this she was referring to all
the elders and prior generations whose knowledge of the land, history,

culture, and resources was synthesized for the application. Staff from the Department of Natural Resources and Culture (most notably Courtney Krossman) conducted new interviews with tribal members, and earlier testimony was gathered from treaty negotiations, land claims efforts, ethnographic and archaeological records, and historical accounts. In addition, Patricia Whereat Phillips's book *Ethnobotany of the Coos, Lower Umpqua, and Siuslaw Indians* provided a meticulous compendium of historical community knowledge. Margaret believes that one of the key accomplishments of the TCP process has been to create a mechanism by which new generations can interface with these prior documents and gain familiarity with community knowledge. The proposal itself was a rich recognition and celebration of culture, illustrated with images of gathering, weaving, harvesting, and cooking, all of which are tied to ceremonial practices. A major desire was to document the importance of the land, so that the significance of any additional impact upon the resources—which have already been degraded by nearly two centuries of US settlement—would be clear. The implication is that further environmental degradation—in the immediate or long-term future—will impair the ability of the community to continue its process of reconnecting with the land and the cultural knowledge that comes with its use.

The nomination document for the Q'alya ta Kukwis shichdii me TCP was recognized as eligible by the State Advisory Committee for Historic Preservation on February 22, 2019. The State Historic Preservation Office then allowed a period for property-owner objections. While the CTCLUSI provided public information to clarify that a National Register TCP designation was sought primarily to require federal agency consultation with the Tribes to determine the impact of proposed commercial, industrial, or recreational use (when such projects involve federal approval or permit) and, in actuality, would place few restrictions on individual private property owners, a majority of property owners within the TCP boundary submitted notarized objections to the TCP.[21] Nevertheless, the State Historic Preservation Office ultimately forwarded the nomination to the National Park Service on May 23, 2019. In July 2019 the nomination was returned by the NPS to the State Historic Preservation Office without a determination of eligibility, citing procedural and documentation shortcomings—but not rejecting the nomination. While the door remains open for resubmission, the formal process of establishing a National Register TCP is essentially on hold; the CTCLUSI continues to work with its partners to protect important resources tied to culture, cultural heritage, and way of life.[22]

Margaret Corvi, when I spoke with her in October 2019 about the status of the Q'alya ta Kukwis shichdii me TCP, took the long view: "The assertions of the TCP will stand with or without the [designation of the] National Park Service. Those things will be carried forward by future generations of tribal members. Whether or not they are recognized in the federal sense through the more formal process [of the TCP], they will be recognized and internalized by our tribal members today. They [know] all those places exist and that those places belong to them. . . . That's the most important thing, regardless of that formal recognition." Ultimately, Margaret's hope and that of the CTCLUSI leadership is that the knowledge embedded in the Q'alya ta Kukwis shichdii me will thrive, alongside and inseparable from the places and the people them-selves. As she summed up: "I really hope it empowers people to carry forward that all those people and all those resources belong to them, and they have a right to them, and they have a right to protect them."

Being able to exercise one's right to protect the resources requires access to and time on the land. Chief Doc Slyter, whose great-great-grandparents were Jane and James T. Jordan, after whom Jordan Cove is named, has been involved with fellow tribal members for years in efforts to regain a land base (partially achieved with the Western Oregon Tribal Fairness Act of 2018). In talking about the effort of the Tribes over decades to regain portions of their homelands, Doc spoke about how critical a land base is for his community's well-being: "The importance of the land base is so that we will have a larger area, that tribal members can become part of the land. . . . For the tribal people to get back into the ancestors' way, they need to learn that respect for land. The only way that you're going to learn that is the time you're going to spend on it. That's one tiny step, to get a larger land base, to grow that tribal com-munity. I think that's going to truly grow the spirit of the people."

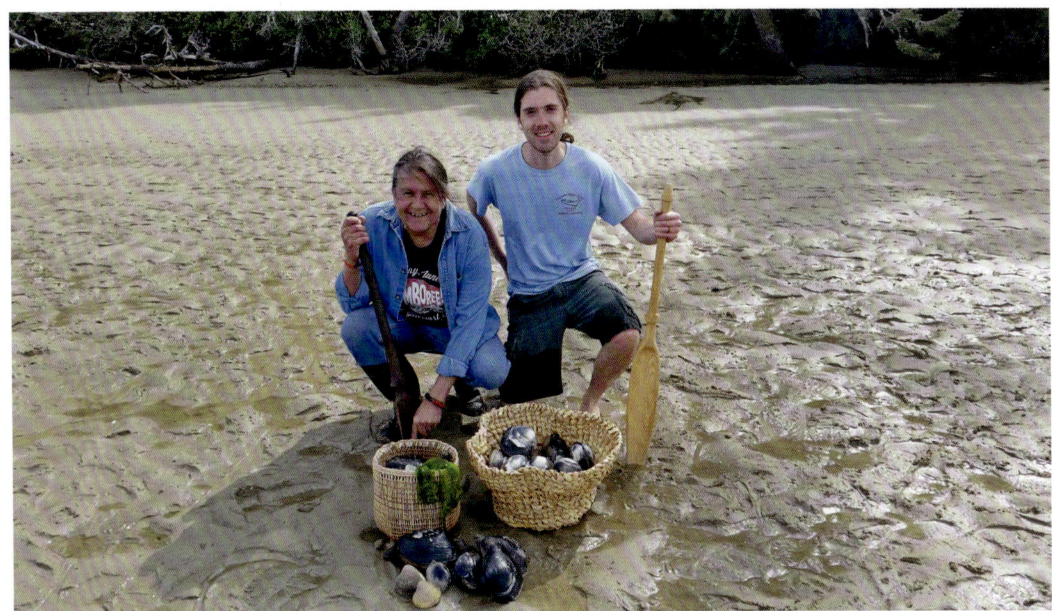

Chief Doc Slyter and Mark Petrie with baskets made by Ashley Russell, 2017. Photograph by John Schaefer. Courtesy of the Confederated Tribes of Coos, Lower Umpqua, and Siuslaw Indians.

CHAPTER 3

POTLATCH AS A WAY OF LIFE

The Coquille Indian Tribe

"Potlatch, for me, it's way beyond a tradition or ceremony, it's a way of life," said Anne Burnette Niblett, a Coquille tribal member born in the 1970s, in a conversation with Denni Hockema, Coquille cultural anthropologist, and Brenda Meade, Coquille tribal chair, the December afternoon following the 2015 winter solstice dance, or NeeDash.[1] I had begun the conversation thinking I would hear primarily about particular events at which the gift-giving associated with potlatching takes place; in the hours that followed, our talk took a more profound turn, centering on ways potlatch values infuse contemporary tribal lives.

The term *potlatch* is said to be derived from a Chinuk Wawa (in English, Chinook Jargon) term for a "giving" based in turn on a word from the Nuu-chah-nulth language spoken by the people of the western coast of Vancouver Island.[2] Variations of potlatch ceremonies were and are practiced all along the Pacific Northwest Coast from present-day southeastern Alaska through British Columbia to southern Oregon. Potlatches, speaking very generally, are events filled with dancing, ceremonies, and extensive gifting of food and goods by hosts to guests; through reciprocity (acts of giving and receiving), they establish and reinforce social relationships. The potlatch has been studied by generations of anthropologists, most famously by Franz Boas and his research associate George Hunt (raised among the Kwakwa̱ka̱ʼwakw, of Tlingit and British heritage), who focused on the complex customs of the Kwakwaka'wakw of Vancouver Island.[3] Outsiders often fixated on the giveaway itself, the accumulation, distribution, and sometimes destruction of wealth that was seen as so bizarre by Western colonists and settlers in the nineteenth and early twentieth centuries. Potlatching in southwestern Oregon was traditionally a more generalized form of feasting and gift-giving, not as elaborate as that practiced farther up the Northwest Coast, where it was governed by clan-based social organization. Nevertheless, as Niblett emphasized, potlatch at Coquille is a way of life, more than just gift-giving occasions associated with any one particular event.

As the conversation unfolded in the Coquille Tribe's government center, it became clear that to these tribal members, the principles of the potlatch are understood to have deep roots not just in social organization but also in an even more fundamental relationship: that between land and people. At the core of the land-people relationship is a dynamic of harvesting and caregiving, receiving and tending. The abundance of the land is shared with and conserved for others; productive conditions are generated by taking (harvesting) while giving (tending).[4] The land's gifts to people, people's acceptance of those gifts, and the reciprocal caregiving relationship between land and people can be understood as a model for the social relationships enacted in potlatching. The occasions at which potlatches occur for the Coquille are times when the harvesting, preparation, and consumption of traditional foods reinforce the relationship between people and the land. The ethic of potlatch—abundance shared—offers the potential for transformation and renewal of both society and environment.

The Ethic of Potlatch

For the 2008 *Art of Ceremony* exhibition the Coquille Tribe contributed a selection of regalia used in the NeeDash, the dance that had just been held the day before our December 2015 conversation. The NeeDash, or Nee Dosh, depending on community usage, is a world renewal ceremony held at winter and summer solstices that is also conducted by the Tolowa of northwestern California and the Siletz of western Oregon, who, like the Coquille, are tribal groups with Athabaskan heritage (see chapter 7, "World Renewal—The Nee Dosh: The Confederated Tribes of Siletz Indians"). The participants repair the world by performing the NeeDash, in which the story of creation is recounted by an orator, and the community's youth and young adults are outfitted in elaborate regalia for several rounds of dances. The ceremony provides the opportunity for people to give thanks to the Creator for the abundance of life and to acknowledge responsibility for tending the earth that provides it. Each community performs the NeeDash or Nee Dosh with the belief that it is necessary for the health of the relationship between people and the natural and spiritual world.

The regalia for the 2008 display was primarily made by Brenda Meade, then a tribal employee in elder services, and her husband, Lyman Meade. Coquille tribal members today are descended from the peoples who lived in the Coquille River watershed, at the mouth of the

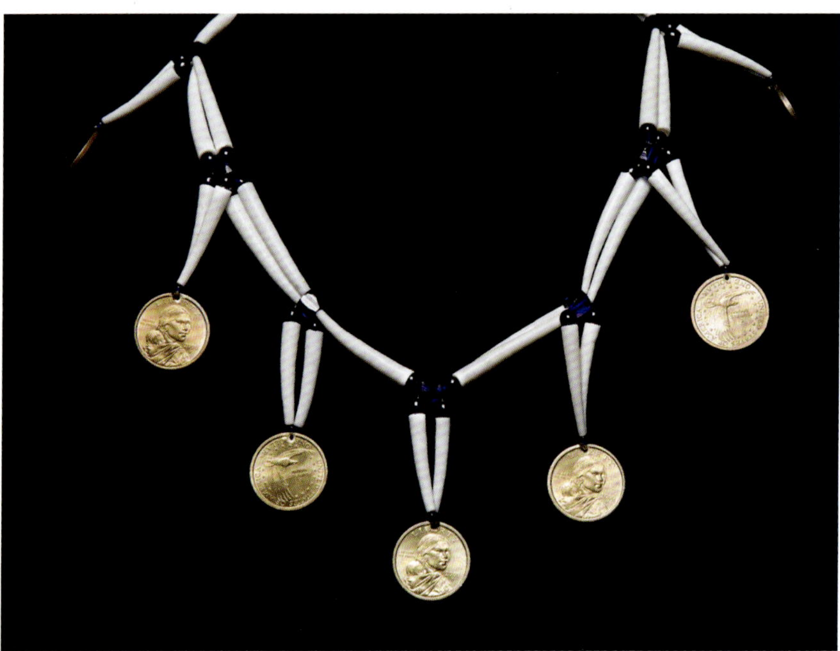

Necklace, 2007. Brenda Meade. Dentalia, glass beads, Sacagawea US dollar coins. This necklace was made by Meade to honor her great-great-great grandfather, Charlie Ned, and his daughter, Lily Ned, for whom Charlie made a gold coin and dentalium necklace, which was buried with Lily according to traditional practices when she died in childhood. Collection of the Meade Family. Photograph by Frank Miller. Courtesy of Frank Miller and Willamette University.

river at present-day Bandon, and along a portion of Coos Bay at South Slough.[5] The Coquille were among the many tribal groups in what is now southwestern Oregon shattered in the nineteenth century by the regional gold rush and Rogue River War. Most tribal members were forcibly relocated to the Coastal (or Siletz) Reservation in the 1850s by the US government. A few Coquille women married to white men managed to stay in their homelands, and they and their descendants maintained a quiet presence in the aftermath of extreme cultural destruction. Then, in 1954, the legal existence of the Coquille Tribe, along with that of many other tribal groups, was terminated by the federal government. Only after decades of daunting effort did the Coquille secure federal recognition in 1989; the challenging work of restoring a nation began.[6]

A key milestone in the rebuilding process was the 2005 completion of the tribal plankhouse, where the dances are held twice a year, at the winter and summer solstices. Many youth now participate, and the community has enough regalia for more than twenty dancers. Brenda Meade, born in the 1970s, explained how there has been a shift from the need to explicitly teach the young people about the philosophy and meaning of the NeeDash to a sense that it has become theirs: "They own it. It's not like it's something that's taught now." The generations who have been born since restoration learn from living the dance. "They are getting it from everyone that's coming together and doing things together." In 2014, she explained, the young dancers felt it was time to potlatch for NeeDash, to honor all those involved in rebuilding the ceremony: "It was time to just stop everything and to invite everyone in, but it was a time to recognize all the folks that have supported that event, that ceremony happening, because there's so many people that have just come in and done things to make sure that that happened and to support those young people. It was a time when they worked on gifts, and we talked about all those amazing people and who we wanted to recognize."

Although the focus in *The Art of Ceremony* exhibit was on the NeeDash celebration and its regalia, Meade explained that the Coquille Tribal Council agreed that for this book the focus was to be on potlatch as a fundamental guiding philosophy as well as its practice. It was easy to reach this consensus, Meade said, because potlatch is something the Coquille have "shared through generations" and continue as part

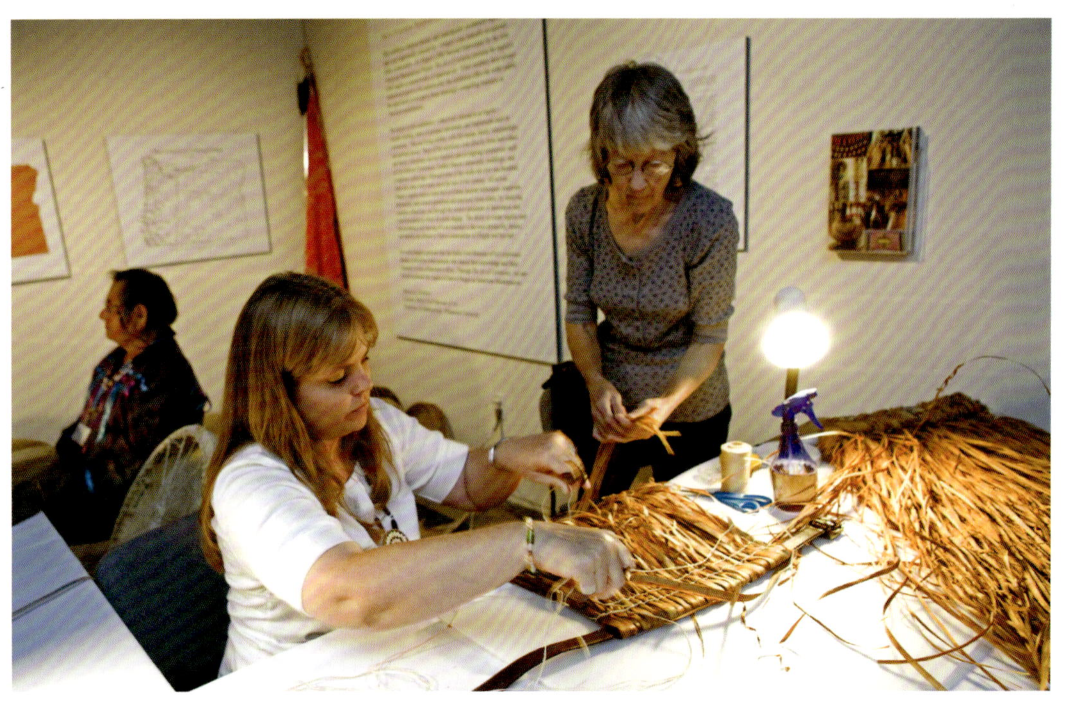

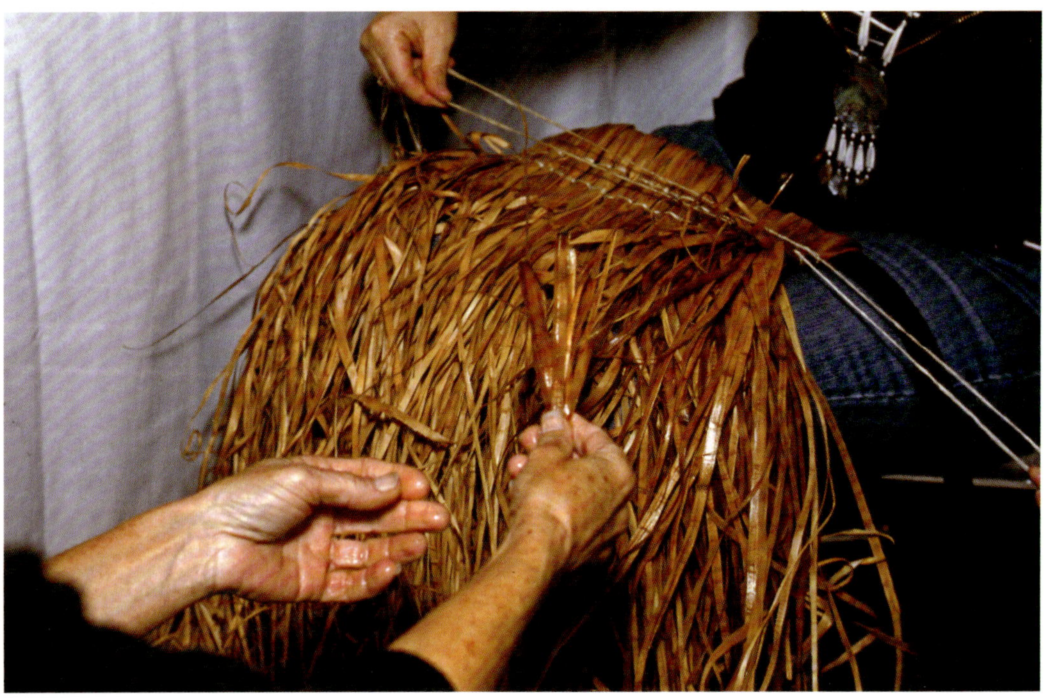

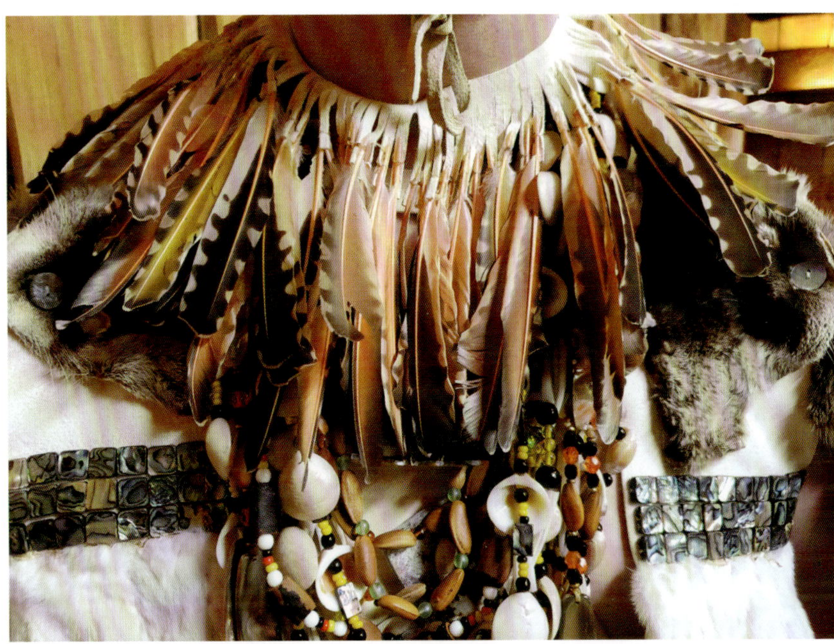

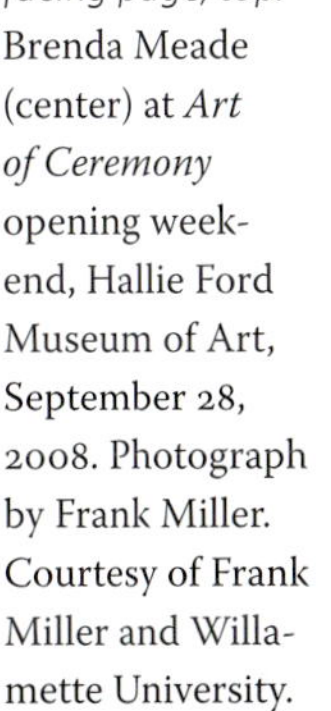

Flicker feather collar, worn with shell, bead, and pine nut necklaces, and fur and abalone deerhide vest, 2006. Lyman Meade. Photograph by Anne Burnette Niblett. Courtesy of the Coquille Indian Tribe.

facing page, top: Brenda Meade (center) at *Art of Ceremony* opening weekend, Hallie Ford Museum of Art, September 28, 2008. Photograph by Frank Miller. Courtesy of Frank Miller and Willamette University.

facing page, bottom: Maple bark skirt making, at Hallie Ford Museum of Art, September 28, 2008. Photograph by Frank Miller. Courtesy of Frank Miller and Willamette University.

of the ongoing rebuilding of their nation. The Coquille Tribe actively seeks to create opportunities for its citizens to return to the Coos Bay area, and the dual ethic of abundance and conservation informs the rebuilding process, as Meade relayed: "As we raise our kids together and as we bring our tribal membership home, it's such an intricate piece of how we treat each other and how we treat people around us in our community too."

Denni Hockema, born in the 1950s and of the generation that grew up in the termination era, explained that, for her, potlatch has "always been there." Hockema's family, which includes grandfather George B. Wasson Sr. (1880–1942), an early leader of efforts to regain lands and rights for western Oregon Indians, lived out lives of service to others, although Hockema stressed that such generosity of spirit is "part of everybody here." To this, Anne Niblett added that potlatch marks her family "in the way that we interact with other people" and said that both of her parents, one of whom is non-Indian, embodied that spirit. Niblett said the potlatch ethic is an "understanding of responsibility that when you have a lot and you are a leader, part of the responsibility that comes with that is to serve and to take care of others."

Like many in the generation born in the 1970s just before restoration, Niblett was born in the Coos Bay area but left as a youth and returned as an adult. When she returned, she saw the values of potlatch "lived out in the lives of the people here and then saw it in my relatives too." She realized: "Oh, that's where that's from!" Niblett sees this in the ways members help out others in their community, giving the example of a recent request for help from the family of a disabled child that was met almost immediately by tribal employees. "This is the thing," she explained. "We do things as a Tribe. Part of the reason that works and that's real is because [people] live it out on an individual level." So it is "lived out, in big ways that lots of people see" as well as in much more private ways that go unmarked. Hockema quietly affirmed: "It's part of life."

The people's relationship with the land is in a sense the first teacher of the potlatch ethic. The land offers abundance; there is a human responsibility to take those offerings, though not more than is needed, and to offer thanks not just in ceremonial acts but also in tending and caretaking. Both Hockema and Meade remarked on how Niblett's experience of returning as an adult to Coquille ancestral lands around Coos Bay heightened her awareness of the relationship with the land that tribal people had had for generations. The two older women had lifelong access to this relationship given that they had grown up on the land. One of the places Niblett is strongly drawn to and visits with her children is the Susan Adulsa Wasson allotment, now part of the South Slough National Estuarine Reserve, in the Coos Bay area. The land was originally allotted to Susan Adulsa Wasson, the daughter of Upper Coquille and Miluk Coos parents and the wife of George R. Wasson, an American settler, as part of the late nineteenth-century federal policy of allotment. This policy imposed a system of individual land ownership upon Tribes.[7] Niblett recalled the experience of visiting at a time when berries were ripe:

> I realized that the land had something to offer and not only did it have something to offer—it had fruit—it wanted us to take it. There was what it had to give, and it was a blessing that somebody would come along and take what it had to give. All of us as human beings have different giftings in our life and ways that we're supposed to bless one another. When we have the opportunity to give that, it blesses us as well. We all have something, everybody

does. You see that in a tribe, there's different gifts and different things that everybody has. When you understand that you have something to give, and it's going to be unique and different from everyone else, it blesses you too. When people will take it from you without thinking "Oh, it's an imposition," but just understand it's your gift to give, then you're both blessed.

The experience of gathering gifts of the land at the Wasson allotment reinforced Niblett's understanding of the ethic of potlatch: a process that continually unfolds, must be practiced, and involves both having gifts to give and having those gifts received by others.

Responding to Tradition

When Hockema talks about contemporary cultural practices in her community, she likes to use the term *respond* (as opposed to revive) to indicate the relationship between past traditions and current practices. Today's community *responds* to what is known about traditional knowledge, which was fragmented by the speed and severity of

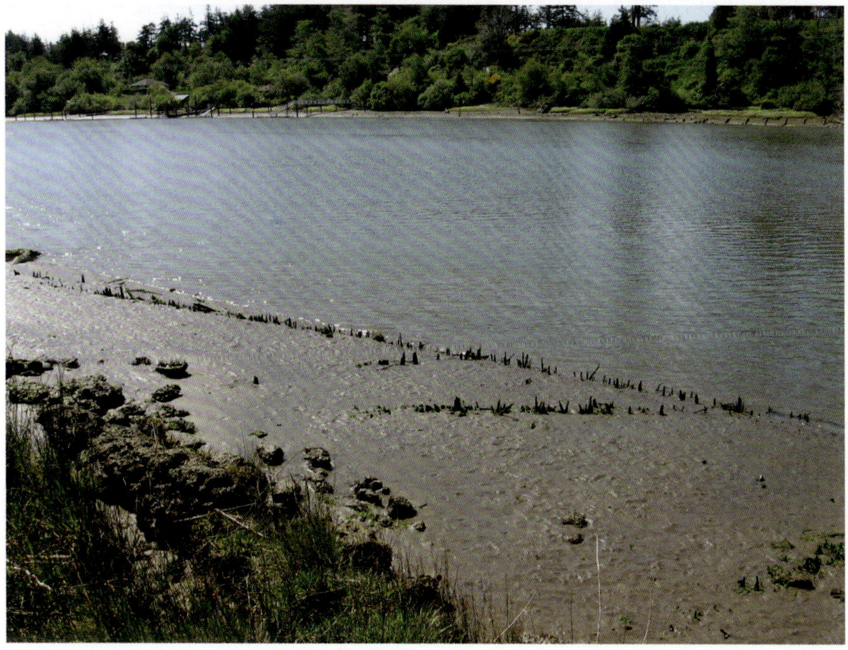

Coquille River, with remains of traditional fishing weirs in the foreground, 2000. Photograph by Jonathon Ivy. Courtesy of the Coquille Indian Tribe.

the destruction the Coquille people experienced with the arrival of
Euro-American society in the 1800s. Responding is qualitatively different than replicating or reproducing or even reacting, and involves flexibility and creativity from the twenty-first-century Coquille community,
who of course are not themselves homogenous.

One example of a contemporary response to the tradition of potlatch is the now long-standing Restoration Day Feast, celebrated every
year on the anniversary of the signing of the Coquille Restoration Act,
June 28, 1989. The Twenty-Fifth Restoration Day in 2014 was a major
watershed event for the Tribe. In addition to a week of tribal community events, a public celebration was held, where friends of the Coquille
people—ranging from federal, state, and tribal government officials to
city and county representatives, and a wide range of others—were recognized by tribal chair Brenda Meade with gifts handmade and accu-
mulated by tribal members over the prior months.

Every Restoration Day includes a salmon bake, although this is not
simply a way to get everyone fed. It's a form of service and thanksgiving, and photographs of Restoration Days going back decades feature
the salmon firepit with elders and others on their knees, preparing to
feed the community. Meade described those images as a "symbol of an
elder in service." She reflected on the impact of the early Restoration
Day celebrations in the 1990s during her young adulthood: "Everybody's
working on that pit, they're teaching the young people that were there.
I know we were around, and we were being told what to do. There's so
much that comes from preparing foods." The preparation of foods, from
harvesting to cooking, offered instruction by example in the tribal value
of service, according to Meade: "When I think of our people on their
knees at the salmon pit, they're just giving every ounce of themselves."

Other specific events characterized by potlatching include internal
community occasions for tribal membership and families. The Midwinter
Gathering held annually in January is one example. Over three days
tribal members and their families gather at the Coquille's Mill Casino
and Hotel for conversation with and reports from tribal leadership and
staff, traditional craft and youth activities, and celebratory meals. The
weekend culminates with a feast and potluck at the Coquille Community
Plankhouse and a giveaway of elk and salmon to tribal heads of households. According to Meade, this is a time to bring together the Tribe as

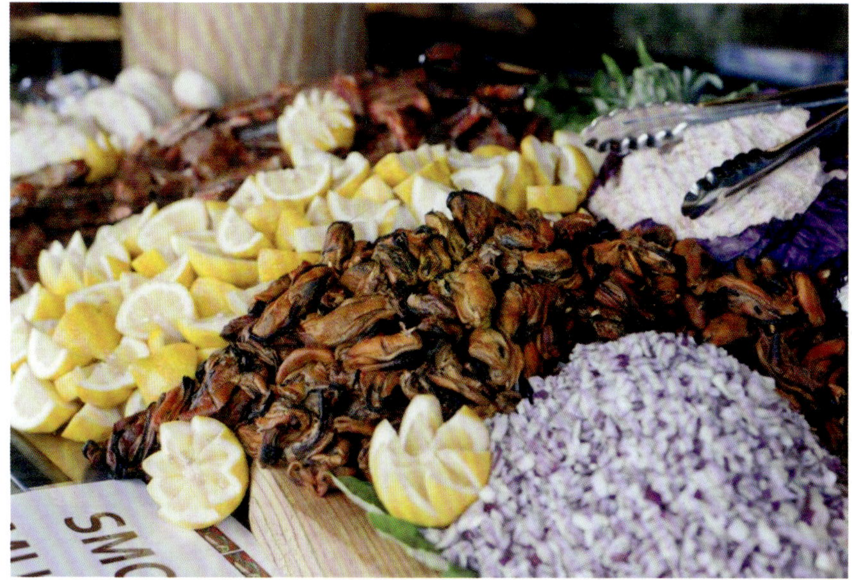

Smoked mussels and other foods for Twenty-Fifth Restoration Celebration Feast, 2014. Photograph by Jonathon Ivy. Courtesy of the Coquille Indian Tribe.

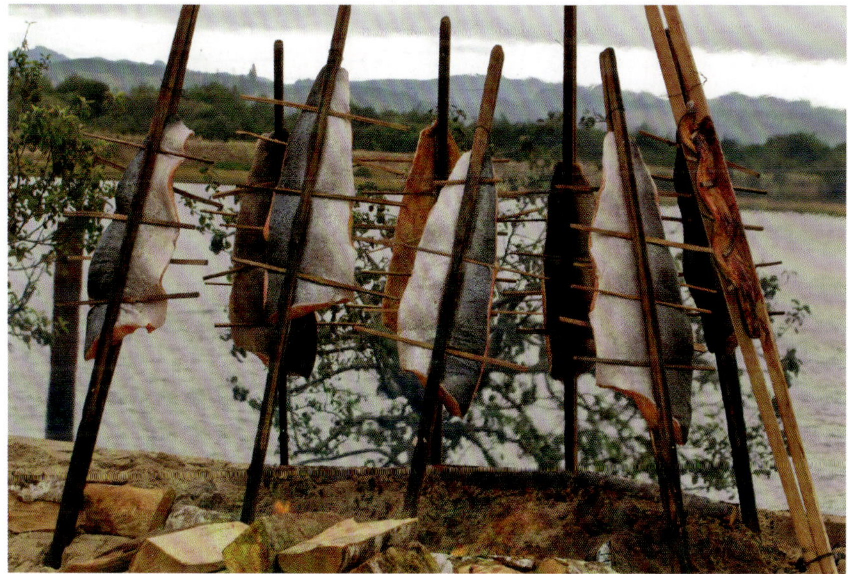

Salmon bake, 2014. Photograph by Jonathon Ivy. Courtesy of the Coquille Indian Tribe.

a family, "a time to bring folks in and talk about how things went over the last year, what's coming up for the next year. Give them information, giving that connection again, for our community." The Midwinter Gathering, with its sharing of information and food, nurtures the connections tribal members have with one another and manifests the

relationship-building dimension of potlatch. Scholars have long emphasized how potlatching connects those who practice it in a dynamic
network of relationships through which gifts circulate.[8] Relationships are
what are being given, and these intangible yet embodied connections
are marked with tangible gifts such as the traditional foods.

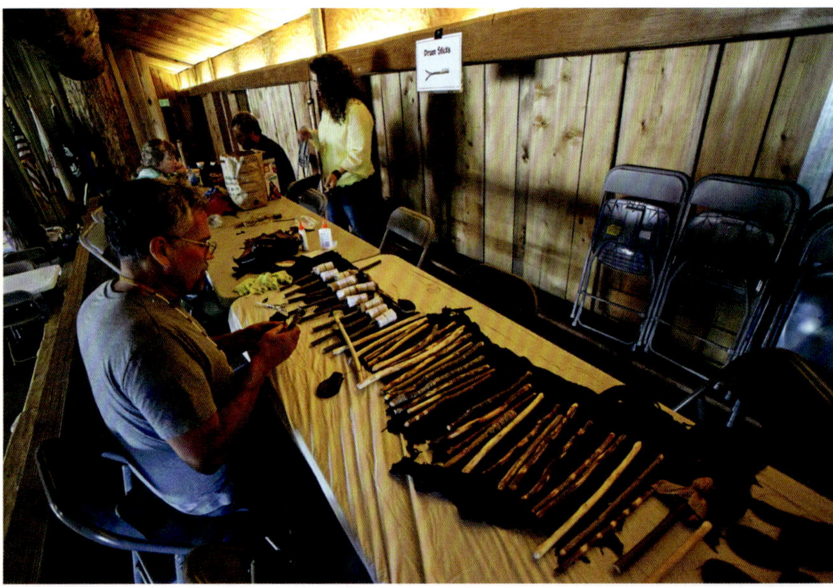

Drumstick making at the Coquille Tribe Community Plankhouse, 2016. Photograph by Frank Miller. Courtesy of Frank Miller and Willamette University.

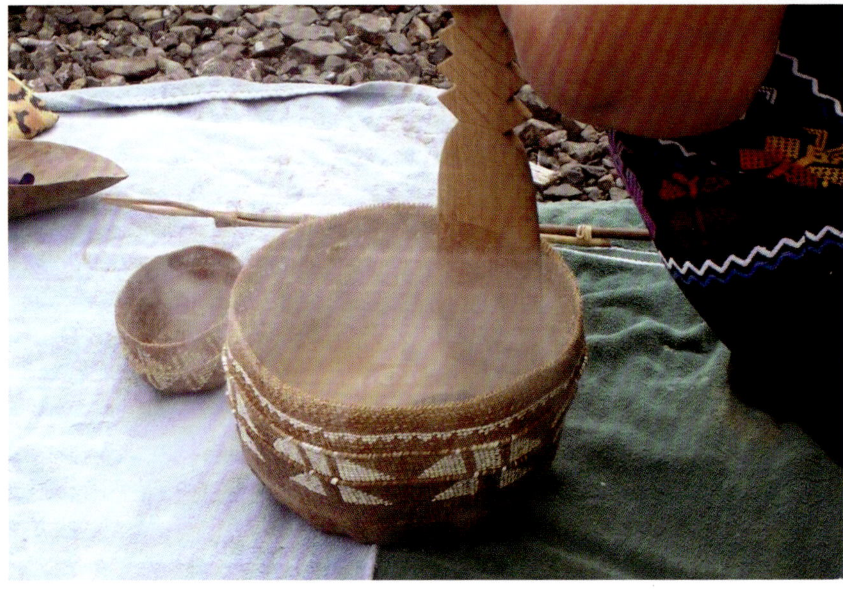

Acorn mush in cooking basket with paddle, 2000. Photograph by Donald Ivy. Courtesy of the Coquille Indian Tribe.

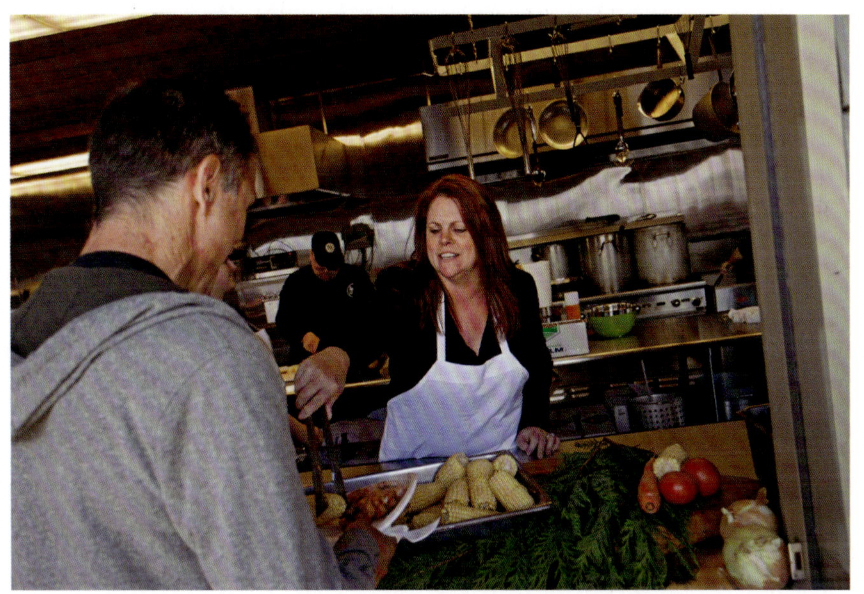

Tribal chair Brenda Meade serving food, Twenty-Seventh Restoration Anniversary celebration, 2016. Photograph by Frank Miller. Courtesy of Frank Miller and Willamette University.

In 1997 the Coquille Tribe hosted its first intertribal potlatch since the mid-nineteenth century as part of a very intentional process of relationship-building with regional tribes. The occasion for the potlatch, held at the University of Oregon, was the sharing of the initial results of the Southwest Oregon Research Project (SWORP). Spearheaded by the Coquille Tribe, SWORP began in 1995 as an innovative effort to repatriate intellectual property held in Washington, DC, archives concerning the many tribes and bands of southwestern Oregon and northwestern California.[9] These documentary resources—full of linguistic, cultural, and territorial information—had essentially been inaccessible to their communities of origin. SWORP was initially conceived by George B. Wasson Jr., son of George B. Wasson Sr., the Coquille land-rights advocate mentioned earlier and the grandfather of Denni Hockema. The younger Wasson, then a graduate student of anthropology at the University of Oregon, had knowledge of the archives' holdings and envisioned making copies of such documents, bringing them home to Oregon, and providing them to regional tribes and scholars for research—research that in turn could strengthen the continuing process of building tribal sovereignty by contributing to everything from the protection of sacred sites to curriculum development.[10]

The Coquille Tribal Council supported these efforts beginning in 1995, and several Coquille scholars—including Hockema—participated in the first summer of research, which yielded almost sixty thousand pages of historical documents dealing not only with the Coquille but also with other tribes in Oregon and California, whose histories are linked through Indigenous cultural ties as well as colonial processes. In order to distribute copies of the SWORP collection to the other tribes, the Coquille Tribe decided to host a contemporary potlatch, until then an interrupted tradition. Documented in the film *A Gift of History: The Potlatch Returns* (Coquille Tribe, 1997), the potlatch drew nearly 350 people, including representatives of the Smithsonian Institution, one of the locations of archival research. A second SWORP research trip to Washington, DC, in 1998—this time joined by scholars from the Coos, Lower Umpqua and Siuslaw, Grand Ronde, and Siletz Tribes—yielded another fifty thousand pages of materials. It, too, was followed by a potlatch in 2001 at the University of Oregon to which all forty-four tribal groups whose histories are reflected in the SWORP materials were invited.[11]

SWORP inspired another vehicle for intertribal sharing, the Coquille Cultural Preservation Conferences, in their own way a form of potlatching. Begun in 1997 and continuing through 2006, the conferences brought together members of tribes, the general public, and scholars— an increasing number of them Native American—to share the results of research, whether drawn from SWORP documents or from other sources. In addition to presentations, field trips, and demonstrations of traditional arts and technology, the conference published selected proceedings in a journal, *Changing Landscapes.*[12] In 2002 the John F. Kennedy School of Government at Harvard University granted SWORP and the Coquille Tribe the Honoring Nations Award for Excellence in Tribal Government, in recognition of the project's success in promoting tribal self-determination.[13] In large part underwritten by the Coquille Tribe, SWORP very intentionally circulated a wealth of information through the potlatches. The events facilitated the homecoming of the archival materials and the building of a network of relationships, not merely the distribution of documents—the latter a process that could have been achieved any number of ways. By gathering people together for the SWORP giveaways and the Culture Conferences, the Coquille creatively responded to the custom of the potlatch and reinvented it for the present.

Potlatch on the Oregon Coast: The Story of Face Rock
As told by Denni Hockema

Four coast tribes were hosting a potlatch for the inland tribes led by Chief Siski-you. He had a daughter that came with him. Of course they prepared for days and days and caught dozens of fish and elk and deer and camas and just everything. They cooked for days and days, down at Bandon. When the guests got there, there was a lot of celebration and one of the first things that they were told was, "Don't go down to the beach by yourself and especially not at night." Because they were from inland, they didn't know about the ocean and how powerful the waves are. Nothing is more powerful than the ocean. The adults were having fun and eating and fell asleep. The daughter had brought her dog and a basket of baby raccoons. So she took the baby raccoons and the dog and went down to the beach, where she ran and played. It was a full moon. She kept thinking, "What are they talking about? This is not dangerous. Why should I be worried?" She decided she'd go swimming, put that basket of raccoons on the beach, and the dog was sitting there. So she gets out in the ocean a ways and she sees a big black thing rising up out of the ocean. They had told her about the sea monster, Se-at-co, and they told her, "Don't look into his eyes because that's where his power is." So she tried her best not to look. She looked away, but he grabbed her. So she's turned to stone down there at Bandon. You can see her face looking up at the moon. And her dog and the raccoons are turned to stone down the beach.

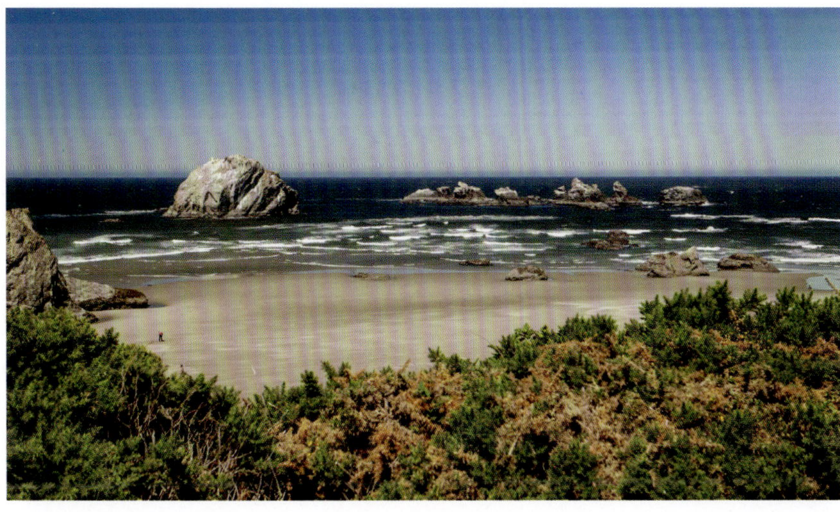

Bandon, Oregon, 2016. Photograph by Frank Miller. Courtesy of Frank Miller and Willamette University.

Potlatch as Guiding Principle

Because relationship enhancement is understood by Coquille tribal members to be at the heart of potlatching, with the goal of strengthening existing relationships, creating new ones, and extending them into the future, it is easy to recognize that the Tribe's approach to land management and planning for the future is being guided by the values of potlatch. Although restoration is formally celebrated once a year, the work of restoration is an everyday, ongoing process of nation-building fundamentally tied to ancestral lands. When the Tribe was restored to federal recognition in 1989, no land base was included. Persistent effort resulted in the transfer of the 5,400-acre Coquille Forest to the Tribe under the Oregon Resources Conservation Act of 1996. In the years since, other parcels have come under tribal control, bringing the total to approximately 10,000 acres. Meade, from her perspective as tribal chair, emphasized that restoration is "not something that just happened in the past. One reason we're so blessed and so healthy as a community is that when we went through all of those things, termination and restoration, it was a fight. It was a fight and people were suffering, and our folks recognized that we weren't taking care of our elders and we weren't offering things to our young people. We've had the time now to get people back together, and the resources to get our people back together, and get our elders back on the land, and our young people, and luckily we're back on our ancestral homelands."

This latter point is all the more significant because of the Coquille Tribe's history of forced removal; reclaiming land offers tribal members the possibility of renewed ties with tribal homelands even after environmental and political ruptures. According to Meade, "Things come back to people in ways. We're gathering in the same places for basketry materials and clam digging and berry picking and all the things we do every year now, as the seasons go through." Tribal members are relearning and teaching one another the land-based skills by *performing* them. During trips for gathering basket and food-plant resources, Meade noted, cultural leaders like Hockema emphasized gratitude by asking tribal members: "Did you make sure you gave thanks to the land for what it gave you and how lucky we are that we are still here and that we're still gathering at the same places our ancestors did?" And now, a generation into

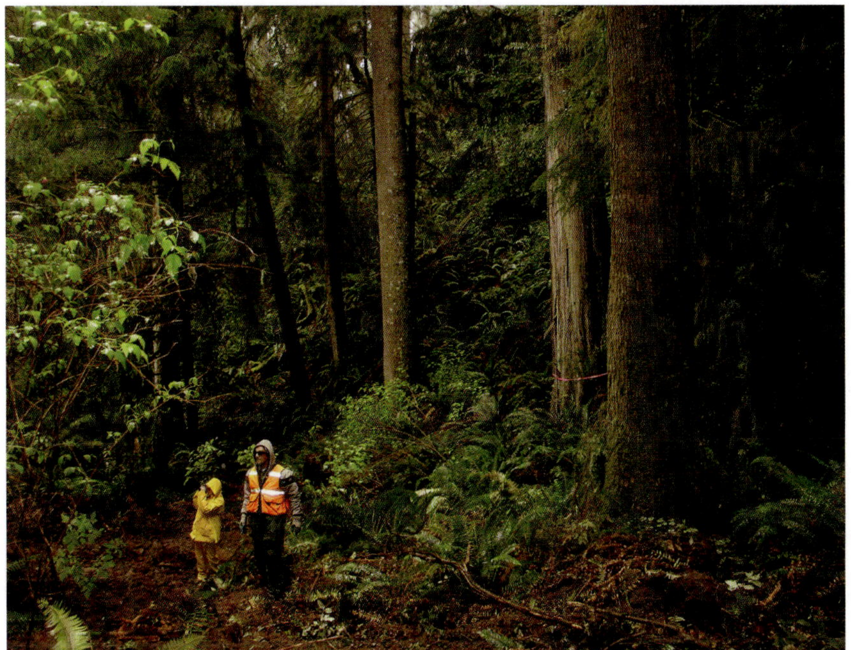

Coquille Forest blessing, Chief Don Ivy in orange vest, 2006. Photograph by Christopher Tanner. Courtesy of the Coquille Indian Tribe.

restoration, with more ancestral lands under tribal ownership, Coquille youth have the opportunity to learn these lessons from an early age.[14]

Reflecting upon the lessons learned that come from being out on the land and harvesting from it, Hockema explained that people have to use what they receive, steward the resources with sustainable practices, and offer thanks, so that the land and sea are able to continue to produce. "We've always learned that we just take what we need and leave the seeds," she said, "so more will grow back the next year and thank the plants and thank the land. Take care of it or it won't be there, and respect it and the same way with the First Salmon Ceremony. That's the same thing. Thanking the fish for bringing us food, putting the bones back so they will go out and tell the other fish that we're okay people." The First Salmon Ceremony Hockema referred to is conducted, along with other first-foods rituals, in various ways by many tribes to honor the resources that reappear annually to sustain life; the Coquille incorporate their First Salmon Ceremony into the annual Restoration weekend.

Having access to ancestral lands means having access to potential growth and renewed relationships to the land, recast for today. Talking about Tribal Council priorities, Meade related that every time the

Council is together, they discuss two priorities: "opportunities for tribal membership and access to their lands." For example, she elaborated that the Tribal Council doesn't say that members should or must go out to do basketry or other traditional arts, but instead the Council has to "make sure they can get to a place that has everything they need" if they choose to do so.

The Coquille Tribe numbers more than a thousand citizens, and with only about half living in the five-county service area around Coos Bay, getting people back onto the land and into the community is an urgent priority. There is a consciousness on the part of the tribal leadership that the future of the Tribe depends on the land-people relationship. To that end, one of the goals of the Tribe is to continue to expand its land base. An example of an acquisition is the 2015 purchase of the 3,200-acre Sek-wet-se Forest, formerly known as the Sixes Forest, in Curry County, from Ecotrust Forest Management, which had purchased the property in 2006 with the goal of transitioning it to tribal ownership.[15] Within a month of its purchase, the Tribe brought elders and youth up to meet the land and renew its acquaintance as part of the planning process. In the management of Sek-wet-se (the traditional name for the Sixes River) as well as the Coquille Forest, the Tribe involves its membership, archaeologists, and foresters as part of a conversation that tries to balance revenue-generating activity (timber harvest) with cultural uses (traditional food and plant harvests, fishing, and hunting).

"We talk about that balance again," Meade said, "of needing to have revenue and being able to harvest timber on that property, but also to keep in mind all the traditional uses and gathering spots that are easy to get to, for elders." The Tribe anticipates its members will want to peel cedar bark for baskets, harvest acorn to make traditional acorn mush, and collect beargrass for weaving and pick berries; all such uses are incorporated into the forest management plan. Meade continued:

> We're just working in those opportunities and making sure we're not destroying anything. You can have it all, you can have old growth, you can have willow for basketry, you just have to make sure what you take, you put back. It has to be sustainable. We've looked at it and we utilize science today. We look at the rivers, the roads, we look at everything before we have any activity on those

lands. Then we look at it afterwards, and make changes. Our harvest schedule is an eighty-year rotation, which is something that has been deemed as sustainable, so it will always be there for tribal membership, we'll always have old growth.

Meade explained that as the Coquille Tribe seeks to purchase other lands, one of its goals is simply to demonstrate to others through their land-use management proposals that it is possible to create management plans that balance what are often seen as competing uses. "You can manage lands for all uses, not just one or two," she said. "You can have old growth without having rotten trees on the land. And you can always have clean water even if you are accessing things up there. Public access doesn't mean that it's being damaged or that people aren't taking care of it. Public access is important for the land just as much. We have to harvest those berries that are being offered, it can't be closed up. There's better ways to do things. We're going to have that conversation through that process." As an indicator of its success in sustainable management, the Coquille Forest received Forest Stewardship Council (FSC) certification in 2011, making the Coquille Tribe one of only three American Indian tribes at the time to have met the FSC's high standards for balancing environmental, social, and economic objectives.[16]

Listening to Meade, Niblett reflected:

So what Brenda's talking about on that level is partnering with the land, not viewing it as something to be taken over and owned. But saying we're a partnership here: you have things to offer and I have things to offer. And working together, when you have a relationship like that, a partnership, it works really well. When you just have exploitation and domination, it doesn't. You see that in human relationships. I think the whole world needs this understanding and different Indigenous groups and other people all over, anyone who has had that relationship, those ties, where they've cared for land and the land has cared for them, get it.

Pausing briefly before finishing her thoughts, Niblett explained: "I think one of our most important messages as Indian people is this understanding that we are here to work together. Only take what you need, let the people downstream have some, and understand that we are all working together. Not you over there and me over here. We're all connected and we're connected with the earth too. If we can get that instead of me and you and it, imagine what can happen."

Marking the Heart Places

A place that demonstrates those connections and the possibility of working together is the Nasomah Memorial in the Old Town section of Bandon, Oregon, begun in 2013 and completed in 2015. The memorial marks the site of an ancient Coquille village that was disturbed during a construction project on Port of Bandon property in 2011. Nasomah was the name for the band of people who once lived at the lower Coquille River and who were among those violently displaced from their homelands in the mid-1800s. The Coquille Tribe calls this a "heart place," a location where ancestors lived and for which those now living have a responsibility to care. The Tribe worked together with officials from the City and Port of Bandon, the US Fish and Wildlife Service (which oversees the Bandon Marsh National Wildlife Refuge), and archaeologists from Southern Oregon University to plan the memorial, which features a garden with native plants significant to the Tribe, pavers utilizing a traditional basketry pattern, and large fragments from the "Grandmother Rock," a monolith of blue schist that once loomed high above the mouth of the Coquille River but was destroyed to create the river's jetties in the early 1900s.[17]

The garden's centerpiece is a sculpture created by artists Shirod Younker (Coquille) and Tony Johnson (Chinook) made of a red cedar tree root wad embedded with five carvings of stylized artifacts significant to the people: an adze (a woodworking tool), a mussel shell used as a spoon, a fishing spearpoint, an awl used for basketry and hide work, and a dentalium shell used as currency and for adornment. These outsized objects, painted ochre red, reference the artifacts lying just below the surface in the village site, and the sculpture overall evokes a tree from the village that had been uprooted, revealing that its roots had grown around similar artifacts placed by countless generations of ancestors.

The sculpture is titled *Weli:t'ea*, or *Gifts for the Spirits to Take to the Land of the Dead*, a reference not only to the embedded objects but

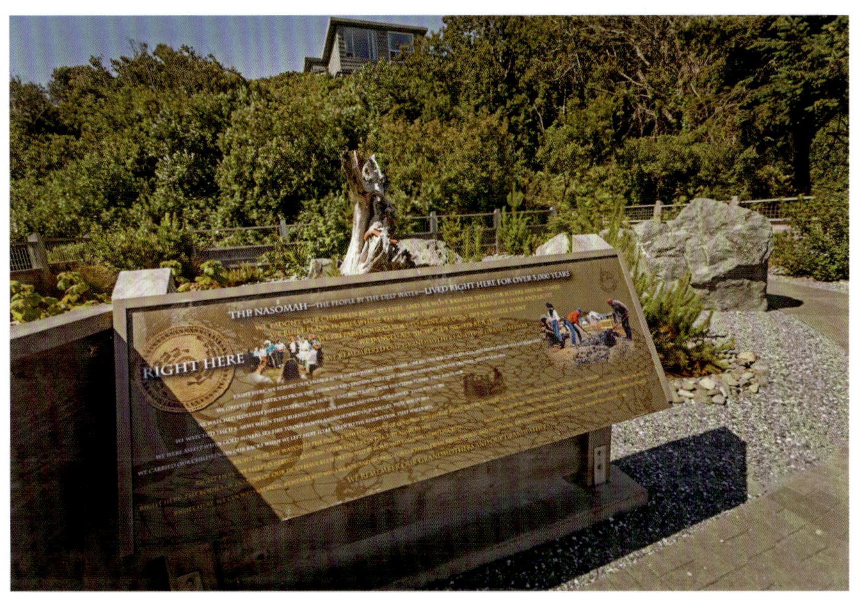

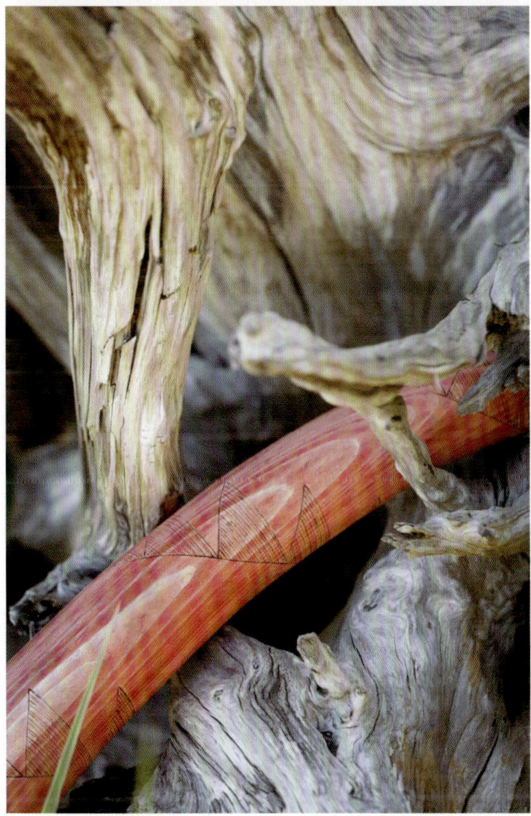

above:
Nasomah sculpture signage, 2016. Photograph by Frank Miller. Courtesy of Frank Miller and Willamette University.

left:
Nasomah sculpture (detail), 2016. Sculpture made by Tony Johnson (Chinook) and Shirod Younker (Coquille). Photograph by Frank Miller. Courtesy of Frank Miller and Willamette University.

also to the gifts to come, as the artists intended it to be used as a kind of altar or place of remembrance where tribal members and other visitors would pay their respects to those who came before. In the spirit of potlatch, the Nasomah Memorial Garden is a gift whose development gave community partners the opportunity to work together and whose presence offers the chance for the living not only to fulfill the responsibility to remember the ancestors but also to continue to build relationships with one another and the land.

CHAPTER 4

THE HUCKLEBERRY PATCH AS A SPIRITUAL GATHERING PLACE

The Cow Creek Band of Umpqua Tribe of Indians

For centuries Native families have been gathering every summer at a huckleberry patch—or to elders, the Patch—atop the divide between the Rogue and Umpqua Rivers, about twenty miles west of Crater Lake. Longtime tribal chairperson Sue Shaffer (1922–2017) called the Patch "a spiritual gathering place" and in doing so referred equally to its material and spiritual resources.[1] In August 2014, I traveled to the Cow Creek Band of Umpqua Tribe of Indians tribal government offices to meet with Rhonda Richardson, cultural development and language coordinator, and members of the tribal board of directors, to begin to understand the importance of the Huckleberry Gathering in the life of the Tribe. The next day, following Rhonda and her family, I made the long drive up into the mountains along US Forest Service roads to attend that year's gathering. I returned twice in 2015 to meet again with Rhonda and other tribal members from several generations to hear stories about "Huckleberry," as some refer to the annual event.

In September 2020 we continued our conversations through virtual means with additional tribal members who wished to contribute their perspectives to this account of the significance of the Patch.[2]

To a non-Indigenous outsider, picking huckleberries may seem far from ceremonial. Yet the Cow Creek Umpqua people, in coming together annually and harvesting nourishment from lands their ancestors have related to for millennia, engage in a process of self-creation. As tribal elder Mary Dumont Howren explained in the 2020 conversation, going to these places is "sustaining": "Whether it's at the Patch or South Umpqua Falls, I have these special places that I have always felt I am never alone. The past still lives. There are very special places that the past and present are very, very close." In both mundane and profound ways, the actual gathering and eating of berries feeds the tribal body—the Cow Creek Umpqua nation—as well as its individual members.

The annual Huckleberry Gathering forms Cow Creek Umpqua culture in another way: through the stories tribal members tell about huckleberry gatherings of the past. In other words, both the experience of and narratives about these events are a key way many Cow Creek Umpqua people understand and portray themselves to others.[3] The ongoing telling of stories about the Huckleberry Gathering, along with the continued experience of going to gather at the Patch, have shaped the future of the community in a very concrete way through the achievement of the designation of a special interest area of more than nine thousand acres of huckleberry fields by the US Forest Service (USFS). This chapter explores the intersections of storytelling, people, plants, and place, and concludes with a discussion of the special interest area agreement to protect these relationships, finalized in 2006 between the Cow Creek Umpqua Tribe and the Umpqua and Siskiyou National Forests.

In her role as cultural development and language coordinator, Rhonda Richardson is often in the position of telling the story of the Huckleberry Gathering, as she did for me when I met with her and fellow tribal members Elizabeth Gipson and Cindy Grizzle for a conversation in August 2015. "Families would go up there and camp for a long time, weeks," she said. "Decades ago, they would ride horses up there, camp up there, that's where they would meet once a year. They would catch up. They'd pick huckleberries and catch up on what who-and-who is doing, what's going on. I imagine that was going on forever. It's

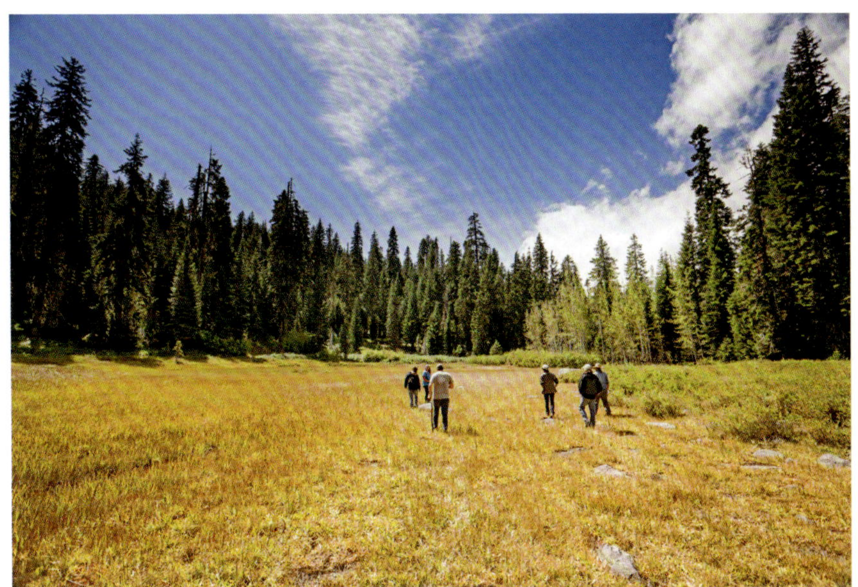

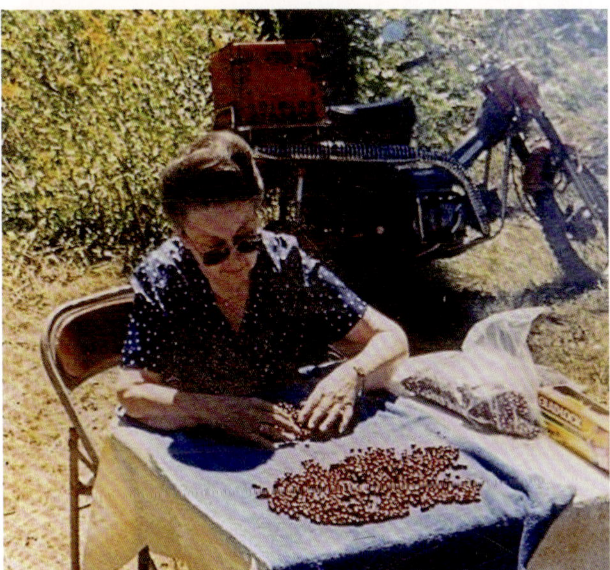

a major meeting place, the top of the divide." Other tribes in southern Oregon, especially the Klamath, Modoc, and Yahooskin Paiute, also historically used huckleberry fields in the area and continue to do so on a regular basis, as anthropologist Douglas Deur documented in his 2002 study of contemporary and historical traditional uses of huckleberry fields in the Rogue River National Forest.[4] The cultural and natural significance of the Patch to the Cow Creek Umpqua Tribe is what led to the special interest area designation—with its important protections—for these particular grounds at the top of the rivers' divide after years of advocacy by tribal leaders.

The annual Huckleberry Gathering is a time for the renewal of kin and community ties, both to one another and to the land. Every August, tribal members, with their families and friends, come together for berry picking, drumming and singing, picnicking and visiting. Today the gathering still involves a pilgrimage through miles of forest, although folks drive their trucks and cars along logging roads instead of walking or riding horses on ancient trails. Most people drive up just for the day, while some families still camp for extended periods of time during the summer months at South Umpqua Falls campground, not far from the Patch. Once folks have arrived and set up the meal, an elder leads the group in prayer, followed by others offering words of gratitude. In 2015, Rhonda explained, the group came together in a circle and joined hands while Ralph Young (born in the 1930s) led the prayer, which was completed by Cindy Grizzle (born in the 1960s), who is able to introduce herself in Takelma, the Penutian language that the tribe embraces as its language of heritage; the last fluent speaker, Francis Johnson, died in 1934. Then, as Rhonda remembered: "We went around the circle and said what everyone was grateful for, our own little piece in there."

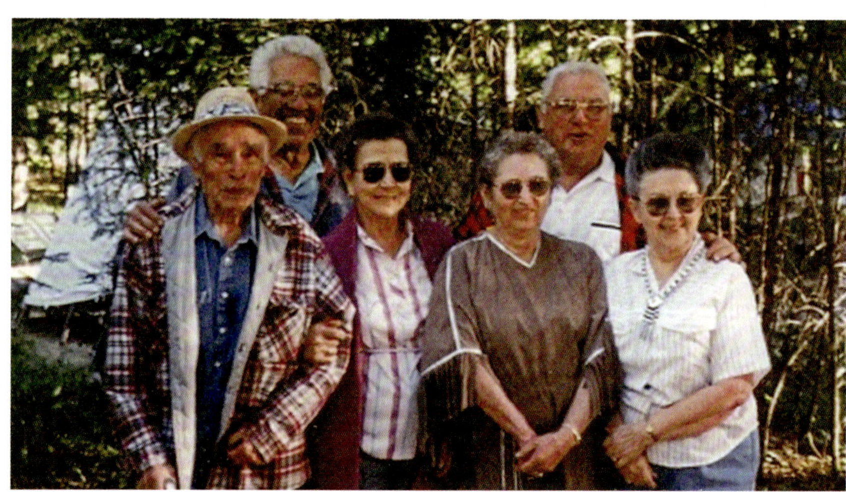

Elders at Huckleberry Gathering, July 1995. Left to right: Wallace Rondeau, Buster Rondeau, Emily Rose Kranz, Rena Cox, Tom Rondeau, Sue Shaffer. Photograph by Michael Rondeau. Courtesy of Cow Creek Band of Umpqua Indians.

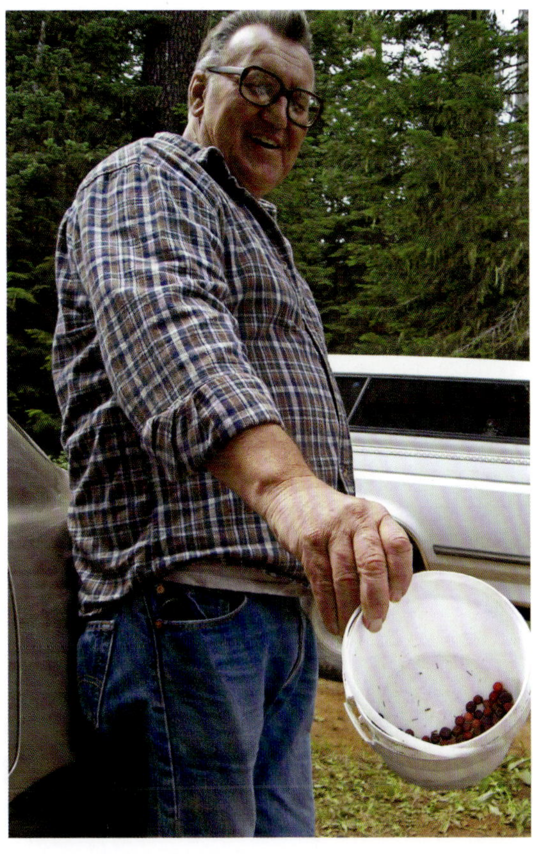

Ernie Volkman, with harvested huckleberries, date unknown. Photographer unknown. Courtesy of Cow Creek Band of Umpqua Indians.

The tribal drum has a central presence at the gathering. The Dancing Thunder Drum group, a core group of drummers and singers from several generations, gathers weekly to drum and sing, and plays at occasions such as this. Up at the Huckleberry Patch, anyone present is invited to join in, with a special emphasis upon children's participation. Rhonda described the spirit of inclusion that characterizes the gathering and the way that spirit reproduces the vitality of the tradition: "Seems like every year we get new tribal people or tribal family. It's good because that's how it stays alive for us. It *is* alive for us." After several songs, small groups of family members make their way out into the meadows and woods to gather huckleberries and to explore the ridge's meadows and wetlands. Others, having brought camp chairs for a day of visiting, stay close to the picnic spot, catching up on news of the community and old friends.

Generations of Gathering

In 1853 the Cow Creek Umpqua were one of the first tribes in what was then the Oregon Territory to negotiate a treaty with the US government, and a year later it was one of the few to have a treaty actually ratified by the US Senate.[5] The treaty provided for a temporary reservation of about five thousand acres, and the location, near the mouth of Council Creek, was occupied by the Quintoosa band from 1853 to 1855. The band members fled, however, under threat from hostile attacks by the US Army and settler militias during the outbreak of the Rogue River War. Because a permanent reservation was never established, after 1855 the Cow Creek Umpqua became landless. From then on, the US government failed to fulfill the treaty's promises of land, housing, and services, and essentially ignored the existence of the Tribe until the Western Oregon Indian Termination Act of 1954, which ended federal relations with sixty tribes and bands. The irony of the act for the Cow Creek Umpqua people is that it finally "recognized" the Tribe for the purpose of terminating their legal status, a status that had never been acknowledged in a meaningful way in the first place.

While it was the ultimate insult and was done with no prior notification, the federal government's act of termination was at least an admission that the Tribe had existed. In 1982, after decades of persistent organizing, the Cow Creek Band of Umpqua Tribe of Indians received federal recognition, although no land base was provided in the decree. In 1984 the Tribe won a lands claim case in the US Court of Federal Claims that provided a settlement of $1.5 million for the lands taken but never paid for as had been promised in the 1853 treaty. The Tribe insisted on investing the lump sum in an endowment instead of dispersing it in per-capita payments, a decision that has secured the long-term well-being of its citizens by creating strategic economic development opportunities. The Cow Creek Umpqua purchased twenty-nine acres at Canyonville in 1984 that were legally taken into trust status as reservation land in 1986; this is where the Seven Feathers Casino Resort and related tribal enterprises are located.[6]

The significance of the annual Huckleberry Gathering must be understood in light of this history. By continuing to come together at the Huckleberry Patch in the twenty-first century, Cow Creek Umpqua people harvest food resources and reinforce traditional values and bonds of identity, away from the pressures to conform to mainstream society.[7] In centuries past the time spent in the meadows was essential to procuring food for the coming year—not just berries but also other plants, game, and fish. After Euro-American contact transformed the Indigenous subsistence economy and forced tribal members to comply with the schedule of the wage labor economy, the food-resource-harvesting dimension of the gathering lessened in significance. Yet the gathering at the Patch remained and remains powerful as a place to experience tribal belonging and where, as Deur noted in his study, "families still bring children to teach them what it means to be Indian."[8]

One of the ways the significance of the gathering is reinforced is in the stories told about it by elders. An important account widely circulated among tribal members is one written by Emaline Lerwill Young (1905–1982) in 1980.[9] The Huckleberry Gathering figures prominently in her account of her family's history and her childhood:

> As long as I can remember the Rondeau family and our other Indian family friends went to the Huckleberry Patch each year. This was an annual event that lasted from about the first of August until the first frost, with the different families coming and going during that time. . . . I well remember from all the family stories, that this had been the meeting place of these same Indian families for as many generations back as oral tribal history went . . . back to the time when the mountains started throwing rocks at each other. History records this as the volcanic eruption of Crater Lake.[10]

The archaeological record resonates with Emaline's account, providing material evidence that Indigenous peoples occupied the region around Mount Mazama long before it erupted 7,700 years ago to form Crater Lake. Klamath oral traditions also provide evidence of occupation at the time of eruption.[11] Many tribes' stories about gathering huckleberries and other plant resources on the flanks of the mountain stretch back to time immemorial.[12]

Emaline remembered that in her childhood, families would come up on horseback. Her brother once counted eighty horses in the camp corral, a number that suggests the scale of the event for people attending the encampment in the early twentieth century, believed to be in the hundreds for the entire area, if not at the Huckleberry Patch itself.[13] Berries were abundant and were dried on a large flat rock heated by the summer sun. The warmth sped the drying process, and the berries were ready for storing after two days. Other foods Emaline recalled gathering included hazelnuts (sometimes picked while on horseback), camas root (*Camassia quamash*), and Indian carrot (*Lomatium macrocarpum*). Elk and deer meat was dried, while every other "part of the deer was used, nothing went to waste. The hides were all saved to later be made into moccasins, gloves, pants and coats as well as smaller 'what not' items. . . . The brains were used for tanning the hides and the horns were used for buttons. The hoofs were boiled down and used as glue."[14]

The food gathering and processing activities during the long daylight hours were complemented by evening social gatherings. From Emaline's account: "At night everyone managed to get together and had a dance around the big bonfire. . . . Everyone sang our Indian songs and chants and danced around the fire. They would sing really loud and then suddenly stop and listen as the mountains sang back to them. Of course, what they were hearing was the way the echoes came back." Some dancers wore "fancy buckskin outfits . . . decorated with lots of quill work, beads, fringe and embroidery."[15] Something that stood out to Emaline was the spirit of celebration and gratitude that characterized the community created at the Huckleberry Patch, expressed all the way up to the moment the gathering came to a close. "As the families would leave the berry patch," Emaline wrote, "they would whoop and yell as they went down the mountain side. The ones still at the Patch would give an answering yell and this would continue as long as they could be heard. This was the time to give thanks for a good harvest, a good time and a meeting of good friends, from our own tribe and from other acquainted tribes as well."[16]

The children of Emaline Young—Clementine Young Rice, Clara Young Keller, and Ralph Young, themselves elders when I met with them in 2015—had clear memories of going to the Huckleberry Patch with their mother. I spoke with all three, along with several other elders, at a regularly scheduled weekday senior lunch at Seven Feathers Casino Resort in September 2015, where I had been invited to talk with elders who wished to share recollections of Huckleberry.

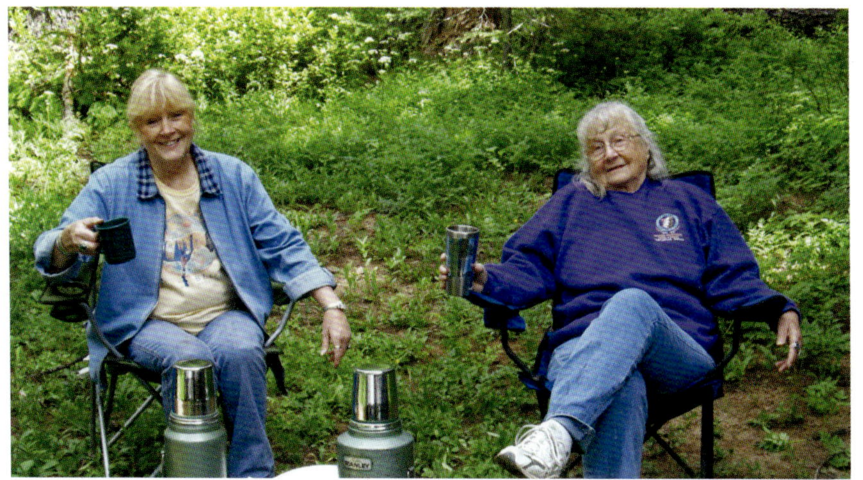

Clara Young Keller and Clementine Young Rice at Huckleberry Gathering, date unknown. Photograph by Rhonda Richardson. Courtesy of Cow Creek Band of Umpqua Indians.

Clementine (1928–2019) recalled, "Our family went every year. Mother wouldn't miss going. She'd go if she had to walk. They would pack in with horseback and stay a couple of weeks." The family always camped and brought everything they needed. In hindsight, Clementine said she and her sister, Clara, realized this entailed exceptional creativity on her mother's part: "We were just talking about this the other day. We just had a car, and how my mother got we kids in there, bedding, food? We always had plenty to eat. I don't know how she did it." Clara added: "We always took our grandmother. She was in a wheelchair." This meant there was yet more equipment that had to be brought along.

Clementine explained that for the Young family, along with many others, the time spent camping at the huckleberry fields included harvesting and storing a variety of resources for the rest of the year: "They did a lot of drying their stuff and preparing for the winter. A lot of them came in from the Klamath side, too, and they exchanged things. So it was kind of a meeting place, a get-together." Many Cow Creek Umpqua tribal members of all ages refer to the long-standing connections with the Klamath Tribes by telling the story of a stand of quaking aspens thought to have been planted by Klamath people at the Patch as a gesture of friendship and as an ongoing gift. Used in the hide-tanning process, the white bark of aspen trees produces particularly soft buckskin and was collected during the annual gatherings by both tribes' members for later use. Similarly, although many of the huckleberries harvested were eaten on the spot, large quantities were dried to be enjoyed throughout the coming year. And, as Ralph (1934–2021) remembered, "We always took a rifle. We always had meat." Deer and elk were abundant in the area, drawn to the ripe huckleberries. The game provided ample meals during the gathering but in addition much of it, like the berries, was processed for later consumption. The Young siblings, for example, remembered their mother bringing a pressure cooker along so she could cook and then can the meat.

Others from the generations born before termination in 1954 are likely to have grown up going to the Huckleberry Patch during the summers. As Larry Davis, born in the 1940s, recounted: "Last time I can remember being up at the Huckleberry Patch was when I was six, seven, eight years old. Somewhere along in there. My dad, aunts, and uncles would go up there every year. Seems to me it was shortly after the Fourth of July." He remembered his father explaining that "when there was a war with the whites, our tribe went up in that area," likely referring to the time of the Rogue River War of the 1850s, when Cow Creek Umpqua people were forced to take refuge in the foothills and mountains east of Canyonville during the winter months when typically they would have lived there only during the summer harvest months.

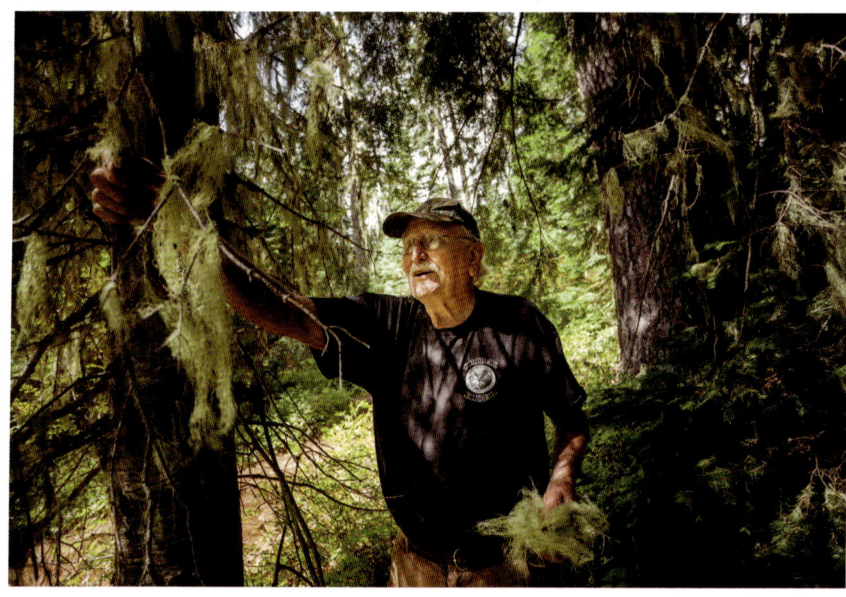

Ralph Young, gathering lichen at Huckleberry Gathering, 2015. Photograph by Frank Miller. Courtesy of Frank Miller and Willamette University.

Larry and his wife, Elaine, who have known one another since they were three years old, spent the majority of the past fifty years in Boise, Idaho, and moved back to the Canyonville-Roseburg area in 2015. While living in Boise, they occasionally returned for visits, and from afar they kept "on top of things that were happening" through correspondence with relatives. Now that they have returned, Larry is eager to resume going to the Huckleberry Gathering. In talking about the Huckleberry Patch, Larry remembered that there and elsewhere in the tribal homelands other plants, such as camas, wild onion, and chinquapin (*Chrysolepis sempervirens*) were picked. Elaine reminded him that it was his mother and other women who did much of that gathering and processing and who did "all the hard work." Other elders in the room chimed in, naming other plants such as wild hazelnut (*Corylus cornuta*), wild ginger (*Asarum caudatum*), and plants used to make teas.

Among those I spoke with in 2015 was Charles "Chuck" Jackson (1934–2017), who had played an important role in the long quest to secure federal recognition for the Cow Creek Band of Umpqua Tribe of Indians and served on the Tribal Council. When he introduced himself to me, Chuck described himself as "older than a box of rocks" and put the food gathering and hunting practices others were describing in a broader context by remembering what he was told as a child by the older people around him. "You can't starve to death here, you can't," he said, recalling those elders' words. "Because you just take a deer, and eat what the deer eats, and the deer is fat. You can eat anything they eat and you can survive here. You can't starve to death. It might get rough, you're not used to this, but," the elders instructed, you will survive. Chuck grew up learning to fish and hunt across a wide range of ancestral territory and contrasted the conditions of his youth with those of 2015. "When I was a kid, the old-timers, there was no hunting season," he said. "You hunted when your family needed food. That was the way of life. Our tribe was very rich. They had everything they wanted to eat. They had the bear and the deer and the elk and all the animals. They had the eels and all kinds of fish, and the creek had the crawdads. I remember the creek and all the crawdads, hundreds of them." At the time I spoke with Chuck, he considered himself lucky to see even one crawdad in a creek; much of the abundance of his childhood landscape has been decimated.

Chuck remembered knowing that his great-grandmother, Susan Nonta Thomason (1839–1912), conversed with her peers in five languages: English, French, Athabaskan, Takelma, and Chinook Jargon. Eventually becoming renowned as a keeper of tribal history himself, Chuck said that as a child, he was "the one that was interested in what the old-timers were talking about. Other kids would be playing and fighting, but I'm over here with the old people, I wanted to hear what was going on. To me that was interesting. You could play later but you couldn't always talk with the old people later. A lot of them were the old Indians; a lot of them were the old white people. I wanted to hear what they said. This kid don't give up; if you didn't give up, they'd talk to you." In Chuck's youth his elders and many other Cow Creek Umpqua tribal members were still able to move from place to place rather freely, living in different locations at different times of the year or in different life stages of their families. They met their basic needs through subsistence hunting and gathering supplemented by wages earned through participation in the timber industry or other aspects of the local economy. The late-summer gathering in the huckleberry fields high up on the Umpqua-Rogue River divide was an annual punctuation in that cycle, as it brought people together for fellowship and mutual assistance in procuring highly valued foods that were essential to the everyday well-being of Cow Creek Umpqua families throughout the rest of the year.

The next generation, those Cow Creek Umpqua tribal members born after World War II whose formative childhood and young adult years overlapped with the decades of termination (the 1950s through the 1970s), did not necessarily grow up going to the Huckleberry Patch. Their lives were impacted by a variety of factors, including legal racism. Del "Red Hawk" Ansures (1954–2017) quipped: "Yes, I was born during termination. I'm an illegal alien, if you really look at it." He explained his reasons for referring to himself this way: his parents, one white and the other American Indian, were married before 1951, when such a union was technically illegal in Oregon. The state's 1866 antimiscegenation law prohibited interracial marriages, including those between whites and people of at least one-half Native American ancestry. The law was finally repealed in 1951. Emphasizing the irony of his service in the military given that his family was seen as somehow less than fully legitimate, both in terms of his parents' "illegal" marriage and the terminated status of the Cow Creek Umpqua that impacted their family citizenry, Del said, "I'm an alien but I served my country. I was in Vietnam, but I'm happy."

The termination era, officially ushered in with the Western Oregon Indian Termination Act of 1954, had an impact on the ability of families to make the annual pilgrimage to the Huckleberry Gathering. In my earlier conversation in August 2015 with Rhonda Richardson, Cindy Delay Grizzle, and Beth Gipson, we discussed the diaspora, the geographic scattering, of the Cow Creek Umpqua community following termination as families moved to make a living elsewhere. Cindy, born in the 1960s, grew up at a distance from the Cow Creek Umpqua homelands—in the mid-Willamette Valley, where her father had found work. Cindy did not go up to the Huckleberry Patch until midlife. "My grandma always talked about it," she explained. "But until I moved here in 2008 I hadn't ever been there. That's the first year Rhonda took me up there. We had a Yukon [SUV] and I don't know how many kids stuffed in the back. Rhonda had foster kids."

By 2015, just seven years later, Cindy had become one of those who play a leading role in the continuation of the Huckleberry Gathering. And she is among the many tribal members who are returning to live within reach of Roseburg, the site of tribal government offices, and Canyonville, where the Seven Feathers Casino Resort is located along with other tribal enterprises. Cindy, who now works for the Cow Creek Umpqua Tribe in elder services, explained: "We've been encouraging families who have moved away to come back, to come home. There are benefits [of employment and housing] when they are in our counties." Since Cindy's own return in 2008, she said, "my daughter and granddaughter have moved here. I'm still working on the other family. My sister just moved back here. When my parents move back, I know [the rest of] my siblings will."

Federal recognition was won in 1982, and the generations born after that year are key to the contemporary revitalization of tribal traditions. Beth Gipson, born in the 1980s and raised in the Canyonville area, went to her first Huckleberry Gathering in 2014. "I had been wanting to go for many years," she said. "I've been getting more and more involved. Being self-employed now, I've been really pushing my way through to be more involved with the girls and the tribe." Her self-employment gives her the flexibility to take part in cultural activities and facilitate the learning of tribal traditions by her grown children and young grandchildren. "I've always been raised saying it's important to get our children involved," she said. "We have to keep our heritage going, learning. I loved it as a kid, [but in] my teen years I stopped dancing. . . . I wanted [my children and grandchildren] to know more than me." The Tribe's investment in its members' education and employment, supported with the endowment created by the land claims settlement in 1984 as well as with revenues generated by contemporary enterprises, has benefited Beth's family. She explained that it was important to her, especially since she became a mother and grandmother relatively young, to get her two children "educated and go from there. They are both graduated and working. . . . I feel really blessed. There's always something new around the corner, some new program, benefit. . . . It's truly a blessing. I look forward to a lot."

That hope and gratitude are shared and generated by many, especially those in the Dancing Thunder Drum group, of which Beth is a part. She explained that the group members "meet up weekly and we learn all the songs we grew up on plus more. . . . I didn't drum much as a kid, until I drummed a few times as a teenager at a powwow. . . . Kids weren't really doing too much then. Now we do involve our children and teach them early. . . . We've even got a child that's eight years old that knows how to lead his own drum group, with kids." Beth stressed repeatedly how important it is to her that children are involved at the drum: "When I sit there and I drum, you'll see me smile profusely when there's children. And they're new and they know the songs already because we've had, besides our own groups, we've had other groups to teach them."

Beth explained that playing the drum—like picking huckleberries—at the Patch provides another avenue for teaching children about what it means to be Cow Creek Umpqua. "We bless the drum before we get started," she said. "We teach them the traditions, little pieces here and there. . . . We . . . drummed with the kids and they mess up and you just put it back where it needs to be with the beat." Listening to Beth reflect on the children's participation in the 2015 Huckleberry Gathering, Rhonda chimed in: "They'll have memories of Huckleberry and drumming there . . ." Beth finished the thought: "That I didn't have." Rhonda came back to say, "But you have them now!" She offered the

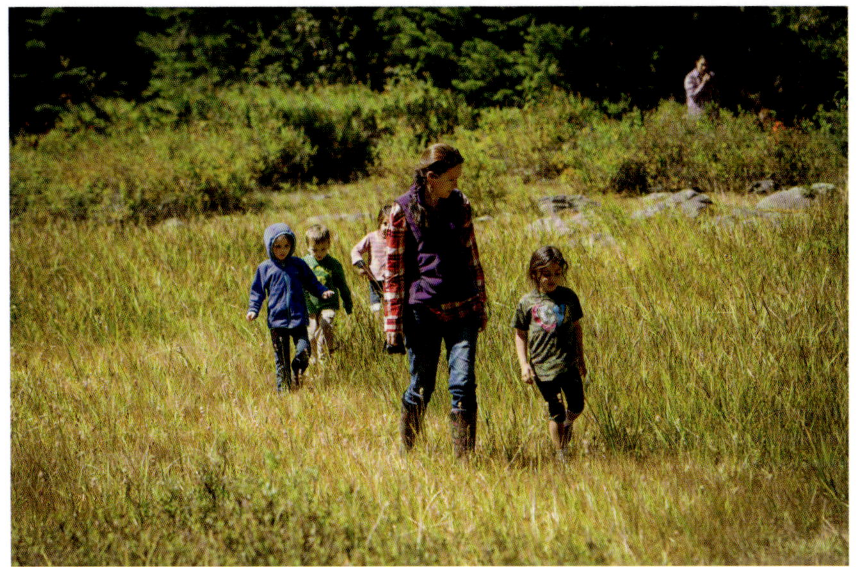

Tribal member Jessica Bochart with children at Huckleberry Gathering, 2015. Photograph by Frank Miller. Courtesy of Frank Miller and Willamette University.

broader view: "We talk about *our* elders talking about Huckleberry and these little ones are going to see *us* as their elders." Then, Rhonda went on, the children will someday say, "We came here with our elders and they drummed here." Rhonda, Beth, and Cindy agreed that going to the Huckleberry Gathering is something the children today know and to some degree take for granted as part of what it means to be a member of the Cow Creek Umpqua community. There is a sense of accomplishment and well-being that comes from being able to provide this security to the rising generations.

In addition to participating as a drummer and singer, Beth is expanding her repertoire of clothing customs and other knowledge and skills. In 2015 she became the first Cow Creek Umpqua tribal member in decades to make a traditional southwestern Oregon–style dance skirt and apron. She learned to tan the hides and got help from tribal members and relatives. "Sheila and Jim Rich are the ones who taught me," Beth recalled. "I asked friends to keep their hides for me. We wrapped them up and froze them a special way until we had enough warm weather. I went up there on my uncle Ralph Young's property. We learned a bunch of different ways. He taught me to use the lye and the water and let it soak for a few days. He had me even scraping all the membranes and the hair off, and then soaking it in an actual pig brain mixture."

Beth continued: "Then we wring them out. He splices a bunch of areas to put them on a frame. We stretch them all out until they're fully dry in the sun, when it's very hot." During this long process, Ralph brought out a copy of his mother Emaline Young's account of her memories of tribal traditions and Huckleberry Gatherings, mentioned earlier. Ralph wanted Beth to take the time to read it out loud, in effect having her recount stories as told by an ancestor while enacting elements of those stories, lending weight to the occasion. Laughing, Beth explained the irony of being interrupted while trying to carry out a tradition by being asked to *read* about traditions. "I had to redo that hide," she said "because he stopped me to read out loud. He's an elder so you have to respect your elders. So I sat down and read." She did complete the tanning process, and in the coming weeks created the dance skirt and apron, decorating them with pine nuts, dentalia, and abalone. Beth's hope is that "in the future we'll get a few more [tribal members] to get out there and learn the old traditional tanning and go from there."

Stewardship for Future Generations

The Cow Creek Band of Umpqua Tribe of Indians long advocated for protection for the area that includes the Patch so that it continues to be a place where huckleberries, other natural resources in the ecosystem, and future Cow Creek Umpqua generations thrive in ongoing relationship with one another. In our 2020 conversation, Sherry Shaffer, Sue Shaffer's daughter, remembered this long struggle as seeming to take a "lifetime of trying" and of being pleasantly shocked when the effort resulted in an agreement between the Tribe and the US Forest Service. In 2004 staff from the Umpqua National Forest began meeting with tribal representatives to discuss plans to designate thousands of acres containing the traditional Huckleberry Gathering grounds as a designated special interest area. According to the Forest Service, such areas are intended to "protect and, where appropriate, foster public use and enjoyment of areas with scenic, historical, geological, botanical, zoological, paleontological, or other special characteristics and to classify areas that possess unusual recreational and scientific values so that these special values are available for public use, study, or enjoyment."[17] Special interest areas are distinct from wilderness or research natural areas, in which the Forest Service may limit human interactions with the land in keeping with the tenets of conventional conservation biology. In contrast, a special interest area designation recognizes the human community's active relationship with the land in order to facilitate its continuance.

In January 2006, after a required period of research and public comment, the Forest Service took administrative action to set aside a total of 9,497 acres in the Umpqua and Rogue River–Siskiyou National Forests as a special interest area.[18] This decision encourages "management activities that would benefit the recognition of the cultural, historic, and traditional values" of the Huckleberry Patch to tribes and to nontribal users, including activities that promote huckleberry production and continuance of existing cultural practices such as the annual gatherings.[19] Furthermore, the decision requires "appropriate tribal consultation for projects on the Forest," thus codifying an important partnership between the two National Forests and the Cow Creek Umpqua Tribe.[20] When the special interest area was designated in 2006, Sue Shaffer, then tribal chair, said:

> From time immemorial, the Huckleberry Patch has been a spiritual gathering place of Cow Creek Umpqua Tribal members. This is the place where traditions, history and what it means to be Cow Creek were passed down from our elders to the present generations. Families gathered every year from August until first frost to harvest and prepare berries, deer, poo-eat-sic [*an edible tuber*] and other traditional foods for the year. Today, the Huckleberry Patch continues to provide a place of quiet communion with nature and the Great Spirit; a place where Cow Creek families congregate; and a place for harvesting sustenance. The designation of a Huckleberry Patch Special Interest Area is important to the Cow Creek tribe, memorializing our continued use of this area and ensuring future generations will experience this spiritual gathering place. This location, huckleberries and more, deserves distinct consideration in both the Rogue and the Umpqua National Forests management plans.[21]

Shaffer's choice of words—her emphasis on the Huckleberry Patch as a "spiritual gathering place" for "quiet communion with nature and the

Great Spirit" where "Cow Creek families congregate" for "harvesting sustenance"—points toward the ways physical and symbolic dimensions intersect at the Huckleberry Gathering.

In coming together at this particular place in the ancestral homeland, harvesting and eating the fruits of that land, the Cow Creek Umpqua people engage in a process that makes them who they are bodily, culturally, and spiritually. The fact that this age-old set of practices continues and has continued over generations made possible the designation of the special interest area, an administrative mechanism through which the Cow Creek Umpqua Tribe can now partner with the US Forest Service, the land manager of the Huckleberry Patch. Such a process is far from isolated on the world stage, as Indigenous peoples globally are more and more successful in their struggles to participate in the management and use of customary territories no longer under their jurisdiction.[22] Seen from this perspective, the annual Huckleberry Gathering achieves new relevance as a representation of the Cow Creek Umpqua Tribe's continuing influence on ancestral lands, an influence that extends well beyond berry picking.

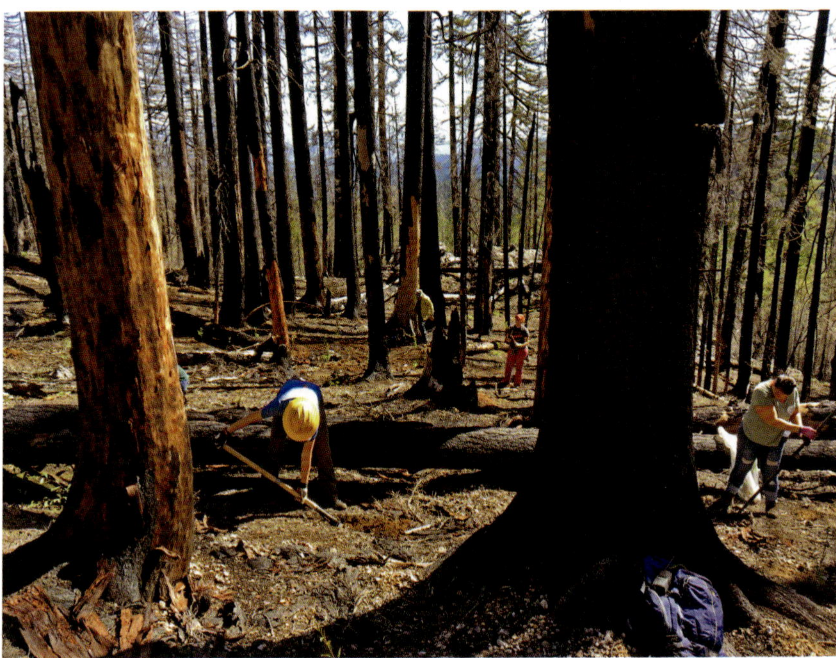

Tribal members replanting after wildfire in ancestral lands now part of the Umpqua National Forest, 2019. Photograph by Kelly Coates. Courtesy of Cow Creek Band of Umpqua Indians.

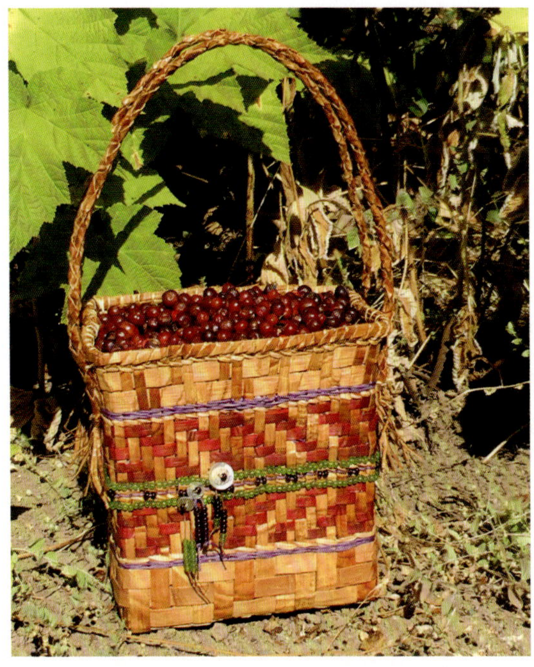

Basket with huckleberries, woven by Jennifer Bryant of cedar with glass beads and shell, 2019. Photograph by Jennifer Bryant. Courtesy of Cow Creek Band of Umpqua Indians.

Experiencing the intersection of people, plants, and place at the Huckleberry Patch, as well as the telling of stories about the Huckleberry Gatherings over time, are central to the way the Cow Creek Umpqua people understand and portray themselves to others. At the close of our conversation about the 2015 Huckleberry Gathering, Rhonda Richardson reflected: "Huckleberry will always be a significant place and it's already being passed on. Some of our kids are going to be not knowing how significant it is unless we talk about it, we tell them, tell other people. We have even elders who want to go back, because it's that important of a place. We have our kids, it's generational. So it's obviously being talked about. We have to keep it alive." The Huckleberry Patch and the stories about gathering there give substance to and strengthen the Cow Creek Umpqua Tribe.

CANOE FAMILY, DIG DEEP

The Confederated Tribes of Grand Ronde

In a Clackamas Chinook myth from northwestern Oregon, Stank'iya, or Coyote, prepares the world and makes it ready for people. Encountering all manner of food-beings who testify to their value to people, Stank'iya responds by giving the plant-, fish-, and animal-people their names. He explains to human beings which ones are edible, at what time of year they appear, and how they should be prepared. In doing so, Stank'iya "made everything good" for the people to come.[1] In the twenty-first century the image of Stank'iya has come to represent the Grand Ronde Canoe Family and his name is given to the group's principal canoe. Just as Coyote prepared the world and explained to people the use of its resources, *Stank'iya*, the canoe, provides a space for learning to thrive in this world. Coyote, at once a creator-transformer and a maker of wildly inappropriate mistakes, brings needed balance and levity to a world that can be imbalanced and burdensome. His example is one that offers endless lessons for the complexities of life's journey.

In 2008, *The Art of Ceremony* exhibition featured an installation representing the Grand Ronde Canoe Family, then still quite new, having participated in its first Canoe Journey in 2005. Held regularly since 1993, Canoe (or Tribal) Journey is a summer event that involves tribal canoe families launching from their home territories in Oregon, Washington, and British Columbia, and traveling to that of a host community for several days of feasting, celebration, and sharing of cultural protocols. Along the way canoes are hosted by local tribal communities, to whom paddlers offer song and dance in return for their generous hospitality. The entire endeavor has come to last for weeks and to involve a hundred or more canoes and thousands of people, not only paddlers but also support crews traveling by road and in motorized boats. Throngs of people, Native and non-native, from infants to elders, greet paddlers when they arrive at the final destination. The impact of the Canoe Journey has spread through the Pacific Northwest and beyond, drawing attention and participation by Indigenous groups from other parts of North America and as far away as New Zealand.

The Art of Ceremony installation at the Hallie Ford Museum of Art included a lower Columbia River Chinookan canoe, called *Ul-iymits*, or Old Nose in Chinuk Wawa (the creole language shared among many Northwest tribal groups), whose special origins are recounted later in

Chinook and Grand Ronde Canoe Families, in *Ul-iymits* (center) and another canoe (at right) belonging to the Chinook Nation and the Tony Johnson family. Grand Ronde Canoe Family, Journey to Elwha, Port Angeles, Washington, 2005. At bow, Bobby Mercier. Photograph by Dave Fullerton. Courtesy of *Smoke Signals*, the independent publication of the Confederated Tribes of Grand Ronde.

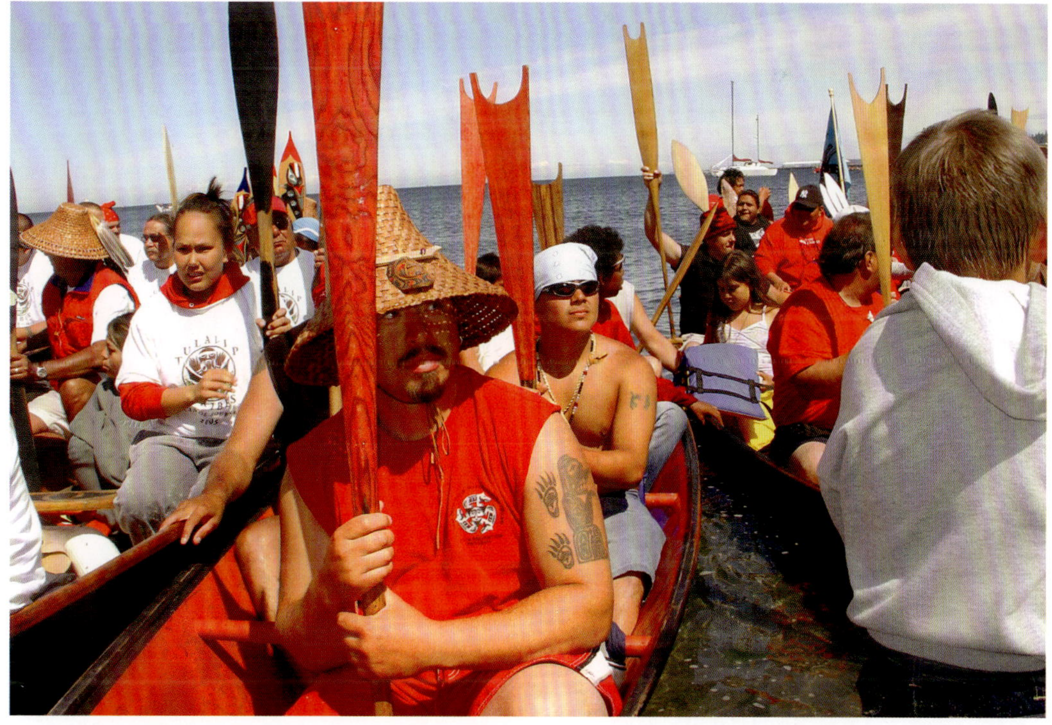

this chapter. Inside the canoe were figures of paddlers wearing sweatshirts bearing the Canoe Family's motto, "Dig Deep," referring to the imperative to find the individual and collective strength to paddle hard. During the course of the exhibition's run, Grand Ronde tribal members shared weaving traditions in public programs at the museum. In May 2016 three members of the Canoe Family who have been involved since those early years—Cristina Lara (born in 1984), Lisa Leno (born in 1968), and Bobby Mercier (born in 1976)—came together at the Grand Ronde Tribe's Chachalu Museum and Cultural Center to have a conversation with me about tribal members' experiences in the Canoe Journey movement.[2]

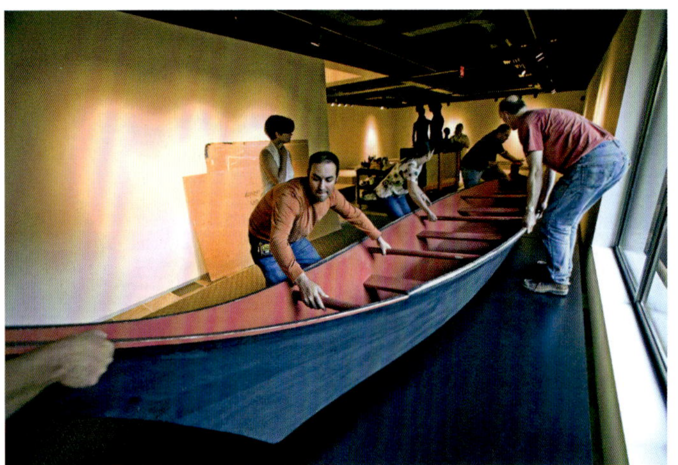

Installation of *Ul-iymits* (Old Nose) at the Hallie Ford Museum of Art, 2008. Out of the frame at left, Tony Johnson guides in the canoe; museum staff Jonathan Bucci and David Andersen are on either side, and Bobby Mercier is at the rear. Photograph by Frank Miller. Courtesy of Frank Miller and Willamette University.

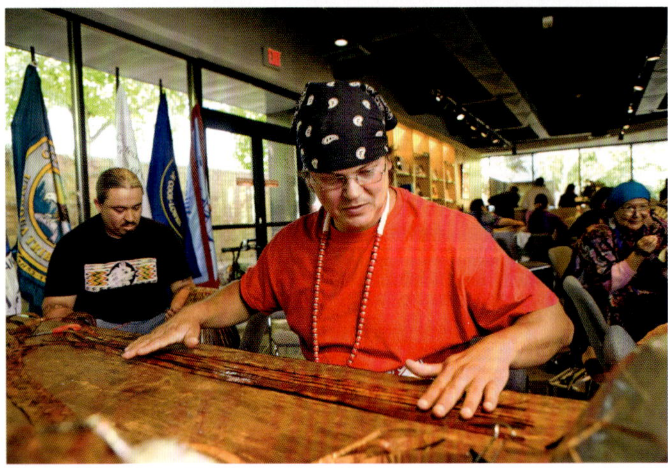

Brian Krehbiel preparing cedar strips for weaving at a public program in association with *The Art of Ceremony* exhibit, 2008. Photograph by Frank Miller. Courtesy of Frank Miller and Willamette University.

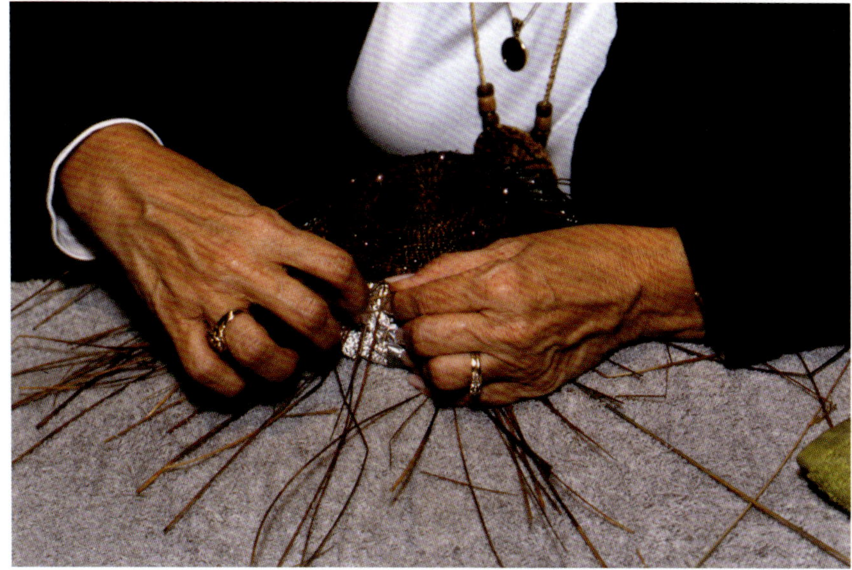

Connie Graves (1955–2019) demonstrating weaving at a public program in association with *The Art of Ceremony* exhibit, 2008. Photograph by Dale Peterson. Courtesy of Dale Peterson and Willamette University.

The Canoe Revival in the Pacific Northwest

Cristina "Tina" Lara, who at the time of our 2016 meeting was a member of Tribal Youth Prevention's program staff at Grand Ronde, was an intern in the Tribe's youth education department in the mid-2000s. Her first exposure to Canoe Journey was in 2005, when she met the Canoe Family at Suquamish, Washington, north of Bainbridge Island, during a stopover on its way to the final host, the Lower Elwha Skallam Tribe at Port Angeles. Tina had no idea what to expect; when she witnessed the canoes landing and saw "families . . . asking for permission to come ashore, I was hooked!" Floored by the experience, she wondered to herself, "Where has this been my whole life?" The sight of hundreds of Native people, especially youth, pulling the canoes up, engaging in traditional protocols, rituals in which visitors ask permission to land and are formally welcomed by the home community, led to a clear conviction: "This is where it's at. This is where you need to be."

Tina returned to Grand Ronde and became involved with the Canoe Family, which for her "fulfilled some of whatever I was missing" since she, like many other tribal members, had been cut off from the practice of cultural heritage as a consequence of destructive historical interventions. To Tina, the Canoe Family became a new kind of extended family, and she felt "safe, because I was with people I trusted and because it felt good." Bobby Mercier, then and now Grand Ronde's Canoe Family skipper, remembered that her enthusiasm and commitment drew in other youth; he called Tina "the magnet for the rest of them."

The modern Canoe Journey movement was launched with the 1989 Paddle to Seattle, organized by Emmett Oliver of the Quinault Nation to celebrate and draw attention to the continued sovereignty of Native communities during Washington's centennial year.[3] Canoe contingents from two coastal Washington tribal communities (Hoh and La Push) journeyed around the Olympic Peninsula to Seattle, where they were joined by canoes from several other Puget Sound tribes as well as Heiltsuk paddlers from British Columbia. At that event the Heiltsuk issued an invitation for canoe nations to come north to Bella Bella in 1993. Native communities across the Northwest were transformed by the experience of preparing for that journey over the following four years.[4] Canoe Journey has continued almost every year since, with ever-increasing numbers of participants.

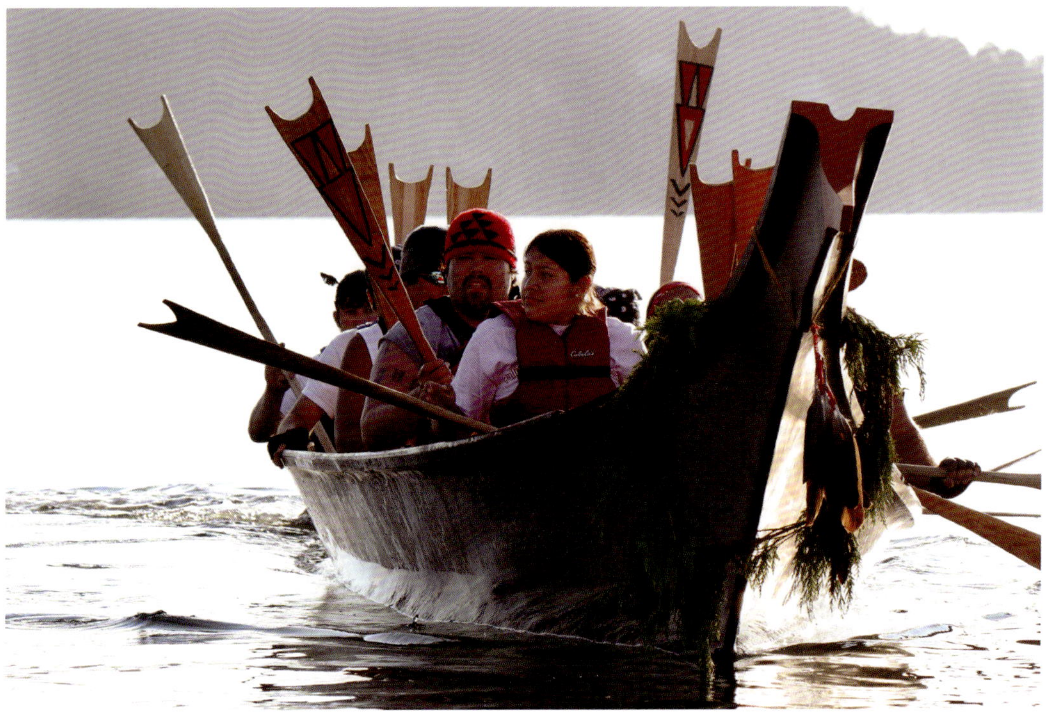

The majority of tribes participating in Canoe Journey are from Washington and British Columbia, with communities positioned right on the waters of Puget Sound and Canada's Pacific Coast. Joining the journey might not be seen as an obvious step for Grand Ronde, whose reservation in the western Willamette Valley has no major waterways running through it. But the Grand Ronde confederation is made up of thirty tribal bands whose ancestral territories stretched from the Columbia River south to northwestern California and east to the Willamette Valley and the foothills of the Cascades, and who historically had canoe traditions associated with their pre-reservation locations on bays and rivers or on the Oregon coast. A series of federal policies and interventions from the mid-nineteenth century onward profoundly disrupted not only the tribes' historical relationships to their aboriginal waterways and associated canoe traditions but to their heritages altogether. In the mid-1850s, these tribes were forcibly removed by the US military to the Coast Reservation; shortly afterward, in 1857, the Grand Ronde Reservation was legally established by presidential executive order.[5] By 1901, Grand Ronde Reservation lands had been divided into individual tribal member allotments or sold as "surplus" lands to non-Indians. Then, in 1954, Grand Ronde was terminated along with other tribes, ushering in an era of further cultural and family destruction. Grand Ronde achieved restoration in 1983 and, like other restored tribes, has since been engaged in a process of nation-building in governmental, economic, social, and cultural realms. Seen from the context of this historical trajectory, the Canoe Family is integral to the process of developing contemporary Grand Ronde cultural identities.

Among those dispersed in the 1800s to Grand Ronde were members of Lower and Middle Chinookan tribes, who navigated the Columbia and Willamette Rivers in canoes.[6] Many Grand Ronde tribal members today can trace some Chinookan heritage.[7] But some Lower Chinook families remained in their aboriginal territory at the mouth of the Columbia River, including that of Tony Johnson, Chinook Nation tribal member and, since 2014, tribal chair, who worked at Grand Ronde from 1997 to 2011 as a linguist and educator.[8] Along with linguist Henry Zenk and Grand Ronde tribal members, Johnson was instrumental in developing a language-immersion program for children in Chinuk Wawa (known in English as Chinook Jargon), the historical lingua franca of the many tribes that made up Grand Ronde, few of whom otherwise shared a common tongue.⁹ In 2002, Johnson collaborated with John McCallum of Applegate Boatworks in Veneta, Oregon, to build a replica of the Chinook canoe made by the Scarborough family in the nineteenth century, held in the collection of the Oregon Historical Society and now on display as a key element of the permanent *Experience Oregon* exhibit that opened in 2020.¹⁰ McCallum used a taped-seamed plywood method to craft the canoe, and Johnson carved the nose and tail from an 1,180-year-old western red cedar; hence, the canoe was named *Ul-iymits* (Old Nose) in Chinuk Wawa.

During the time Johnson was bringing *Ul-iymits* to life, he and Bobby Mercier were coworkers in Grand Ronde's Cultural Resources Department. For a few years Mercier had been encouraged by tribal members in Washington to become involved in Canoe Journey, and in 2003 he and a small group of others from Grand Ronde came to witness the journey landing at Tulalip. The experience convinced them to form a Canoe Family of their own, and once they returned home, a dozen or so began paddling the Tribe's canoe in local waters in preparation. Partnering with Johnson and the Chinook Canoe Family, the Grand Ronde Canoe Family had its first official Canoe Journey in 2005, when they paddled Puget Sound from Squaxin Island to the Lower Elwha Klallam Tribe. When they returned home, they shared their compelling stories and photographs, and this generated further support from the Grand Ronde Tribal Council toward the significant expenses involved in Canoe Journey.¹¹ The Grande Ronde Tribe commissioned a thirty-three-foot Chinookan-style canoe from McCallum of Applegate Boatworks, the one described at the opening of the chapter, called *Stank'iya* (Coyote). It was ready for the 2006 Paddle to Muckleshoot Canoe Journey.

Canoe Journey as Metaphor: Building a Healthy Community

The process of building a canoe family is a process of healing and of reckoning with the destruction wrought by colonization and displacement. It involves developing physical and emotional discipline as well as the historical knowledge and cultural creativity needed to represent one's people in the intertribal protocol of the Canoe Journey. Sobriety and healthy living are core emphases among Canoe Journey participants, as are intergenerational relationships. Many tribes have utilized the Canoe Journey as a practice as well as a metaphor in the development of addiction prevention and intervention programs for Native youth.[12] Canoe Journey has become an effective intervention, whether youth go on an actual paddle or are introduced to it as a metaphor for life's journey. Elizabeth Hawkins and June La Marr, who wrote about the *Canoe Journey—Life's Journey* curriculum project developed in collaboration between University of Washington and the Seattle Indian Health Board, have explained:

> Simply put, anything you would need on a Canoe Journey you also need in life's journey. On a Canoe Journey, you need to be in balance emotionally, mentally, physically, and spiritually in order to be a useful and valuable participant. You need problem-solving skills, measured thinking, goals, a plan, communication skills, and emotional regulation. On a life's journey you need exactly these same skills. On the canoe, you have paddles and pullers to move you forward on your journey. In life's journey, you need to develop the skills and social support necessary to navigate through what life gives you and meet the challenges and barriers set before us.[13]

This metaphor has deep roots in many Northwest Coast tribes, some of which refer to the tribe as a canoe and the water it plies as the events of life: the members of the canoe must work together to navigate the waters, whether calm or turbulent, aware that the actions of one have impact upon all.[14]

The Canoe Journey offers the chance for these lessons to be discovered experientially. Lisa Leno has worked in Youth Prevention since 1995, where she has long wrestled with the questions of how a tribal program can "build resiliency and attachment" and encourage "healthy lifestyles" among youth, particularly those considered at risk. She came to Canoe Journey from that position of responsibility and has found that the experience gives youth and all those involved a way to heal, to belong, and to be connected to a strong community without overreliance on just one person, as can happen in a conventional therapeutic relationship. Bobby Mercier echoed that the job of adults involved in the Canoe Family is to model "healthy living and healthy relationships." One of the strongest lessons of Canoe Journey, according to Leno, is that every person—

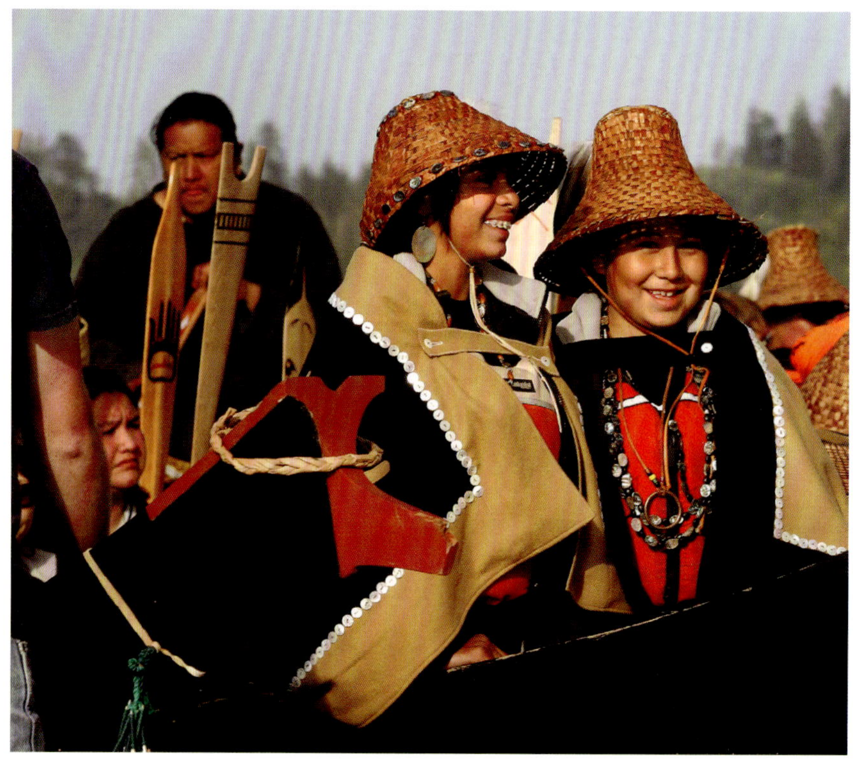

Paddle to Makah, Neah Bay, Washington, 2010. Grand Ronde Canoe Family members, right front, Raven Harmon; middle, Mataya Holmes; left rear, Doug James (Quinault). Photograph by Michelle Alaimo. Courtesy of *Smoke Signals*, the independent publication of the Confederated Tribes of Grand Ronde.

whether youth, adult, or elder—has "something different that Canoe Journey brings for them" and strengths that they bring to it. Various skills are needed—paddling, cooking, camping—and there is enough flexibility to allow people to gravitate to tasks at which they excel.

Mercier described how, for him, one of the best things about Journey is seeing how attitudes of the youth are transformed as they paddle from the first to the last day, arriving in the final host community perhaps two or more weeks later. As Lisa Leno explained, "Canoe Journey is a lot of wonderful things, but it's also a lot of work and . . . stress." Young people must accept being told what to do, meet expectations, deal with many unknowns, stay up late for protocol, and get up early to paddle. But now, more than a decade in, many Grand Ronde youth have grown into adulthood having participated in Journey. As a result, as Mercier emphasized, they have social networks that extend "up and down the coast," and some have even "married into other communities with canoe families of their own." These connections enrich the larger Grand Ronde community. Leno added that for the youth who have been involved, "their lives have been changed forever," and even if they discontinue direct participation in Journey, many return home and make positive contributions. To Leno, that's a key goal: "We focus on Journey, but we're also focusing on building a healthy community."

Since 2009, Māori paddlers from New Zealand have joined the Grand Ronde on Canoe Journey, through invitations that developed out of meetings during *The Eternal Thread* in 2005 and *The Art of Ceremony* in 2008 (see the introduction).[15] The Māori visitors have been sponsored by Toi Māori, the Māori arts organization supported in part by the New Zealand government, and are members of its Ngā Waka Federation, the committee devoted to the art and culture of the waka (*oceangoing canoe*). In ways parallel to the Pacific Northwest, New Zealand has been transformed over the past several decades by the self-determination struggles of its Indigenous people.[16] During Journey, the Māori guests become part of the Canoe Family, and there is a great deal of knowledge-sharing about traditions related to canoes, carving, weaving, and protocols. According to Tina Lara, however, the real learning comes from the relationships that grow out of living together over the weeks of paddling and camping; while it is the "similarities that bring you together, it is a relationship that makes those similarities important." Just as Canoe Journey brings Northwest Coast nations together in a demonstration of embodied sovereignty, the inclusion of the Māori makes manifest the international dimensions of Indigenous resurgence and provides youth with further examples of self-discipline and leadership, broadening their sense of a wider—even global— community of support.

Canoe Journey demands a serious commitment of time and physical endurance, and today nearly a hundred Grand Ronde youth and adults directly participate in some way, although of course the majority of tribal members cannot take part every year. Although many paddle some portion of the route, others, such as elder Delores Parmenter, drive to join the Canoe Family in camp. Parmenter has gone on every journey since 2006, driving her pickup truck to each stop, to be onshore for the arrival and to share in the evening gatherings. Her presence offers the Canoe Family a deep sense of support and accompaniment. At the end of the 2011 Journey to Swinomish, Parmenter summed up

the emotion she and other elders felt upon watching the Grand Ronde
Canoe Family conduct protocol: "We're honoring our ancestors, it's
overwhelming. Our ancestors would be honored the way everyone
worked together for the journey."[17]

Building Culture: Carving, Weaving, and "Catching Songs"

Becoming a canoe family demands the development of a range of
knowledge and skills—from the making and use of the canoe, paddles,
and other physical components of the journey to the cultural knowledge needed for the enactment of canoe etiquette and onshore protocols. Just before coming ashore, the skipper of a canoe is expected to
announce the group's arrival, speaking his or her Indigenous language
and acknowledging ancestors on both sides, and then ask permission
to land. In the days of feasting and celebrations that follow, each canoe
family (which may number up to one hundred in the final host community) performs songs and dances, often going on into the wee hours
of the morning. Dancers and singers wear regalia, carry hand drums,
and present gifts of thanks.

At the first Canoe Journey Grand Ronde made in 2005, Bobby
Mercier recalled: "We were standing there, at protocol, in Port Angeles.
We only had a few songs, and those were songs that we had from old
wax cylinders that were from here."[18] Songs are a key element of protocol in that they are understood as gifts being given in exchange for
the generous hospitality of the hosts, as well as being an essential representation of one's nation. Yet the Grand Ronde contingent had only
a few songs and no dancers or regalia that first year. Mercier and the
others reassured their hosts: "We told them, 'Next year we're gonna
bring more people, we'll have more songs, we'll share dances with you.'
And we did, we came there with a handful more people and a bunch
more songs."

In the 1990s, when he was in his teens, Mercier began making trips
north to the Puget Sound area and was exposed to Northwest Coast
songs and longhouse culture, which gave him a template for the acquisition of songs. "That's where that singing like just attached itself to me,"
he recalled. In addition, Mercier's and other tribal members' efforts to
learn and teach Chinuk Wawa as a language of heritage had brought

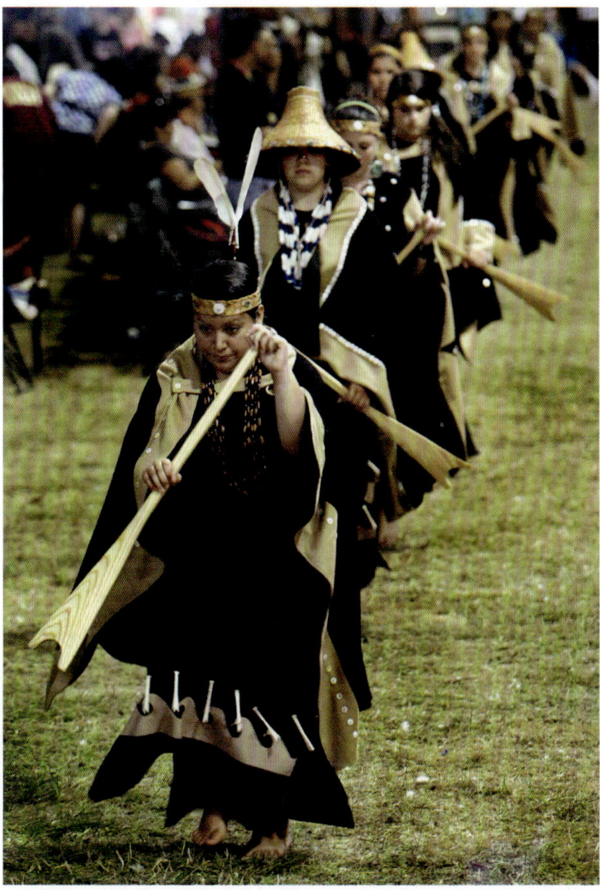

Grand Ronde Canoe Family members dancing, Paddle to Swinomish at La Conner, Washington, 2011. From front, Bee Foster and Kyoni Mercier. Photograph by Michelle Alaimo. Courtesy of *Smoke Signals*, the independent publication of the Confederated Tribes of Grand Ronde.

with it an emphasis on Lower Columbian–style song, dance, and art, which are more closely related to styles further north than are those of the tribal groups from what is now southwestern Oregon that are also part of the Grand Ronde confederation. But many Grand Ronde tribal members, such as Lara, didn't have prior experience with Northwest-style singing and dance, so developing a canoe family meant working with everyone to learn what was needed. According to Mercier, there were "plenty of stumbles along the way" as the group built a repertoire of song and dance, and that very struggle was part of what strengthened the group.

Across the canoe nations of the Pacific Northwest, knowledge has had to be relearned and created anew in order to participate in Canoe Journey; the practice of this knowledge is guided by protocol.

Mique'l Dangeli, a Tsimshian scholar, dance artist, and Canoe Journey participant, describes protocol as an "artistic lens" through which sovereignty-asserting performances are created.[19] Dangeli argues that protocol is much more than "boundaries" or "a set of restrictions"; an understanding of it allows for the governing of conduct but also for the creation of new songs, dances, and oratory.[20] In Grand Ronde's situation, developing protocol involved a process of recovering traditions from home (such as the songs recorded on wax cylinders) as well as engaging in learning through relationships with other tribes.

Mercier explained that as other tribes saw that Grand Ronde was developing a canoe family, they gifted them songs. He gave the example of Maria Parker Pasqua (Makah), who composed a song for bringing girls onto the floor to dance—something they did not have. Pasqua gave it to them during a Canoe Journey, and they've been singing it ever since. Other songs were gifted to them, and Grand Ronde incorporated those into their repertoire, along with accounts of the circumstances of the gift. The process led them to understand how alive and dynamic the process of song creation is. When one person would realize there was need for a dance for a particular reason (saying, for example, "We'd really like to have a dance for this or that"), then someone would make a song.

This process of bringing songs home and adding them to the "handful of songs" they already had from Grand Ronde has "led to so many other things," according to Mercier: "That's how we ended up with all these songs." Youth as young as four years old in the Canoe Family create songs, a process they call *catching songs*. The process of catching songs is intertwined with the development of dance. As Mercier described: "The ladies are sitting around, talking, and all of a sudden going, 'You know what? That song makes me want to dance like this.' And pretty soon there's dances that go with the songs." The Grand Ronde Canoe Family process of song and dance creation is a dynamic one that involves not just taking from other groups and not "just sitting around making stuff up." Rather, it is laid upon a template of movement and rhythm with a foundation in Lower Columbia and Willamette River cultural traditions.

This template includes protocol about "carrying" songs: who can and can't sing them, who owns them, and how or whether they are

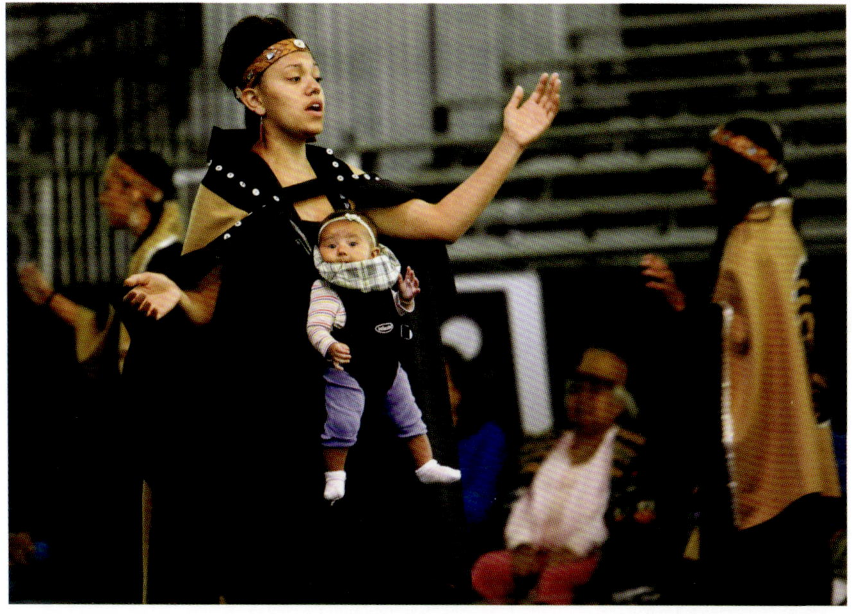

Grand Ronde Canoe Family members Kimberly Roybal and daughter Eva Jurado, dancing, Paddle to Squaxin Island, Kamilche, Washington, 2012. Photograph by Michelle Alaimo. Courtesy of *Smoke Signals*, the independent publication of the Confederated Tribes of Grand Ronde.

shared. For example, Grand Ronde youth became interested in a song and dance from the Vicky and Tully Kruger family of the Squaxin Island Tribe. Mercier explained to them that they could not perform another group's song and dance without permission. So they asked if they could "buy" the song, and the Kruger family agreed. The Grand Ronde Canoe Family traveled to Squaxin Island for one of their canoe meetings and presented gifts such as elk hide robes, jam, canned fish, paddles, cedar baskets, and blankets. Laying these gifts at the feet of the family, they asked, "We'd like to have the rights to that song and dance." The family gave permission and, speaking to those assembled, pointed out that there were plenty of witnesses to verify the gift and the right of the Grand Ronde Canoe Family to perform it anywhere, as long as they recognized the Kruger family when they did so. Such songs are living performances of those relationships with others, as well as of the relationship the Canoe Family has to Grand Ronde's own multistranded heritage. Recalling the time he stood in Port Angeles at the end of their first Canoe Journey in 2005, Mercier marveled: "It's because of those first things that we did and even the first songs that we've received from other tribes that have sparked everything you see today."

At Grand Ronde, as with many communities across the Pacific
Northwest, Canoe Family participants had to learn to make things that
had not been made in living memory—or perhaps ever at their reservation community. The paddles Grand Ronde uses are typical of river
tribes and are generally made of Oregon ash, known as isik-stik
(*paddle tree*) in Chinuk Wawa. Its wood is harder than cedar and there-
fore preferable for paddles, which need to be rigid to have a strong
pull. They have a notched tip with two points, useful for harvesting
riverbank food sources such as wapato (*Sagittaria latifolia*) and for
pushing a canoe away from shallow wetland plants. Regalia is another
necessity. Weaving styles of the tribes removed to the Grand Ronde

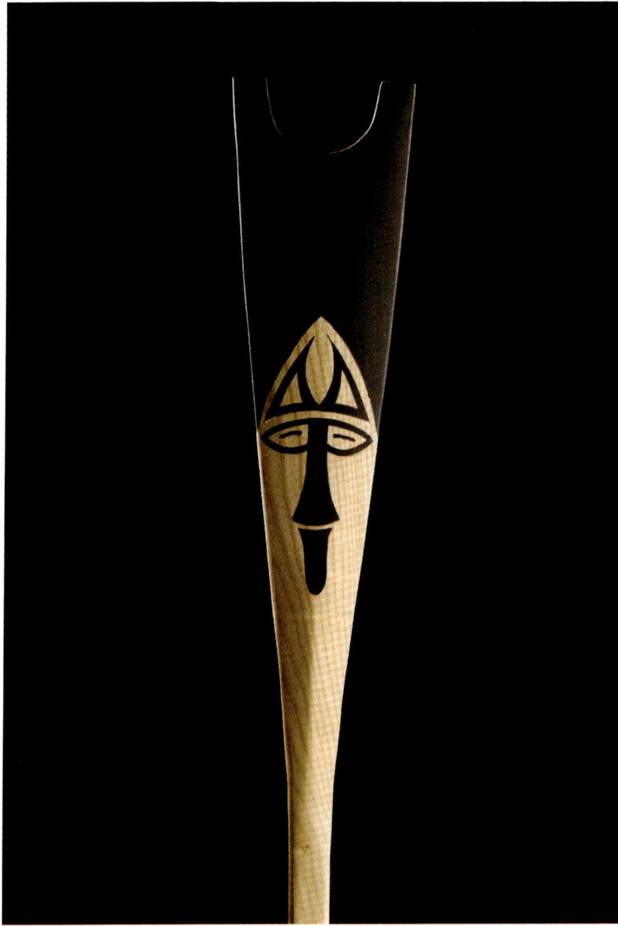

Paddle made for
dance by Jesse
Petite, before 2008.
Oregon ash, paint.
Collection of Bobby
Mercier. Photograph
by Frank Miller.
Courtesy of Frank
Miller and Willa-
mette University.

Reservation were associated with their original ancestral homelands and cultures, but once settled there, weavers tended to make baskets with locally abundant plant materials (juncus, hazel, willow) in forms functional for the newly imposed sedentary life (market and laundry baskets, for example). In contrast, most nations participating in annual Canoe Journeys historically use cedar bark to plait hats, make capes, and even twine rope. Those objects are now needed by Canoe Family members, so Grand Ronde weavers have increasingly used cedar to make hats and capes for paddlers.

Another Northwest Coast cultural tradition is the button blanket, conventionally made of dark-blue wool with red appliquéd designs and pearl buttons and/or abalone shell, a garment associated with tribes such as the far northern Haida, Tsimshian, and Tlingit, where designs usually represent a family or clan crest. These capes, whose production flourished after European trade brought an influx of wool blankets, are worn at feasts and other celebrations and, like many other elements of Northwest Coast culture, have also been the subject of a twenty-first century resurgence. To outfit their female dancers, the Grand Ronde designed button blankets distinguished by black-and-tan color combinations and symbols representing the notched-tip paddle and other elements of lower Columbia River iconography, including petroglyph designs.

Finally, canoe carving itself is being nurtured, particularly of canoes to launch on rivers close to Grand Ronde, not just for the annual Journey in the relatively distant waterways of Puget Sound and Vancouver Island. In 2011 the Grande Ronde Tribe partnered with the Willamette Heritage Center in Salem in the creation of an exhibit called *The Grand Ronde's Canoe Journey*, to tell the history of the contemporary Canoe Journey renaissance as well as the canoe cultures that are historically part of the Confederated Tribes of Grand Ronde: the Kalapuya of the Willamette Valley and the Tillamook of the northern Oregon coast. The Heritage Center collection included a Kalapuyan shovel-nosed canoe perhaps three hundred years old that had been found in the 1960s on the banks of the Santiam River near Tangent, Oregon, after floodwaters removed layers of soil concealing it. In the months leading up to the exhibition, tribal members designed and carved a Kalapuyan-style canoe from a cedar log donated by the Willamette National Forest, the first such canoe carved at Grand Ronde in contemporary times. The carving took place both at the reservation and at the Heritage Center in Salem. And, acknowledging the importance of the return of canoe traditions, the Heritage Center gave the historical Kalapuyan canoe to the Grande Ronde Tribe at the conclusion of the exhibition.[21]

The growth of the Canoe Family has coincided with other key cultural developments at Grand Ronde, such as the 2010 opening of a traditional plankhouse, *Achaf-Hammi*, a Kalapuyan-Tualatin word for such a house. Made with hand-split cedar planks, the house provides a gathering place as well as a site for performance and reinforcement of tribal identity. This was followed by the long-awaited 2014 opening of Chachalu, the Grand Ronde Tribal Museum and Cultural Center, at the site of a former elementary school. According to the Tribe, *Chachalu* is a Kalapuyan word meaning "the place of the burnt timbers," referencing a forest fire that wreaked havoc in the area in the mid-1800s. The name evokes the resilience of both land and people, recovering and even thriving after devastations both natural and social.

Canoe Family Dancers, second birthday celebration at *Achaf Hammi,* the Grand Ronde Plankhouse, 2012. Photograph by Michelle Alaimo. Courtesy of *Smoke Signals,* the independent publication of the Confederated Tribes of Grand Ronde.

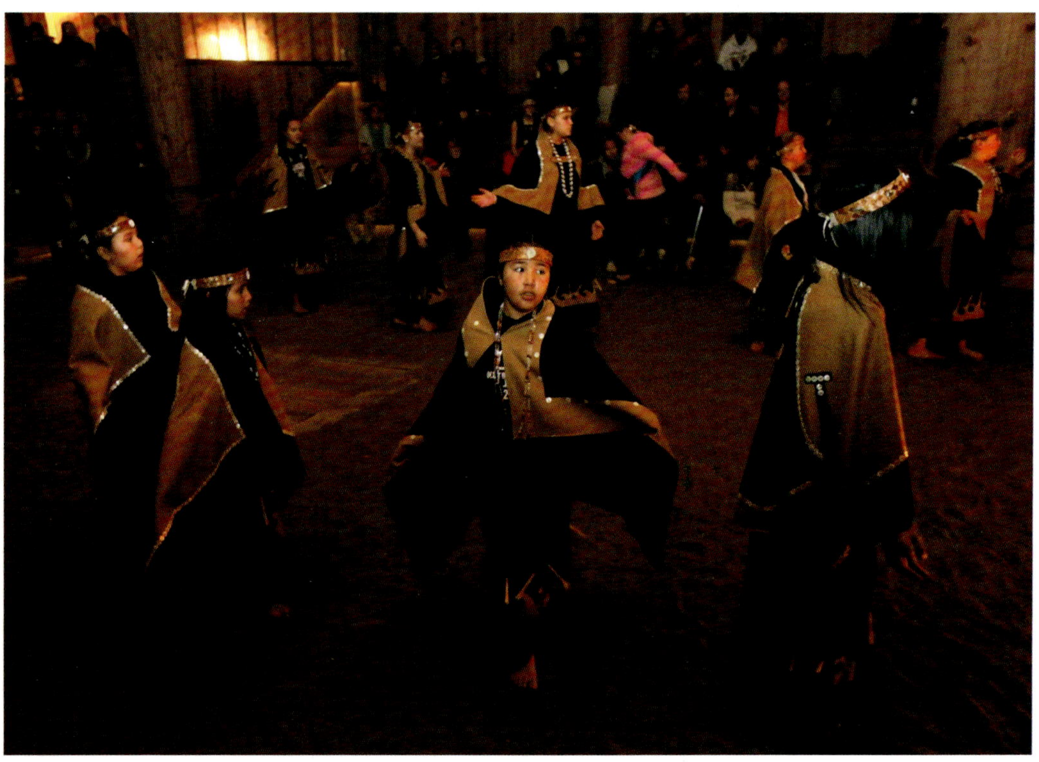

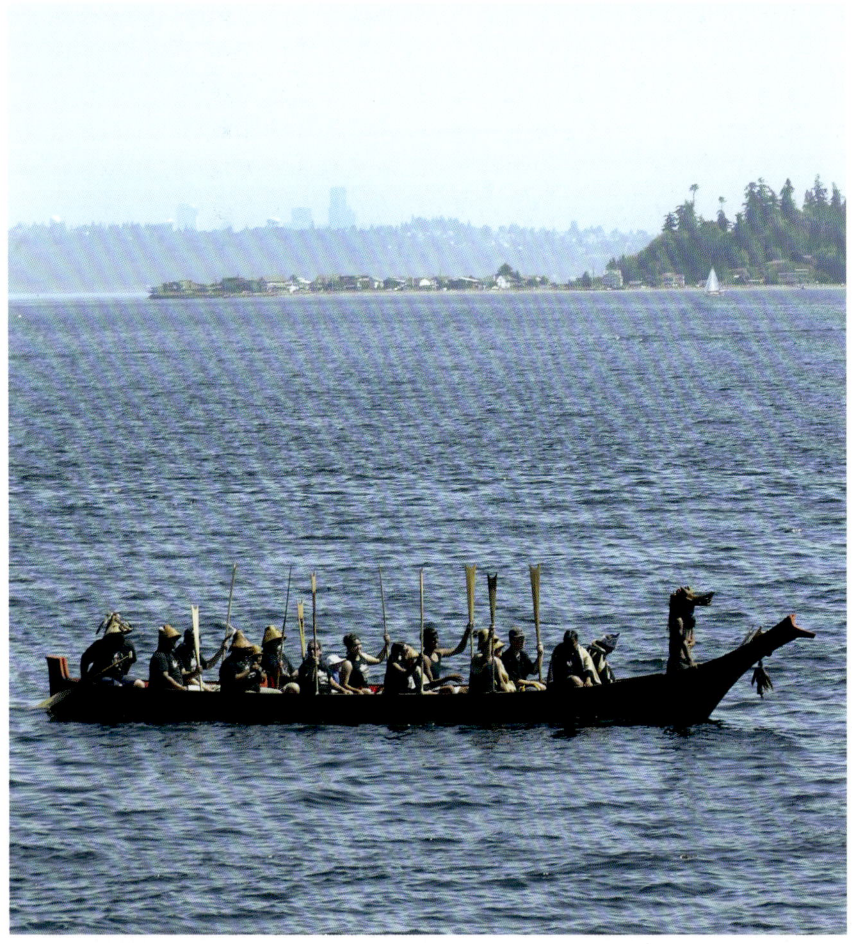

Grand Ronde Canoe Family in *Stank'iya*, Paddle to Suquamish, Washington, 2009. Photograph by Michelle Alaimo. Courtesy of *Smoke Signals*, the independent publication of the Confederated Tribes of Grand Ronde.

Healing the Past

It has been only a short time historically since the restoration of the Confederated Tribes of Grand Ronde in 1983; the opening of the Tribe's primary economic resource, the Spirit Mountain Casino, in 1995; and the beginning of the Grand Ronde Canoe Family in 2005. In the *First Oregonians* chapter on Grand Ronde, Brent Merrill and Yvonne Hajda report how elders emphasize that termination should not be forgotten in the restoration era.[22] As with all tribal communities, there is an imperative to be self-sufficient through education, self-governance, and economic development. The impact of the investment of time and knowledge into Canoe Journey is yet to be fully felt, although there is well-founded hope that extraordinary leaders will emerge in the rising generations. As Lisa Leno put it: "Our young people who have grown up in Canoe Family are so much stronger than they would have ever been without that." They learn "I can do it," the very definition of self-sufficiency.

The generations who directly experienced the assault of policies of removal, the reservation and allotment era, and termination had few opportunities to experience the kind of public and private affirmation of identity facilitated by Canoe Journey. The damage done is lasting but not entirely irreparable, as Tina Lara sees it: "A huge part of this is not only that we're building healthy communities but we're healing those past. We're healing our past. We're healing our elders who missed out on that." Leno elaborated, explaining that tribal members have said that the Canoe Family brings back some of what many feel were the "old values" of the Grand Ronde community: people gathering, visiting, sharing food, singing, dancing. Lara, who was born just one year after restoration, summed up: "Our generation, we're in a really great kind of place that we get to learn about that kind of stuff. We get to learn about how important it is to heal. We're that generation that is connecting this with this. And it's a great place to be."

CHAPTER 6

THE RETURN OF C'WAAM CEREMONY

The Klamath Tribes

Upwards of a hundred people gathered on the banks of the Sprague River, near the former site of the Chiloquin Dam, on the last Saturday in March 2016. The morning had dawned cold in the small town of Chiloquin, the headquarters of the Klamath Tribes (the Klamath, Modoc, and Yahooskin), with the possibility of snow thick in the air. Winters are long in the high-elevation Upper Klamath Basin, a land of marshes, streams, and rivers in the eastern rain shadow of the Cascades. People bundled in jackets formed a loosely woven circle around a generous fire; elders sat within the range of the fire's warmth in camp chairs, laps draped in blankets.

All were there for the Return of C'waam Ceremony that calls to the c'waam, also known as the Lost River sucker fish, as they migrate from the quieter waters of Upper Klamath Lake to spawn in the gravel beds of the more rapidly flowing Williamson and Sprague River systems from March through May. Once abundant across the region, the c'waam were a major food source for Native peoples as well as the first white settlers in the 1800s. But because natural stream flow and water quality have been drastically altered by agriculture, dam construction, and the timber industry, the c'waam population has been reduced to

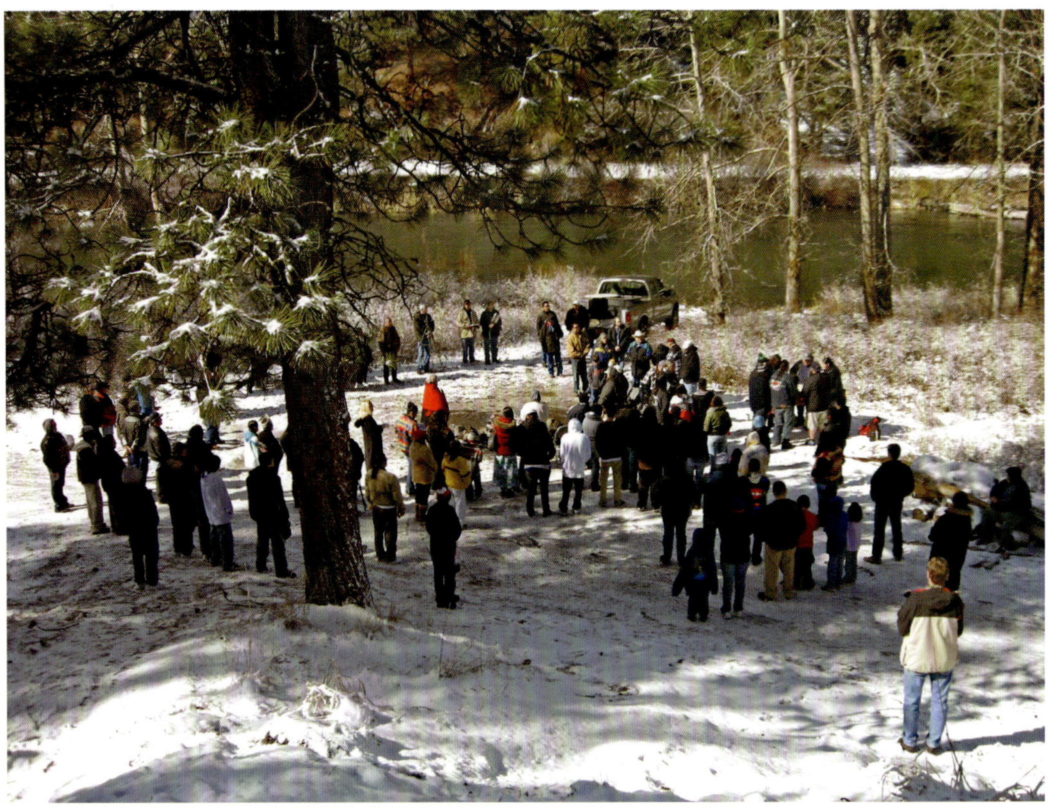

a fraction of its former range and the species' very existence is threatened. Compounding the habitat destruction is the fact that the c'waam, which can live forty years and reach three feet in length and a weight of ten pounds, do not reach sexual maturity until age nine on average. Few juvenile fish now survive into reproductive years. Since 1988, the c'waam have been listed as an endangered species.

I attended the Return of the C'waam Ceremony at the invitation of the director of the Klamath Tribes Culture and Heritage Department, Perry Chocktoot, who first told me about the event when we collaborated on *The Art of Ceremony* exhibition in 2008.[1] He explained that the ceremony not only calls the c'waam back to their birthplaces to spawn but also "allows us to carry on as a people." The ceremony, conducted since time beyond memory, went into dormancy during the decades of termination (1954–86) but has been held annually since 1989, when tribal elders called for the resumption of the ceremony to restore the

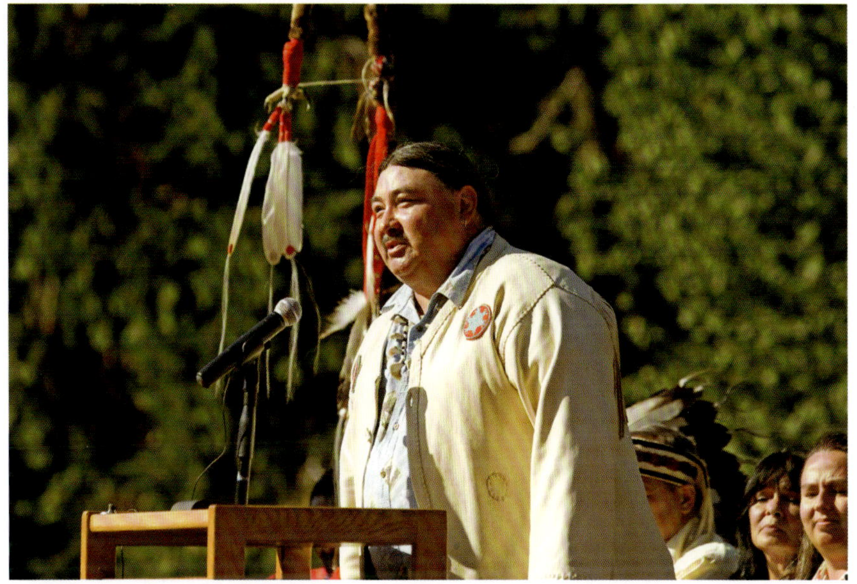

Perry Chocktoot, *The Art of Ceremony* opening events, 2008. Photograph by Frank Miller. Courtesy of Frank Miller and Willamette University.

health of both the fish and the Tribes and, by extension, all of creation. The story is one not only of a renewed ceremony but also of the inextricable connection between the well-being of the fish and the Klamath Tribes, and the restoration of the ecosystem they share.

Ceremony: What It Means to Be Fish People

Preparations for the Return of the C'waam Ceremony begin well in advance. While Chocktoot and his staff coordinate the day's events, he is the first to acknowledge that many people contribute to its success. Early in the morning, Chocktoot starts the fire at the site, where generations of Klamath tribal members camped and fished for c'waam, right up through the mid-twentieth century. The location is downriver from the old Chiloquin Dam, built in 1914 and dismantled in 2008 in an effort to provide access to upstream spawning grounds for c'waam and other species.[2] Well before the ceremony begins, tribal fisheries staff deliver a large tub with the c'waam, a long-nosed fish with a dark back and light underbelly, along with other, nonthreatened sucker species. Ironically, because so few of the endangered c'waam can now make the migration up the Sprague River, this step is needed to ensure that the fish are present for the ceremony. A few blocks away at the Chiloquin Community Center, tribal members prepare a feast to take place after the morning's rituals. Following the feast, where elders and others are honored, a powwow is held at the Chiloquin Elementary School gym.

On this particular day in 2016, by around 10:30 a.m. all was ready. Perry Chocktoot welcomed everyone and explained a bit about what was to take place. Then Harold Wright, who also works with the Culture and Heritage Department as a Native language instructor, offered a prayer in the Klamath language, followed by a hand-drum song led by three younger men. Following contemporary protocol, the next person to speak was Don Gentry, the current Tribal Council chair, who addressed how important the ceremony is to the community spiritually and thanked the elders for being present. Gentry acknowledged the role of elders in guiding and teaching younger generations and, looking their way, said it was they who had long recognized that everything people have was placed on earth by the Creator. That was the reason for gathering as a community, to honor these gifts. Gentry spoke of the need to come together, with young people present, and ask Creator to restore the fish, because "we all know that without these fish, part of us is missing."

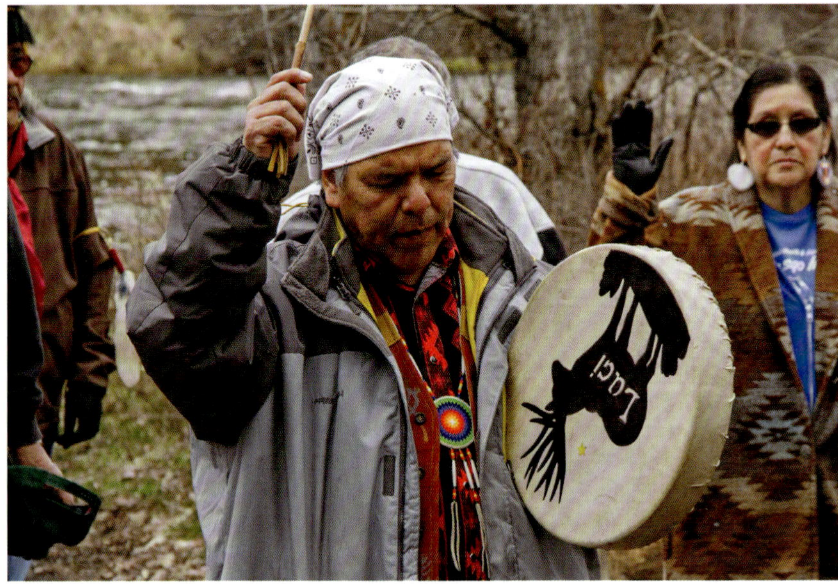

Harold Wright offering prayer at the Return of C'waam Ceremony, 2016. Photograph by Peter Murphy.

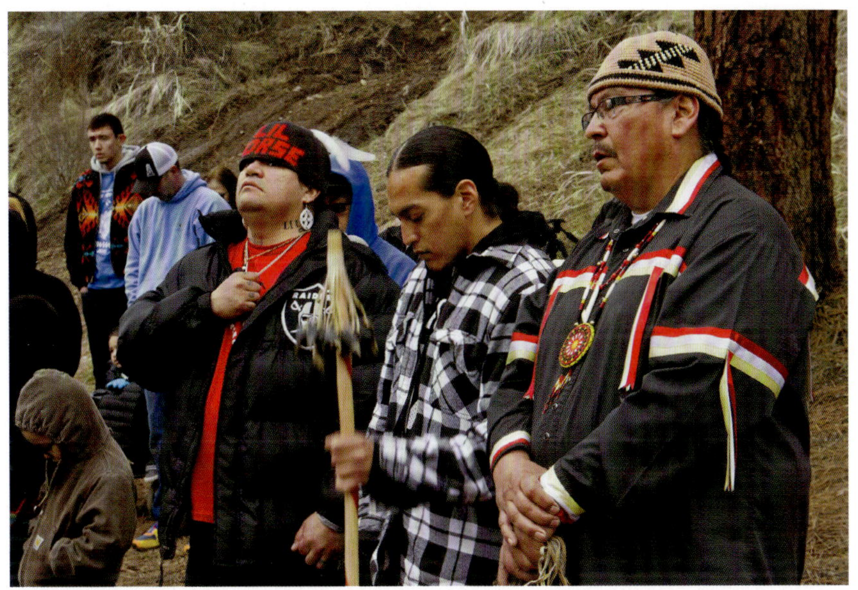

Return of C'waam Ceremony, 2016. Jeff Mitchell at right, with Ian Gallagher, far left, and Nats Wright, middle. Photograph by Peter Murphy.

After another hand-drum song, Jeff Mitchell, a Klamath tribal leader with experience on the Tribal Council and its water policy team, spoke, saying how much he always looked forward to this day. "We're fish people," he affirmed, meaning all the Klamath, Modoc, and Yahooskin peoples who make up the Klamath Tribes.[3] All across their ancestral homelands, Mitchell said, "wherever there were fish, you'd find our people." He stressed that many good things have happened since the reemergence of the ceremony. Mitchell explained that he wanted to share two songs, the first a "calling" song, one that calls out to the Creator and to the ancestors to be present, to listen, and to witness what is to take place. Concluding that song, he introduced another, a welcoming song. Mitchell acknowledged that there were people present who had never been at the ceremony before, but that in coming together, everyone (both familiar and new) was in a sense already changed, in ways not yet possible to know. The song welcomed everyone and recognized that "there's change that's going on in this world" and that "nothing stands still." Mitchell sang the welcome song, making way for a story about the creation of the c'waam.

The story goes back to the time not long after the Klamath peoples were placed on the land by the Creator, Gmukampc. At the beginning,

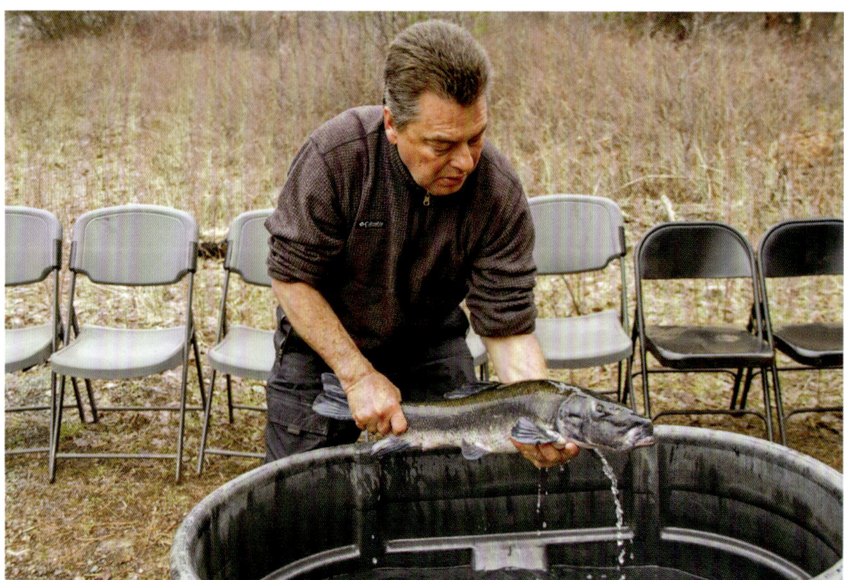

things were very good and the people lived well. But, Mitchell paused and then said, "This land is a hard land here, at times." Winter can be long, and by the season's end food difficult to find. People then as now depend on the land "to take care of us." In the time long ago, drought and famine struck, and people had a hard time finding enough food to feed themselves. People were suffering and realized they had to do something if they were to survive.

So a call went out to all the villages to come together, at a place called Nilocks, now known as Barkley Spring on the eastern shore of Upper Klamath Lake, about fifteen miles south from where we stood on the banks of the Sprague River. The holy men gathered at a lodge there, to sweat and pray, and asked Creator for help. Gmukampc, who sat on a ridge nearby, listened and knew the people were hurting. All the while, the people kept praying.

In addition to the terrible famine, another threat faced the people: a large serpent was devouring people and animals. This giant snake came moving along the ridge near Creator; Gmukampc pulled out his obsidian-blade knife and slew the snake. He cut its body into many pieces and threw them into Upper Klamath Lake. There, they became the c'waam, and multiplied, providing food for the people to thrive.

Creator told the people that he was giving them "this gift of life," the c'waam, the fish that would be first to come up to spawn in the rivers after the long, cold, and sometimes hungry winter. Gmukampc explained how to watch for signals that the fish will soon return. Begin watching for the c'waam when you see the fish constellation, the three stars that make up what is called Orion's belt in Greek mythology, come up in the southwestern horizon in the evening sky. Watch also for the time when snow falls in large flakes, called c-waam s?am skodas. These are signs that the c'waam are returning; they will give you life, the Creator said.

Gmukampc explained that there was just one law the people had to follow: they had to respect and honor the fish and perform this ceremony every year. He gave instructions about how to honor the first c'waam, how to respectfully prepare it for offering on a fire. Creator emphasized that the people must do the ceremony so that the fish will continue to come to relieve winter's hunger. He warned that the fish would go away without the ceremony, and if the fish go away, so will the people.

Concluding the narrative, Mitchell spoke directly to the young people present, reminding them that someday this ceremony would be their responsibility to carry forward. He lamented that there was a time during the decades of termination that the people did not perform the ceremony, and that the Tribes—and the fish—suffered. The elders recognized the need to do the ceremony and reinitiated it. Mitchell expressed his gratitude to them and to everyone there for paying respect to the Creator and to creation and for their presence.

After Mitchell closed with a prayer in the Klamath language, Chocktoot again addressed the crowd, explaining what was to happen next. One fish—a nonthreatened sucker rather than an actual c'waam—was to be released to the fire, ultimately to burn into ash, as an offering to Creator. First, the still-living fish was brought to the elders who, touching it, blessed it one by one. Then, using an obsidian-blade knife, Chocktoot processed the fish, as one would when preparing it for eating, carefully taking out the bies, or gall. If broken, the gall contaminates the meat with a foul taste, rendering it inedible. Chocktoot recollected stories told by tribal elders of early white settlement in the 1850s, when tribal fishers offered already prepared sucker fish to the newcomers, who were starving. In later years, when the settlers caught and

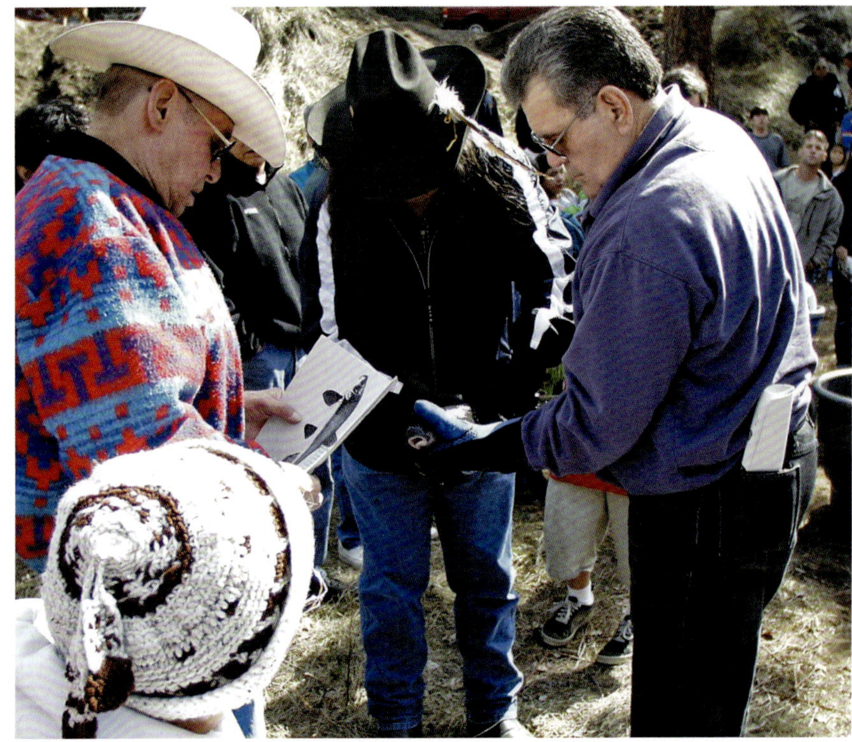

Return of C'waam Ceremony, 2004. At center, elder Bobby David (1934–2008) praying over fish, with longtime fish handler Rayson Tupper (1947–2019) at left and then tribal chairman Joseph Kirk at right. Photograph by Taylor R. Tupper. Courtesy of the Klamath Tribes News Department.

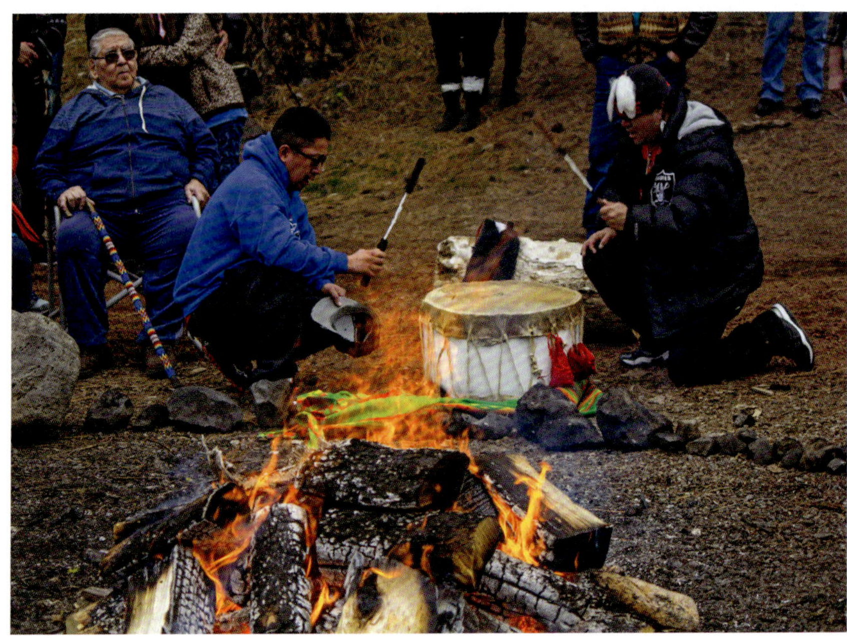

Fire in foreground, with drummers and seated elders in background, 2016. Photograph by Peter Murphy.

processed the c'waam just as they did other fish, they pronounced them "trash fish." Never consulting with the Tribes, they ruptured the gall and found the fish distasteful. This derogatory attitude about the c'waam persists into the twenty-first century and is one of the tensions between the Klamath Tribes, who see the fish as a sacred gift from the Creator to be protected along with its ecosystem, and many of the descendants of the settlers, who view such protection as impeding their agricultural interests, which rely—as do the fish—on Klamath Basin water.[4]

After the fish was cleaned and placed in the fire, the crowd was invited to come forward to take a pinch of cedar leaves, offer them into the fire, and send up prayers to Creator. Slowly, people moved into place, lining up, murmuring to one another in quiet but happy conversation. After passing by the fire, many, some with infants and children in tow, went to greet the elders, who remained seated close to the warm flames, receiving embraces and offering laughter.

C'waam and the Klamath Tribes

In the story of the creation of the c'waam, the Creator transforms a threat—the murderous serpent—into a food resource, in response to the hunger and need of the people. In return, the Creator requires only that the people continue to conduct the ceremony. First-food ceremonies, such as this one, are conducted annually to honor the food resource at its "first" reappearance and to give thanks to the Creator for its original creation and ongoing sacrifice. In writing about Klamath tribal history, anthropologist Douglas Deur has discussed how first-food ceremonies, carried out at specific harvest sites, "acknowledged the enduring relationships between particular human communities and particular plant and animal communities over successive generations."[5] In tribal cosmology, plants and animals are living, spirit-possessing beings, and human relationships with them call for "ethical and reciprocal relations."[6] The living food resources give of themselves to sustain the human community, while people reciprocate for their sacrifice through both environmental and ritual actions that "ensure the health and fecundity" of these plant and animal species.[7] First-food ceremonies thus point toward a host of responsibilities people have to meet the needs of the species that give of themselves to support human life.

To understand the contemporary layers of meaning of this ceremony and the depth of the responsibility felt by the Klamath Tribes, we turn to the story of the Klamath Basin's complex water issues. Tribal chair Don Gentry, who has a background in natural resources, laid out the historical interconnections among Klamath water, Tribes, and fish in a statement made before the US Senate's Committee on Energy and Natural Resources in June 2014.[8] He explained that the Klamath Tribes, a confederation that represents three historically distinct peoples—the Klamath, the Modoc, and the Yahooskin Band of Snake Indians (Northern Paiute)—negotiated a treaty in good faith with the United States in 1864. That treaty ceded more than twenty million acres of ancestral homelands and reserved about two million acres of the Upper Klamath River Basin, a key habitat for c'waam and other sucker-fish species. The treaty also reserved the Tribes' fishing, gathering, hunting, and trapping rights on their original lands in perpetuity. But these rights can only be meaningfully exercised if natural resources continue to thrive so that they may be harvested. In the case of the c'waam and other fish species historically harvested by the Klamath Tribes, these rights have not been exercisable for many decades. The Tribes recognize the c'waam's precarious condition and have not fished for them since 1986. This loss ruptures the cultural and spiritual relationship between people and the fish; its restoration requires not only ceremonial action but also environmental and political intervention.

Early in the twentieth century, the federal government began making competing promises to provide water to different parties: agricultural interests through the Bureau of Reclamation's Klamath Project, a series of wildlife refuges now known as the Klamath Basin National Wildlife Refuge Complex, and homesteaders encouraged to settle in the arid, rural region. The Klamath Project involves a complicated system of irrigation canals, dams, and reservoirs that diverts water to farms and ranches from the bodies of water in the Upper Klamath Basin as well as from the Klamath River and some of its tributaries. All these commitments were made on top of those resource-harvesting rights guaranteed by treaty to the Klamath Tribes and other Tribes downstream on the Klamath River into California, setting up inevitable and potentially explosive conflicts of interest over access to water.

By the early 1900s the private energy company now known as Pacifi-Corp began building dams and power plants along the Klamath River, a system that became the Klamath River Hydroelectric Project (not to be confused with the Bureau of Reclamation's Klamath Project just described). This dam system, extending from Oregon through north-western California to the Pacific Ocean, fatally impacted the salmon and steelhead runs to the Klamath Lakes, cutting the Tribes off from the traditional harvest of species that provide both spiritual and physical nutrition. And although the dams did not entirely eliminate the salmon runs in the Lower Klamath River, the home of the Hupa, Karuk, and Yurok Tribes, the impact was catastrophic, affecting tribal, commercial, and recreational fishing.

The federal Klamath Termination Act of 1954 dealt another enor-mous blow to the Klamath Tribes, ending the Tribes' federally recog-nized status and resulting in the transfer of their remaining reservation lands to private and government owners, with half a million acres eventually becoming the Winema National Forest.[9] Ironically, the Klam-ath were targeted for termination because their tribal economy—built largely upon the reservation's forest-products industry—was thriving and thus, from the perspective of federal policymakers, tribal members were prime candidates for assimilation into the mainstream. Yet the communal holding of a land base and its resources was, as Gentry put it in his statement, the "heart of that success." Eliminating it through termination "precipitated severe economic and social devastation from which we are still struggling to recover."[10]

Nevertheless, like many other terminated tribes, the Klamath did not lose an understanding of themselves as a nation and made a suc-cessful case for restoration, which was won in 1986. Incredibly, given the size of the Tribes' pre-termination reservation, the reinstatement of the political and legal relationship with the federal government was not accompanied by restoration of a land base. To this date, the Klamath Tribes have been able to reacquire only a tiny percentage of their ances-tral lands, in scattered parcels. Though rendered essentially landless, the Klamath Tribes push to exercise their treaty rights to harvest resources on former ancestral homelands, interpreting that to mean the right to protect the habitats (including waterways) that their traditional food resources need in order to thrive.

Just two years after tribal restoration, in 1988, the c'waam as well
as the quapdo (*shortnose sucker*) were listed as endangered under the
federal Endangered Species Act. The primary reason for the decline
was given as habitat degradation resulting from the modification of
the watershed for agriculture, grazing, logging, and road construction,
and related erosion and sediment problems that impact water quality.
The drainage and contamination of the historical Upper Klamath Basin
wetlands resulted not only in lower water levels but also in excessive
algae blooms that reduce oxygen in the water. These conditions are
particularly hard on juvenile c'waam. While c'waam are very long-lived,
with life spans of thirty to forty years, biologists from the US Fish and
Wildlife Service (USFWS) determined that their populations were
made up of primarily older individuals, with few juveniles surviving into
reproductive age, which begins between six and fourteen years. More
than 95 percent of the population had been decimated.[11]

In the early 1990s the USFWS began implementing a recovery plan,
which included setting a minimum water level in Upper Klamath Lake.
As there was simply not enough water to go around for both the fish
and the farms, the various stakeholders for Klamath Basin water were
put into direct conflict with one another. Droughts in the semiarid
region heightened tensions. A decade of often open hostilities followed,
particularly between the Tribes, who advocate for the protection of fish
habitat, and farmers, whose livelihoods depend upon irrigation. In 2001
the Klamath "water war" received national attention when the Bureau
of Reclamation restricted water for irrigation, citing the need to protect the fish, and farmers and ranchers staged protests. Then in 2002 a
massive salmon die-off in the Klamath River, coinciding with low water
levels, stunned the region's tribes, commercial fishers, and the public.
Tragically—and avoidably—this ecological and social disaster repeated
itself in 2021, with a major die-off of juvenile salmon in the Klamath
River, due to drought conditions that in turn have resulted in deadly
parasitic infections in the fish population, and with heightening tensions between farmers and the Tribes in the Klamath Basin.[12]

Beginning in 2000, with a deadline of 2006, the Klamath River dams
were up for relicensing, a process that requires the operator (in this case
PacifiCorp) to provide fish passage and related environmental improve-
ments, at the cost of hundreds of millions of dollars. As an alternative to

such costly modifications, dam removal, though also expensive, began to be discussed in earnest. These conflicts and crises threatened social relations and economic life in the region; they continue to do so in 2021. In the early 2000s many understood that solutions were sorely needed, and by 2010 diverse constituencies including the Tribes, farmers, conservationists, fishers and hunters, and several levels of government came together to negotiate the Klamath Basin Restoration Agreement (KBRA) and the Klamath Hydroelectric Settlement Agreement (KHSA). In March 2013 the Oregon Water Resources Department issued an order determining that the Klamath Tribes hold the senior water rights in the Upper Klamath Basin, rights based upon the "the needs of plant, wildlife, and fish species the Tribes reserved the right to harvest in the Treaty of 1864."[13]

That order, long expected, brought needed clarity to the negotiations. The KBRA and the KHSA were followed in 2014 by the Upper Klamath Basin Comprehensive Settlement Agreement (UBA) and Senate Bill 2379, the Klamath Basin Water Recovery and Economic Restoration Act. While the latter legislation, which encompassed the various agreements, was supported by diverse signatories, it languished in a deadlocked Congress and was allowed to expire at the end of 2015. So a comprehensive settlement for the Klamath Basin remains elusive. In April 2016 state and federal officials signed an amended version of the KHSA that pledges to remove four dams along the Klamath River, an action critical to restoring salmon and steelhead runs, and a second, new agreement that supports irrigators by offsetting costs associated with protecting fish once they return to the Upper Klamath Basin and keeping the cost of electricity for irrigation low even after dams are removed. Key elements of these agreements—notably funding for the irrigators and securing a land base for the Klamath Tribes—have yet to be worked out.[14] Nevertheless, a major step toward the removal of the four dams took place in June 2021, when the Federal Energy Regulatory Commission approved the transfer of the hydroelectric licenses for the dams from PacifiCorp to the nonprofit Klamath River Renewal Corporation and the States of Oregon and California. If the next steps in the process proceed as expected, dam removal could begin in 2023.[15]

Regardless of the uncertain future of specific agreements, the Klamath Tribes remain focused on meeting their responsibilities to the plant and animal species that have sustained them for millennia. In generations past the Return of the C'waam Ceremony coincided with the harvest season for the fish and "consecrated" that harvest.[16] Today, as an endangered species, the c'waam cannot be taken. As noted, the Klamath Tribes make a choice in the ceremony to sacrifice one of the other sucker species that is not endangered, an indicator of the degree of reverence they hold for the c'waam. In large tubs adjacent to the fire, the c'waam attend and witness the Klamath people's fulfillment of their responsibility; they are returned live to the tribal hatchery, where ongoing research into factors impeding the survival of the species is conducted in collaboration with federal agencies.[17] Youth are reacquainted with the fish at the ceremony each year, rather than getting to know them through a long fishing season as earlier generations could do while camped by the Sprague River at the very same location. Instead of marking the initiation of the harvest, the ceremony now focuses on the fulfillment of a promise and the rekindling of hope for future return. The fish that once saved the people's lives in a time of famine now quite literally rely on the Klamath Tribes for their lives.

Pursuing water and treaty resource rights holds promise for the return of the c'waam and the people. Just as Gmukampc transformed the threatening serpent into the life-giving c'waam, the Klamath people—and other stakeholders in the Klamath Basin—hold out the possibility of transforming the threat of environmental collapse into the possibility of a renewed ecosystem and the threat of social turmoil into an expectation of mutual tolerance and respect.[18]

Watchmen: Making Way for Renewal

Creator gave the people signs to watch for—the fish constellation and the large-flake snowfall—to alert them when the c'waam would begin migrating up the Sprague River to spawn. In tribal stories it is said that watchmen "were placed along the riverbank to see exactly when the fish would return." Once the fish were spotted, a shaman initiated preparations for the ceremony. This practice of having a shaman lead the ritual is thought to have continued up to the 1930s, when Lee Snipes, a revered shaman also known as Captain Sky, last did so. Since the ceremony was renewed in 1989, its coordination has become the responsibility of the Tribe's Culture and Heritage Department, now directed by Perry Chocktoot, assisted by many tribal leaders and elders.

The Klamath Tribes' contribution to *The Art of Ceremony* exhibition in 2008 featured two sets of regalia—one from an early twentieth-century shaman, David Chocktoot (1880–1960), and the other from Gerald Skelton Jr., Culture and Heritage director prior to Perry Chocktoot's appointment to the position in the early 2000s. Gerald is the great-great-grandson of David Chocktoot, and Perry is his great-grandson. Juxtaposed, these sets of regalia speak to the complexity of the relationships between the Klamath Tribes and the settler society that came to engulf them, and to tribal members' ongoing efforts to advocate for the health and well-being of the community and environment, as represented in the life events of Skelton and the elder Chocktoot.[19]

In early 2008, during a break in that winter's heavy snowfalls, I traveled over the Cascade Mountains to Chiloquin from the Willamette Valley to talk with Perry about Klamath participation in *The Art of Ceremony*. He drew my attention to a stack of documents in his office, pulling out a small brown pamphlet titled *The Old Ox Yoke*, written by Dr. Andrew Albert Soulé in the 1940s.[20] Chocktoot pointed to a photograph of David Chocktoot dressed in an intricately constructed elk-hide shirt and sitting in front of an American flag, and began to tell the story of this fascinating man.[21] David Chocktoot (also known as Mona Stynas Maqlaqs, or Big Hearted Indian) was a renowned kiuk, or doctor, in the first half of the twentieth century. His father was Tom Chocktoot, one of the signers of the 1864 treaty between the Klamath and Modoc Tribes and the US government, and his mother was YaYa Noneo, from an influential Yahooskin family. According to Perry, David Chocktoot played a major role at Klamath in bridging the gap between the worlds of Indian and Western medicine and was an advocate for Indian people when they visited the offices of the basdin (*Euro-American*) doctors. Chocktoot also served as a tribal policeman, a position that likely strengthened his role as an intercultural mediator.

David Chocktoot apparently developed a particularly close relationship with Soulé (1882–1976), the basdin doctor at the Klamath Indian Agency from 1912 to 1954.[22] Soulé, who had been born in California and received his medical degree from Willamette University in 1911, first worked as a government-employed doctor on the Crater Lake highway project and in 1912 became the doctor at the Klamath Reservation, a post he held until termination in 1954. David Chocktoot helped his community develop trust in Soulé by accompanying them during visits to the doctor and the hospital. Soulé seemed to have developed respect for his Klamath patients and their beliefs.[23]

At some point David Chocktoot's regalia was given to Soulé, a gesture that reflected the respect Chocktoot and other members of the Klamath Tribes must have had for the basdin doctor. Perry Chocktoot and Skelton surmise that it likely happened toward the end of David Chocktoot's life in the late 1950s. Soulé died in 1976, and the outfit passed on to his children. In 1990, Soulé's children donated the outfit to the Klamath County Museums. Perhaps by that time, the genealogy of the outfit had become muddled, since the information written by the Soulé heirs accompanying the gift states that it was Lee Snipes who gave Soulé the doctor's regalia. Yet the existence of the photograph in the 1941 pamphlet suggests with some degree of certainty that Chocktoot was the owner of the outfit, since traditionally no man would have worn another's doctoring outfit without risking harm to himself.

For nearly two decades, the doctoring outfit—with no mention of Chocktoot—was displayed at the Klamath County Museum in a corner of a diorama-type exhibit about Soulé, featuring his early twentieth-century medical paraphernalia and office furniture. The inclusion of David Chocktoot's regalia in *The Art of Ceremony* marked the first time it had been seen outside of the medical office diorama display since 1990. When I went to pick up the outfit from the Klamath County Museum in summer 2008, Gerald Skelton joined me, and together we prepared his great-great-grandfather's outfit for its journey to the Hallie Ford Museum of Art.

In a quiet room in the cavernous museum, Skelton held David Chocktoot's elk-hide shirt and explained that the three eagle-claw amulets and two painted head-scratchers attached to its front served as the shaman's personal medicine and assisted him in curing. Metal bells were suspended from the fringed shirt and accompanying pants, which made attention-arresting sounds when moved. Another element of the regalia, a deer-hide hand drum, was painted with five small stars

surrounding one large star and a cartoonlike owl on a crescent moon.
The design may have its origins in the 1870 Ghost Dance as well as in
tribal cosmology; the 1870 Ghost Dance came to the Klamath from the
Northern Paiute and was the predecessor of the better-known 1890
movement of the same name. Symbols associated with it include crescent moons and stars.[24] In tribal beliefs the number five is significant,
and the crescent moon is often referred to as the "Gambler's Moon."
Owls are commonly viewed as harbingers of death, sickness, or bad
luck but also can symbolize good gambling power. In this instance the
owl on the crescent moon is likely a powerful symbol of the shaman's
skill and expertise. The final element of the David Chocktoot outfit was
a beaver-pelt headdress, graced on the front with orange-and-black
flicker wings; Skelton explained that only shamans were allowed to
adorn themselves and their regalia with such feathers.

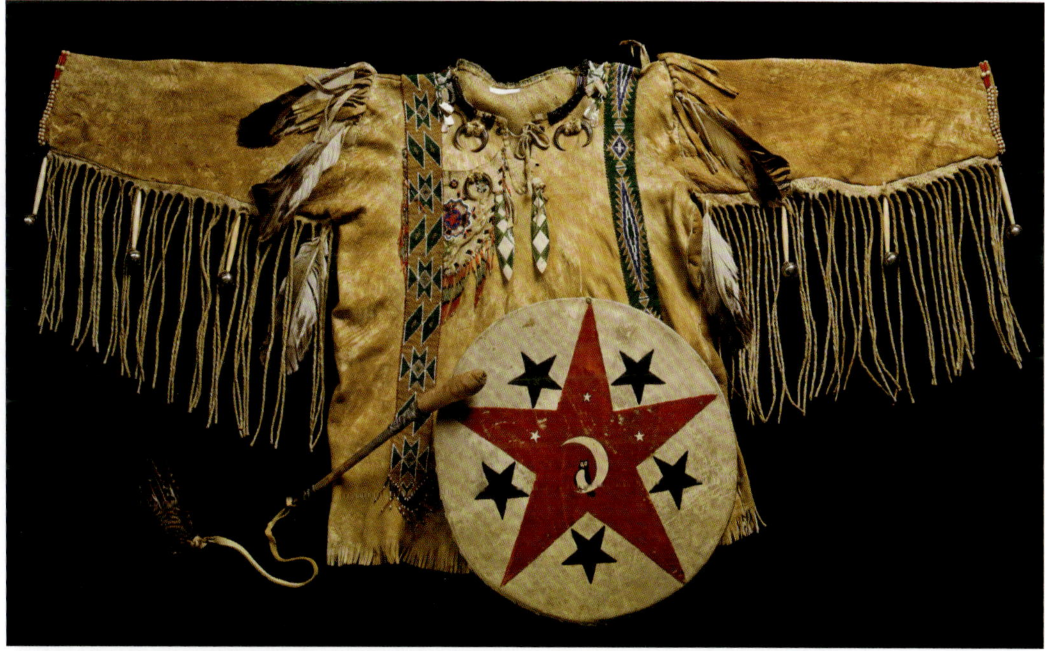

David Chocktoot's doctoring shirt with drum and drumstick, ca. 1915. Klamath Tribes artist(s);
possibly family of David Chocktoot. Elk hide, glass and bone beads, abalone, elk or deer
bone, eagle feathers, eagle claws, metal bells. Collection of the Klamath County Museums,
gift of the children of Andrew Albert Soulé, MD. Photograph by Frank Miller. Courtesy
of Frank Miller and Willamette University.

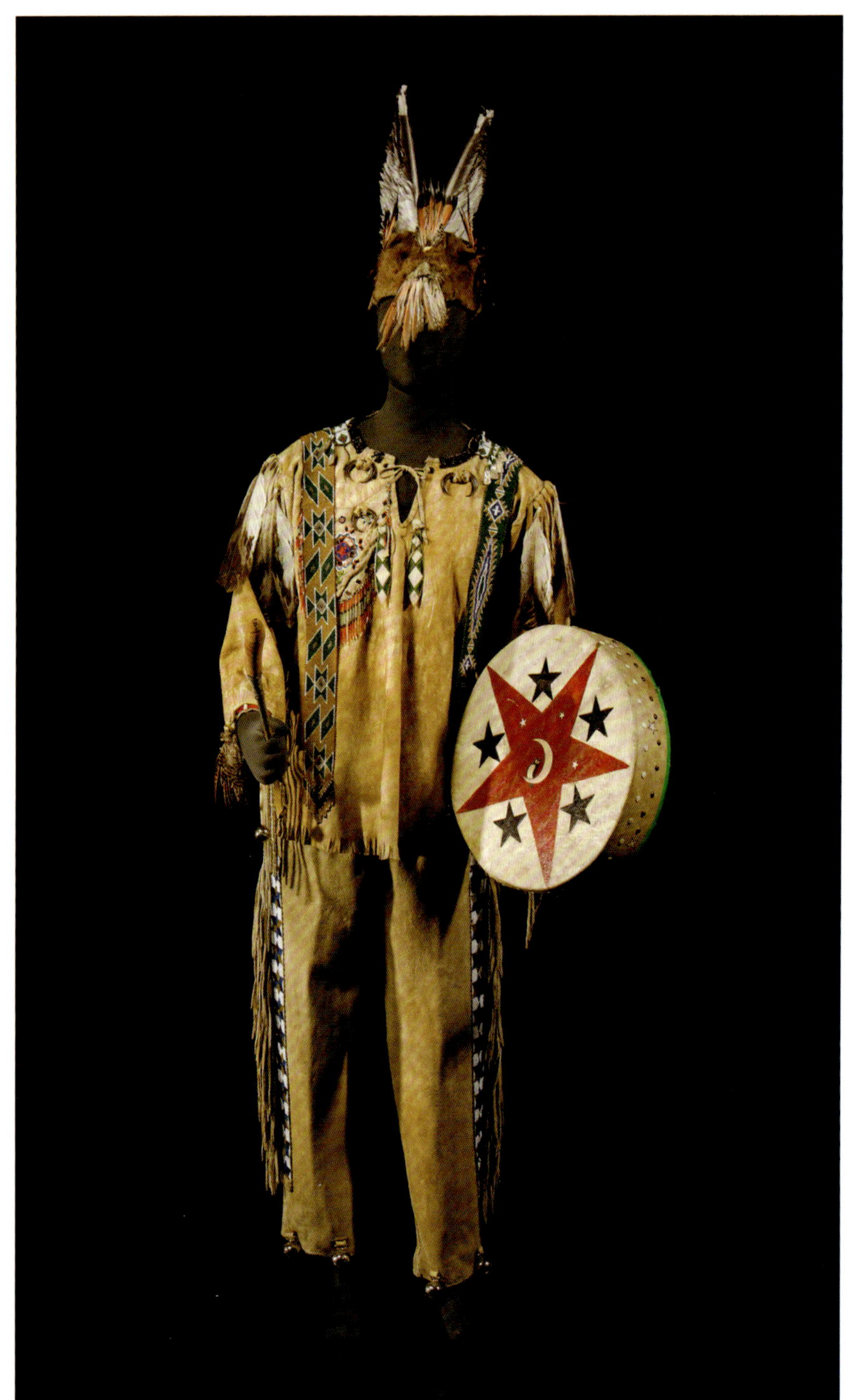

David Chocktoot's doctoring regalia, ca. 1915. Klamath Tribes artist(s); possibly family of David Chocktoot. Collection of the Klamath County Museums, gift of the children of Andrew Albert Soulé, MD. Photograph by Frank Miller. Courtesy of Frank Miller and Willamette University.

Skelton had also brought along his personal regalia, which he was loaning to the exhibit as a means of representing contemporary Klamath ceremonial leadership. The outfit included a pair of jeans, a red cotton shirt, a vest of Pendleton wool, a pair of moccasins made by his cousin Perry Chocktoot, as well as necklaces given to Skelton by the Klamath Tribal Council, an inmate at the Oregon State Prison in Ontario, and the Native American Studies program at Southern Oregon University. In addition, mirroring David Chocktoot's regalia, there was a simple hand drum and beaver-pelt headdress adorned with ermine, abalone, and an eagle feather. Skelton used all these items while he was Culture and Heritage director in the early 2000s, when called upon to coordinate ceremonies such as the Return of the C'waam and to represent the Klamath Tribes in meetings with outside agencies.

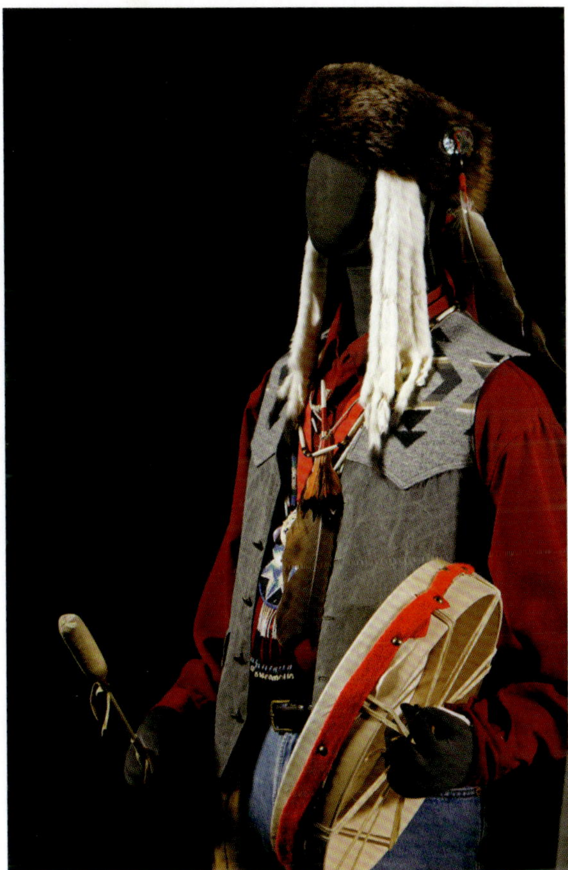

Headdress and other regalia worn by Gerald D. Skelton Jr., early 2000s. Headdress by Gerald D. Skelton Jr., 2004. Beaver pelt, ermine, eagle feather, abalone medallion, glass beads. Photograph by Frank Miller. Courtesy of Frank Miller and Willamette University.

In 2004, Skelton wore his headdress at a meeting in London with the executives of Scottish Power, then in control of hydropower in the Klamath Basin through their subsidiary, PacifiCorp (since 2006, PacifiCorp has been owned by Berkshire Hathaway Energy). Skelton was there along with representatives of several Tribes from Northern California to protest the failure of PacifiCorp to install fish-passage systems around the Klamath River dams. The meetings drew the attention of the international media and were an embarrassment to Scottish Power.[25] Although no immediate steps to modify the dams were then taken, the protests contributed momentum to the long chain of events that brought various stakeholders together to begin working toward the dam removal agreements that were finally signed in 2016.

The watchmen of the past alerted the shaman after seeing signs of the returning fish, setting the stage for ceremony. Circumstances have changed; the c'waam are drastically reduced in number, and shamans no longer lead the ceremony. But new generations of Klamath tribal members watch and advocate for renewal of the c'waam, whether on the banks of the Sprague River or in the boardrooms of utility companies, and by so doing contribute to the well-being of the Klamath Tribes.

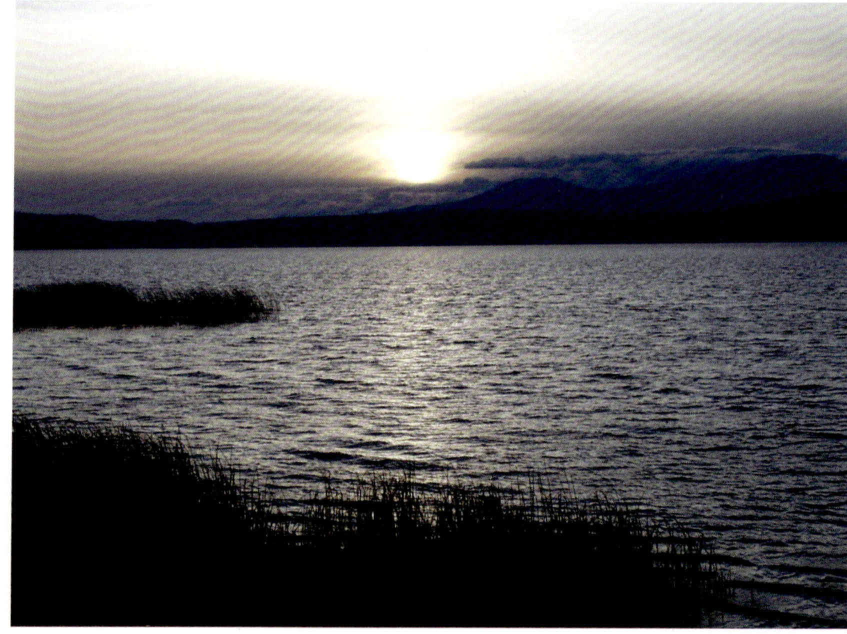

Upper Klamath Lake at sunset, 2004. Photograph by Taylor R. Tupper. Courtesy of the Klamath Tribes News Department.

At the Return of the C'waam Ceremony, when Jeff Mitchell sang a
song of welcome to newcomers at the banks of the Sprague River, he
reminded everyone how change was at that moment taking place. The
very act of meeting meant that all those gathered would change, in ways
not yet known but already set in motion. By gathering and participating
in ceremony, renewal of the shared human and environmental landscape in the Klamath Basin is made more possible against tremendous
odds, along with much-needed healing for the Klamath Tribes and their
homelands.

CHAPTER 7

WORLD RENEWAL— THE NEE DOSH

The Confederated Tribes of Siletz Indians

The abundant regalia of Siletz feather dancers spills out of the frame of a photograph taken during Fourth of July festivities in the early 1900s in coastal Newport, Oregon. In the center Ella Spencer is laden with seemingly endless strands of dentalia-shell necklaces, in a display of traditional wealth. Martha Johnson, third from left, wears an apron heavy with trade beads; the same garment is worn today by young Siletz women in some Feather Dances. The inclusion of so many tall feather headdresses, complemented by matishes (*feathered wands*) held downward by most in the photograph but upright when danced, signals that this was an occasion when the community brought out its most prized treasures. These treasures, every one of the dozens of regalia items, were being kept and cared for, mended as needed, somehow sheltered from decades of disruption that characterized the Siletz experience since Euro-American settlement began in the early 1800s. This resilience and creativity in the face of fragmentation characterizes the story of the Siletz Nee Dosh.

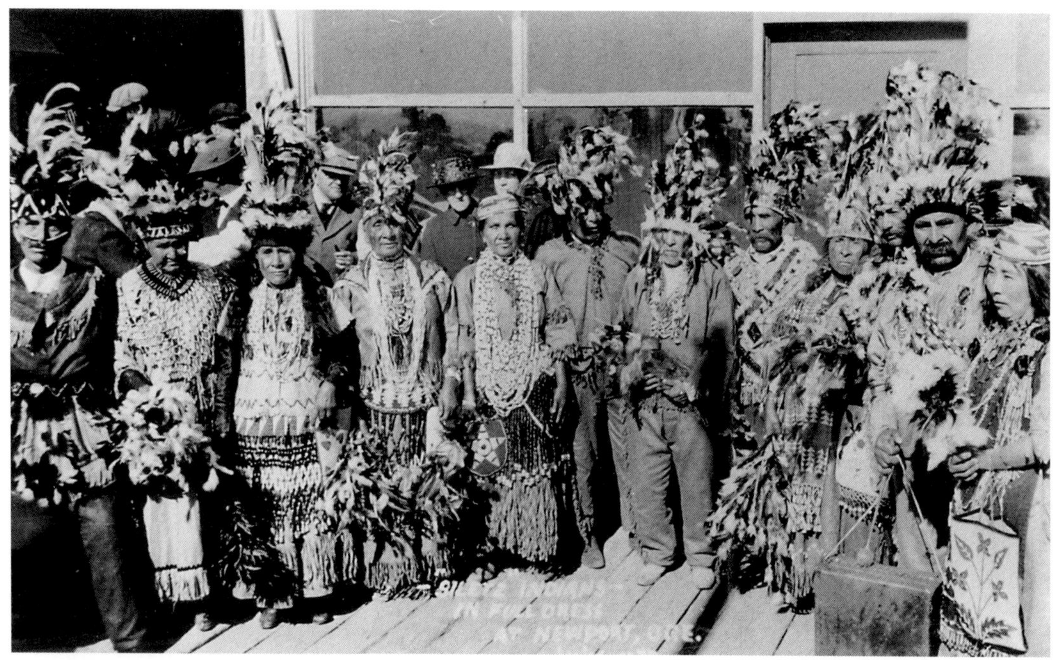

Siletz feather dancers in Newport, Oregon, for Fourth of July festivities, early 1900s. Individuals represent every southwest coastal band of the Siletz confederation from Northern California to the Alsea River. From left: Baldwin Fairchild, Annie Fairchild, Martha Johnson, Coquelle Nellie Lane, Ella Spencer, Jim Watts, Simpson Billy, Ed Bensell, Mary Rooney, Billy Metcalf, Hank Johnson, Sadie Cook. Photographer unknown. Courtesy of the Confederated Tribes of Siletz Indians.

The Nee Dosh, or Feather Dance, is a world renewal ceremony, understood by its participants to "fix" or repair the world, to remind people to give the Creator thanks for creation, and to carry out the human responsibility for tending to its well-being. In doing both— giving thanks and taking responsibility for caretaking—the dance nurtures hope that the world will be brought into greater balance and wholeness for another cycle. Assembling the community for these core purposes of the Nee Dosh reconstitutes the interpersonal world as well, mending and renewing the Siletz social fabric of relatives and friends.

In June 2015, I traveled to Siletz to attend the last of the three nights of the summer Nee Dosh, first sharing a meal in the Tribal Community Center on Government Hill, the site of the old Siletz Agency, where the federal government headquartered its administration of the reservation for decades.[1] Densely forested with Douglas fir and the highest point in the municipality of Siletz, the hill opens up to a circle of grassy pow-wow grounds that are flooded with light from the summer sun, though perpetually shaded by trees at the circle's perimeters. After dinner, we walked a few dozen yards to the cedar-plank dance house, tucked into the woods close to a bend in the Siletz River, its privacy protected. Over the course of the evening, I joined the women and girls in the dance house dressing room for conversation as they changed regalia for each of three rounds, the final one only concluding well into the wee hours of the morning. The next day I visited with Alfred "Bud" Lane III, Siletz Tribal Council vice chairman and traditional arts and language instructor, his wife, Cheryl, and their daughter Alissa (both of whom at the time were Siletz tribal employees in accounting and education, respectively), and Robert Kentta, Tribal Council member and director of the Cultural Resources Department, at the Lanes' home on the banks of the Siletz River, where the previous night's regalia lay out drying on the deck in the sun. Our conversation that afternoon was later supplemented by reflections written by Kentta, selections from which are included in this chapter. Along with the background Charles Wilkinson provides in his history of the Siletz Tribe, *The People Are Dancing Again*, these sources inform this account of the Feather Dance.[2]

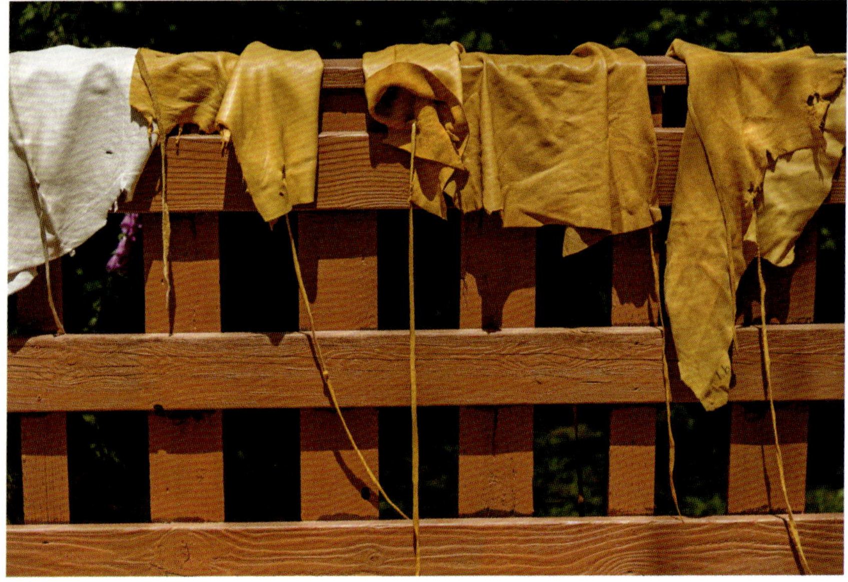

Men's deer-hide regalia drying at Lane family home, Siletz, Oregon, 2016. Photograph by Frank Miller. Courtesy of Frank Miller and Willamette University.

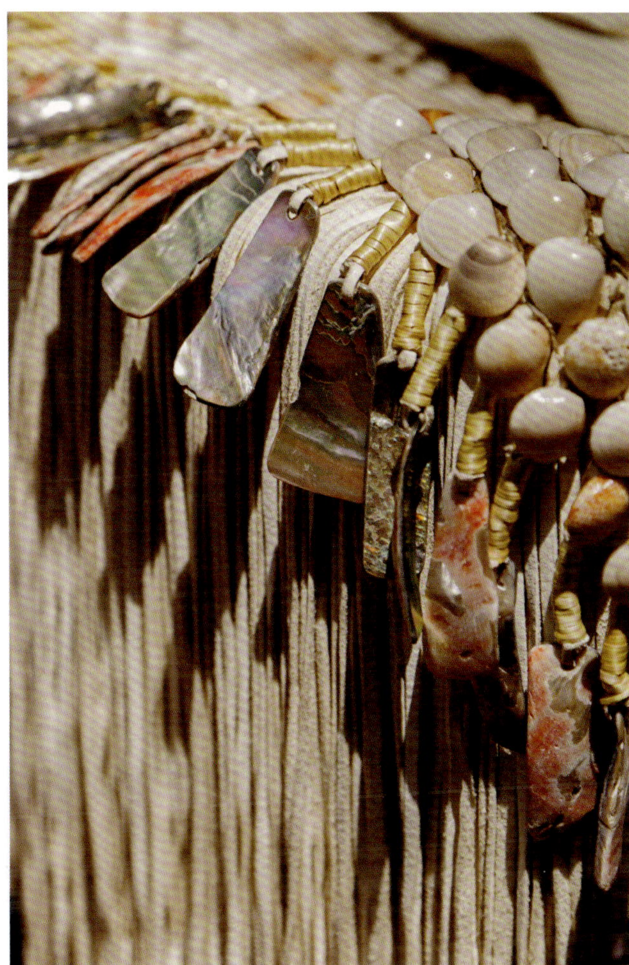

Women's deer-hide dance dress, with abalone pendants and shell decoration, Lane family home, Siletz, Oregon, 2016. Photograph by Frank Miller. Courtesy of Frank Miller and Willamette University.

The History and Resurgence of the Nee Dosh

The concept of renewal, central to the dance from time beyond memory, is essential to what has made possible the strengthening of the Nee Dosh in recent decades. In precontact times, across what is now northwestern California and southwestern Oregon, tribal groups along the Klamath and Smith Rivers all the way up to Coos Bay practiced a category of dances called world renewal ceremonies by early twentieth-century anthropologists, a term that is now used by tribal members themselves.[3] The various dances have some common threads.

Typically they take place over many days' time, each event increasing in elaboration and intensity from day to day, with the aim of renewing and rebalancing the world. World renewal dances demonstrate appreciation for creation and commitment to continued right relationships between creation and the human and spiritual worlds. As Robert Kentta wrote to me, in personal communication, shortly after the June 2015 Nee Dosh:

> The philosophy of our ceremonial dances make the most sense of anything I've heard in the world of spiritual beliefs. We rely on our Creator to make life possible for us and our future generations as a people. Though we may not produce children ourselves, we help take care of, teach, and guide our young people, through living productive lives, through passing on these values of life into the future, and responsibility to our Creator to give thanks, to care for and care-take that which has been put here for our use, and to make sure that the younger people also feel that responsibility. Our philosophy does not teach of impending doom and looking to the hereafter. It's what you do here that matters. That means for your descendants, whether direct lineal or the future members of your community, life will continue to exist.[4]

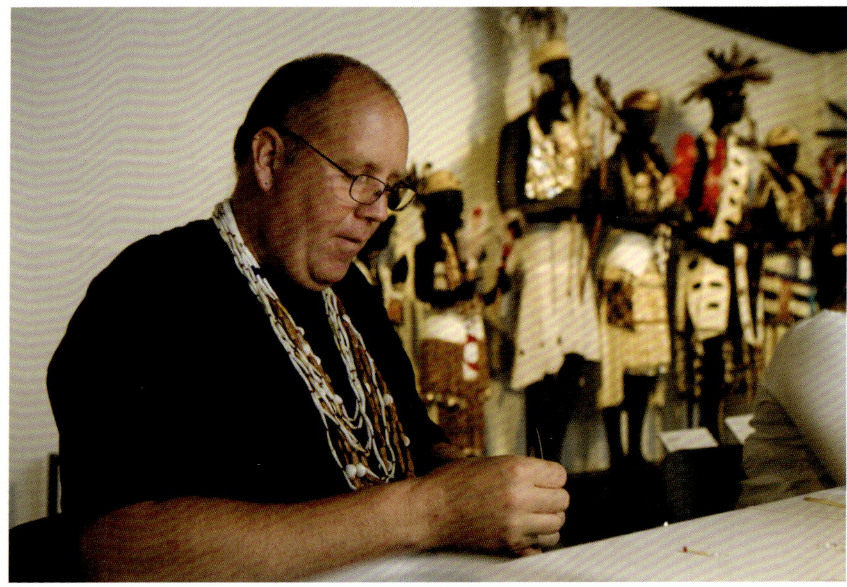

Robert Kentta making earrings at a public program for *The Art of Ceremony* exhibit, 2008. Photograph by Frank Miller. Courtesy of Frank Miller and Willamette University.

Another key characteristic of the dances is that they involve the display of wealth, not strictly through material possessions themselves but through the power manifested in those treasures and their use and presentation. As Bud Lane explained, traditional wealth "is a sacred thing, meant to be used and loaned and revered," not stored away untouched.[5] Regalia, especially when worn in ceremony, are infused with generosity, family status, and symbolic value. The spiritual power of the dancers in their regalia is shared with the audience, who by receiving it magnify and reflect it back.

By the mid-nineteenth century the lives of the tribal peoples who practiced world renewal dances were to change dramatically. The discovery of gold along southern Oregon's Rogue River in 1850 brought a flood of lawlessness perpetrated by miners and other settlers. Open hostilities between the newcomers and Indians in the region led to the Rogue River War, and under its pressure tribes and bands in southwestern Oregon negotiated numerous treaties in the 1850s with federal agents, only some of which were ratified by the US Senate. Out of this complex process, the Coast (or Siletz) Reservation was established in 1855, a swath of land that stretched more than a hundred miles south to north, from Cape Perpetua to Cape Lookout. The federal government aimed to remove most Indians from southwestern Oregon to clear the way for white settlement there, believing that the more difficult-to-access coastal terrain with its wet, cool climate would be less coveted by settlers.[6]

In 1856 the first of many forced removals from western and southern Oregon to the Coast Reservation began for several thousand Indian people who represented twenty or more tribes and bands, spoke several mutually unintelligible languages, and had distinctive belief systems. They were joined by other groups from north coastal areas and the Willamette Valley. Suddenly all these groups (from the west, south, north coastal, and Willamette Valley areas) were compelled to live together and conform to sedentary, agricultural lifestyles in remote and ill-equipped reservation settlements.[7]

It is amazing that any elements of the Nee Dosh survived this upheaval, but its practice was brought to the reservation by some of the Athabaskan-speaking groups who were removed there, such as the Chetco and Tututni, who originally inhabited the coastal region from

Smith River in present-day Northern California to the Coquille River in Oregon. In the twenty-first century, descendants of all the groups that make up today's Siletz tribal confederation now share the Nee Dosh, and in essence it has become a core embodiment of what it means to be Siletz.[8]

In his account of Siletz history, Wilkinson traces the ways other religious practices provided a medium in which the eventual resurgence could grow.[9] One was the Ghost Dance, the revitalization religion originating among the Paiute of Nevada in two waves (1869 and 1889), which preached that Indian people should return to Native values and practice round dancing in order to bring back tribal strength and return lost ancestors from the dead. The Ghost Dance was introduced to Siletz in 1873 by a Shasta Indian from Northern California, and six "Warm Houses" were built on the reservation for the dance. With its affirmation of Indigenous beliefs and message of social renewal, the Ghost Dance was perceived as a threat by Indian agents across the West. Siletz was no exception: the federal government burned down the dance houses in the late 1870s, making a devastating impact on the open practice of any traditional ceremonies. Government suppression as well as disillusionment with the failure of the dance to resurrect the dead resulted in its decline.[10]

Even though official federal Indian policy from the late 1800s to the 1960s emphasized the suppression of traditional language, religion, and communal practices, somehow Siletz tribal members found ways to perpetuate elements of the Nee Dosh. Photographs of Siletz tribal members in Feather Dance regalia in public settings, like the one in Newport, date from the late 1800s. These occasions, such as the Fourth of July or other national holidays, must have been experienced as relatively safe times to assert and display one's "Indianness" in the face of this history of suppression, even if the public reading of such displays might have confined the Native participants to a supporting, exotic role in the main event.

One of the elders who passed along much traditional knowledge of language and dance against the pressures of assimilation was Nellie Orton (1913–2001). From childhood, she suffered from a disability that left her unable to walk easily, so she "couldn't run and play outside with the other kids," as she recalled to Robert Kentta.[11] Orton thus

spent a great deal of time at home in the company of elders, many of
whom conversed in Athabaskan, assuming she could not understand.
Yet Orton grasped more of the language than they realized, and toward
the end of her life she became one of Bud Lane's language teachers.
Orton's parents hosted Feather Dances in their home, where they moved
out the furniture, invited folks inside to dance, and then later broke
out fiddles for entertainment. These memories became invaluable when
the Nee Dosh began to be renewed.

The middle of the twentieth century brought another wave of assimilation policies with the Termination Act of 1954, which ended the federal
trust relationship with the Siletz and most tribes in western Oregon.
Many Siletz people dispersed in order to survive economically, moving
to urban centers in Oregon and beyond. Members of terminated tribes
were no longer considered Indians in legal and political terms; outward
expression of Native identity was curtailed as a result. Yet some Siletz
families, such as that of Archie Ben, kept traditions alive during the
decades of termination by hosting dances in their homes and occasionally in public locations. By the 1970s powwow culture provided one
acceptable means to express "Indianness" in public. Many Siletz people
participating in powwows began to ask themselves what was distinctive
about being Siletz. In looking back at that time, Lane reflected: "That
journey for me really started with singing on the powwow drum here.
It started the question in our heads: What were *our* dances and what
was traditional to *us*?"[12] In this way powwows, by being a place where
being Indian was affirmed but where a longing for specific tribal identity
also grew, provided another impetus to reclaim the Nee Dosh.

This exploration took place in the context of the quest for Siletz
tribal restoration, achieved in 1977 after heroic efforts by dozens
of tribal members and allies over many years' time. Once restoration
was secured, a complex process of postcolonial nation-building began.
Many people at Siletz actively sought ideas and assistance from other
tribes, especially those with whom many Siletz families share an Athabaskan linguistic and cultural background. In the mid-1980s the visit
of Smith River Rancheria tribal members to Siletz to teach the Tolowa
language helped fuel a growing interest in Native language learning.
That interest was intertwined with a desire to renew ceremonial and
dance traditions at Siletz and the weaving and regalia-making skills

that facilitate those practices. Elders such as Nellie Orton were moved by the experience of hearing the Smith River Rancheria visitors speak the Tolowa language and dance the Feather Dance, and as Bud Lane remembered, "I think it triggered Nellie to become involved again."[13] Bud's daughter Alissa (born in the 1980s) remembers Nellie and other elders. As Alissa works with even younger generations of dancers, she explains to them that "yes, [the dance has] been restored, but it was alive in all these other Siletz people and Siletz families. They were just waiting to talk about it."[14]

In the 1980s and 1990s members of Siletz and various tribal communities in northwestern California and southwestern Oregon intentionally shared cultural knowledge, regularly visiting one another's ceremonies and developing in their capacity as dance makers.[15] These efforts planted seeds for future growth, including today's Siletz Tribal Language Project that teaches what has come to be called the Siletz Dee-Ni (or Athabaskan) language in the K–12 Siletz Valley School, community classrooms, and online. While few tribal members can speak Dee-Ni fluently, many are comfortable with the vocabulary and phrases used in the dance and other ritual occasions, and thus keep the sounds and sentiment of the language alive.

The 1990s also saw the beginning of rebuilding of cedar-plank dance houses in northwestern California and western Oregon, with one constructed at Siletz in 1996. The dance house movement has responded to—and facilitated—the flourishing of interest in traditional practices. In the first decade of the twenty-first century, plank houses were built at Coquille, Coos, Lower Umpqua and Siuslaw, and Grand Ronde, and their presence cradled the growth of community ceremonial practices. In preparation for the dedication of the Siletz dance house, Robert Kentta, director of the Cultural Resources Department, and staff member Silene Rilatos researched museum collections in search of Siletz heirlooms to inspire the making of contemporary regalia and also to be brought home to dance. At the National Museum of the American Indian (NMAI), Kentta and Rilatos located a historical Siletz woman's dance skirt and apron in sound enough condition to be danced. They requested the regalia be loaned for the first Nee Dosh to be held at the new dance house. As Kentta asserted, regalia was made to be used, and using it in ceremony would fulfill its purpose as well as the community and museum's responsibility to utilize it in the way it was meant to be. The NMAI agreed to the Siletz request and, according to Susan Heald, the conservator who accompanied the regalia to and from Siletz, the dance garments were returned to the museum in better condition than they left, as she and Siletz regalia-makers mended and stabilized them for the rigors of dancing.[16]

The opening of the Siletz dance house in 1996 represented the beginning of a new era in the cultural life of the community. More than two decades later, an entire generation has grown up within its walls. For them, the dance and the dance house have always been there. But as Cheryl Lane tells the young people she guides in the dance, at some point their understanding of their role in continuing the dance will deepen: "When you get older, you're going to realize all the things that were done to us as a people still didn't stop this song, it didn't stop this dance. Even when they burned the dance houses, it was done in homes. It survived the removal, the termination, all of it. We're still here. You guys are part of that, to keep it going. Despite all of that, that just goes to show what a strong people we are."[17]

Regalia, Land, and Creation

Regalia materially manifests the relationships people have with creation. Each object is made *from* the land, and in the Nee Dosh, is worn *for* the land and the people, embodying, renewing, and strengthening their interrelationship. Cheryl Lane explained this when she relayed what she tells Siletz youth who ask her for help composing essays about their culture. "One of the places that epitomizes so much of it is this dance," she said. "Because you tie everything back to the land. From digging spruce, gathering hazel, to the shells that were picked up to make a necklace. The language that's spoken, the songs that are sung, the creation story. Everyone has their favorite song, whether it's about Yaquina Head or the whale in the mouth of the Klamath River. That dance has it all."[18]

One way of thinking about regalia is to start with the resources, imagining the pathway they took from their origins to being worn in ceremony. The resources come from the abundant offerings of forests, rivers, and the ocean. Plants—beargrass, pine nuts, hazel sticks, maidenhair fern, maple bark—are incorporated into basket caps and dance skirts. Hides and skins from deer, river otter, ermine, ringtail cat, and even sea otter become transfigured into dance skirts and aprons, hair ties, men's wraps, cloaks, and headdress ornamentation. Flickers and other woodpeckers provide feathers and scalps for adorning headgear. The ocean yields iridescent abalone, clamshell, and prized dentalium. Volcanic outflows in mountains and deserts hold stores of obsidian for oval blades, held by men as emblems of strength. Referring to the concept that regalia represents wealth, Kentta wrote of its origins in creation's abundance:

> The materials all represent "wealth," in a sense, and when brought together and made into regalia, that piece has the added value and status of the work and effort that went into making it. New regalia has its own appeal and status, but when something has been danced multiple times, you can smell the smoke of past ceremonial fires, you can see the signs of use, and feel that it is a living thing, with history and significance. When I say that the materials represent wealth, I mean that the materials are symbols of the plenty that is provided for us, and that we are responsible for passing along to the next generations. We are responsible for allowing the resources to exist, responsible for caring for and enhancing them through our daily activities, through our way of walking in the world, and through how we interact with them. The regalia, as symbols of plenty, are more representative of "prosperity" than "wealth" in my mind, and as that is what we are praying for in our ceremonies, . . . then the regalia is a manifestation of the plenty our people have prayed for and received in the past, and pray for and receive in the present.[19]

The resources are carried along both environmental and social pathways shaped by forces of historical change. In precontact times dentalia from the seas around Vancouver Island was traded widely from its original ecosystem into much of the Pacific Northwest, California, and the Plains. It represented wealth, as did the regalia itself, along with the social and kin relations embedded and reflected in the wearer. Some objects were prized for their kinesthetic and auditory qualities—how they moved and sounded once on the regalia and the body. Postcontact goods such as thimbles and other metal objects like coins, bells, and

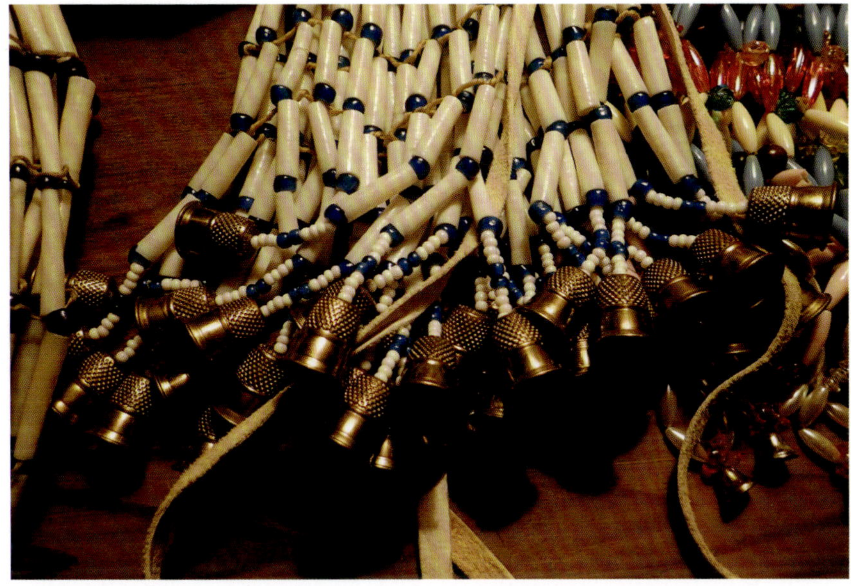

Women's denta-
lium apron with
brass thimbles and
glass beads, Siletz
dance house wom-
en's dressing room,
2016. Photograph
by Sara Siestreem
(Hanis Coos).

scrap fragments make pleasing sounds when danced. Glass and ceramic beads took the place of, or joined, pine nut beads on dresses and necklaces.

The routes that many resources travel from point of origin to use in a finished object of regalia have been forcibly altered since colonization. As just one example among many, the habitat of many fur-bearing mammals has been drastically reduced over two centuries of non-Native settlement and the accompanying environmental destruction, making traditional harvesting of species such as ringtail cat and mink exceptionally difficult. Compounding the issue of scarcity is the near-total social transformation of the subsistence-based economic systems of those peoples indigenous to what is now Oregon, which involved a seasonal round of movements throughout ancestral homelands, in systematic pursuit of resources for food, technology, and art. Today, very few individuals are economically able to live a lifestyle in which there is ample time and enough schedule flexibility to devote to the tending, gathering, and harvesting of resources that make up regalia. Regalia-makers have responded to these constraints with creativity, using fur culled from roadkill, purchased online through sources such as eBay, and traded through personal networks. These adjustments are not understood as concessions that somehow render regalia less worthy but as resilient responses to social and environmental forces that threaten yet fail to overwhelm those makers who carry on customs.

The Confederated Tribes of Siletz Indians have not passively accepted these compromised environmental conditions. As Kentta noted, a key message of the Nee Dosh is that the human community has the responsibility to create conditions for resources to thrive by caring for and enhancing the lives of plants and animals, fish, and fowl. This responsibility is taken very seriously and is not merely a matter of philosophy but also of tribal law and policy, as the Siletz tribal government works systematically with state and federal natural resources agencies to advocate for the well-being and protection of ancestral lands now under the jurisdiction of those agencies. One prominent example of such collaboration is between the Siletz and the Willamette National Forest, a 110-mile-long corridor on the western slopes of the Cascade Mountains. There, Siletz Cultural Resources Department staff has worked with the US Forest Service on enhancing habitat for traditional foods such as camas and huckleberries and for basketry and regalia resources such as beargrass. In western Oregon's coastal range the Siletz coordinate beargrass protection with the Bureau of Land Management (BLM) and the Siuslaw National Forest, and, in the Rogue Valley, work with the BLM and the Nature Conservancy to promote protection of vegetation in the Table Rock area, considered a sacred site by tribal members. These ongoing efforts, along with the broader conversations taking place around the incorporation of traditional ecological practices such as controlled burning to create greater biodiversity and to help suppress catastrophic forest fires, are embodied ways the Siletz Tribe meets its responsibility to renew the world as emphasized in the Nee Dosh.

Preparation and Performance

The resources, natural and cultural, that undergird the Nee Dosh mean that its preparation is measured not just in days and weeks but also in decades and generations. There comes a moment, though, when ritual time begins, in real time at the summer and winter solstices. The solstices punctuate the earth's seasonal cycle and also coincide with

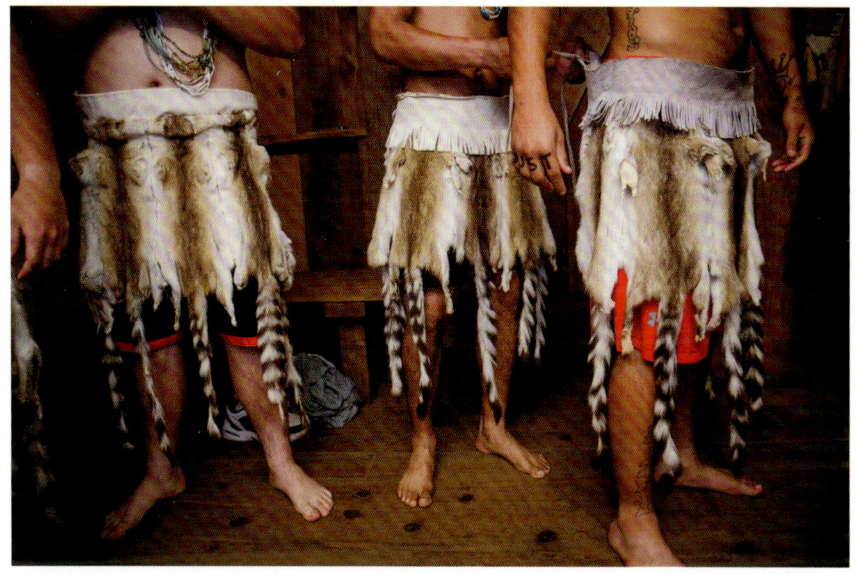

Men preparing to dance in ringtail cat skirts, Siletz dance house men's dressing room, 2016. Photograph by Frank Miller. Courtesy of Frank Miller and Willamette University.

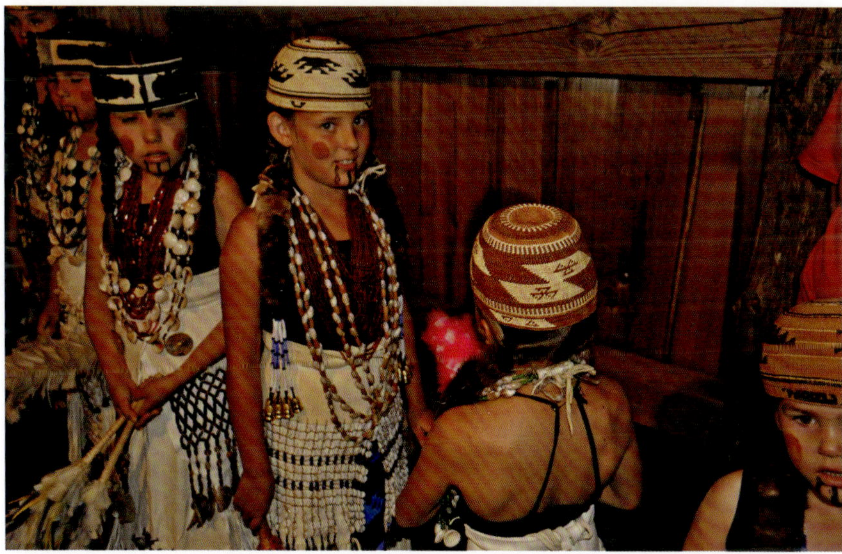

Girls wearing xee-tr'at, caps made of hazel sticks, spruce roots, and beargrass (with maidenhair fern and dyed porcupine quill decorative elements), Siletz dance house women's dressing room, early 2010s. (Left to right) Sierra Steere, Lilly Whitehead, Teonna Johnston, Halli Lane, Sahaylee Mason, Beyonka Bell-Tellez. Photograph by Alissa Lane.

calendrical pauses in modern society, the end of the US school year in June and the winter holidays of Christmas and New Year's. Conveniently, this schedule may make it easier for dancers and singers to come home to Siletz if they live far away. The dances take place over three nights, from Thursday through Saturday, and on the third an abundant meal is served in the Siletz Tribal Community Center, like the one I enjoyed in summer 2015. That night, the kitchen crew prepared an overflowing table that included now-traditional meats, vegetables, and salads as well as highly valued Indigenous foods such as seafood, roasted camas, acorn mush, and huckleberries. No one rushed through the meal, and as folks moved through the room, laughter and greetings reverberated in an atmosphere akin to a family reunion. While the meal took place, dancers of all ages—from preschoolers to teens to middle-aged adults—were already congregating at the dance house, where the stores of regalia were brought into the dressing rooms by the families that own them. Soon the walls and shelves of the dressing rooms were lined with regalia carefully organized by category and size. The dance house is cared for all year round, and keepers make sure it is ready to host the dance. A fire tender ensures there's ample firewood, as the fire must provide not only warmth but light for the audience to be able to see the dancers.

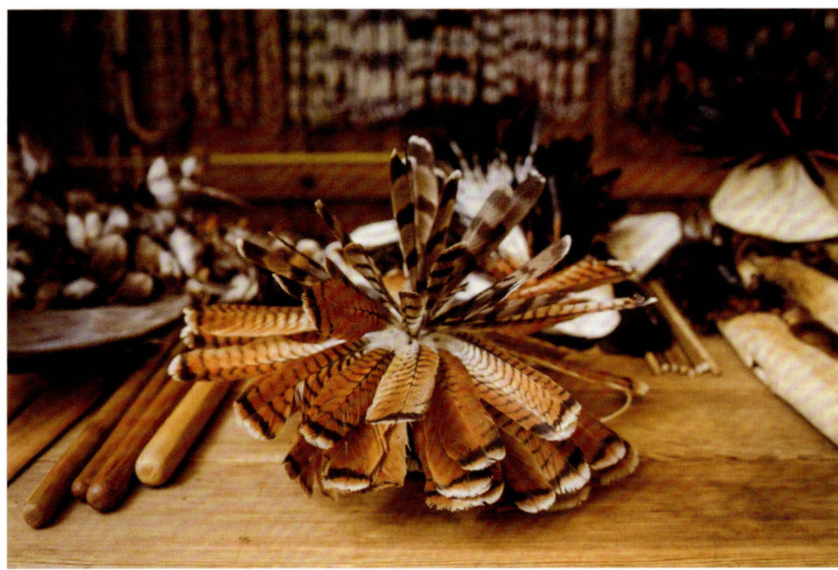

Headdress, with rows of necklaces in background, Siletz dance house men's dressing room, 2016. Photograph by Frank Miller. Courtesy of Frank Miller and Willamette University.

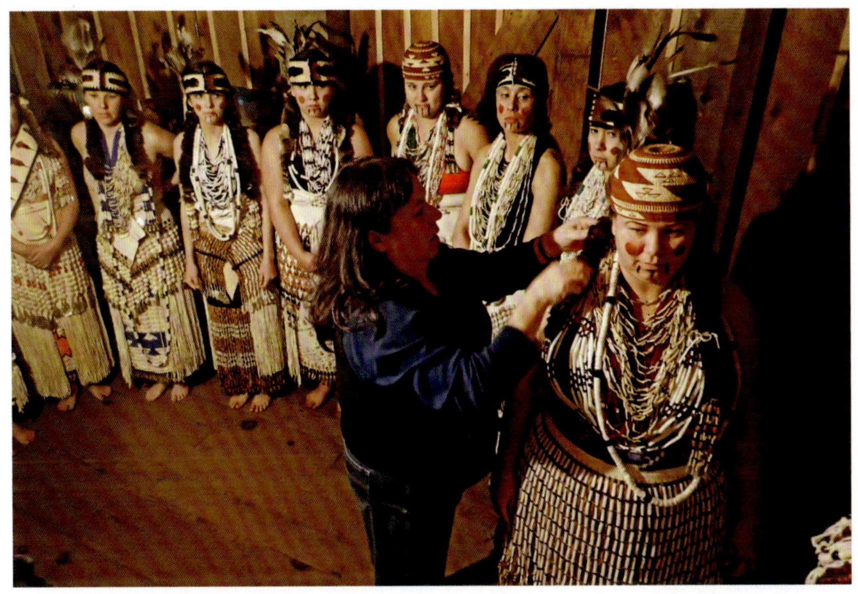

Cheryl Lane adjusting a hair tie made of river otter fur, Siletz dance house women's dressing room, 2016. (Left to right) Alissa Lane, Sierra Steere, Miakoda Scott, Tasha Rilatos, Sarah Butler, Teila Jurado, Alicia Keene. Photograph by Sara Siestreem (Hanis Coos).

Behind the dance house two prayer fires burned, one for women and one for men, right outside the doors to the dressing rooms. The fires are places for the dancers to pause between rounds, relaxing, talking, and warming up. Relatives and friends who were not dancing—mothers, fathers, sisters, cousins, grandparents—came and went from this area, their presence particularly encouraging to the youth. Two hours before the first round began, the women and girls began preparations. As in other tribal communities that practice world renewal ceremonies, Siletz has a dance maker family (the Lanes) who serves as outfitters of regalia and choreographers of the dance, but many families contribute and take responsibility for the continuity of the dance. In each dressing room the dance maker and assistants inventory both the dancers— who is here tonight to dance?—and the available regalia, making certain there is enough right-sized gear for every dancer. There is a great deal of hanging around, waiting one's turn to be dressed, and, once dressed, waiting for others to finish. Even the youngest dancers waited patiently and without irritation for what added up to many hours over the course of three days. It is a privilege to wear regalia—it is not "clothing" in any common sense—and it is put on with great care by the outfitters, with reminders in word and gesture about how it is to be worn.

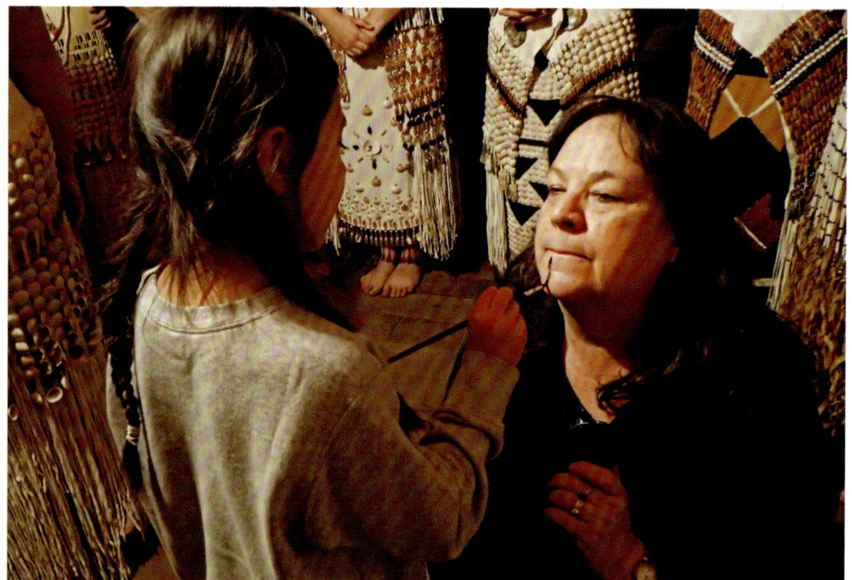

Eva Jurado painting Cheryl Lane's chin with three vertical lines, a traditional chin tattoo design for Siletz women, Siletz dance house women's dressing room, 2016. Photograph by Sara Siestreem (Hanis Coos).

Among the women and girls, hair ties went on first; wrapping braids tightly with strips of otter fur is a quiet, lengthy process. Next, aprons and dresses were tied firmly around the waist so there would be no chance of their loosening during the controlled but intensely percussive movements of the dance. Basket caps were sized to heads, again with the need to have a snug but not-too-tight fit. Among the men and boys, ringtail and deer-hide wraps went around waists, and headgear was secured. On both sides, layers of dentalium, clamshell, and bead necklaces were laid on, and finally faces were painted. Here and there, instructions were given in unfolding conversation about what the dances are about, the renewal of the world, the needs of the earth and the people to be in relationship with one another, and the role of the dancers in making this relationship right.

The men's voices rising in song from their dressing room signaled it was time for a round to begin. Inside the dance house the people gathered. From the outside the semi-subterranean house looks much smaller than it does within, where rows of built-in benches dug down into the earth hold dozens of community members and guests. Always, there are guests—folks who regularly come from other tribal communities or non-Indian visitors invited to engage on a deeper level with this

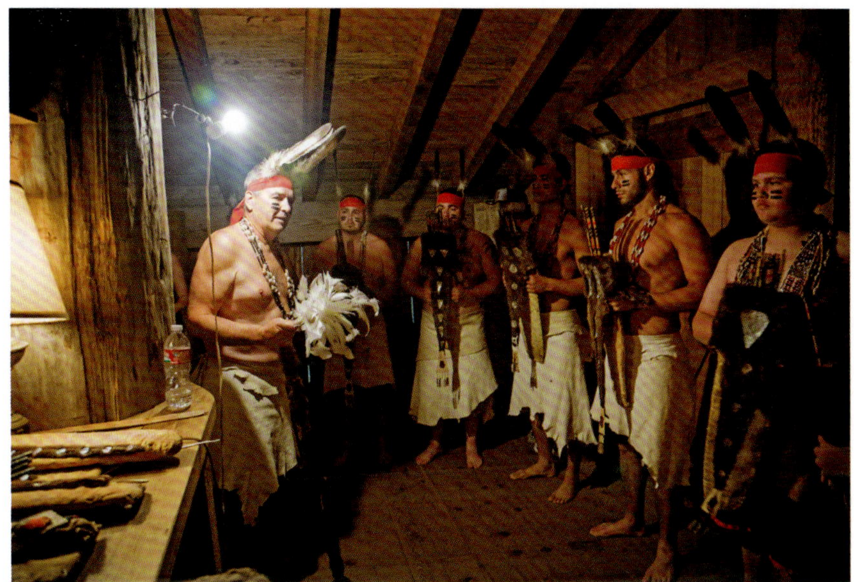

Bud Lane speaking with the men and boys as they prepare to enter the dance house, Siletz dance house, 2016. From left to right, Bud Lane, Justin Mason, James "Jimmy" Williams, Jesse Cordova, and Ebyn Jackson. Photograph by Frank Miller. Courtesy of Frank Miller and Willamette University.

community. This congregation makes a contribution through their witness and participation, responding to dancers, offering prayers, socializing between rounds, supporting and encouraging family members and friends. In these ways those gathered carry out a crucial role in fixing the world and renewing social ties within community and family networks. Bud Lane has spoken of these two components of the Nee Dosh as a "dual track": yes, it is intended to repair the world, but it also "plays a role in the harmony of our people, getting along together, something that we can do together without huge political division." Reflecting on how the Nee Dosh helps the Siletz function as a cohesive tribal group even though internal differences will always persist, as they do with any community, Lane summed up: "I think if you can't fix your own issues between yourselves then you're never going to fix the world."[20]

The men and boys emerged first from the dressing room, whose door opens directly into the house, walking along the top row of benches and down onto the dance floor. The women and girls arrived next from their dressing room on the opposite side of the house, similarly arranging themselves in the dance line. The male dance maker began most rounds with a prayerlike speech, passages from the story or scripture of creation, and then led the dancers and singers in song. Directly

opposite the dancers, seated with the audience, the women dance
makers shouted out names and instructions; dancers leapt into motion.
After each dance the audience audibly supported with applause, sometimes expressing delight about the performance of the youngest dancers
during the dance itself. The Nee Dosh, though deeply serious, is not
solemn. The dances sometimes include girls or boys only and at other
times both. Girls may dance arm in arm, in twos and threes, passing one
another in a crisscross pattern. Boys, with quivers and arrows in hand,
and in some rounds with deer antler headdresses, make the motions of
hunters. There is a productive tension between male and female: boys
may bring girls out to dance, but the girls set the pace of the movements. The dynamic pairings come in and out of balance and represent
the possibility of new generations.

All the regalia has to be sturdy enough to endure the kinds of movements that are expected: stepping and jumping up and down, moving
quickly across the dance floor. The Siletz dance "dress" and "apron" for
girls and women share traits common to tribes of northwestern California and southwestern Oregon. The apron is a rectangular panel, worn
in front, and tied at the waist. Over it, also tied at the waist like a skirt,
is a dress, a much larger panel of buckskin that meets at the front of the
midsection but is open enough for the apron within to be seen. Historically the lower portion of the apron was largely fringed, using beargrass
braids, pine nut beads, and abalone pendants; later, glass beads and
thimbles were incorporated. The dress is a solid surface at the top, then
fringed and highly ornamented all the way around. Kentta wrote to
me about how the ornamentation is arranged so that regalia becomes
part of the singing of the dance:

Dance dresses, aprons, necklaces, hair ties, even quivers with
pendants, all have their own individual sound, and often layers of
sound within a piece. The pendants are of similar size and thick-
ness on a particular piece, and the shells or pine nut beads are
prepared similarly, so when they rattle and rustle together, they
make a song for that piece, and then each of the many pieces
in the line adds to the song that's being sung. When the women
turn and join the line in dancing, that is when things are complete,
and the song is whole . . . and I feel medicine is being made.[21]

The jingling and rustling of the pendants on regalia make music with every movement of the dancers, creating sounds evocative of ocean waves and flowing water.

In that final night of the 2015 Nee Dosh, there were three rounds of dances, though sometimes there are five (three and five being sacred numbers in Indigenous western Oregon). Between rounds there were long breaks that are themselves vital to the dance. During these pauses visiting happens inside and outside the house, and the dancers dialogue about the dance itself around the prayer fires. All this is part of "fixing the world." At the end of the breaks the dancers don more regalia, with the men's changes being somewhat more dramatic, in that their headgear is distinctively different each round; then by the last round both men and women wear prized feather-laden headdresses. All throughout that night, and into the early morning, the fire keeper played a crucial role, continuing to stoke the fire, filling the house with light and heat. In the very last dance of the night, the tempo shifted to one of exuberance, a last explosion of energy and affirmation.

Men's regalia waiting to be worn, including breast plates with abalone and glass bead pendants that make audible sounds when in motion, Siletz dance house, 2016. Photograph by Frank Miller. Courtesy of Frank Miller and Willamette University.

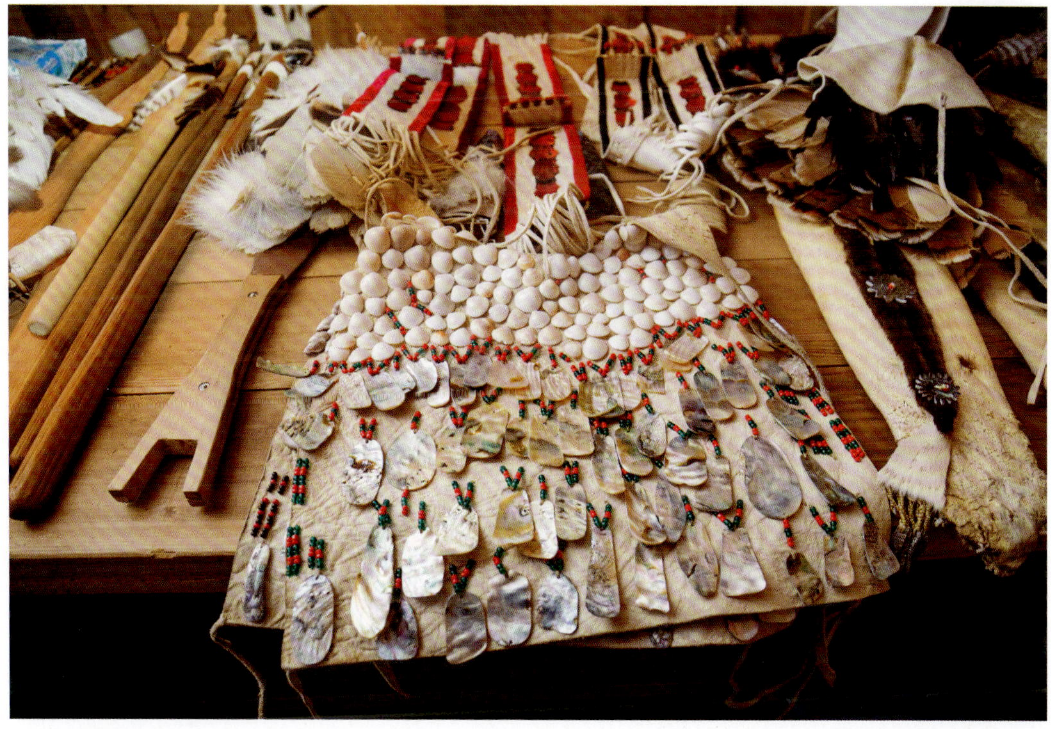

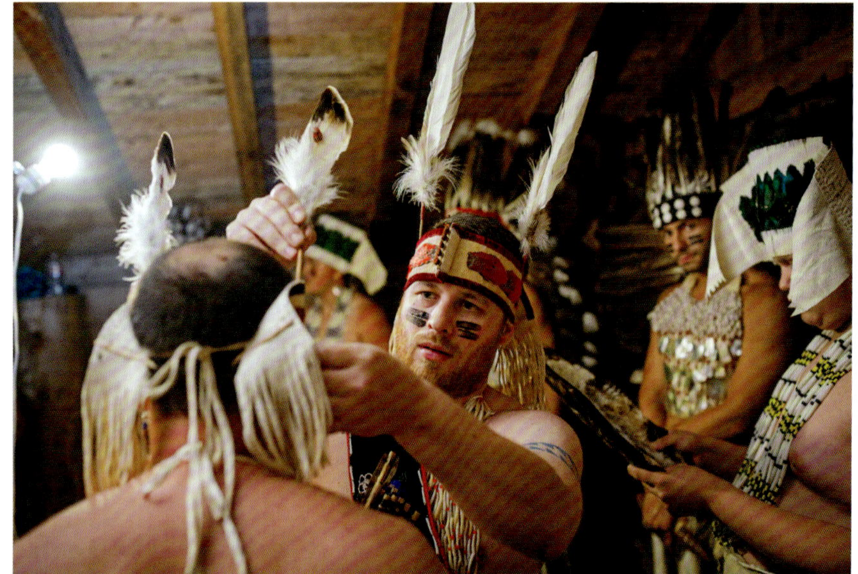

Alfred "Buddy" Lane IV securing a headdress for one of the final dance rounds, Siletz dance house, 2016. Photograph by Frank Miller. Courtesy of Frank Miller and Willamette University.

Regeneration

Ultimately regalia is but the tangible manifestation of the intangible themes at the core of world renewal. Although regalia is important to wear as a good way "to approach the Creator," as Bud Lane has said, the focus of the Nee Dosh is on the ongoing process of renewal that creation models and human beings require to thrive.[22] Anthropologist Thomas Buckley, drawing from his experiences with the Yurok of northwestern California, has written about world renewal dances as having always been "open processes" that provide recurring ways to work out difficult questions of being and belonging and becoming.[23] To participate in the dance is "to both express one's Indianness and to become more Indian," and those notions are not fixed but emergent for every generation.[24]

At Siletz, to take part in the Feather Dance is to express one's "Siletz-ness," something that has old roots but must also be renewed. In talking about what he thought was perhaps most important about the Nee Dosh today, Bud Lane stressed: "The larger thing is that the dance can remain relevant to young adults and those young folks that are coming into it. We can present those beliefs and they actually mean something to the young people, not just dressing up and getting out there

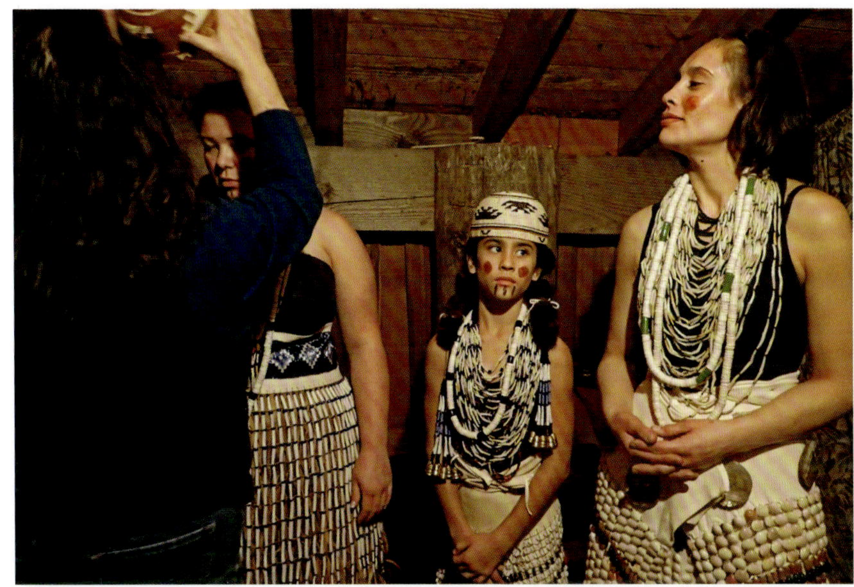

Girls and women receiving a fitting of their caps, Siletz dance house, 2016. (Left to right) Alicia Keene, Tenaya Cordova, Sarah Butler. Photograph by Sara Siestreem (Hanis Coos).

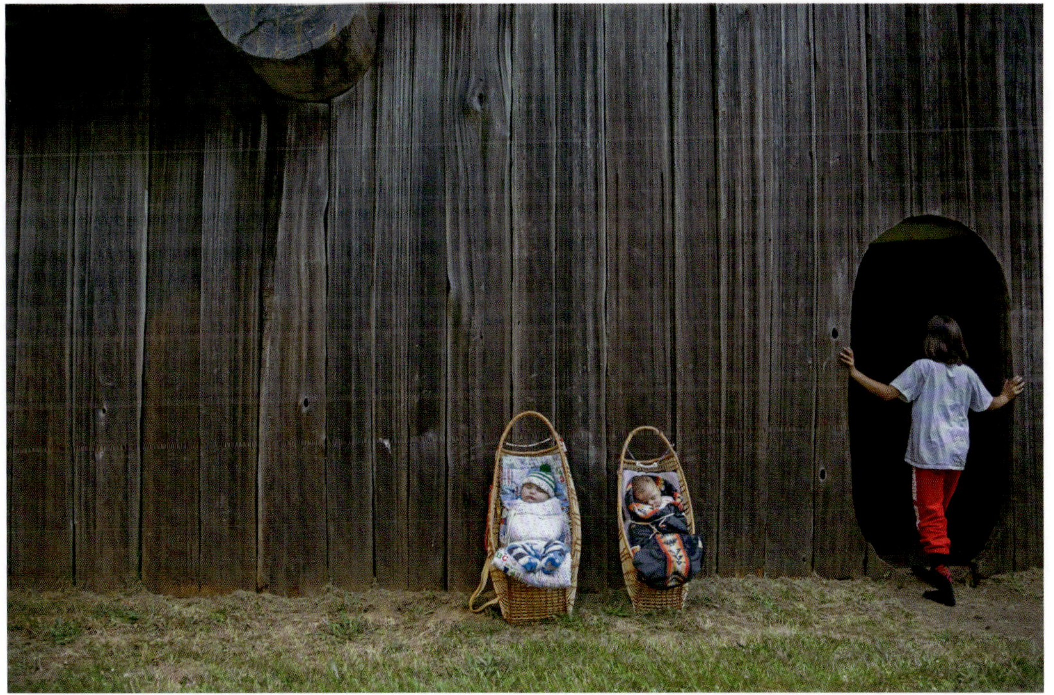

Entrance to Siletz dance house with babies in traditional baby baskets, before Nee Dosh begins, 2016. Photograph by Frank Miller. Courtesy of Frank Miller and Willamette University.

looking fierce and dancing. We could be standing out there naked with no regalia, and do the dance, and it could be the same thing. It won't be as pretty but it will be the dance with the same meaning. It has this core to it that is besides the regalia."[25] The Nee Dosh is an open process that reaches back before living memory and forward to the children yet to come and holds the promise of remaining relevant for every generation that will dance to renew the world.

CHAPTER 8

MAKING SWEAT, CHASING SMOKE

The Confederated Tribes of the Umatilla Indian Reservation

Toby Patrick began the story of the creation of the first sweat, as told to him by his grandfather Ike Patrick, who had been renowned for his traditional knowledge: "This is important. This is the most important part of my entire life. The things that Gramps explained to me about sweat, that tell me about all of us as Indian people, Natítayt. We started off as a family, and in the very beginning, we shed our skins."[1] There was a time when that family was congregated, as one, in the center of North America. The people were animals. To become human, they had to shed their skins. But becoming human brought opinions and differences, and soon the people learned how to fight and quarrel. Their families grew and became crowded. The Creator looked at the people, saw fighting going on, and came down to earth. Spilyáy, Coyote, came to Creator and said, "Something is going on, I can't control these people." The Creator decided to disband the people, family by family, throughout the land, to become separate tribes across the continent. The Creator told the people that in the future, when any one of their brothers came to visit, "You will be the one to help them understand your part of the land."

Creator also gave the people other instructions. Shedding their skins to become human had presented the people with a problem. The animals knew how to teach each other to stay clean. A deer licks its whole body. The mother, as soon as her fawn is born, licks and cleans it. As spirits, in animal skins, the people also knew how to keep themselves clean. But when they shed their skins, they had a new problem: they began to smell bad and be unclean. They went to Spilyáy and asked, "What do we do? We're in this form now, how do we clean? What do we do?" Spilyáy went to the Creator, who sent down the instructions for the sweat. Spilyáy showed the leader of the people how to sweat, where to place the lodge, the purpose of the rocks and the fir boughs used for the floor, and why to sweat: to give thanks, to cleanse, and to be reborn. To learn to love and to respect all that was "amongst us, under our feet, above our heads, surrounding us." Each of the dispersed groups was to have a distinctive way to sweat, a different set of beliefs, but for all it was to be a source of balance.

Telling this story, Toby emphasized that his grandfather taught that sweat is "something you give to the Creator, the Creator gives to you." The entire process, of preparing for and experiencing the sweat, is spoken of as "making sweat." In doing so, reflected Toby, "you're taking care of the land, and giving thanks for being reborn into this land yet again. When we go into the womb of the Mother Earth, when you sweat here, this is going in to clean your mind, your heart, and your body." Coming out of the sweat, each person washes with čúuš (*water*)—itself a sacred food—becoming refreshed and new. As Toby put it: "This is you, with your glow, that you earned, that you worked for. Nobody gives it to you. Nobody put it on you. The Creator put it on you but you have to work for it. You have to keep that mind, from the very beginning to the end, when you're making sweat."

The Oldest Teaching: The Sweathouse as a Vessel

In early 2016, I traveled to the Confederated Tribes of the Umatilla Indian Reservation to meet with staff at the Tamástslikt Cultural Institute, with whom I had worked on *The Art of Ceremony* exhibition project. Although this community is widely renowned for its extraordinary beaded regalia associated with horses, on public display every

year during the Pendleton Round-Up, the Tamástslikt staff decided
that instead their contribution to the exhibit would include less ornate
implements related to fundamental ceremonial practices of the Columbia River Plateau peoples: seven hand drums, used to call the people
into the Longhouse, as a core element of the Wáašat religion; simple
white buckskin outfits for men and women representing spiritual
rebirth and renewal; and an eagle staff, commissioned especially for
the exhibit, carried by leaders, often veterans, as a traditional symbol
of the tribal nation. Displayed separately, on a simple round platform,
were elements of the sweat lodge: a cast-iron pail of water and a dipper
made of elk horn, a small tule mat, a wooden bucket holding medicinal
plants wrapped in a bandana, a mound of rocks, and antlers. This latter
element was considered to be the core of the installation, and for this
book, Roberta "Bobbie" Conner and Malissa Minthorn Winks of the
Tamástslikt staff chose to focus on the sweat as the most fundamental
and oldest of teachings.

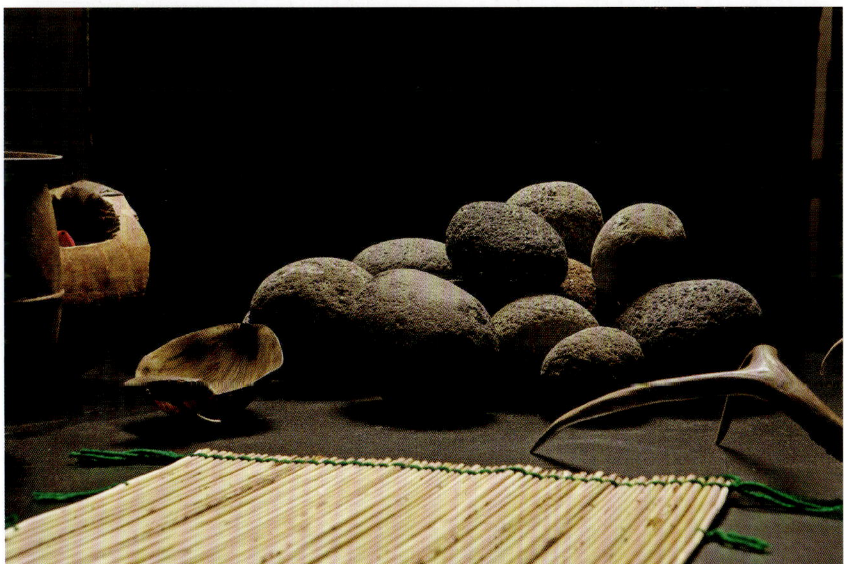

Sweat lodge elements, *The Art of Ceremony* exhibition installation, 2008. Sweat lodge rocks
collected by Victor Bates, Umatilla tribal member, from Hood River, Oregon. Tule mat, wooden
bowl, elk horn spoon, antler picks, and sweat rocks from the collection of the Tamástslikt
Cultural Institute, Pendleton, Oregon. Photograph by Frank Miller. Courtesy of Frank Miller
and Willamette University.

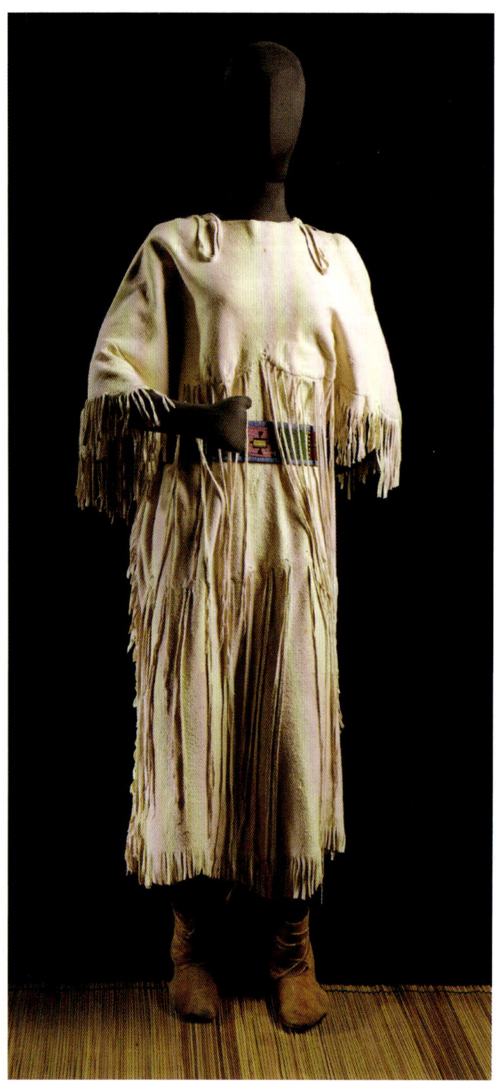

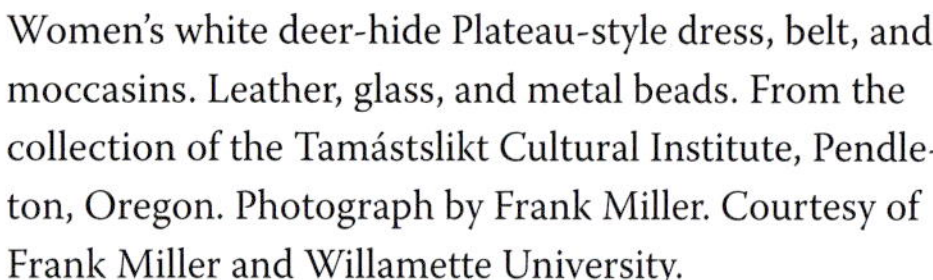

Women's white deer-hide Plateau-style dress, belt, and moccasins. Leather, glass, and metal beads. From the collection of the Tamástslikt Cultural Institute, Pendleton, Oregon. Photograph by Frank Miller. Courtesy of Frank Miller and Willamette University.

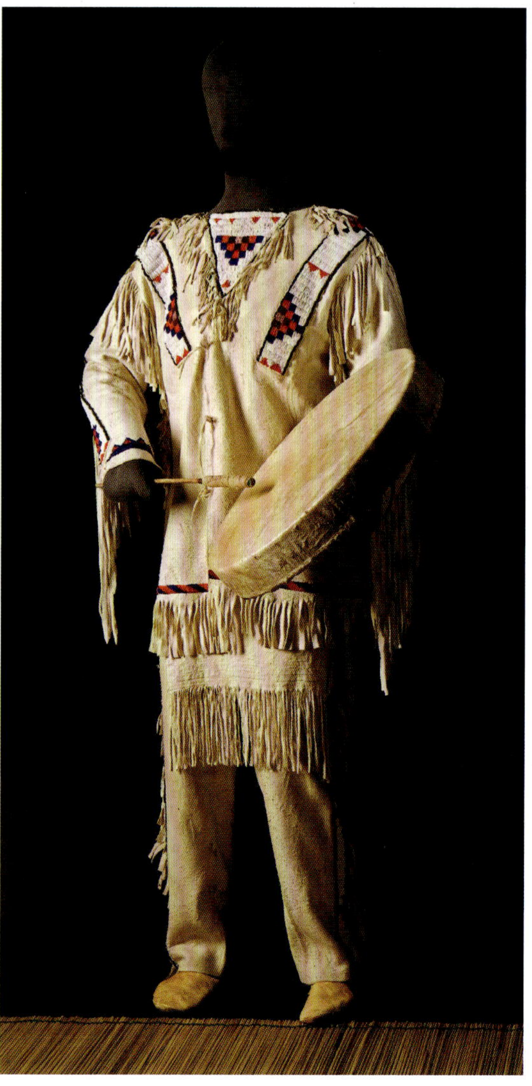

Men's white deer-hide Plateau-style shirt and leggings. Deer hide and glass beads. From the collection of the Tamástslikt Cultural Institute, Pendleton, Oregon. Hand drum and drum stick made by Les Minthorn, CTUIR member, 2007. Photograph by Frank Miller. Courtesy of Frank Miller and Willamette University.

Bobbie and Malissa invited nine community members, men and women from several generations, to Tamástslikt to engage in conversations about their experience with making sweat. Bobbie, Malissa, and I generated questions together, then Malissa and I were involved in conducting the conversations. Over three days in January and February 2016 we met with Marjorie Waheneka (born in 1953), John Bevis (born in 1957), and Toby Patrick (born in 1969) for individual conversations, and with elders Les Minthorn (born in 1933), Alphonse Halfmoon (1922–2016), and Dr. Ronald Pond (born in 1939) and his daughter Lona Pond, as well as Linda Jones (born in 1945) and Ramona Yeager (born in 1955) in small group sessions. Those involved in the conversations were concerned about the appropriation and misuse of the sweat lodge by non-Indians, a popular phenomenon in the United States in recent decades, perhaps most infamously resulting in the deaths of three people and injuries to many others in Arizona in 2009, at a for-profit retreat conducted by James Arthur Ray, a white man eventually convicted of negligent homicide.[2] The tribal members contributing to the conversations wished to convey the essence of making sweat, an essence that is seen as being beyond appropriation, and very explicitly did not want their accounts interpreted as "how-to" instructions for conducting a sweat.

The three Tribes that make up the Confederated Tribes of the Umatilla Indian Reservation (CTUIR)—the Cayuse, Umatilla, and Walla Walla—are all Columbia River Plateau peoples, who traditionally oriented themselves to the seasonal round and the appearance of first foods, including salmon, game, roots, and other plants. After the rapid incursion of white missionaries and settlers in the 1800s, the Tribes signed a treaty with the US government in 1855 that reserved a fraction of their original 6.4-million acre homeland, along with rights to fish, hunt, and gather in usual and accustomed places. Reservation lands were subject to further diminishment through allotment policies beginning in 1885, and tribal members were significantly impacted by other federal assimilation measures, including boarding schools and the 1950s urban relocation program. Throughout the twentieth century, CTUIR leaders maintained tribal sovereignty, resisting termination and advocating for the free exercise of reserved treaty rights, though struggling with pervasive poverty and the paternalistic constraints of the Bureau of

Indian Affairs. Since the 1970s and the ushering in of the era of self-determination, the Tribes have been systematically developing economic, political, and cultural resources and restoring key ecosystems within their homelands, perhaps best symbolized by the return of salmon after nearly a century to the Umatilla River basin.[3]

Throughout all these historical transformations the people of this community have continued to build and participate in the sweat lodge. The sweat physically relies upon the primary elements of earth, water, fire, and plant and even animal life, while spiritually offering cleansing and rebirth to participants. The sweat lodge itself is referred to as Qíiwn, the Old Man. His ribs are the boughs, harvested as young willow or lodgepole pine or chokecherry; his "skin" can be a variety of materials, including gunnysacks, canvas, blankets, or carpets. People enter the lodge by kneeling down and then, after turning around, backing in, showing respect to Mother Earth. Inside the lodge it is as dark as the womb, the beginning of time, and people are naked, as naked as the first people after shedding their animal skins. Each time the sweat experience is a symbolic rebirth: people leave the lodge headfirst because, as John said, "that's how you were born." In older times sweat lodges were earth-covered subterranean places, often embanked into a hill and framed inside with cedar poles, reflective of how profoundly "we believed in the Mother Earth," according to elder Dr. Ron Pond.[4]

Going into the darkness of the lodge separates you from the world outside with all its distractions. Yet, there in the darkness, the Creator can see you—or, in the words of Linda and Mona, can "recognize" you. John explained that Qíiwn, the Old Man, is not precisely the Creator, but the conduit to the Creator: "The sweathouse is a vessel. He's a vessel to the Creator. I always tell people when you shut that door, the darkness that envelops you inside is kind of the opposite. A light goes on. He can see everybody that's down in your lodge. You give thanks for that time you're being together." In the darkness is where you are seen. John made the point that making sweat does not require special knowledge and talent, unlike Wáašat singing and services or traditional dancing or, in these times when English has all but erased Indigenous tongues, speaking one's language: "Everybody can do it that wants to. . . . Everybody has a gift for sweat. All you have to do is give your sweat, is show up. It's the best deal in town."

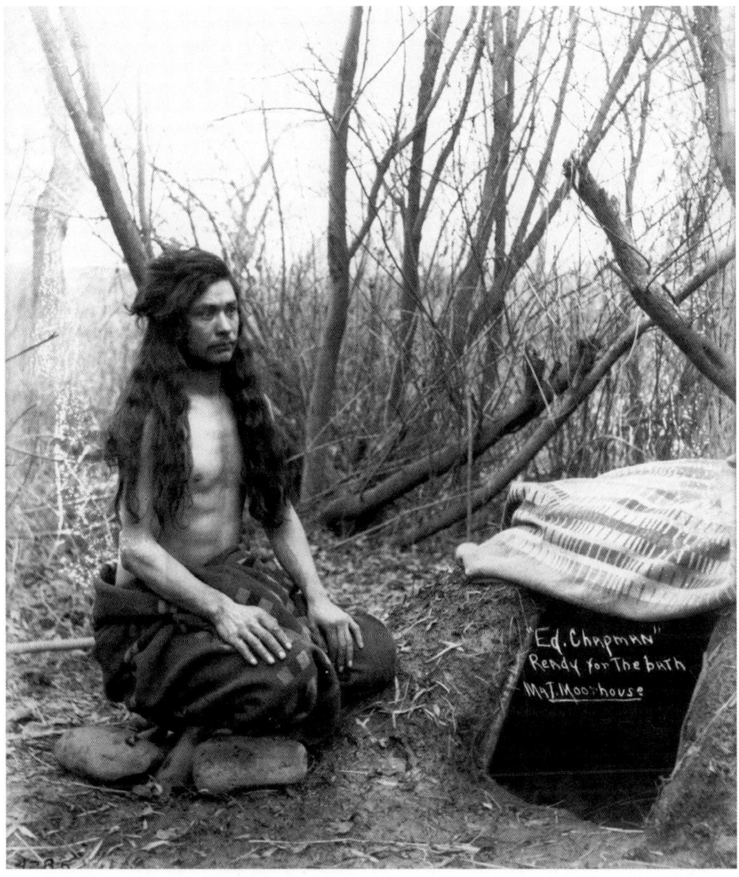

"Ed Chapman Ready for the Bath," ca. 1900–1910. The man identified as Ed Chapman sits outside a subterranean-style sweat lodge, constructed by digging into the earth. A Pendleton blanket is folded back over the top of the lodge and serves as a door. Photograph by Thomas Leander "Lee" Moorhouse. Lee Moorhouse photographs, PH036_4285, Special Collections & University Archives, University of Oregon Libraries. Courtesy of Tamástslikt Cultural Institute, Pendleton, Oregon.

Preparation: Getting What Is Needed

Making sweat involves a profound relationship with place. "Place" connotes much more than mere location. The traditional lands of the Tribes, the basins and ranges of the Blue and Wallowa Mountains, hold the teachings and bodies of the ancestors, the first foods that sustain life, and the resources for every ceremony, including those of the sweat.[5] Because of this relationship, the sweat lodge can never fully be appropriated by outsiders, and as practiced in this community, it is not a spa or a retreat for relaxation and self-indulgence. One does not go into the sweat to ask for something; rather, one offers gratitude. The experience embodies a responsibility to self, others, and to the land and its resources.

The basic elements of the sweat are very straightforward though deceptive in their simplicity. Gathering the resources for sweat was compared by many with gathering resources for food. In making this connection, Les reflected: "Gathering [food] is where I learned the principle of gathering, preserving, and sharing." He continued: "I learned the same for preparing the sweathouse." As Toby explained, "With making sweat, you don't use a whole lot, you use what you need. Just like gathering food: you don't go out and get all the food, you go out and get what you

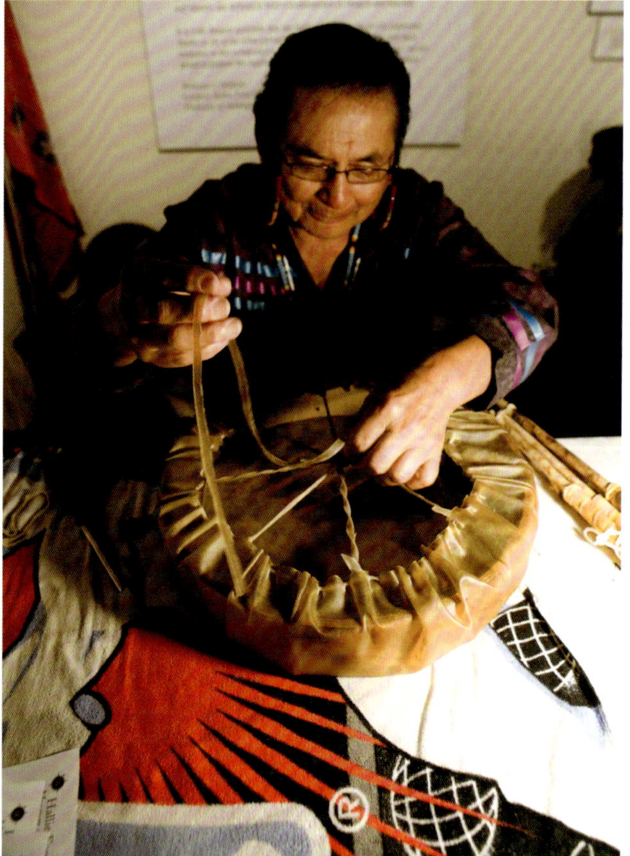

Les Minthorn, drum making during the opening weekend of *The Art of Ceremony*, September 28, 2008. Photograph by Frank Miller. Courtesy of Frank Miller and Willamette University.

need." Toby emphasized that you get what is going to help you, "what you can take care of, what you can manage. . . . Everything in our lives is like that." Les made the point that especially in today's economy in which many tribal families suffer from high unemployment, the need to gather, preserve, and share resources is as pressing as ever.

Participants in the conversations described variations made in the physical structures and material resources used in sweat as well as variations in protocol. Rather than seeing this as a problem, with one variant more or less valid than another, Malissa stressed that such diversity dispels the myth that there is only one way of doing things. She suggested that the sweat lodge tradition allows room to be independent, for choice in which practices a family or other group will follow. As John succinctly put it, although there's sweathouse etiquette, there is also "a lot of freedom."[6]

The location and materials used for the sweat lodge are flexible. Today many lodges are covered with canvas, carpet remnants, or blankets. Families place one somewhere on their property, ideally close to a stream or river, but even a garden hose in the backyard can be the source of water for making steam in the lodge as well as for bathing afterward. As mentioned earlier, the frame is made from young, pliable tree growth, sometimes collected in favored places. The ground within the lodge is covered with fragrant fir boughs, whose frequent replenishing is a good "excuse to go to the mountains," according to John.

Outside the lodge a fire tender makes an intensely hot though not necessarily large fire; making a good fire is one of many responsibilities involved in making sweat. Rocks are heated until orange-red and then "caught" with antlers, an iron pitchfork, or long sticks and carefully placed in a pit dug into the ground inside the lodge, usually to the left of the door for men and to the right for women. In the fire the rocks represent the grandmother, or woman; once in the lodge, they become part of the Old Man, whose face (the rock surface), according to Ron, is cleansed of ash from the fire with the first streams of water. The best rocks are of volcanic origin with relatively high iron content, as they are already tempered and less likely to explode and send burning fragments onto exposed skin. In addition, flat volcanic rocks are placed underneath as well as on top of the heated rocks, to provide a way to diffuse the water when it is poured, a technique felt to create better steam.

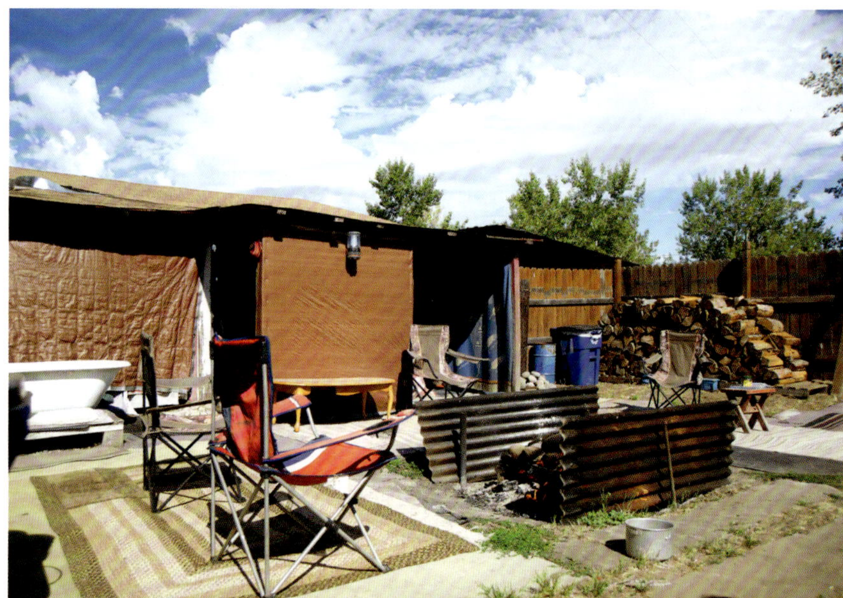

Backyard sweat lodge at the home of Victor Bates, CTUIR member, 2016. Photograph by Patrice Hall Walters, CTUIR member.

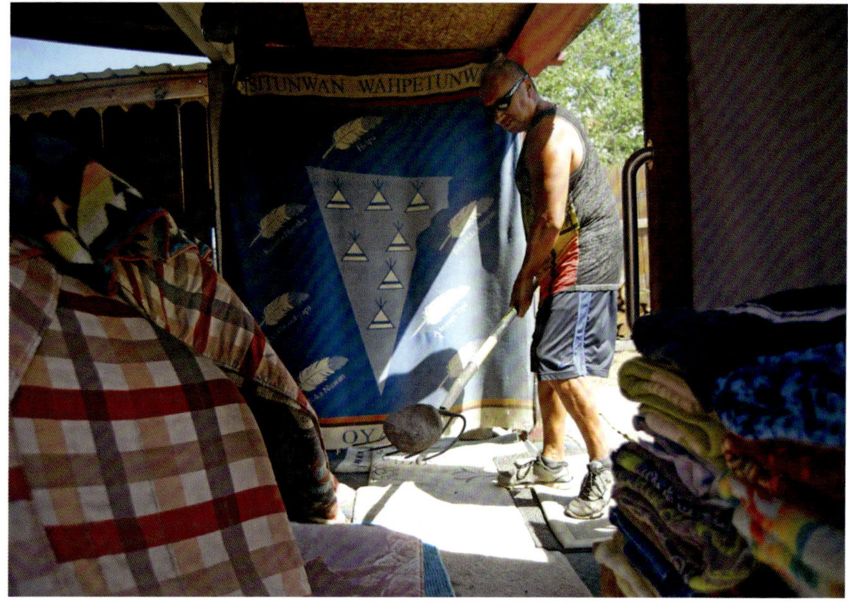

Sweat lodge at the home of Victor Bates, CTUIR member, 2016. Photograph by Patrice Hall Walters, CTUIR member.

Les told of going to a favorite streambed to collect sweat lodge rocks that have descended over the ages down the slopes of volcanic Mount Hood, then offering them for ceremonial giveaways at the Longhouse, a measure of their high value.

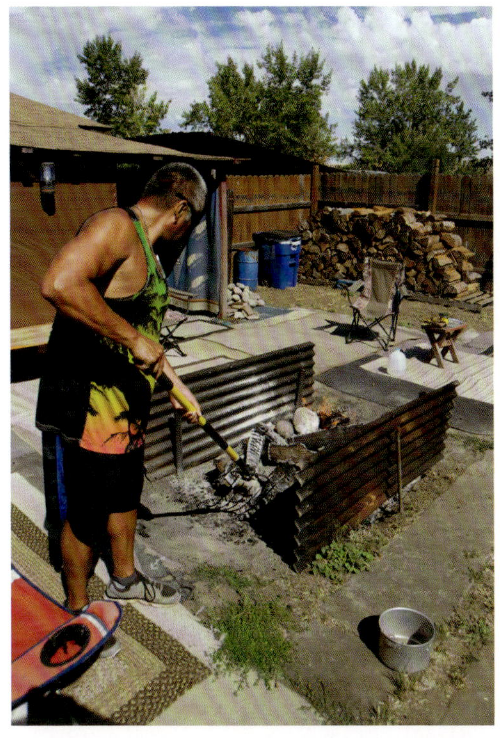

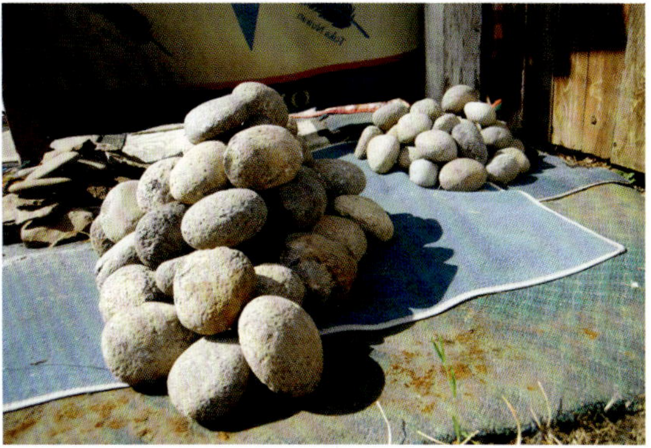

left:
Victor Bates tending fire, 2016.
Photograph by Patrice Hall Walters,
CTUIR member.

above:
Rocks prepared for heating in fire,
2016. Collected by Victor Bates.
Photograph by Patrice Hall Walters,
CTUIR member.

In addition to flexible shoots for the frame and logs for firewood, other plants are harvested for elements of the sweat. Wild rosebush is considered sacred and purifying, "a big medicine for us," said Ron, who explained how brooms made from rosebush were traditionally used to sweep the ground around the sweat "to cleanse the ground spiritually, every day." Other medicinal plants are used inside the sweat; almost everyone spoke of qawšqáwš (*bear root*), an aromatic root with astringent properties, often being placed in cloth bags and then into the bucket, to infuse into the water. Many people referenced other plants—mint and yarrow among them—as similarly being used to enhance the steam.

Participants go in and out of the lodge in order. The sequence of the entry and position once within can reflect status and respect. For instance, the role of bucket man or woman is one of the most important, often going to the eldest one present, as he or she has control of the duration and pacing of the sweat by deciding when water is to be ladled from the bucket onto the hot rocks. Most people spoke of having three rounds, each with several ladles of water to create steam. John relayed that in his experience the first is for the Old Man, the second is for singing medicine songs and for praying, and the final is for visiting, for sharing good humor. The door, usually a flap that can be opened by being thrown up over the top of the dome, is tended by a doorkeeper who usually doesn't open it until the sweat is complete. The door usually faces east, so that as people enter backward and exit headfirst, they are facing the direction of the rising sun. Yet more than one participant described sweathouses with west-facing doors, a direction, Mona remembered her grandfather saying, that allowed participants to "collect for wisdom."

Sweat through the Life Cycle

Many of those in the conversations who were born before 1950 grew up with sweat as part of their childhoods. Linda recollected: "It was one of the first things after learning to walk and to talk, the way we grew up. I was born in 1945, the third-oldest of fourteen children. We lived with our grandparents, my mother's parents. We had no indoor plumbing, no running water, nothing like that. We used [sweat] as a means of bathing."

For those born into homes with no electricity or running water, the sweat was a dimension of hygiene. Les remembered bathing in a galvanized steel washtub filled with water heated on a wood-burning stove until he and his siblings were too big to fit into the tub. Then they were told, "Go to the sweathouse," and his father and older brothers guided them in what to do. As one of the eldest children, Linda recalled, it fell to her to teach younger ones what to do; the girls in her family "grew up sweating with each other, with our aunts, with our grandmas." Not only was sweat a vehicle for hygiene (like adults, children would bathe in a stream or with water ladled from containers after the sweat) but for developing self-discipline and physical and mental strength. Elders expected children to tolerate the heat of the sweat; it was "not a playground," said Marjorie. In addition to the benefit of getting clean, Marjorie remembered going to sleep easily at night as a child after the warm, relaxing experience of the sweat, something she still relishes doing as an adult.

Others who grew up practicing the sweat reflected on how they learned "by watching, by experience," as Ron explained, with "everybody making you do things on your own if you watched enough." Les added that as a child he didn't understand or know reasons why things were done as they were, and that "as you grow older, you begin to understand some of those principles that they were trying to show you." This extended to understanding language as well. Lona remembered that, in her childhood, Native language was spoken inside the sweathouse with English reserved for the outside. Children were expected to follow along and learn; today, even though fluency in Native languages has been severely impacted by official federal policies of linguistic suppression, many practitioners of the sweat possess a specialized vocabulary of Native terms drawn from the reservation's Sahaptian languages.

By the 1960s indoor plumbing became the norm, and fewer children grew up in households that relied on sweat for hygiene. Teaching young people to sweat became more intentional. Born in 1969, Toby was chosen at about age seven by his grandfather Ike Patrick to be his apprentice in the sweat. Toby was the youngest of his brothers and cousins, and had been with his grandfather, father, uncles, and brothers in the sweat since early childhood. Ike sat in the sweat with Toby and said, "You're the last one, and I need you to listen to what I'm saying. Somebody's got to pick this up and take this beyond." Toby remembered: "I'm sitting there looking at Gramps, and I'm saying, I want to be there. I want to be old, respected, loved by everybody in the world." This invitation came at an optimum time: Toby had just seen *Star Wars*, released in 1977, and in his imagination saw himself as a young Luke Skywalker at the feet of a Jedi master, eager to receive this knowledge.

Toby's explanation of how his grandfather and father taught him about preparing and carrying out the sweat is a meditation upon Native pedagogy: "They allowed me my mistakes. They allowed me to do the things I did good. You get complimented, but the things you needed to work on, you were told 'you need to work on that.'" When he would ask his father how to do something related to the sweat, his father would turn the question back upon him and first ask Toby to reconstruct what he remembered. Toby went as far as he could, and only then would his father give him the "answer," thus simultaneously reinforcing and expanding Toby's base of knowledge. He felt he could make mistakes but not be ridiculed; he was encouraged to work on learning.

Ron, from a generation before Toby, also remembered learning by doing and good work being reinforced: "With the menfolks, if you make sweathouse by yourself, you have to kind of earn your way. You watched, took part, you knew to make fire. . . . If you do this all yourself, then you put the rocks in by yourself, then that shows something." He continued: "Seems to me that the elders kept a watch on you. If you had experience in there, you're doing good, they kind of assign you [to do more]." In these ways, as Bobbie related, elders select youth who are receptive, who are thinking people, who demonstrate an eagerness to learn. The young person is encouraged to embrace his or her own strength but also to recognize—and minimize—weakness.

While Toby learned at the sides of his grandfather and father, others such as John came to the sweathouse as teenagers through a culture camp sponsored by the CTUIR in the 1970s, where community leaders such as Ron set up sweathouses and instructed a new generation. John considers himself a latecomer to the sweat. He was fifteen when he learned to sweat at camp but became hooked for life, carrying the practice with him into adulthood, eventually making a sweat lodge in his own backyard after becoming a grown man with his own home.

Women in the Columbia Plateau sweat separately from men and generally after them. Although some women spoke of earlier times when women might have had separate sweathouses, in living memory most women use the same structure as men, and because they usually sweat after men, they are less directly involved in the preparation of the sweat itself, although they have essential responsibilities that make the sweat possible, such as cooking the meals served after the sweat and taking care of children. Those women participating in the conversations spoke of the sweat lodge as being a place where they learned about being a woman, a mother, a wife, and could discuss life challenges. Marjorie remembered her experience as a child and young girl: "There was always a lesson or something you went away with, if you were lucky enough to sweat with the older ones." Now that she is an elder, she has had a "good opportunity to talk with some of my nieces in the sweathouse" about how important it is to be a woman and a mother and eventually a grandma, and to take care of yourself and your children.

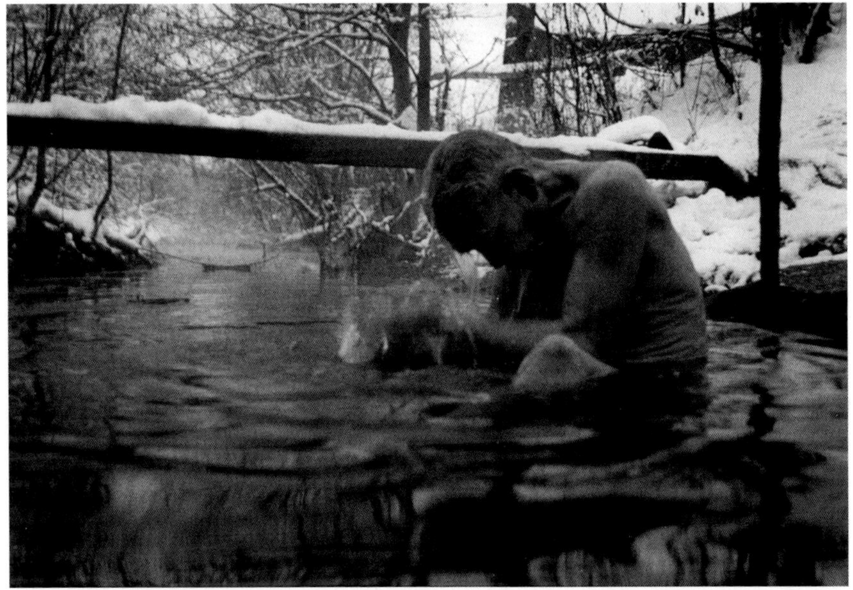

In the dim light of a winter sunset, Atway Ike Patrick splashes in the cold spring after a session in the sweathouse, 1977. Photograph by Joel Davis. Courtesy of Joel Davis and Tamástslikt Cultural Institute, Pendleton, Oregon.

Women spoke of the sweat lodge as a place where troubles can be released and the self unburdened. Linda said she heard this referred to as "taking troubles to the Old Man":

> We'd use it not only for gossiping and laughing, but also, like you probably heard people say, confessing. Whatever is bothering you, you let it go. Our mother used to always tell us, when we became adults with our own lives, you'd get troubled, everybody gets troubled, bothered with something, and she'd always tell us, "Well you need to go sweat, you need to go and just let it go, go talk to the Old Man." I heard a lot of people have problems, and for the longest time I never knew what she meant until I got to that point and it's like "Oh!" It's like a light bulb goes on, when you go release whatever is bothering you. She said, "Let the Old Man take your troubles, you'll be better." For whatever reason, when you hear words like that they stay with you and then when it happens to you, it's like "Oh that really did help." It's probably better than going and sitting and talking to a mental health expert!

Linda acknowledged that those with whom you sweat become confidants with a special bond of trust. "What you say stays there," she said.

"Nobody takes it and repeats it. Whenever I was bothered, I felt good that I could share that with somebody."

Another lesson from the sweat is that one learns to remain thankful, even in the face of loss or grief. Toby was explicitly told by his grandfather that one of his roles as a keeper of the sweat would be to provide sweat for just such reasons, to offer others a place to go in times of need or trouble and to access the teachings Toby received from Ike. Ike told Toby that he needed to make sweat every day, not just when he was hurting, because he couldn't know "when [something hard] is going to happen." Doing this meant that tribal members coming home to the reservation from time away—whether serving and doing combat in the military, living in urban areas, doing time in prison—would have a way of reintegrating back into the community and "dealing with their demons." For Toby today, keeping up this consistent practice may mean he is the "only one sweating, for months on end," until someone reaches out, often out of need. Toby spoke of how his grandfather emphasized how important it was to be consistent in practicing the sweat, because "there's things that are happening in the world today we have no control over."

Those who have practiced sweat for a long time report a sense of "craving for sweat," both the physical cleansing and the camaraderie and spiritual strengthening. Ron remembered Ike getting to a certain time of day and then expressing a craving that he could feel in his body, which would perspire in anticipation. As John explained, "It gets addictive after a while; your body will tell you need a sweat. I will go, not just for the body, but for your heart and your mind." Linda echoed her sense of this need: "When you grow up with it, like I have, it's like you miss it. I miss not only the cleansing part and all [but also] the visiting part. That's what we would do is visit and catch up, just laugh and have a good time. Tell stories on each other."

Today on the Confederated Tribes of the Umatilla Indian Reservation, there are several sweathouses, although all participants in the conversations readily acknowledge that only a small proportion of tribal members regularly sweat. But those who do sweat regularly believe that the practice remains relevant to younger family members and generations. John, who has younger people, including his own adult children, join him in the sweat, sees the experience as providing "something to believe in." He clarified:

The sweathouse gives them something to believe in, like a release valve. Sometimes you can see the confusion in them, when they lose a friend or a crisis comes to them, you can see the panic in them. That's where you go deal with your panic. That's where you're going to find your answers. You always hear that in Indian Country: You come here for a reason. You may not know what it is, but the Old Man brought you here at this moment, for a reason. It's up to you to find that reason. When things are bothering you or, vice versa, you feel grateful. I was blessed with good happiness and good feelings, there was something great happening in my life. I want to give things. You always do that, you want to cover all bases. Thank you for my life, thank you for my breath, thank you for my mind.

John concluded the reflection by adding that asking for being humble and asking for forgiveness was also a resource that every generation needs: "I hope I didn't hurt anybody; I ask for forgiveness if I have. Maybe it was me that pointed the finger without thinking, maybe it was me that caused pain. You don't want to live with that. You want to cover all bases." Making sweat releases you.

Sweat as Ceremony

Making sweat was spoken of as being distinct from the practice of going to the Longhouse for regular Sunday Wáašat services and special occasions. As Toby put it, the sweat and the Longhouse are in the same world but are "two separate entities"; one indicator of this relationship is that sweats are usually not conducted on Sundays. Making sweat is a more private expression than going to public events at the Longhouse, as it can even be done alone and takes place quite literally in the dark. Anyone who wishes can join in; while some understanding of protocol is needed, the participant simply needs to show up and follow instructions, whereas the Longhouse relies on a ritual structure with the singing of Wáašat songs and the guidance of knowledgeable leaders. In contrast, as John pointed out, there is a simplicity in the sweat: "Just going through the act makes it holy. Just the idea, 'I'm going to go make sweat' makes it holy. And so when you follow through with it, you're

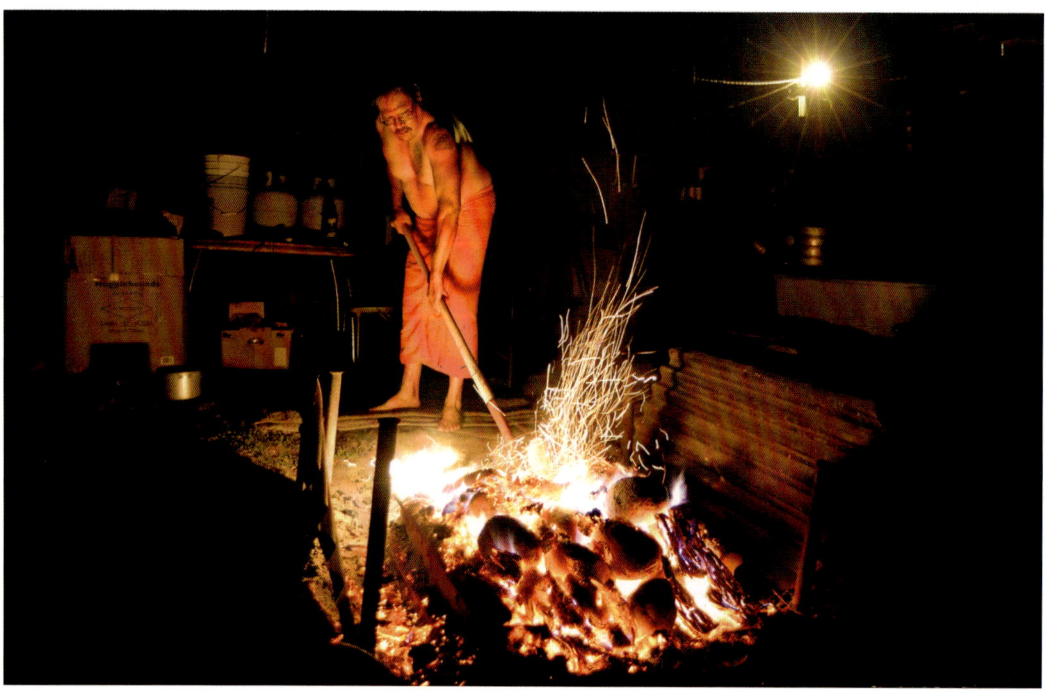

Virgil Tsosie preparing sweat at night. Victor Bates sweat lodge, 2016. Photograph by Patrice Hall Walters, CTUIR member.

already on your way." That said, making sweat is a foundational element of ceremonial life. Before gathering or hunting, people were expected to sweat. Ritual practitioners, such as medicine singers, sweat before conducting ceremony. When someone dies, sweat is essential to mourning and healing for the living left behind.

Several women relayed the teachings they received about the importance of making sweat in preparation for gathering, especially at the initial seasonal harvesting of first foods, such as roots, berries, and other plants. Throughout her life Linda has practiced her mother's instructions. "One of the things she always told us," Linda recalled, "you need to go sweat before you go gather our foods. You have to cleanse your body, cleanse your soul. We'd go in there and cleanse our body. At the same time, we're cleansing our soul by confessing to our Púša [*grandfather*]. I still believe that. The young women that come out and gather the food with us, it's just now starting to grasp in their mind what we're talking about when we say that. When we go out to get our food that's coming back new, we have to be of clean mind and spirit." Marjorie remembered that when she was asked to step into her mother's role as a food gatherer, she "had to sweat five days in a row before the sun came up." She recounted teachings she had learned from her grandfather, who emphasized that to gather one had "to be clean. Your thoughts, your body, everything." Malissa recounted traveling from her childhood home in Portland to gather huckleberries on Mount Adams in the summer and participating in sweats as part of that experience. This association between traditional resource gathering and the transmission of cultural knowledge is continued through a huckleberry gathering camp that Toby and his partner, Julia, have hosted in summer at Mount Adams since the late 1990s, where they introduce new generations to making sweat.

Before hunting, boys and men were expected to sweat. Alphonse remembered sweating before fall hunting, at hunting camp, as a boy in the 1920s. Mona recalled that her grandfather expected boys and men to sweat for three days before hunting. One reason given was that it was important to sweat so that the prey would not smell you and know you were coming. Linda's mother always told her brothers, before they went hunting, to sweat: "Cleanse your body, cleanse your soul before you go out there. If you don't do that, whatever you're going after is going to know you're coming because you're dirty."

When someone dies, family members are encouraged to sweat for several days for cleansing and for release. And those who tend to, or "dress," the dead by washing and dressing the body as part of funeral services are to sweat for cleansing and protection as a dimension of those responsibilities. Those who tend the dead were traditionally restricted from doing certain things for themselves during times when they are actively caring for someone recently deceased, sometimes including preparing the sweat itself. Mona remembered that in her childhood, her family provided daily sweats for Molly Minthorn, who held that traditional role, thus assisting her and the whole community by making it possible for Molly to fulfill her ritual duties.

When someone who is the keeper of a sweathouse or who is otherwise closely associated with a sweathouse dies, that house is to be burned down. A lodge may be rebuilt in the same location or a new location, depending on the best judgment of those who may carry on that lodge. As Les stressed, doing so is "a way of cleansing" and of recognizing that "not only did they physically pass away, their spirit needed to be cleansed from that house." In talking about this practice,

Ron highlighted that these steps and others are taken in part to emphasize the importance of life while acknowledging death. Through these measures people place the focus on the living and on the earth as the eternal home of the ancestors.

Toby had a powerful interpretation of the significance of burning down and rebuilding a sweat lodge after an elder's death, as happened with his grandfather. "When [Ike] passed, we burned it down," he said. "Everything that he did, that he taught, goes up with him. It's up to us to rebuild, to remember everything that he said. And when we rebuild and we bring back what he said, then it becomes ours." The elders' knowledge becomes part of the new generation through its practice and renewal.

Prayer is integral to every sweat, and in that sense every sweat is ceremony. Over and over again, people emphasized that prayer is not understood as asking for something but instead is about expressing gratitude. "Everything that I've come across in my life had something to do with sweat," Toby reflected. "You don't go there to pray for something that's better. You go there for what it is, you're thankful for the day. You're thankful that things are going to get better. You're thankful that you've earned teachings. You're thankful that you remember teachings. You're thankful you're gonna teach. You're thankful that somebody might remember your teachings. You don't know if any of that is going to happen but you have to go in and pray for it."

Ron's uncle taught that in prayer one was to "give thanks, pray for your people. That's the real purpose, acknowledging the Creator, having good thoughts for your people." When discussing the variety of prayers that might be offered in the sweat lodge, Les reinforced the flexibility of the practice: "Whoever is in there has their own prayer words, nothing seems to be rehearsed, just whatever comes out of your heart, the need you have to express yourself to Old Man, Qíiwn." He continued: "The principle's always the same. Take care of your body, take care of your heart, all your relatives that are living, those that are sick, get you through the day. If you can't get yourself healthy, you can't help your elders, your brothers, your sisters." Going through the act of making sweat is ultimately a ceremony of thanksgiving and caretaking, of self and others.

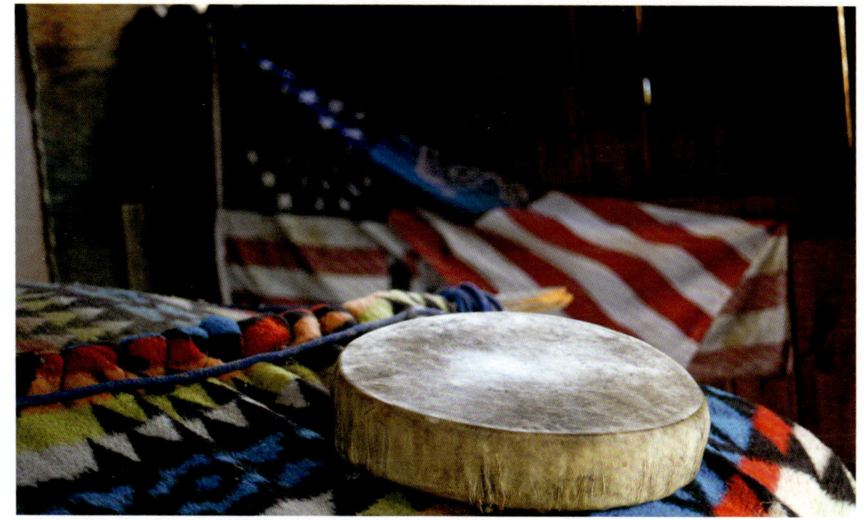

Drum resting on top of sweat lodge, with American flag in background, 2016. Out of view to the left is the flag of the Confederated Tribes of the Umatilla Indian Reservation. Photograph by Patrice Hall Walters , CTUIR member.

Re-creating for a New Day

In the story of the creation of the sweat at the beginning of this chapter, Spilyáy tells the people not only how to sweat but also why: for giving thanks, for cleansing, and for the chance to be reborn. After retelling the story in our conversation, Toby summed up the renewing power that the sweat offers: "It's the beginning, it's the creation, it's the creation of who you are. You're re-creating yourself for a new day, for a new time, to move on. Everything that happened from before you sweat that day, the sweat before, everything that happened within that time, that's going into the Old Man, the Creator. That's going to take it, that's going to comfort you." Through the experience of entering the womb of the lodge and emerging at the end of the sweat, the self is reborn, prepared for another day of life.

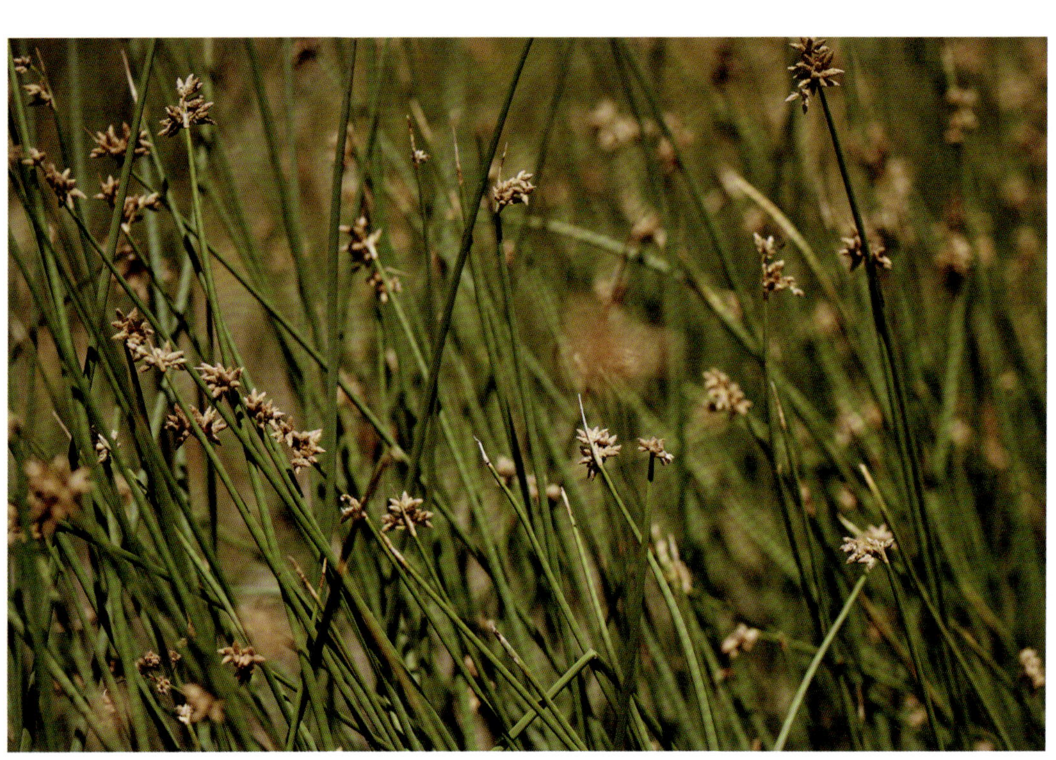

CHAPTER 9

TULE IS EVERYWHERE, FROM BIRTH TO DEATH

The Confederated Tribes of Warm Springs

Tule is everywhere, explained Brigette McConville: "It's from birth to death." Mats made from tule stems are essential elements of weddings as well as other ceremonies held and experienced by Warm Springs people from the time they are born until the moment their bodies are readied for burial.

Brigette, joined by fellow Warm Springs tribal members Rosalind (Rosie) Johnson, Rayann Katchia Satanus, and Natalie Moody, told me more about these customary practices. These women explained that large tule mats are used at naming ceremonies; at weddings; at feasts in the longhouse, where they are laid on the floor as tables; and at funerals to wrap the body of the deceased. Smaller tule mats are used for placemats, decorations, purses, headbands, and necklaces. The largest tule mats become coverings for pole-frame lodges, sheltering the bodies and families of the community. The tule plant, when young, can even be eaten. At weddings a large tule mat, usually made by the bride's family, is an essential element of the ceremony, with bride and groom stepping onto it for their vows. "We stood on one, when we got married,"

facing page:
Tule growing on the Confederated Tribes of Warm Springs Reservation, 2021. Photograph by Frank Miller.

recounted Brigette. "When you come together on your mat, you are two people. When you get married, you step back onto the earth as one. The mat is the place that brings you together."[1]

This conversation unfolded at The Museum at Warm Springs, in Warm Springs, Oregon, over the course of a day in August 2015, where curator Natalie Moody had invited these tribal members to talk with me about contemporary wedding traditions. While our talk wandered

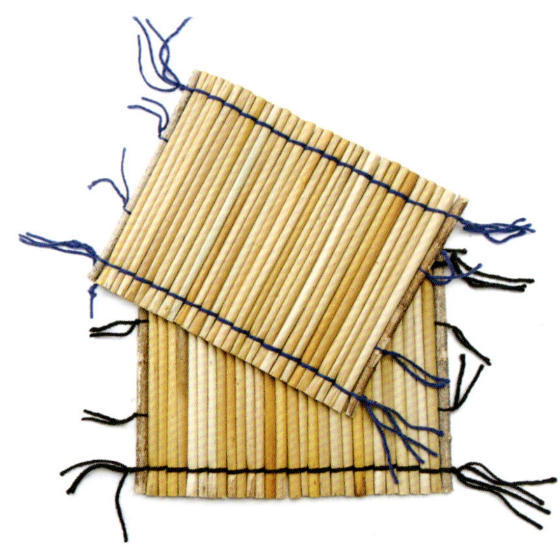

Tule mats, 2021. Rosalind (Rosie) Johnson. Tule, yarn. Photograph by Frank Miller.

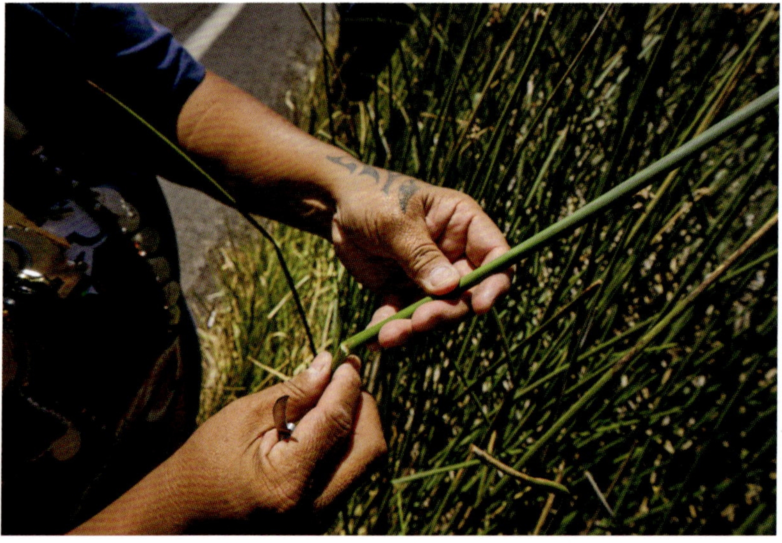

Rosalind (Rosie) Johnson of Warm Springs cutting tule to reveal its interior, 2021. Photograph by Frank Miller.

across many elements of wedding preparations and events, the women kept circling back to the humble tule. Also known as bulrush, tule is a member of the sedge family native to the western United States and is ubiquitous in the Columbia River Plateau region, inhabiting wet areas such as marshes, swamps, shorelines, and roadside ditches. Its insulating and cushioning qualities are what make it so useful and versatile—the semirigid stems are composed of spongy tissue that is full of air pockets. When joined together in mats, tule stems can serve as cushions for sitting or sleeping, and as siding and roofing for traditional pole-frame longhouses. In winter the stems absorb moisture and then swell, keeping out wind, cold, and precipitation. In summer the stems shrink, allowing for circulation on hot days.[2]

Mats made from tule accompany Warm Springs people through life as tangible markers for rites of passage, often providing a foundation or stage for the event itself, as they do at weddings. The major life events of the new family created by a marriage—children's births, namings, first hunts, first fish caught, first roots gathered, adult children's marriages, funerals—are often underlined by the presence of tule mats. In Brigette's words, the mat is "the place that brings you together," not only for the singular occasion of a wedding but again and again through the course of family life.

Just as tule mats are foundational to traditional Warm Springs weddings, so is what the community refers to as "Indian trading" and what early ethnographers and pioneers oversimplified as "bride purchase."[3] Typically, the groom's family presented the prospective bride's family with high-value goods such as horses and dried meat or fish in shaptakai (*painted hide cases or parfleches*). The bride's family reciprocated by agreeing to the marriage as well as with gifts to the groom's family of objects associated with women's work and knowledge, such as woven bags containing prized foods that might include dried roots.

The Museum at Warm Springs staff curated the community's contribution to the 2008 *Art of Ceremony* exhibit: a fully outfitted wedding party with figures of the bride, an adult female helper, two young girls, and a groom with a male helper. The decision to focus on weddings grew out of the fact that the museum had long featured a similar installation that had been prepared after many years of community conversations and input, so the staff felt comfortable in having this ceremony

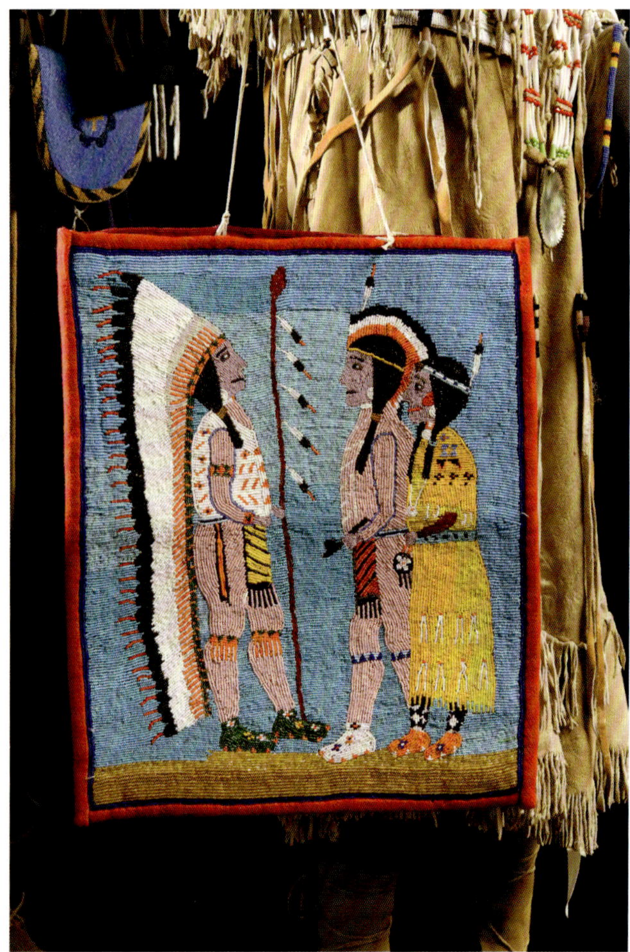

Beaded bag depicting a wedding party, date unknown. Beads, wool felt, corduroy, buckskin. Collection of The Museum at Warm Springs. Gift from Ursula Little. Photograph by Frank Miller. Courtesy of Frank Miller and Willamette University.

become the portrait for their community. All the regalia was borrowed from The Museum at Warm Springs collection, itself made up of tribal families' heirlooms. One of the most treasured objects in the display was the mid-twentieth-century dentalium bridal veil donated by elder Adeline Moses Miller, who had received it as a keepsake from her aunt. The veil is a symbol of the bride's family status and traditional wealth and is a manifestation of the customary knowledge carried by the bride. Front and center in the display, perhaps unnoticed by many visitors or seen merely as a backdrop, was a long and narrow tule mat, heaped with trade goods such as shaptakai, corn-husk bags, and Klickitat-style berry baskets. The effect was one of lavish abundance.

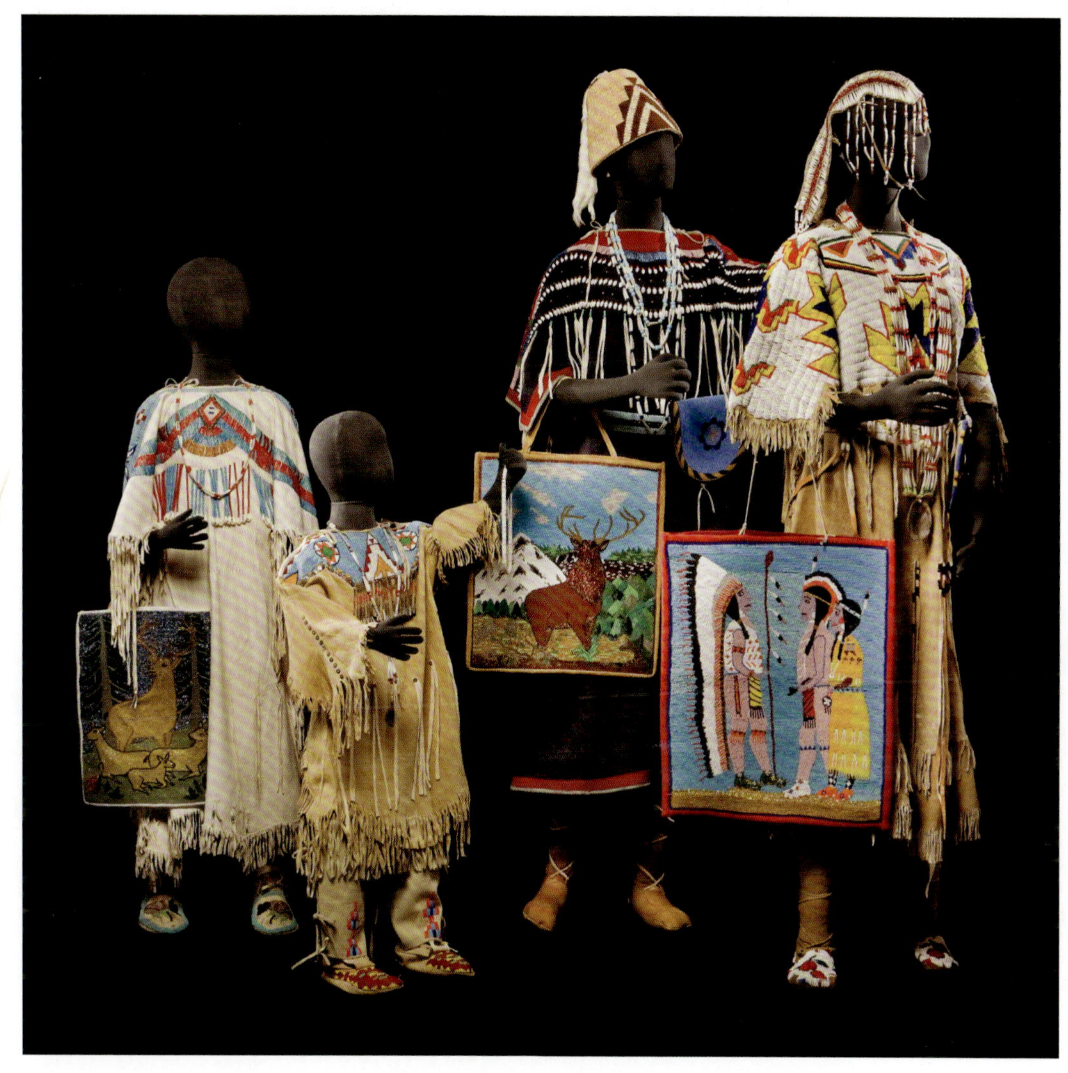

Bride's wedding party, dates unknown. All regalia, Collection of The Museum at Warm Springs.
Photograph by Frank Miller. Courtesy of Frank Miller and Willamette University.

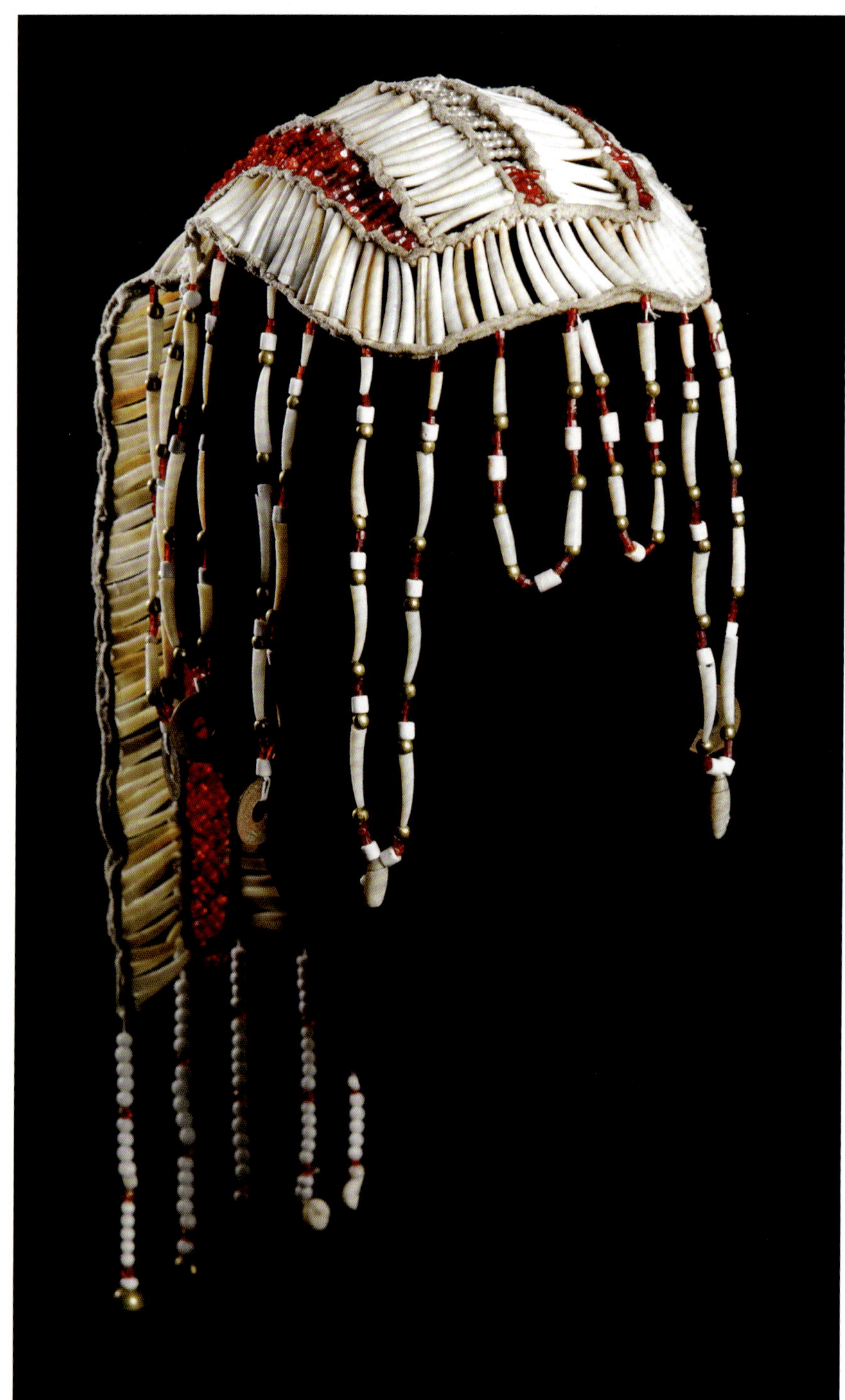

Wedding veil, early 1900s. Dentalium, metal coins, beads, deer hooves. Collection of The Museum at Warm Springs. Gift from Adeline Miller. Photograph by Frank Miller. Courtesy of Frank Miller and Willamette University.

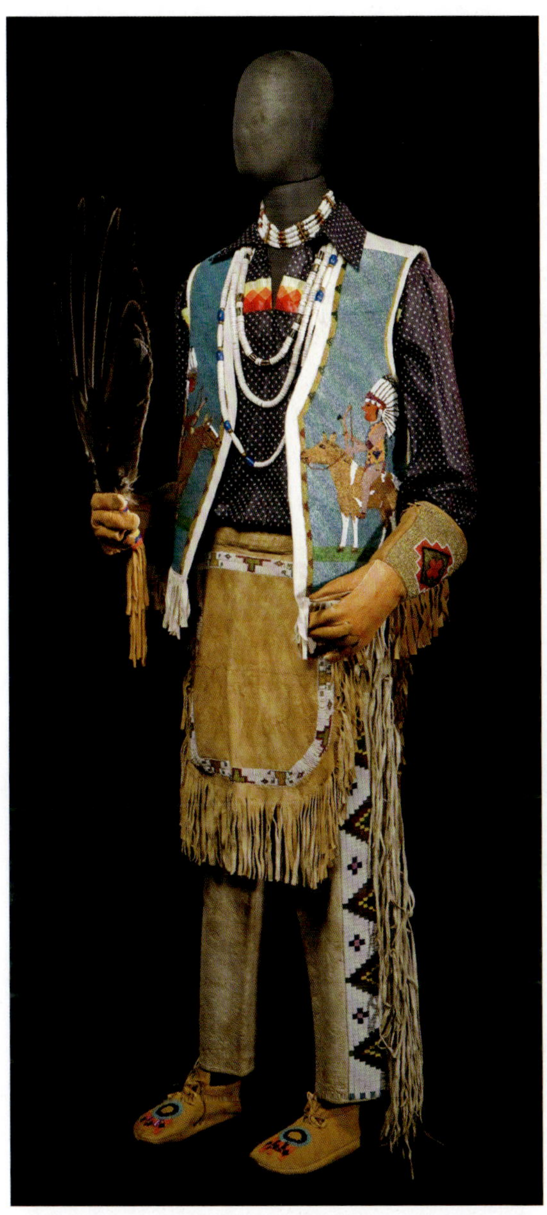

Groom's outfit, date unknown. All regalia, Collection of The Museum at Warm Springs. Photograph by Frank Miller. Courtesy of Frank Miller and Willamette University.

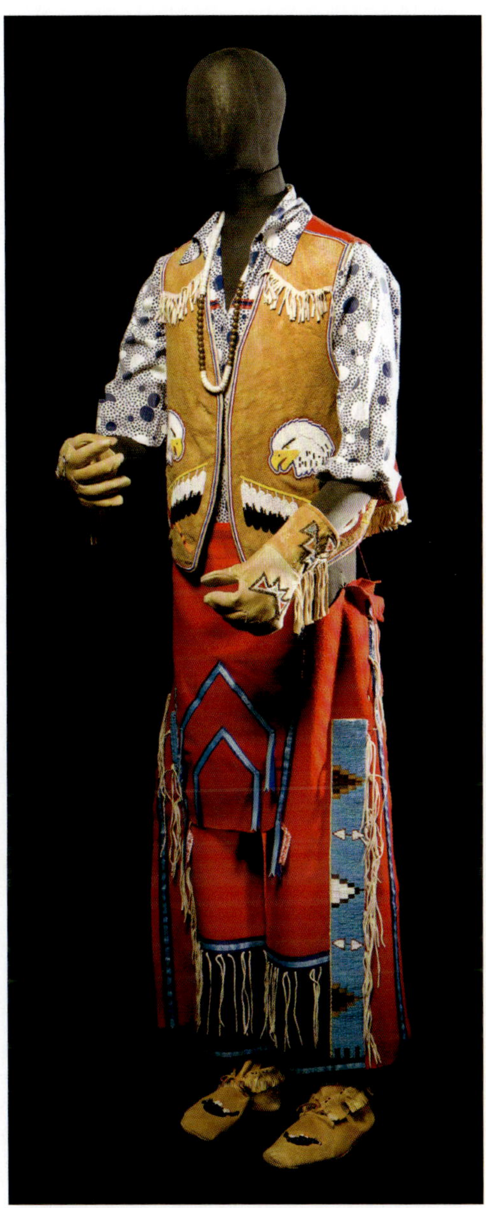

Groom's helper's outfit, date unknown. All regalia, Collection of The Museum at Warm Springs. Photograph by Frank Miller. Courtesy of Frank Miller and Willamette University.

When we came together in summer 2015 to talk about weddings, the women emphasized the preparations involved in creating the events of the day and the dynamic exchange of gifts, foods, and knowledge between extended families of newlyweds, an exchange that in their experience continues well after that day has concluded. This is part of a larger system that Elizabeth Woody, a Warm Springs poet and, since 2018, director of The Museum at Warm Springs, calls the "gifting economy," a system of reciprocal relations between people that also involves people's reciprocal relationships with the land and its resources.[4] While the reciprocal social relations underlying gift-giving in Native American and other societies have long been noted by non-Native scholars, Woody's inclusion of land and species as actors participating with people in the formation of those social relations expands the reach of the concept and is more reflective of the way many Warm Springs people live their experience. The accounts shared in this chapter reveal the way preparations for weddings and the associated trading between families can bring people into reciprocal relations with one another as well as with the land and its resources.

Trading through the Lifetime

Brigette grew up in an extended family rooted in such a system of reciprocity. Her parents, Brenda Kalama Scott and Gordon Scott, were married in 1966, at sixteen and twenty-one years respectively. Throughout their married life, Brigette's father joked, "I raised my wife," a statement her mother found irritating. Brigette described theirs as an arranged marriage in which her father's family chose her mother because of her family's chiefly line (Brenda Kalama's father was Paiute chief Nick Kalama). Both families were also descended from the Klickitat, Yakama, and other groups associated for generations with lands along the Columbia River. The marriage endured for their lifetimes, reinforced by the exchange of resources and knowledge across family lines.

By the mid-twentieth century, when the Scotts married, the reservation of the Confederated Tribes of Warm Springs was home to diverse groups of people whose original homelands had extended from the Columbia River on the north to the arid high desert of southeastern Oregon on the south. In a treaty signed in 1855 two distinct groups of

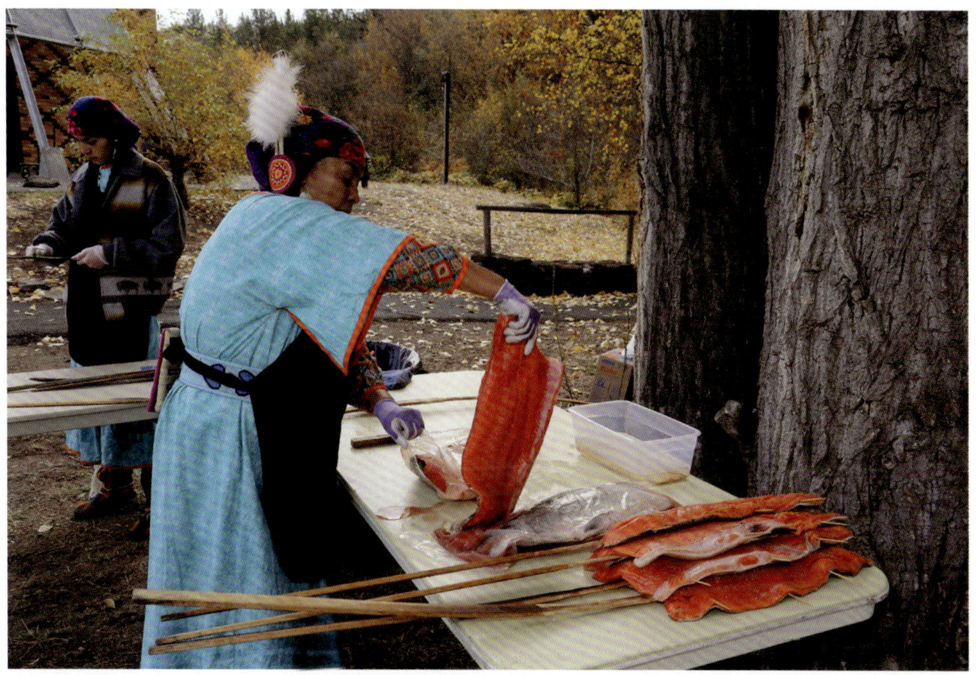

river-based peoples—the Chinookan-speaking Wasco of the Lower Columbia and the Sahaptian-speaking Tenino or Warm Springs bands from farther up the Columbia, near The Dalles and the Deschutes and John Day Rivers—ceded their nearly 10 million-acre territory for an inland reservation of about 640,000 acres of timber and high desert. This relocation destabilized the pre-reservation livelihood and status of the Wasco and Warm Springs Tribes, which were interdependent upon their respective geographic positions on the Columbia River and its tributaries. Each had a salmon-based economy and thrived on strategic trading that took place at Celilo Falls, the Columbia River market and gathering place that drew tribes from hundreds of miles away. The Wasco groups lived in cedar-plank houses akin to those up and down the Pacific Northwest coast, while the Warm Springs bands, in their arid easterly homelands, moved with the seasons, following the flow of natural resources, erecting tule mat–covered dwellings for shelter.[5]

The ancestral land of the Paiute people was the Great Basin, a desert environment that supported fewer persons per square mile than the Columbia River and its inland plateau. The Paiute spoke a language

Brigette McConville, preparing salmon for traditional barbecuing, 2018. The Museum at Warm Springs Treaty Conference, Warm Springs, Oregon. Photograph courtesy of The Museum at Warm Springs.

from the Uto-Aztecan family, which extends over a very large geographic area from present-day Montana to Mesoamerica. Today, Paiute peoples are associated with several reservations in many western states. The US Army moved groups of Northern Paiute to the southern part of the Warm Springs Reservation in 1879 and 1884. One of the ironies of these moves is that, historically, the Northern Paiute and the Wasco had been rivals if not enemies. But by the late 1930s they and the Warm Springs Tribes had officially formed a confederacy and a tribal council form of elected government under the Indian Reorganization Act of 1934. In recognition of Indigenous leadership systems, the confederacy retained a structure of hereditary chiefs from each of the three Tribes, in addition to the elected tribal council.[6] It is from these hereditary chiefly lines that both Brenda Kalama and Gordon Scott descended.

The Scotts married in the 1960s, in the decade after the 1957 flooding of Celilo Falls caused by the completion of the Bonneville and The Dalles Dams over the protests of the Columbia River fishing tribes. The 1855 treaties signed by these tribes reserved rights to fishing, hunting, and gathering in their usual and accustomed places in ceded territories, and that foresight on the part of the treaty signers has been essential to the ongoing subsistence, commercial, and ceremonial economies of the tribes. Brigette's livelihood today is tied to these rights. "When my parents came together, both families were fishers," she said. "This is a continued tradition we practice today."

Knowledge about fishing and about the river was only one type of resource that Brigette and her siblings inherited from their parents' union. From her parents' wedding onward, each side of the family had someone responsible for carrying out trading. These two women—her paternal relative Elizabeth "Lizzy" Rhoan and her maternal grandmother, Viola Kalama—made sure that every key time in the children's lives was recognized with a celebration—sometimes formal, sometimes informal—that was accompanied by an exchange of gifts. For example, when Brigette and her sisters and brothers had their first traditional food-harvesting experiences, she remembered, "Our first gatherings, those were trade times. First hunting, fishing, were trade times. Whenever it happened, it was a cause for trade. It wasn't always great big, wasn't a big shindig at the longhouse." Instead of an elaborate production, the emphasis was upon acknowledging the occasion and expressing gratitude for it.

The two women in charge of trading also made sure Brigette and her siblings received a traditional education by arranging for them to receive training from knowledgeable people and by compensating those people with gifts. As Brigette recalled: "They would even come together and they would take us to people. There was this lady in Yakama, her name was Hazel Umtuch. They would give her things to show us how to do something. That was the family coming together to learn, to teach us. So we would go over there every year and go gather that little Indian carrot [*Daucus pusillus*]." Year after year, Hazel took Brigette and her sister to gather at Medicine Valley, on land that turned out to be their father's. The land was ultimately inherited after their father's passing, and the daughters have continued to use and share the knowledge of the land they developed in childhood.

Brigette and her sister learned other traditional skills, such as how to make and bead moccasins. As she remembered: "Another celebration or trading was with another woman [at Yakama], Rosanna Iukes, who would teach us how to make moccasins. We would sit with her for a week and make a pair of moccasins the way she did it. Then they'd come together, Lizzy and my grandma; they'd either take us over there or come to pick us up, and they'd always have a bundle. There were several people like that." The bundle contained gifts for the teacher who had so generously given of her knowledge to Brigette and her sister.

Brigette referenced another experience from childhood to illustrate how her grandmother and mother impressed upon her the value of tradition:

When I was eight years old, my grandma held up eight dollars and a corn-husk bag. And I wanted the eight dollars. My mom pinched me: "You go get that bag!" So I was like, "I'll take the bag then," all upset. Then she put the money in the bag! Then, every year after that on Christmas and our birthday, my sister and I go pick something out. Since I was eight, I've taken a corn-husk bag. And my sister has taken these big pictorial [beaded] bags. She has all elk and deer. When Shawn and I got married, [Grandma] said, "I have one corn-husk [bag] left that will go to his mom." So she put stuff in it. She was telling them the story of how [I have] all [her] corn-husk bags! So through time, she's given a lot away. They went to good homes; we take care of them.

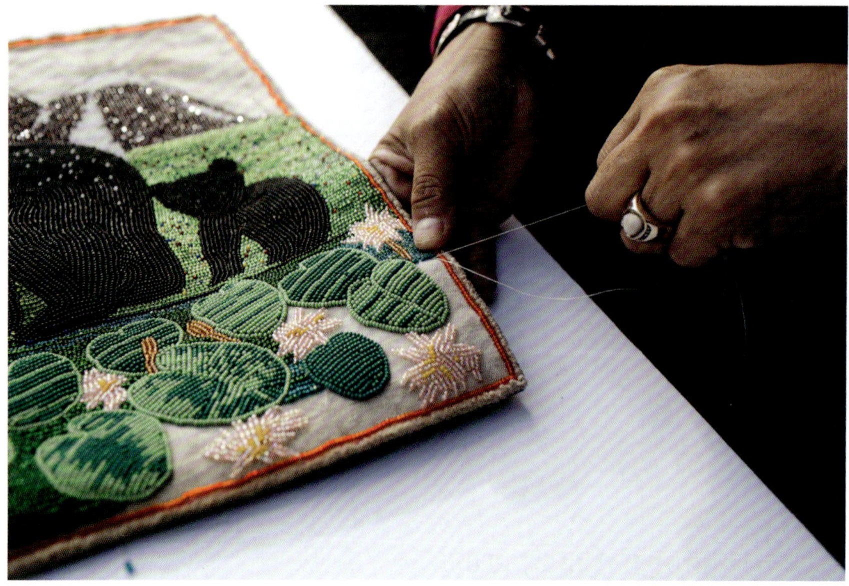

Brigette McConville, beading a flat bag, 2016. Pictorial design of a mother bear and cub, with a foreground of water lilies and background of mountain peaks. Photograph by Micah Fischer. Courtesy of WildCraft Studio School.

Later, Brigette continued these traditions when she had children of her own. When her daughters were given their Indian names as babies, "they got traded on" with celebrations happening in the home. Once again the elder women in the family "made sure it happened." Before Brigette's son turned a year old, he was given the Indian name of his great-grandfather, a Paiute chief. She explained: "It's a big responsibility to carry a name like that." In recognition, the naming was held in the Warm Springs Agency Longhouse, with many people in attendance. Her son, now an adult, is a commercial fisherman, and in Brigette's eyes he has lived up to the high stature of his name in the way he works hard and lives his life with integrity.

Longhouses on the Warm Springs and other Columbia River Plateau reservations (including the Umatilla) are home to the Wáašat or Seven Drum religion, considered a way of life by those who follow it. Most practitioners are of Sahaptian background; the system is grounded in ancient traditional beliefs about the responsibilities of the people toward creation and the Creator. Weekly Sunday services are held in longhouses, as are ceremonies celebrating first foods and rites of passage. Hand drums, usually seven in number, commence the services, and bells are rung in concert with the singing of Wáašat songs. Wáašat followers may also attend Christian churches, and elements of Christian beliefs are present in longhouse services. Architecturally, contemporary longhouses are fully modern buildings that evoke the rectangular pole-frame and tule-mat lodges for which they are named; in addition to a central meeting space, longhouses have large kitchens equipped to cook meals for sizable groups.[7]

Although both regular services and those for major life passages take place in the longhouse, according to Brigette, other occasions are "more personal" and unfold in the settings where they occur. She recalled her daughters' first root-gathering, an important event in a girl's life and a marker of her progress toward adulthood: "My daughters, their first gathering, we ate the roots with the elders. Lizzy just happened to be with us and Grandma, my mom and my sister and two aunts, I and my two daughters. And we danced and sang with her roots and ate them right there in the root fields." In this instance the "trade" received for the girls' first harvest was the companionship and sharing of traditions by four generations of Warm Springs women. In Brigette's family Indian trading has been a dynamic reciprocal system of knowledge and resource sharing that has spanned the full course of several generations. Weddings themselves are a single point in time, and a generative one in a stream of many others.

Portraits of Contemporary Weddings

Today, wedding ceremonies at Warm Springs range from noontime courthouse weddings tucked into a workday to services held at the reservation's Baptist or Catholic or Presbyterian churches, the Indian Shaker Church, or one of the longhouses. Rayann Katchia and Kurtis Satanus decided to have a traditional longhouse wedding, on very short notice. Most such weddings require at least a year's worth of planning, whereas they held theirs at the Warm Springs Agency Longhouse in October 2014 with only two weeks' preparation time. Rayann reflected on why it was important to the couple to have a longhouse wedding even though they had been legally married by a judge in a simple ceremony in Madras the week before: "The whole point of the wedding, the ceremony, we didn't look at it like it was for us. It was like getting this side and this side and putting it as one. That was the whole core of it that we wanted. The week before the whole wedding thing we were legally married, but we wanted to make it about just the family."

Rayann explained that it was her husband who wanted to have the traditional wedding—and wanted it quickly. The rush was based on a practicality: the couple wanted to work toward buying a home and had learned that financing a loan would be easier if they were married, something they already had decided to do. At a family barbeque, after being asked when they were going to get married, Kurtis announced: "In two weeks." Right then and there, members of the two families sat down and began to "figure out who was going to make what." As Rayann remembered: "We went around the table to figure out what people could do. We put my sister at the end of the table and we said you have to write this all down." Rayann called her sister "the glue" who kept everything organized. The families got to work sorting things out: "Everything kind of fell into place."

Both families contributed. "What I liked was my husband's family stepped up right away," Rayann explained. Kurtis's aunt offered to make the bridal dress, while Rayann's aunt wanted to be the one to stitch the shells on it. Having each side of the family involved in creating her dress meant "it's like two on one." Another relative made all the ribbon shirts

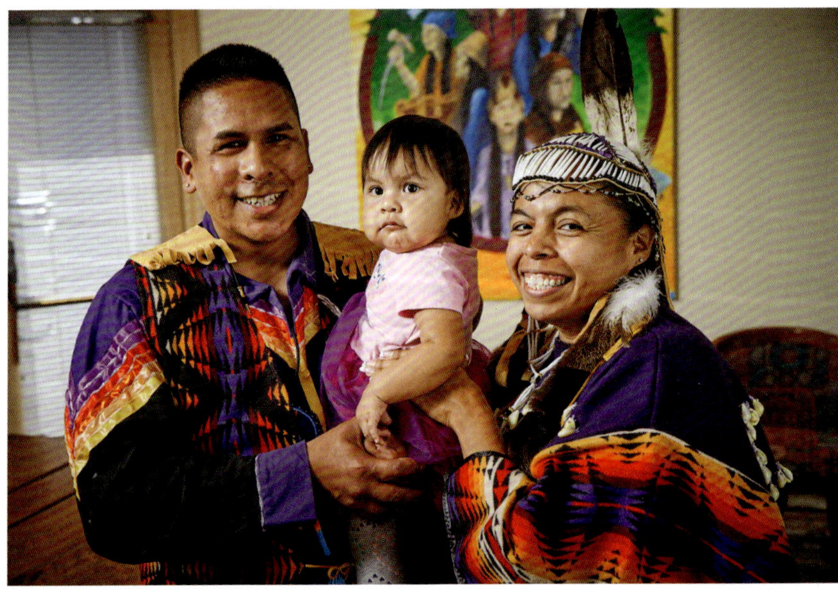

Kurtis and Rayann Satanus in their 2014 wedding outfits, with daughter Kataleya, 2021. Photograph by Frank Miller.

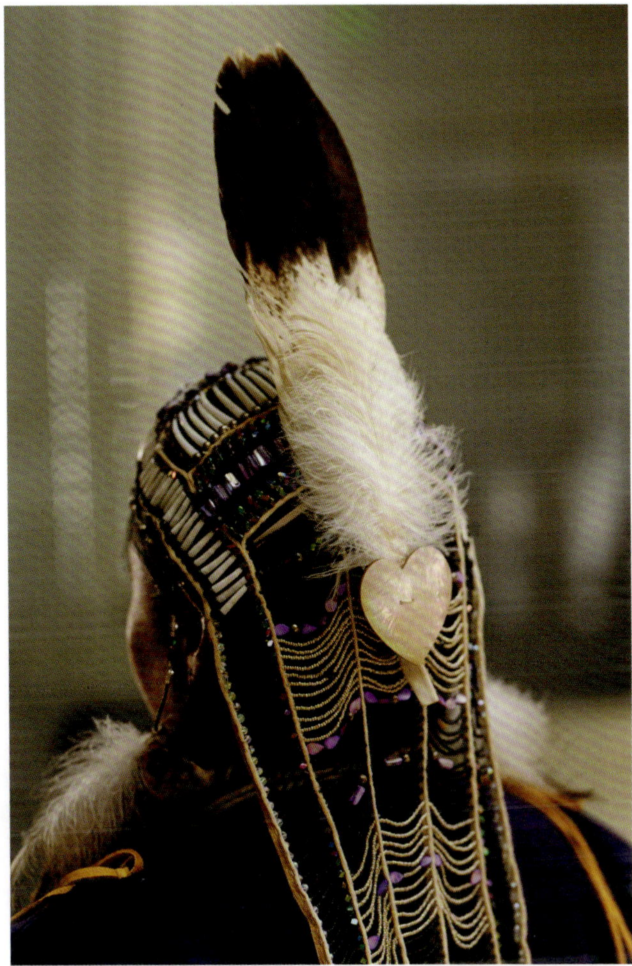

Rayann Satanus's wedding veil, made by her maternal aunt, Andrea Kalama, 2014. Photograph by Frank Miller.

for the groomsmen, and yet another made the dresses for the women and girls in the wedding party. Customarily the bride's mother would make the veil, but Rayann had lost her mother when Rayann was thirteen. Her mother's sister made a traditional veil with dentalia and beads, providing a connection to her mother and a way of having her present at the wedding.

While the veil and other elements of the wedding party attire were the responsibility of female relatives from both sides, the men of Rayann's family provided gifts as well. After the wedding was announced, Rayann's brother and her sister's boyfriend went hunting and came back with two deer, which they dressed, smoked, and divided into parcels. They also prepared gift bags to hand out to Rayann's husband's side of the family at the wedding. As Rayann explained: "That was from our side going to them."

The short notice for the wedding left little time for all these preparations. Many elements fell together at the last minute on the wedding day. Rayann's father asked a relative who lived in the Willamette Valley to make the all-important tule mat. When Rayann arrived at the longhouse, the mat was nowhere to be seen. She remembered: "Everyone started panicking because it wasn't there yet. Of all people to walk in, Grandma Millie walked in and she stared at me and I was just looking at her and she said, 'Where's your mat?' [I said,] 'Um, it's coming.' She said, 'I'll be back.' So she left and she came back and she said, 'I have two that were given to me. I'm going to hang onto them. If they don't show up, pick which one you want to stand on.'"

Rayann knew that "you can't do anything without that mat there." She had to leave the longhouse to pick up the men's shirts, and by the time she arrived back, the purpose-made tule mat had arrived. "But it came," she recalled. "We did stand on it." With relief, she and her husband said their wedding vows as they took their place on the tule mat. The officiant was a longtime coworker at the Warm Springs Tribes' Forestry Program, whom Rayann considers to be a grandfather figure. Having lost both of her grandfathers several years ago, Rayann chose this older man as someone who was close to "fitting in those kind of shoes," someone she respects and looks up to.

Rayann had never before attended a traditional wedding until going to her own, even though she had been raised going to Wáašat services in the longhouse. But that upbringing alone could not have prepared her to be familiar with all she needed to know, as would be true of many young people getting married in most American religious communities today. Nor was her husband fully knowledgeable. With the wedding and in her married life since, Rayann explained, "I'm learning as I go along. I was brought up traditionally, but that's with feasts at the longhouse. I wasn't taught every single thing. It's a learning process. So I'm taking everything that is around me, I'm taking it in. I've got to remember this, I got to remember this for me, because when me and my husband do have kids, I do want them to learn about all of this stuff, I want them to know all of it. I want them to grow up with it, with everything that we were taught."

In their discussions about how they want to raise their children, Rayann and her husband agree they want to infuse their family lives with traditional practices: "When we talk about kids," she said, "that's what we both want. We do want them to have that traditional thing in their life, from the day they open their eyes." Rayann is humble about the limits of her own knowledge and realistic about how much she has to learn: "I'm picking up everything, 'cause I wasn't taught as much as I'd like to know. Even if I don't do it daily, I'd like to know it." Rayann reflected on the reasons she values learning about and nurturing traditional practices:

> I feel tradition is very important. And I heard this on the [reservation] radio: [the announcer] kept saying that the Creator blesses you with something and it's your job to take care of it. You are put here for a reason, and you are responsible to take of this, you have a purpose. So take care of it, otherwise it can be taken from you. That kind of hit the nail on the head. For me, I just feel that the tradition part is very, very important. I look at it like it's gold. It's so precious and it's so secure. It's like your beating heart.

Brigette's relationship to traditional knowledge, particularly regarding weddings, differs from Rayann's as a result of the education she received during her upbringing. In addition, Brigette is a generation older than Rayann. She devoted a year to preparing for her second wedding in 2014, held at one of her family's fishing sites on the Columbia River. "Everything we wore, I made," Brigette recalled. "I made vests for my brothers. The girls were in buckskin dresses." She made her own dress, of satin with a cape adorned with elk teeth, as well as her husband's outfit, complete with beaded leggings. Her mother made her veil, which extends below the waist and is decorated with eagle claws and elk teeth. Brigette explained the significance of the veil's length and complexity: "Grandma always said the elaboration of your veil represents the traditional knowledge you carry. They made it long. They made it nice."

The elements of the wedding feast took Brigette a year to accumulate, because Native foods have to be harvested when they are ready, then dried or otherwise prepared: "[We] provided all the food, it was all traditional, everything. So for the whole year, we put food away. We had moose meat, elk meat, deer meat, then all the fish. Salmon, steelhead, sockeye, sturgeon, eel, smelt. Then all the roots: bitterroot, little carrot, wapato [*an edible aquatic tuber*]. I gathered wapato that October. We made moss [*black tree lichen, prepared by slow roasting*], we made camas [*an edible bulb, also roasted*]. All the berries: chokecherries, huckleberries, serviceberries."

Brigette also made tule place mats for the guests, who took them home as favors along with small gunnysacks filled with dried fish and meat. She made baskets with special food gifts and beaded items for elders she had invited, particularly those who had played a mentoring role for her and her husband in the months as they were preparing to wed. Outside of the wedding itself, there were other forms of giving. As Brigette remembered: "His family told my grandma and my mom and all the women [in my family], you'll never have to fish again. We'll bring you fish, we'll bring you deer. My husband brought four moose back last year. So that was their way of giving. And I do lots of canning for his family. And I make a lot of beadwork for them, and my grandma has given them a lot."

A newlywed couple also receives gifts, and blankets are usually among those gifts. Across Indian country, especially in the greater Northwest, Pendleton blankets are another highly valued gift associated with major life passages.[8] Blankets—like tule mats—are given and received throughout the life cycle, at the birth of children, namings, high school and college graduations, all honorings of any sort, and may accompany the deceased at burial. A Pendleton blanket plays a role during the wedding ceremony. The wedding vows are generally brief and may be similar to conventional Christian vows; they may include readings from the Bible or be written by the couple themselves. At the end of the vows, while the couple is still standing on the tule mat, they may be wrapped in a Pendleton blanket as an expression of their union and new status.

After the wedding itself is long over, giving continues between the now-connected families. Rayann recounted that during the Christmas after their wedding, her husband's grandmother gave him a pair of fully beaded moccasins. Then, she told Rayann, "I need your measurements," to which Rayann responded, "Measurements for what?" Laughing, she gave Rayann a paper bag with which to trace her feet, and said, "Before I go, I want to make sure that all my girls are taken care of." Rayann explained: "That was pretty much telling me that I was one of her girls now, and she told me I don't have to worry about nothing. It shocked me. I was trying not to cry. I never had anybody do that. 'Cause when we were growing up, it was a lot different. Just like that sense-of-security type thing. So it will go back and forth." Given her lack of experience with these kinds of relationships growing up, Rayann said she's now being guided by members of her extended family who do have such a background: "My brother-in-law Corbett, he always reassures me, 'You have to take care of them now. That's how we were raised, you have to take care of them, that's your family now, like they were your own. They're obviously doing the same in return.'"

When Death Separates the Spouses

At one point in the conversation, Natalie Moody reminded us that traditionally, when a marriage continues until the end of one partner's life, the family relationships that scaffolded the couple during their lives come into play to support the mate left behind. Rosalind (Rosie) Johnson, who is an undertaker in the Wáašat tradition on the Warm Springs Reservation, gave a general account of what happens ceremonially when a spouse dies. A dimension of Johnson's role is to assist the family, including quickly making the tule mats needed for elements of the funeral rites.

In Johnson's experience families of both spouses come forward to take care of the surviving mate. On the day of the funeral, very early in the morning, before daylight, family and friends arrive at the couple's home to accompany the survivor through the events to come. The surviving spouse is changed into new, clean black clothes and shoes by helpers of the same gender. Often this change takes place behind the "curtain" of a blanket, which is dropped when the spouse is ready to emerge, dressed for a year of mourning. During the time of preparation, according to Rosie, the assistants are talking, explaining to the bereaved why they are doing what they are doing. One practice is that the hair of a widower or widow is cut, signaling to others, just as the black garments do, that he or she is in mourning. The shorn hair is saved and kept with other hair that has been shed or cut over a lifetime in a custom that continues to be followed today by Rosie and many other Warm Springs people, with the expectation that this part of their bodies will eventually be buried with them.

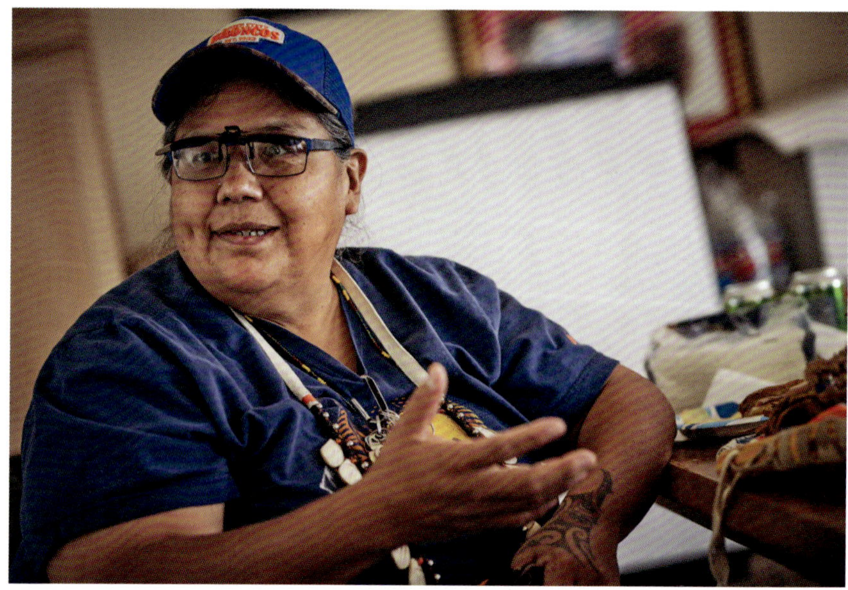

Rosalind (Rosie) Johnson, at The Museum at Warm Springs, 2021. Photograph by Frank Miller.

In funerals held at a longhouse, the body of the deceased will likely be clothed and then wrapped in layers of blankets, hides, and/or a long tule mat, and laid in a casket. A smaller tule mat is placed on the ground underneath the casket, a foundation for this life transition just as in other passages. After the funeral the body is taken to the cemetery, where the tule mat is placed into the grave with the casket. The mourners return to the longhouse, where the officiant leads them in a "cry service" that, as Rosie explained, "opens up their hearts to cry, releasing themselves to hurt." The leader talks about what the person was known for and enjoyed, perhaps showing favorite personal possessions to illustrate the stories. Those gathered weep and let go of their grief, knowing that to do otherwise could make them sick.

A meal and giveaway follow. The leader of the Wáašat service conducts the meal, calling out the traditional foods (roots, berries, game, fish), giving thanks, singing a song of gratitude, and finishing with a call, čúuš (the Sahaptian word for water), at which time everyone drinks water, sacred and essential to all life. A small tule mat with eating utensils is placed at the head of the table for the deceased, whose food is served first before the rest of those gathered may eat. The mat and utensils are later placed at the head of the freshly covered grave.

At the end of the meal, storytelling about the life and impact of the loved one begins. Rosie described what happens, based on a recent experience at a funeral: "They start that side of the table; each one will say something. No one can leave till they say something. You have to sit there, you have to hear every word that has been said. They're encouraging the mate, the children, the grandchildren that are all sitting there. They're encouraging them. They bring out the stories of what things this person did in their life. A lot of them brought out crazy stories, places they traveled with them. Everyone is laughing then. That's part of the medicine, is laughing." The giveaway then begins—or may have even preceded the meal, if the food was not yet ready. Everyone who has helped with the funeral—longhouse leaders, drummers, singers, cooks, those assisting the family in any way—receives gifts and personal belongings from the deceased that have been assembled for the occasion.

During the year of mourning, the extended family prepares for the memorial, held approximately a year after the death, where everyone who has helped is given gifts that range from traditional beadwork or bags to blankets and household goods. The surviving spouse is now encouraged to reengage in social life and discard the black clothing.

Tule, from Birth to Death

Around midafternoon that August day at The Museum at Warm Springs, Rosie brought out big bundles of tule she had harvested the year before, with the goal of having us make small mats. Rayann did not have much experience working with tule, and I had none, so Rosie focused on getting us started by teaching us how to cut the tule evenly and cleanly. She taught us how to alternate the segments so that the broader base ends would complement the narrower tops of the reeds, making a more even mat. Rosie had us use string to weave the mats together—much easier than the old way of using dogbane or Indian hemp cordage, which took a great deal of processing to make. Brigette needed no such instruction; over the course of the day she and Rosie had both described how they made many mats for many occasions, often on short notice if for a quickly organized event, as funerals often are.

Conversation turned to the harvest of tule in wetlands or seasonally wet places. Rosie spoke of her favorite locations on the reservation as well as along highways she frequents on her travels through eastern Oregon and Washington. Rosie and other harvesters like to gather tule in midsummer, after its flowers have gone to seed, but before late-summer heat makes the tule too brittle or the fall rains begin to saturate the plant. While it is not difficult to harvest tule, and children and youth can easily join in, care has to be taken not to break the long stalks as they are bundled to bring home. Once home, cut tule has to be spread out to dry for some weeks; this was one reason we were using Rosie's cache of tule she had harvested the year before.

Ending the long day of conversation by working with the tule underscored the emphasis the women had placed upon the ongoing processes behind weddings, Indian trading, feasting, and funerary rituals. The humble yet simply beautiful tule mat at *The Art of Ceremony* exhibit, though likely unnoticed by most visitors, proved foundational to the story of the wedding and of the entire life cycle, as "the place that brings you together."

CONCLUSION

"Everything emanates from our relationship with the earth," said Roberta
"Bobbie" Conner in 2014. In that conversation Bobbie was referring to
Indigenous peoples' perspectives about ceremony, specifically those of
the Columbia River Plateau, but her statement has come to have many
meanings for me in the writing of this book. As this conclusion is being
written in 2021, we are still in the midst of the global Covid-19 pandemic,
which has resulted in so much loss of life, especially for Indigenous
communities. To protect human lives in pandemic times, many of the
ceremonies described here have not been conducted since Covid-19
began. As they resume, it will be with new resonance for their capacity to
heal and renew. A flurry of ecological crises in the Pacific Northwest and
beyond—from wildfires to ice storms to droughts and unprecedented
heat waves—provide evidence of the threat posed to the earth's inhab-
itants and ecosystems by human-generated climate change. Both the
pandemic and the climate crisis are rooted in and worsened by a global
social-economic system that has relied on settler colonialism, chattel
slavery, and natural resource extraction—the racist legacies of which
have been exposed for all to see, from the militarized police violence at
Standing Rock in 2016 to the murder of George Floyd in Minneapolis
at the knee of a white police officer in 2020. Questions rage about the
nature of humanity's relationships with the earth and with each other.

One of the most powerful insights articulated by Indigenous writers and artists associated with the movement known as Indigenous Futurism is the notion that Indigenous peoples are already post-apocalypse, having experienced the devastation of multiple invasions by colonizing Europeans and centuries of subsequent violence. Indigenous Futurism is an arena of thought, art, and practice that imagines Indigenous-inspired futures while simultaneously reconceptualizing the past and present.[1] The recognition that Indigenous peoples have already suffered through many apocalypses and learned to rebuild and persist is an insight that predated the Covid-19 pandemic but has gained greater potency in the middle of it. In mid-2020 journalist Julian Brave NoiseCat wrote of the power Indigenous peoples' perspectives hold for a globe in grief: "Those who know what it means to lose our world and live might have something to lend to a broader humanity that now faces its own existential crises in the form of disease and climate change."[2] Turning this insight to the accounts in this book, there are deep lessons here about how the work of ceremony is more than ritual expression: it is collective world-making. The art of ceremony makes a difference because it facilitates more than survival; it creates conditions for renewal and constructive responses to even the most devastating of losses, whether environmental, social, or historical. As NoiseCat writes: "In a society built atop our graves, survival has become an act of resistance." He issues an invitation to all readers: "After the pandemic but as the climate crisis unfolds, maybe more people will understand what it means to survive and still dream, like us."[3]

My hope is that this book contributes to the understanding of Indigenous history and survivance and inspires Indigenous and non-Indigenous communities alike to dream better futures. It adds to the growing body of scholarship, anchored in the work of Indigenous authors, that explores how acts of cultural revitalization and reconceptualization heal wounds and support change.[4] Those sharing their stories in this book do not compartmentalize the work of cultural revitalization from other nation-building and world-making efforts: the accounts show how practitioners of Indigenous ceremony knit together environmental, political, legal, linguistic, and cultural dimensions while strategizing for change. The implications of these efforts are profound and extend far beyond the boundaries of the state currently known as Oregon.

The practice of ceremony is both evidence of and essential to Indigenous sovereignty, here defined most broadly in the sense of Indigenous individual and collective well-being. Each ceremonial practice is evidence of Indigenous agency in motion: regalia and other ritual arts such as language, dance, drumming, prayer, and sweat are physical manifestations of this agency. Because this knowledge is land-based and passed down intergenerationally, its practice is inseparable from access to, nurturing of, and control over that land base. This necessitates that tribes exercise their sovereign rights to steward and reclaim land, as recounted so many times in this book, whether from the Cow Creek Umpqua's agreement with the US Forest Service to create a special interest area to protect its traditional Huckleberry Patch or the Confederated Tribes of the Coos, Lower Umpqua and Siuslaw Indians' proposal for a federal Traditional Cultural Property Historic District to protect Jordan Cove in Coos Bay.

Indigenous scholars Michelle Jacob (Yakama) and Cutcha Risling Baldy (Hupa) have written about contemporary cultural revitalization efforts as the work of tribally specific "decolonizing praxis."[5] Jacob writes of the ways that Yakama Nation cultural revitalization activists work both to recover traditional practices and to dismantle oppressive systems, and in doing so, achieve critical healing.[6] Baldy, in her work on the revitalization of Hupa women's coming-of-age ceremonies in northwestern California, emphasizes how decolonization, or Indigenous self-determination and reclamation of epistemologies and land relationships, is made manifest through ceremony.[7] She acknowledges how historical assaults on Hupa homelands, people, and gender relations have impacted how and when ceremony is practiced, yet ultimately its reclamation demonstrates its generative power "as a dynamic and inventive building block of our culture."[8] This analysis echoes Coquille tribal member Denni Hockema's notion of "responding" to what is understood about prior traditions in order to recraft them rather than attempting to replicate a freeze-framed script, discussed in chapter 3. There is tension, of course, between holding on to traditions while also working for change, as Jacob acknowledges; conflict accompanies the dynamic interplay between cultural revitalization and healing from the wounds of colonization.[9] This is made even more complex because of the way colonialism has imposed rigid molds from without as well as from within about what it means to be Indigenous. But renewal—doing things in new ways while in continuity with the past—makes healing more possible in a post-apocalyptic, shattered world. The reclamation of ceremony and all its technology and knowledge is a key vehicle for this exercise of sovereignty.

Yet the English word *sovereignty*, deriving as it does from Western legal traditions, is not adequate to represent the depth of this truth. There is something deeper, that Bobbie Conner would say that people of the Plateau call Tamánwit or that Bud Lane would say is the traditional law at the heart of the Nee Dosh and related world renewal ceremonies.[10] As an outsider, I understand this "something" as the responsibility of individuals in community to uphold the reciprocal relationship between people, their places, and all creation. All of earth's places are under greater threat than ever in human history because of climate destruction. As Jacob has written, all people have inherited the legacy of colonialism and thus all of us need healing education.[11] My deepest hope is that these accounts so generously offered will simultaneously affirm and lift up the work of tribal communities and spark not only respect but also an altered awareness of responsibility from the non-Indigenous public.

Among the most important lessons of the project is how and why it came to be. While on the surface it may seem the result of museum-tribal collaboration initiated by various individuals, it has actually been made possible by local expressions of a global Indigenous resurgence in the twentieth and twenty-first centuries. In a real sense this project emerged over generations, shaped by years of Indigenous activism in and beyond Oregon, and by the impact of this activism on museum practice and non-Indigenous scholars like me. I came of professional age as a cultural anthropologist in the 1990s, the initial years of the Native American Graves Protection and Repatriation Act of 1990 (NAGPRA). NAGPRA provides a process for the repatriation of human remains and certain categories of cultural items held by federal agencies as well as all institutions that receive federal funding to federally recognized tribes. This federal law, with all its flaws, is human rights legislation that arose from the outrage of Indigenous peoples in the United States against museum ownership and display of ancestral remains and sacred items illegally alienated from their communities. NAGPRA took decades of Indigenous activism to enact; it has no statute of limitations and will continue to be transformative.[12]

While collaborative museology projects predated NAGPRA, there is no question that the activists' insistence on dignity and the primacy of Indigenous understandings of history and belonging *coupled with a federal legislative mandate* accelerated communication between non-Indigenous museum practitioners and tribal nations. It certainly did in my case, as in my first two years at Willamette (1996–98) I carried out a then long-overdue NAGPRA inventory and was subsequently involved in the repatriation of human remains and associated burial items that had been in the possession of the university.[13] And in those same years of the late 1990s, the Umatilla and other Columbia Plateau Tribes were calling for the repatriation of the Ancient One, also known as Kennewick Man—a struggle that was resolved only after a generation of legal challenges, with the Ancient One's burial by descendant tribes in 2017.[14]

In turn, NAGPRA has taken place in the context of global Indigenous rights movements, among them the American Indian Movement in the 1960s and 1970s in the United States, the formation of the International Indian Treaty Council in 1974, and the establishment of the United Nations Working Group on Indigenous Populations in 1982. The latter ultimately led to the United Nations Declaration of the Rights of Indigenous Peoples (UNDRIP), approved by the vast majority of UN member states in 2007 but not endorsed until years later by the major settler-colonial nations of Australia (2009), Canada (2016), New Zealand (2010), and the United States (2011). Although UNDRIP does not have the binding force of international law, it is a key articulation of Indigenous rights to self-determination, land, and resources.

Adjacent to these initiatives, face-to-face networking between the Māori of Aotearoa (New Zealand) and Indigenous artists of Hawaii and the Pacific Northwest of North America has been thriving. Beginning in New Zealand in 1995, international gatherings were held to bring together dozens of Indigenous visual artists from all around the Pacific Rim to live and work alongside one another for a week or two at a time. These continue every two to five years and are organized by Te Ātinga, a committee of Toi Māori, a charitable trust founded in 1996, in collaboration with a number of other partners.[15] This foundation in turn facilitated the arrival of the exhibition *Toi Māori: The Eternal Thread* to the United States in 2005–2006, which traveled with a cadre of Māori artists and cultural workers to each of its venues, San Francisco and Seattle, as well as Salem and Warm Springs, Oregon. At each venue of *The Eternal Thread*, the stunning exhibition of feathered cloaks and fiber arts offered the rationale for coming together, but it was the exchanges and shared living (however temporary) out of the public eye that built relationships with enduring dimensions.

The exhibitions *The Eternal Thread* and *The Art of Ceremony* both speak to the potentially empowering nature of museum-based work. Objects—especially when chosen by Native makers and narrated by them—tell stories within and beyond source communities. In both cases the process of gathering these stories and lifting up the objects to the public became a catalyst for deeper, long-term work, work that now spans generations to encompass people who never experienced either exhibition directly. It is a reminder that exhibitions are not an end in themselves but can facilitate the development of relationships that support exercise of Indigenous agency. Many curators who work with Indigenous arts and communities, whether themselves Indigenous or not, have learned to practice what I think of as deep relationality so that after an exhibition is over, relationships are deepened rather than ended.[16]

One thing I've learned by building relationships outside of the museum walls with Indigenous weavers in particular is how inseparable the practice of their art form is from the right to tend and gather cultural plant resources. In an article about traditional gathering in Native northwestern California, Baldy has written about gathering as the exercise of what she calls "biocultural sovereignty" or the tending, gathering, utilization, and management of ecological resources for cultural purposes by Indigenous peoples on their ancestral homelands, whether those lands be on or off current reservation boundaries.[17] This term emphasizes the inextricable relationship among people, lands, and resources and is intended by Baldy to refer to ongoing as well as ancient relationships. She emphasizes that the practice of gathering is also a way of meeting responsibility to the land and to one's ancestors and future generations. Not only are art forms and related knowledge perpetuated but also the land itself is cared for through the tending done by gatherers.

In the past few years I've been involved in collaborative research with members of the Northwest Native American Basketweavers Association to address the challenges such weavers face accessing cultural plant harvests on ancestral homelands now in public ownership.[18] This access is vital for the in situ intergenerational transmission of knowledge so often described in the accounts in this book. In the publications that came out of that research, the other authors and I cited the work of legal scholar Ed Goodman, who argues that the exercise of treaty-reserved gathering rights implies the protection of plant habitat, much as the exercise of fishing rights implies protection of fish habitat.[19] Goodman extends this logic to argue that tribes should have rights to comanage ceded ancestral lands; tribal comanagement of habitat on ceded lands can be seen as a reserved right, so that the resources themselves are available and thriving in order for such gathering rights to be exercised.[20]

Although the legal dimensions of this interpretation of reserved rights is outside my expertise to argue, I am intrigued by the reasoning and its implications. In an age of rapid climate change, conserving habitat directly translates into conserving the resources needed for the practice of ceremony. Just as salmon, other endangered fish (like c'waam for the Klamath Tribes), and their habitats must be protected for tribes to meaningfully exercise treaty rights to fish, so must the other species and habitats be protected so that Indigenous rights to other resources on ancestral lands be preserved. Failing to protect these habitats and species—failing to address climate change—will mean that the customary resources associated with these tribal homelands will continue to disappear, violating tribal rights and impacting the arts of ceremony in the wake.[21]

During the run of *The Art of Ceremony* and throughout my entire teaching career, I have been struck again and again by how little the non-Indigenous US public understands about tribal sovereignty and history. This ignorance is not accidental; as the previous paragraphs suggest, real understanding of tribal sovereignty implies real societal change. While education alone cannot produce such shifts, there has been a major watershed in Oregon state history, with the 2017 passage of Senate Bill 13 (SB 13) that mandated and funded the development of a Tribal History/Shared History curriculum for K–12 schools.[22] This work took generations to achieve and will take more to completely unfold, but it offers a shining example of how tribal activists have moved from being silenced and kept invisible by the broader education system to integrating tribal history into Oregon's K–12 curriculum to reach all children. Because it is a legislative mandate, it is a revolution not unlike NAGPRA and emerges from a similar wellspring of Indigenous human rights activism and intergenerational strategizing. As with NAGPRA, SB 13 and similar measures in Washington and Montana represent ways Indigenous agency and leadership have been exerted. In pages to follow, the staff of the Oregon Department of Education Office of Indian Education offers a reflection on their work and the ways the accounts in this book may contribute to this public education effort.

All these developments—global Indigenous rights efforts, NAGPRA, collaborative exhibitions, exertion of tribal rights, the protection of natural resources, and curricular sovereignty—are not coincidental occurrences but intersecting facets of converging forces. Indigenous systems of knowledge and practice have been sustaining against a backdrop of change, catastrophe, and assault. While the damage endured and the resilience shown has been evident for a long time, the wider US public may only now be beginning to understand as part of a broader reckoning with the history of this country. In 2021, Deborah Haaland (Laguna Pueblo), the first Native American secretary of the US Department of Interior, called for an investigation into the federal boarding school program, the beginning of a comprehensive review of the legacy of the system, with an initial emphasis on understanding the scale of attendance and death at the schools.[23] This inquiry will be very immediately felt here in Oregon, as one of the country's oldest continually operating boarding schools, Chemawa Indian School, is in Salem and has touched the lives of nearly every Native community in the Northwest. And, in a further development that will surely bring greater awareness of Indigenous presence and history to the public, Confederated Tribes of the Umatilla Indian Reservation citizen Charles F. "Chuck" Sams III (Cayuse and Walla Walla) has been confirmed by the US Senate as the first Indigenous director of the National Park Service, a bureau of the Department of Interior.

On a personal level, this project has fundamentally enriched my life. I began many of the relationships that led to these conversations in my thirties and am now in my early sixties. While I never intended to take so long for this book to come to fruition, in some ways its long gestation has allowed for my own maturation and growth, although I remain acutely aware of my limitations as a non-Indigenous, white researcher.

The fact that so much time has passed since the original *Art of Ceremony* exhibition has allowed for a new generation of Indigenous youth to rise, as the Canoe Journeys described in chapter 5 so clearly demonstrate. One reason I felt it crucial to seek voices of differing generations in each chapter was the realization that, while these experiences of renewal have been historically recent, for the youngest it may feel like "this is the way it has always been." Young Indigenous adults today from tribes in western Oregon have been born not only in a post-restoration age but also beyond the very initial nation-building stages of the late twentieth century. The processes of renewal chronicled here may serve to open up even more pathways for rising generations.

Ceremony is a people- and future-making process. My hope is that everyone who reads this will listen to these accounts and, at the very least, be moved by them as beacons of healing, resilience, optimism, courage, and humor. As Bobbie Conner writes in the afterword, they have been shared not with the intention of seeking validation, but instead for renewal of selves, others, communities, and all beings. This is the work of this book. This is the work of ceremony.

Roberta "Bobbie" Conner

Director, Tamástslikt Cultural Institute,
Confederated Tribes of the Umatilla Indian Reservation

Indigenous people the world over have rarely been given their due
by those who colonized us, whether it's our traditional ecological
knowledge, intimate relationships with all that lives in the lands we've
stewarded for millennia, or provisions and assistance shared with newcomers to our lands who had few inklings of how to survive once here.

Indigenous cultures do not wait for or expect corroboration, validation, or recognition of all that we know, contribute, and sustain, let
alone any thought of vindication of the despicable, malicious, and pitiful
stereotypes assigned to us. Instead, we keep on keeping on—doing the
best we can with what we have access to using the ancient teachings
that have sustained us for thousands of years. We do so even when we
must make do on a postage stamp–size acreage compared to our once
vast domains of tended abundance.

Whether it is labeled ritual, practice, ceremony, sacrament, belief,
knowledge, philosophy, values, or standards, little of our cultural teaching is typically considered fact-based, pedagogic, effective, or functional
to the larger world in which we exist. And yet, the lessons learned by
generation after generation after generation living in the same region,
coexisting to the benefit of more than our own species, are pivotal to
understanding this world. These lessons, teachings, and beliefs are
not curiosities to examine as specimens; they are not quaint, folkloric,

uninformed behaviors. They are truths. They have evolved over a very long span of time to protect us, nurture and nourish us, help us help others who rely on our respect and goodness to keep their habitat as well as our own livable.

Most important, we are taught that we are not omnipotent. In our Columbia River Plateau culture the species who are fishes and meats are brothers, while the plants and their fruits are sisters. All that we are reflects this kinship and with the land upon which we all live. Water gives life to us all. For us, there is no ceremony without water. We are not true to who we are without these precious relatives who feed and clothe our bodies. When we have learned these lessons and many more, we can become whole beings endowed with the grace and gift of life, not half-people stumbling and bumbling through the neighborhood with no care for those who come after us.

One of the most fascinating facts that newcomers to our Columbia River Plateau culture miss is that we have our own laws, established long, long before we welcomed strangers to our homelands. These laws teach us to take care of one another. Only take what you need; leave some for those who come behind. All around the planet, other Indigenous cultures have similar tenets, principles, laws. These laws cannot be overturned or diminished. They exist only as long as we uphold them. It is up to us.

In our Plateau culture, like so many cultures around the world, we annually renew ourselves, our kinship with all else that lives, and we make ourselves ready to be anew. We shed our winter trappings, welcome the returning foods—each in their own season—with highest regard. Whether we are shedding our skins, pledging afresh our commitments to ages-old covenants, or coming out of mourning, we embrace, venerate, and celebrate the winter solstice, the spring plants, the animal births, the anadromous migrations, and the warm weather ripening our lives. All, in ceremony.

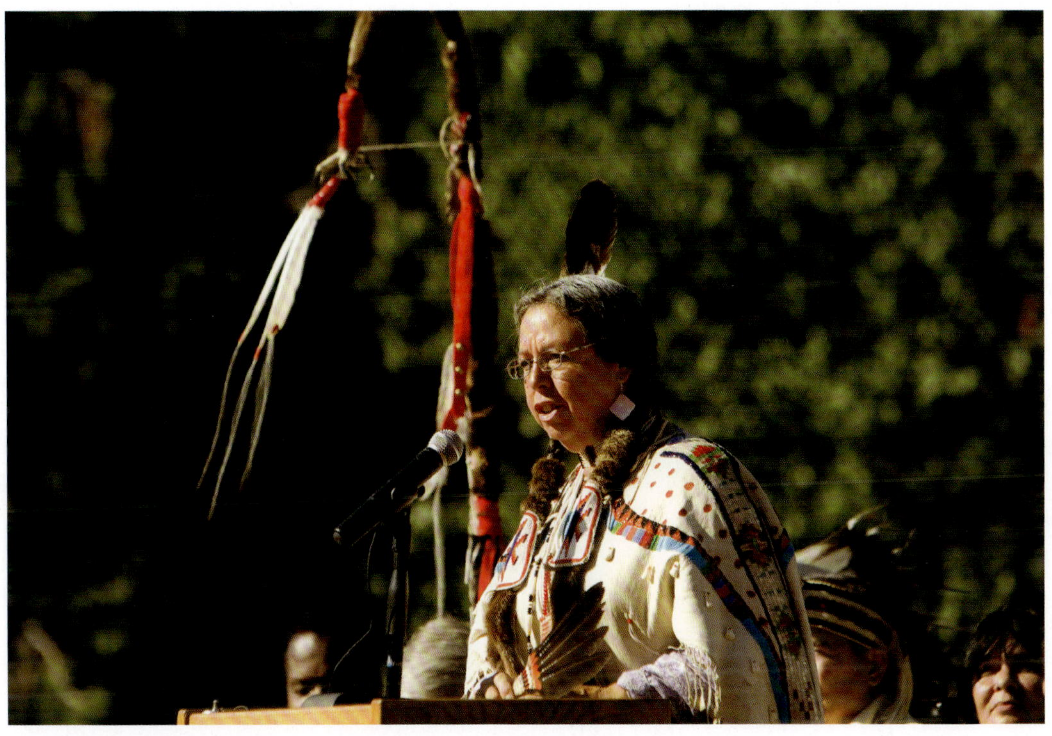

Roberta "Bobbie" Conner at *The Art of Ceremony* opening events, September 27, 2008.
Photograph by Frank Miller. Courtesy of Frank Miller and Willamette University.

REFLECTION

April Campbell, Ramona Halcomb, Trinity Minahan, and Deleana Otherbull

Oregon Department of Education Office of Indian Education

This book comes to publication at an emergent time in Oregon as we are undergoing a transformation of Indigenous education that has been generations in the making. The tireless advocacy efforts of countless Indigenous educators over the years and many other partners in our state came to fruition as the Oregon Legislature enacted Senate Bill (SB) 13 in 2017. This struggle and resilience to courageously continue fighting for a truthful narrative of history, culture, and contemporary portrayal of Indigenous people in our education system will forever hold a place in our hearts as we work to build from the foundation it so diligently provided for us.

These efforts allowed for the implementation of what is now called the Tribal History/Shared History curriculum. This curriculum is a past vision with a new beginning to provide the opportunity to honor the Native American experience in Oregon, tribal sovereignty, and self-determination as well as the history and contemporary status of the nine federally recognized tribes in Oregon. SB 13 directs the Oregon Department of Education (ODE) to create K–12 Native American curriculum across multiple content areas for inclusion in Oregon public schools and provides professional development to educators. The law also provides the ODE resources to provide to each of the nine federally recognized tribes in Oregon to create individual place-based curriculum.

For years the state has been missing a critical opportunity to fully leverage the strengths, assets, and contributions our Native American students bring to their communities. The lack of accurate and complete curricula may contribute to the persistent achievement and opportunity gaps between Native Americans and other students, primarily those students and youth most underserved. Unfortunately, up until the passing of SB 13, public schools in Oregon were not required or equipped to teach historically and contemporarily accurate or culturally responsive curriculum about the Indigenous peoples of Oregon who have lived here since time immemorial. Alas, it is impossible to teach or fully understand Oregon history without including these voices and perspectives of Indigenous people in Oregon.

Over time there have been very few texts or resources created or available to educators and our general citizenry in this state about the nine federally recognized tribes in Oregon. *The Art of Ceremony: Voices of Renewal from Indigenous Oregon* strives to fulfill this need in an authentic, accurate manner. Our hope is that people will read and learn from some of the ceremonies and traditions of the nine federally recognized tribes in Oregon and honor their connection to this land and place we now call Oregon as well as their *survivance* in keeping these traditions alive indefinitely for future generations despite so many attempts at destruction, oppression, and erasure. We are grateful for resources such as this that share a truthful narrative and Indigenous perspective.

In closing, we wish to thank Dr. Rebecca Dobkins for her good heart, extensive research, exceptional patience, and decades-long contributions to cultural and historical preservation, revitalization, and authenticity as well as continual collaboration, service, and engagement with the Indigenous people in Oregon.

The Nine Federally Recognized Tribes in Oregon

See tribal websites for further information regarding the history and contemporary activities of the nine federally recognized Tribes in Oregon. Tribal museums open as of 2022 are listed; other tribal museums and cultural centers are currently in development across Oregon. Additional sources of information may be found in the bibliography.

Burns Paiute Tribe
https://burnspaiute-nsn.gov/
100 Pasigo Street, Burns, OR, 97720–2442
Wadatika Band of Northern Paiutes

Confederated Tribes of the Coos, Lower Umpqua and Siuslaw Indians
https://ctclusi.org/
1245 Fulton Avenue, Coos Bay, OR 97420
Three tribes (four bands): two bands of Coos Tribes: Hanis Coos (Coos Proper), Miluk Coos; Lower Umpqua Tribe; and Siuslaw Tribe

Coquille Indian Tribe
https://www.coquilletribe.org/
3050 Tremont Street, North Bend, OR 97459
Coquille (pronounced *ko-kwel*)

Cow Creek Band of Umpqua Tribe of Indians
https://www.cowcreek-nsn.gov/
2371 NE Stephens Street, Suite #100, Roseburg, OR 97470
Cow Creek Umpqua, also referred to as Upper Umpqua Tribe or
    Cow Creek Tribe

Confederated Tribes of Grand Ronde
https://www.grandronde.org/
9615 Grand Ronde Road, Grand Ronde, OR 97347
More than thirty tribes and bands including the Chasta, Chinook,
    Kalapuya, Molalla, Rogue River, Tillamook, and Umpqua

Chachalu Museum and Cultural Center
https://www.grandronde.org/history-culture/culture/
    chachalu-museum-and-cultural-center/
8720 Grand Ronde Road, Grand Ronde, OR 97347

The Chachalu Museum and Cultural Center opened in phases beginning
in 2014. Chachalu translates from the Yamhill Kalapuyan language as
place of the burnt timbers, referring to a massive forest fire that burned
through the area in 1856 and signaling the way the Tribe, like the land,
is healing from the past as it grows into the future.

The Klamath Tribes
https://klamathtribes.org/
501 Chiloquin Boulevard, PO Box 436, Chiloquin, OR 97624
Klamath, Modoc, and Yahooskin Paiute Tribes

Confederated Tribes of Siletz Indians

http://www.ctsi.nsn.us/

201 SE Swan Avenue, PO Box 549, Siletz, OR 97380

Tribes and bands representing at least ten base languages and
dozens of distinct groups, including Clatsop, Chinook, Klickitat,
Molalla, Kalapuya, Tillamook, Alsea, Siuslaw/Lower Umpqua,
Coos, Coquelle, Upper Umpqua, Tututni, Tolowa, Takelma,
Galice/Applegate, and Shasta

Confederated Tribes of the Umatilla Indian Reservation

https://ctuir.org/

46411 Timíne Way, Pendleton, OR 97801

Cayuse, Umatilla, Walla Walla Tribes

Tamástslikt Cultural Institute

https://www.tamastslikt.org/

Confederated Tribes of the Umatilla Indian Reservation

47106 Wildhorse Boulevard, Pendleton, OR 97801

The Tamástslikt Cultural Institute (opened in 1998) is the tribal museum
and cultural center of the CTUIR. Tamástslikt translates as *interpreter*
in English.

Confederated Tribes of the Warm Springs Reservation

https://warmsprings-nsn.gov/

1233 Veterans Street, PO Box C, Warm Springs, OR 97761

Warm Springs, Wasco, and Paiute Tribes

The Museum at Warm Springs

https://www.museumatwarmsprings.org/

Confederated Tribes of the Warm Springs Reservation

2189 Highway 26, Warm Springs, OR 97761

The Museum at Warm Springs (opened in 1993) was the first tribal
museum in Oregon.

NOTES

INTRODUCTION

1 *Toi Māori: The Eternal Thread* was itself a
model of collaborative curation. In the making
for years, the exhibit was organized by the
Pataka Museum of Arts and Culture (a municipal
museum in Porirua City, New Zealand, where
the exhibition premiered in 2004) in partnership with Toi Māori Aotearoa (an independent
charitable Māori arts organization that cares for
the interests of Māori art and artists at a local,
national, and international level, and is funded in
part by *Creative New Zealand,* the country's
federal arts agency) and Te Roopu Rananga
Whatu o Aotearoa (the Māori weavers' collective,
one of the nine art councils of Toi Māori) of
New Zealand.

2 The fact that Willamette University—founded
upon a missionary history that sought to assimilate
Indigenous peoples—was the institutional location
for these events and the subsequent exhibition
and book has always been front of mind for me.
Since my arrival at Willamette in the late 1990s,
I have had the great fortune to work alongside
many Indigenous students and alumni who have
pushed the university to reckon with the legacy of
its founding and its location on Kalapuyan lands.
Indigenous students helped restore the university's annual powwow, reinvigorated its Native and
Indigenous Student Union, initiated the Chemawa
Indian School Partnership Program, where Willamette students study with and mentor Indigenous
youth at the federal Indian boarding school located
in Salem, and a similar program with Native
youth in Salem-Keizer public schools, and in 2019,
succeeded in getting the university to adopt a land
acknowledgment statement. I acknowledge, with
deep appreciation, all the Indigenous students who
have attended Willamette University and its predecessor, the Indian Manual Labor Training School
(1834–1844).

3 The United Nations Declaration on the Rights
of Indigenous Peoples (UNDRIP) was initially conceived in the 1980s and finally adopted in 2007. In
the intervening decades, the international working
groups that led to UNDRIP's development were
important conduits for global Indigenous networking, particularly before the Internet brought
the possibility of virtual gatherings and immediate
information-sharing.

4   The NEA American Masterpieces grant was for $50,000; in 2007 this was one of the largest single sources of exhibition-related funding available in Oregon. All of the sources of funding for *The Art of Ceremony* exhibition and book are listed in the acknowledgments.

5   The term *masterpiece* is derived from a Western tradition that conceives great artwork as the result of the work of an individual "master" or "genius," who is normatively a man of European descent. This term is woefully inadequate when applied to regalia, living, multidimensional art forms that stem from collective knowledge as well as individual artistry, often the work of women rather than male "masters."

6   The nine federally recognized tribes of what is currently Oregon are the Burns Paiute Tribe; the Confederated Tribes of the Coos, Lower Umpqua, and Siuslaw Indians; the Coquille Indian Tribe; the Cow Creek Band of Umpqua Tribe of Indians; the Confederated Tribes of Grand Ronde; the Klamath Tribes; the Confederated Tribes of Siletz Indians; the Confederated Tribes of the Umatilla Indian Reservation; and the Confederated Tribes of Warm Springs (see the appendix). The term *federally recognized* refers to those tribes which, by treaty, executive order, or other federally sanctioned process, are legally recognized as Indian tribes. Across the nation there are tribes that do not possess this status as a result of various historical events. Many of them, such as the Chinook of the lower Columbia River, are seeking federal recognition; see Daehnke, *Chinook Resilience.* In the case of *The Art of Ceremony*, the decision to focus on the nine federally recognized tribes followed the precedent of other statewide cultural and historical projects, such as the Oregon Council for the Humanities *First Oregonians* book project and the Oregon Historical Society's *Oregon Is Indian Country* exhibition project in 2009. It is important to acknowledge that Tony Johnson of the Chinook Nation was one of the key advisers to the exhibition project and that the Johnson family lent several objects to the exhibition.

7   There is a growing literature on collaborative museology, Indigenous research methodologies, and community-based participatory research, which informs this project and to which this book contributes. This literature is too vast to cite here but ranges from Māori scholar Linda Tuhiwai Smith's seminal manifesto on Indigenous-directed research, *Decolonizing Methodologies*, to reflections on museum-tribal encounters in the age of repatriation, such as that of Krmpotich and Peers, eds., *This Is Our Life*, to the more recent issuance of guiding principles and practice for communities and museums facilitated by Smith, Lamar, and Vallo, *Guidelines for Collaboration.*

8   See Folwell et al., *Hold Everything*, for an example of an exhibition of Native American art that took care to avoid a time-bound definition of *masterpiece* and that involved several Native artists as curators in its development.

9   See Berg, ed., *The First Oregonians*, and Beckham, ed., *Oregon Indians.*

10   All participants in the project gave informed consent, granting permission to be recorded and specifying whether they wished their names to be used. Each tribal representative secured permission to participate in the project, through tribal research permit processes or through their own authority as cultural resources or tribal museum staff.

11   Strong, *American Indians and the American Imaginary*, 1. Entire volumes have been written on photographic representations of and by Indigenous people in North America. For key works on Indigenous photography as the work of sovereignty, see Tsinhnahjinnie and Passalacqua, *Our People, Our Land, Our Images*; Dangeli, "Dancing Our Archive," 262–83; and for an investigation of the ways Indigenous peoples indigenized photography in its first one hundred years, see Strathman, *Through a Native Lens.*

12   Frank Miller, Willamette University photographer from 2002 to 2020, worked very closely with the Hallie Ford Museum of Art and with the tribal curators who came to install their regalia at the

museum during *The Art of Ceremony* exhibition in 2008; in that project his aesthetic was crucial to visually conveying the notion that regalia are masterpieces. Later for the book, Frank traveled to Siletz, Cow Creek, Coquille, and Coos, Lower Umpqua and Siuslaw, to photograph ceremonial events. Two photographers who are also tribal members, Patricia Walters (Umatilla) and Sara Siestreem (Hanis Coos), were commissioned with Oregon Cultural Trust funds to take new photography for the book. Other images were chosen from existing tribal photography collections, including work by tribal member Taylor Tupper of the Klamath and Modoc Tribes and Grand Ronde Smoke Signals staff photographers. The list of all contributing photographers appears in the acknowledgments; I am incredibly grateful for their work.

13 The concept that gathering and its related practices is an exercise of tribal sovereignty is discussed throughout the book and returned to in the conclusion. One of the sources that has been influential to my thinking is an essay by Baldy, "Why We Gather." Baldy builds upon Stefano Varese's work on biological and cultural resistance and adaptation by Indigenous peoples in Latin America. See Varese and Chirif, *Witness to Sovereignty*.

1. BURNS PAIUTE TRIBE

1 I am indebted to Margaret Mathewson, my graduate school classmate at University of California, Berkeley, and now an Oregon-based ethnobotanist, for connecting me with Minerva Soucie not long after I arrived in Oregon in 1996. Minerva worked for the US Forest Service for twenty-four years and retired in her early fifties to pursue weaving and other traditional arts and to teach them to younger generations. For a profile of Minerva, see Briggs, "Tribes Weave the Past into a Stronger Future."

2 Burns Paiute Tribe, "Culture and Heritage Department: Our Tribal Community,"

www.burnspaiute-nsn.gov/index.php/departments/culture-and-heritage (accessed October 25, 2019).

3 Allen, "Malheur Indian Reservation."

4 Burns Paiute Tribe, "Culture and Heritage Department."

5 US Fish and Wildlife Service, Malheur National Wildlife Refuge, "About the Refuge," (accessed October 24, 2019).

6 Teeman, "Cultural Resource Management and the Protection of Valued Tribal Spaces," 626–32.

7 Teeman, "Cultural Resource Management and the Protection of Valued Tribal Spaces," 628.

8 Teeman, "Cultural Resource Management and the Protection of Valued Tribal Spaces," 628.

9 Teeman, "Cultural Resource Management and the Protection of Valued Tribal Spaces," 628.

10 Teeman, "Cultural Resource Management and the Protection of Valued Tribal Spaces," 628, emphasis added.

11 Cowie, Teeman, and LeBlanc, eds., *Collaborative Archaeology at Stewart Indian School*, 5. In this and other passages discussing Puha, the authors refer to an article by Carroll, Zedeño, and Stoffle, "Landscapes of the Ghost Dance," 127–56.

12 Cowie, Teeman, and LeBlanc, eds., *Collaborative Archaeology at Stewart Indian School*, 244.

13 Berg, ed., *First Oregonians*.

14 Teeman, "Cultural Resource Management," 628; and Miller, "Basin Religion and Theology," 66–86.

15 Miller, "Basin Religion and Theology," 80.

16 Soucie, "Burns Paiute Tribe," n.p. Regarding historical and ecological factors in the decline in rabbit populations in the American West, see Brown et al., "History Status and Population Trends of the Cottontail Rabbits and Jack Rabbits," 16–42.

17 Minerva's curatorial approach is evocative of the seminal work of cultural anthropologist Arjun Appadurai on the "social life of things." In arguing that things have social lives, Appadurai urges us to trace the trajectory of objects across space and time to learn how they become imbued with value and meaning through manufacture, use, possession, and trade. Appadurai, ed., *Social Life of Things.*

18 For a discussion of Northern Paiute material culture, including basketry and hidework, see Kelly, "Ethnography of the Surprise Valley Paiute," 67–210.

19 Oard's Gallery and Museum is in the tiny hamlet of Buchanan, Oregon, at 42456 Highway 20 East. See "Oard's Gallery and Museum," https://oardsgallery.com/ (accessed November 12, 2019).

20 "Native American Wild Rose Mythology," www.native-languages.org/wild-rose.htm (accessed November 13, 2019).

21 "Rena Adams Beers, 1918–2018."

22 Burns Paiute Tribe, *Tu'Kwa Hone Newsletter,* www.burnspaiute-nsn.gov/index.php/news-letter (accessed November 5, 2019).

23 Burns Paiute Tribe, "Aboriginal Territorial Protection Policy," 2006, www.burnspaiute-nsn .gov/index.php/resources/natural-resources? format=html (accessed November 13, 2019).

24 For information regarding the work of the Burns Paiute Tribe's Natural Resources Department, see www.bptdnr.com (accessed November 19, 2019).

25 Walker, *Sagebrush Collaboration,* 16–17.

26 Walker, *Sagebrush Collaboration,* 45.

27 Diane L. Teeman, interview with the author, Burns Paiute Culture and Heritage Department, Burns, Oregon, July 12, 2017.

28 Walker, *Sagebrush Collaboration,* 16.

29 Walker, *Sagebrush Collaboration,* 35–36.

30 Teeman interview.

31 Teeman, "Issues in Great Basin Historic Preservation," 2.

32 Teeman interview.

33 Teeman interview.

34 In 2020 linguists Tim Thornes (Boise State University) and Maziar Toosavandani (University of California, Santa Cruz) published a supplement in the *International Journal of American Linguistics* documenting several dialects of Northern Paiute, resulting from their decades of work with Northern Paiute speakers. See Thornes, "Wadadɨka'a (Burns Paiute Reservation, Oregon)"; and

Thornes and Toosarvandani, "Northern Paiute Texts: Introduction." For further information and first-person accounts of Native language teaching and learning in Oregon, see Gross, ed., *Teaching Oregon Native Languages.*

35 Teeman interview.

36 Burns Paiute Tribe, "Language Program," www.burnspaiute-nsn.gov/index.php/ departments/culture-and-heritage/language -program (accessed November 19, 2019).

2. CONFEDERATED TRIBES OF THE COOS, LOWER UMPQUA, AND SIUSLAW INDIANS

1 For a map of the ancestral lands of the Coos, Lower Umpqua, and Siuslaw Indians, see "History: A Brief History of the Coos, Lower Umpqua, & Siuslaw Indians" on the Tribes' website, https://ctclusi.org/history/ (accessed November 1, 2021).

2 Sue Perry Olson, interview with the author, Veneta, Oregon, July 26, 2017.

3 Olson, artist statement.

4 Patricia Whereat Phillips, phone interview with the author, Eugene, Oregon, July 25, 2017. Phillips's groundbreaking book is *Ethnobotany of the Coos, Lower Umpqua, and Siuslaw Indians.*

5 This section on CTCLUSI history draws upon the Tribes' website ("History: A Brief History of the Coos, Lower Umpqua, & Siuslaw Indians," https://ctclusi.org/history (accessed October 16, 2019); and Beck's *Seeking Recognition.*

6 For discussion of the Miluk language and other languages around Coos Bay and the lower Coquille River, see Patricia Whereat Phillips, "Miluk," *Oregon Encyclopedia,* www.oregonencyclopedia.org/ articles/miluk-coos/#.YF0glOd7nIU (accessed October 16, 2019).

7 The Western Oregon Tribal Fairness Act, Pub. L. No. 115–108, was signed into law on January 8, 2018 (www.congress.gov/bill/115th-congress/house-bill/ 1306). It provided for the taking into trust of nearly 15,000 acres of land for the CTCLUSI and approximately 17,500 acres of land for the Cow Creek Band of Umpqua Indians. For the CTCLUSI, the conveyed lands are composed of relatively equal tracts in each of the three tribal ancestral homelands. The majority of the acreage in all cases is made up of timber lands that have been under the management of the Bureau of Land Management. It also amends the Coquille Restoration Act to require that the secretary of the interior manage the Coquille Tribe's forest lands in the same way it does other tribal trust forest lands.

8   On July 24–26, 2017, I interviewed the following CTCLUSI tribal members at the Department of Natural Resources and Culture in Coos Bay, Oregon: Jesse Beers, Margaret Corvi, Courtney Krossman, Ashley Russell, and Don "Doc" Slyter. I also interviewed Brenda Brainard and Patricia Whereat Phillips by telephone from their homes on July 25, 2017. Unless otherwise noted, all quotations in this chapter come from those interviews. Digital recordings and transcriptions of the interviews were shared with the participants and the CTCLUSI Department of Natural Resources and Culture.

9   Don "Doc" Slyter is the elected chair of the CTCLUSI Tribal Council for 2019 through 2023.

10   The program, which Siestreem called the Hanis Coos Traditional Weaving Research and Education Project, had funding support at various times from the CTCLUSI, the Longhouse at The Evergreen State College, the Potlatch Fund, and the Oregon Community Foundation. Siestreem's weaving teachers included Greg Archuleta (Grand Ronde) and Greg Robinson (Chinook Nation), who regularly teach at the Grand Ronde Lifeways program in Portland, where Siestreem took classes.

11   Sara Siestreem, artist statement, "This Is Us Dancing II," 2018, provided to the author. This statement was written in association with a group exhibition at the Pacific Northwest College of Art in Portland, Oregon, titled *The Earth Will Not Abide*.

12   Beck, *Seeking Recognition*, 100.

13   Beck, *Seeking Recognition*, 102.

14   See the CTCLUSI Tribal Constitution, ratified in 1984, at the time of restoration, https://ctclusi .org/tribalcode/ (accessed November 1, 2021).

15   The full text of the proposal "National Register for Historic Places—Traditional Cultural Properties: A Quick Guide for Preserving Native American Cultural Resources," can be found at www.oregon.gov/oprd/HCD/NATREG/docs/ Jordon%20Cove%20-%20TCP/NPS%20Docs% 2023%20May%202019/REDACTED_CoosCounty_ QalyataKukwisShichdiimeTCPHistoricDistrict.pdf (accessed October 28, 2019).

16   Parker and King, "Guidelines for Documenting and Evaluating Traditional Cultural Properties."

17   National Park Service, "Quick Guide for Preserving Native American Cultural Resources," 2012, (accessed October 16, 2019).

18   A timeline and associated documents for the Cape Wind Energy Project, which was ultimately decommissioned in 2017, can be found at "Cape Wind," Bureau of Ocean Energy Management, (accessed October 16, 2019).

19   The Jordan Cove Energy Project proposed building a liquefied natural gas (LNG) export terminal in Coos Bay along with a 230-mile pipeline across southern Oregon that would in turn have connected with the 680-mile Ruby Pipeline project. In late 2021, after years of tribal and community opposition, the project effectively ended after the Canadian company behind the project requested that the Federal Energy Regulatory Commission cancel its permits. See https://www.oregon.gov/energy/facilities-safety/ facilities/Pages/Jordan-Cove.aspx (accessed April 15, 2022).

20   Chief Warren Brainard, as quoted on the CTCLUSI website, "Department of Natural Resources & Culture, Traditional Cultural Property (TCP)," https://ctclusi.org/department -of-natural-resources-culture/ (accessed October 16, 2019).

21   Background to the TCP and a list of frequently asked questions can be found at "Department of Natural Resources & Culture, Traditional Cultural

Property (TCP)" on the CTCLUSI website: https://
ctclusi.org/department-of-natural-resources
-culture/ (accessed October 16, 2019).
22   Oregon Parks and Recreation Department,
Oregon Heritage, National Register, *Q'alya ta
Kukwis shichdii me* (Jordan Cove and the Bay of
the Coos People) Traditional Cultural Property
Historic District, www.oregon.gov/oprd/HCD/
NATREG/Pages/Jordan-Cove-TCP.aspx (accessed
October 16, 2019).

3. COQUILLE INDIAN TRIBE

1   I interviewed Anne Burnette Niblett, Denni
Hockema, and Brenda Meade together at the
Coquille Tribe's administrative offices in North
Bend, Oregon, on December 22, 2015. Unless
otherwise noted, all quotations in this chapter are
taken from a recording of this conversation.
2   Chinuk is the spelling for Chinook preferred by
many twenty-first-century speakers of the language
in western Oregon. Wawa is the preferred term for
language. Chinuk Wawa is a community heritage
language for several Tribes in western Oregon.
For more information on Chinuk Wawa, see Zenk,
"Bringing 'Good Jargon' to Light," 561–69.
3   Boas, "Social Organization and the Secret
Societies of the Kwakiutl Indians." In an exemplary
model of collaborative research, anthropologist
Aaron Glass of the Bard Graduate Center worked
with the U'Mista Cultural Centre and artist Cor-
rine Hunt, George Hunt's great-granddaughter, to
develop the 2019 exhibition and website *The Story
Box: Franz Boas, George Hunt and the Making of
Anthropology* (www.bgc.bard.edu/exhibitions/
exhibitions/88/the-story-box, accessed March 26,
2021) that "explores the hidden histories and complex legacies of one of the most influential books
in the history of anthropology," and provides great
insight into Hunt's role and his efforts to "correct
and expand" the original publication.
4   For a thorough exploration of the notion of
actively "tending" (versus a more limited notion of

"gathering"), see Anderson, *Tending the Wild.*
5   See Coquille Indian Tribe, www.coquilletribe
.org/ (accessed March 15, 2016).
6   See George B. Wasson Jr., "Memory of a People:
The Coquelles of the Southern Oregon Coast,"
in Berg, *First Oregonians,* 80–103.
7   Younker, "Southwest Oregon Research
Project," 2–3.
8   The potlatch has been a subject of study by
many notable scholars, beginning with Boas and
Hunt in 1897. In 1925, French sociologist Marcel
Mauss published his essay *The Gift,* centrally based
on his understanding of the potlatch, which has
been highly influential in understanding reciprocity and gift exchange in human societies. A more
recent essay that explores how the potlatch has
centrally influenced Western thought is Wilner,
"Global Potlatch."
9   In the mid-1990s the SWORP initiative was
unfolding in a broader historical context. Native
American Tribes and activists had been working
for decades to gain access to and control over
intellectual and cultural property and ancestral
human remains held by nontribal entities. Years
of organizing led to the passage of the 1990 Native
American Graves Protection and Repatriation Act,
which mandated that federal agencies and institutions receiving federal funding inventory their
collections of Native American cultural property
and human remains and follow procedures to
consult with lineal descendants of the communities of origin and repatriate those materials if
conditions for documentation were met. It also
mandated procedures for when human remains
are inadvertently discovered, or are exposed in the
course of a planned excavation, on federal or tribal
lands, and further instituted criminal penalties
for the trafficking in Native American ancestral
remains and sacred objects. Though imperfect in
many ways, NAGPRA has had an extraordinary
impact on the relationships and power dynamics
between Indigenous peoples in the United States
and museums and other public agencies. For an
assessment of NAGPRA's impact, see Nash and

Colwell, "NAGPRA at 30." *EBSCOhost*, doi:10.1146/annurev-anthro-010220–075435.

10   Younker, "Southwest Oregon Research Project," 7.

11   Younker, "Southwest Oregon Research Project," 9.

12   See Ivy and Byram, eds., *Changing Landscapes*; Losey, ed., *Changing Landscapes*; and Younker, Tveskov, and Lewis, eds., *Changing Landscapes*.

13   Younker, "Southwest Oregon Research Project," 11.

14   The process described here, though local to Coquille, is an example of a manifestation of global Indigenous resurgence. See Vizenor, ed., *Survivance*.

15   Hansen, "Coquille Tribe Regains 3,200 Acres Forested Ancestral Homeland in Oregon."

16   Wells, "Native American Forestry Combines Traditional Wisdom with Modern Science." The Forest Stewardship Council is an international body, with a US chapter, that offers certification of sustainable forestry practices for forest owners and timber industry businesses. The FSC was officially founded in 1994, in response to the failure of the 1992 Earth Summit in Rio de Janeiro, Brazil, to take decisive action to stop deforestation. FSC certification is a voluntary process that requires an application demonstrating that the applicant (in this case, the Coquille Tribe) meets the FSC's principles and criteria. For an explanation of those principles, see "Mission and Vision," FSC United States, https://us.fsc.org/en-us/what-we-do/mission-and-vision (accessed March 31, 2021).

17   Miller and Pullen with the Bandon Historical Society, *Bandon*, 10.

4. COW CREEK BAND OF UMPQUA TRIBE OF INDIANS

1   Sue Shaffer, chairperson of the Cow Creek Band of Umpqua Tribe of Indians from 1983 to 2010, used the phrase "spiritual gathering place" for the Huckleberry Patch in a 2006 statement associated with the designation of this place as a special interest area. The statement was included in a 2006 PowerPoint presentation prepared by the Cow Creek Umpqua Tribe titled "Huckleberry Patch Special Interest Area," www.slideshare.net/updrugfree/huckleberry-patch-special-interest-area-website (accessed November 15, 2015), see slide 10.

2   Unless otherwise noted, all quotations in this chapter are from recordings of three group conversations. The first one—involving Rhonda Richardson, Elizabeth (Beth) Gipson, and Cindy Delay Grizzle—took place on August 31, 2015, at the tribal administration offices of the Cow Creek Band of Umpqua Tribe of Indians in Roseburg, Oregon. The second took place on September 15, 2015, at Cow Creek's Seven Feathers Casino Resort; those present included Clementine Young Rice, Clara Young Keller, and Ralph Young (children of Emaline Lerwill Young); Larry Davis and his wife, Elaine Davis; Charles "Chuck" Jackson; and Del "Red Hawk" Ansures. The third took place on September 24, 2020, with Mary Dumont Howren, Rhonda Richardson, Michael Rondeau, and Sherry Shaffer meeting together at the tribal administration offices while I joined via video conferencing from Portland. For that meeting, Mary Dumont Howren wrote a reflection on the significance of the Huckleberry Patch that was later provided to me and informs this chapter. Those interviewed in the third session agreed that the following terminology was to be used in this chapter: *Cow Creek Umpqua* as the appropriate shortened term for the Cow Creek Band of Umpqua Tribe of Indians; either *Huckleberry Patch* or *the Patch* for the specific location significant to the Cow Creek Umpqua, and the event itself as the *Huckleberry Gathering* or, in the words of some interviewed, *Huckleberry*. And with reverence, I note that several elders who gave of their knowledge for this chapter have since passed, including Del "Red Hawk" Ansures, Charles "Chuck" Jackson, Clementine Rice Young, and Ralph Young.

3 How stories and expressions of experience have the capacity to frame and articulate life experiences is a subject of long interest within anthropology. Anthropologist Edward Bruner discusses how narratives of experience facilitate the constitution of meaning and shape future possibilities; see Bruner, "Experience and Its Expressions," 6–7.

4 Anthropologist Douglas Deur completed an ethnographic study in 2002, submitted to Frederick F. York, for the National Park Service, regarding traditional uses of Huckleberry Mountain by Indigenous peoples. See Deur, *Huckleberry Mountain Traditional-Use Study: Final Report*. See also Deur, "Most Sacred Place."

5 Mary Dumont Howren pointed out in her 2020 reflections that the term *Cow Creek* was not chosen by the people; the name refers to the location where the treaty was signed. The people's name for themselves was and is *Umpqua*.

6 This historical overview draws from the following sources: Beckham, "History of Western Oregon since 1846," 180–88; and the website of the Cow Creek Band of Umpqua Tribe of Indians, particularly "Tribal Story," www.cowcreek.com/tribal-government/tribal-story/ (accessed November 30, 2015).

7 Deur, *Huckleberry Mountain Traditional-Use Study*, 34.

8 Deur, *Huckleberry Mountain Traditional-Use Study*, 1.

9 Emaline Lerwill Young (1905–1982) composed a five-page, single-spaced typewritten account of her family's history and of her memories of going to the Huckleberry Patch, dated April 14, 1980. I received a copy of this account from Emaline's daughter, Clementine Young Rice, in 2015, as part of the research for this book.

10 Young, family history account, 2.

11 Deur, "Most Sacred Place," 18–19.

12 Deur, "Most Sacred Place," 29–33.

13 Deur, *Huckleberry Mountain Traditional-Use Study*, 1.

14 Young, family history account, 2.

15 Young, family history account, 3–4.

16 Young, family history account, 4.

17 *United States Forest Service Manual* 2361.2, as referenced in "Huckleberry Patch Special Interest Area," PowerPoint presentation, Cow Creek Band of Umpqua Tribe of Indians, 2006.

18 See "USDA US Forest Service, Umpqua and Roque River-Siskiyou National Forests, Decision Notice and Finding of No Significant Impact for the Huckleberry Patch Special Interest Area Forest Plan Amendment Environmental Assessment," as signed by James A. Caplan, forest supervisor, Umpqua National Forest, and Scott Conroy, forest supervisor, Rogue River-Siskiyou National Forest, memorandum published January 24, 2006, 10 pp.

19 "USDA US Forest Service," 2.

20 "USDA US Forest Service," 2.

21 Shaffer statement, "Huckleberry Patch Special Interest Area," PowerPoint, slide 10. Poo-eat-sic, *Perideridia oregona*, is an edible tuber also known as yampa. According to Cow Creek Umpqua tribal member Wallace Rondeau, "Poo-eat-sic grew many different places. Mostly in the prairies in a break in the timber where there was more light. It was eaten fresh or dried and stored for later use." Information provided by Donna Fields, executive administrative assistant for the Cow Creek Band of Umpqua Tribe of Indians, correspondence with the author, November 2, 2021.

22 See, for example, Stevens, ed., *Indigenous Peoples, National Parks, and Protected Areas*.

5. THE CONFEDERATED TRIBES OF GRAND RONDE

1 Jacobs, *Clackamas Chinook Texts*, 58–64, 75–80.

2 Unless otherwise noted, all quotations in this chapter are taken from the recording of a conversation I held with Cristina Lara, Lisa Leno, and Bobby Mercier at the Chachalu Museum and Cultural Center in Grand Ronde, Oregon, on May 11, 2016.

3 While longtime Indian educator Emmett Oliver was central to the Paddle to Seattle, many other people, including David Forlines and Terri Tavenner, were key organizers as well. See Johansen, "Canoe Journeys and Cultural Revival"; and Neel, *Great Canoes*, 3.

4 Neel, *Great Canoes*, 1–12.

5 The history of the formation of reservations in western Oregon is subject to multiple interpretations. For interpretations by Grand Ronde and Siletz scholars, see Lewis and Kentta, "Western Oregon Reservations."

6 The complex treaty and reservation-formation process in the region resulted in Chinookan peoples being enrolled at many modern-day reservations in addition to Grand Ronde as well as being left federally unrecognized. For history of the Lower Columbia and Portland Basin Chinookans, see Boyd, Ames, and Johnson, eds., *Chinookan Peoples of the Lower Columbia*.

7 Lewis, Thorsgard, and Williams, "Honoring Our *tilixam*."

8 Since 2011, Tony Johnson has worked for the Shoalwater Bay Indian Tribe as education director and in 2015 was elected chair of the Chinook Nation, a position once held by his father. The Chinook Nation consists of the westernmost Chinookan peoples, the Lower Chinook, and the Clatsop, Willapa, Wahkiakum, and Kathlamet. The Chinook Nation, whose members assisted Lewis and Clark in the winter of 1805–6, is conducting an ongoing effort to win federal recognition, approved in 2001 under the Clinton administration but rescinded in 2002 after George W. Bush took office. For a discussion of this effort, see Fisher and Jette, "Now You See Them, Now You Don't," and Daehnke, *Chinook Resilience*.

9 The Confederated Tribes of the Grand Ronde offer classes across the lifespan, from preschool to adult. See Zenk, "Bringing 'Good Jargon' to Light."

10 "James Scarborough Occupies Chinook Point on the Columbia River," www.historylink.org/File/7834 (August 15, 2016).

11 In 2009 the Grand Ronde Canoe Family formed a nonprofit, the Canoe Family Cultural Preservation Club, to be able to raise funds autonomously. In recent years the Grand Ronde Tribe financially supports the Canoe Journey through the Tribal Youth Prevention program.

12 Other tribes in Oregon have embraced the Canoe Journey movement, for both youth and adults. The Umatilla Tribe served as a host community in 2000. The Coquille Indian Tribe, the Confederated Tribes of the Coos, Lower Umpqua, and Siuslaw Indians, and the Confederated Tribes of Warm Springs each have canoes of their own. Since 2003, the Coquille Tribe sponsors annual intertribal canoe races at its annual Mill-Luck Salmon Celebration and Canoe Races on Coos Bay. For further discussion of how Northwest tribes have engaged with Canoe Journey, see Donovan et al., "Healing of the Canoe"; and Hawkins and La Marr, "Pulling for Native Communities."

13 Hawkins and La Marr, "Pulling for Native Communities," 239.

14 Neel, *Great Canoes*, 2, 68.

15 The Suquamish Tribe has also hosted Māori paddlers, beginning in 2010, stemming from exchanges that began with *Toi Māori: The Eternal Thread* during the exhibition's showing at the Burke Museum of Natural History and Culture at the University of Washington in Seattle in 2006.

16 For more about the resurgence of Māori arts and culture, particularly as related to museum practice, see McCarthy, *Museums and Māori*. The website for Toi Māori Aotearoa (Māori Arts New Zealand), www.maoriart.org.nz/, is a frequently changing source of information about contemporary Māori arts and practice.

17 Delores Parmenter as quoted in Alaimo, "Grand Ronde Canoe Journey."

18 These wax cylinders were recorded by Melville Jacobs, the anthropologist who also recorded Victoria Howard's Clackamas Chinook myths and stories in 1929 and 1930; see Jacobs, *Clackamas Chinook Texts*.

19 Dangeli, "Dancing Chiax, Dancing Sovereignty," 75.

20 Dangeli, "Dancing Chiax, Dancing Sovereignty," 75.

21   *The Grand Ronde's Canoe Journey* exhibition was awarded an American Association of State and Local History Award in 2012. Willamette Heritage Center has partnered with the Grand Ronde Tribe on several other exhibits since 2011. See Lewis, "Shawash Iliʔi Kənim Ikanum (Grand Ronde Canoe Story)."

22   Merrill and Hajda, "Confederated Tribes of the Grand Ronde Community of Oregon."

6. KLAMATH TRIBES

1   This account is based on my experiences at the March 26, 2016, Return of the C'waam Ceremony and informal conversations with Perry Chocktoot and Don Gentry. Additional background comes from Deur, "The Klamath Tribes"; and Maxwell, "Suckerfish and the Klamath Tribe." Information about the biology of the c'waam is drawn from the US Fish and Wildlife Service, "Lost River Sucker," www.fws.gov/oregonfwo/articles.cfm?id=1494 89443 (accessed May 16, 2016). A four-minute video about the C'waam Ceremony, made in collaboration with the University of Oregon Museum of Natural and Cultural History, is posted on the website of the Klamath Tribes, along with other videos about the Tribes' efforts to save the c'waam and other species; see https://klamathtribes.org/ (accessed March 29, 2021).

2   Juillerat, "Chiloquin Dam Removed."

3   As Deur has explained, prior to the political integration compelled by an 1864 treaty signed with the United States, the Klamath and Modoc "were closely related tribal populations, speaking very similar languages [from the Penutian language family] and together occupying the Upper Klamath basin," with Modoc territory generally to the south and Klamath to the north. The Yahooskin (Northern Paiute), whose language is from the Uto-Aztecan family group, occupied the eastern edge of these Tribes' ancestral territories and are "relative newcomers to the Klamath basin," but became incorporated into the political entity and the social fabric that has become the Klamath Tribes. Many tribal members, Perry Chocktoot among them, have ancestry in all three Klamath Tribes. See Deur, "The Klamath Tribes," 150–56.

4   Maxwell, "Suckerfish and the Klamath Tribe," 2.

5   Deur, "The Klamath Tribes," 151.

6   Deur, "The Klamath Tribes," 151.

7   Deur, "The Klamath Tribes," 151.

8   Donald C. Gentry, "Opening Statement of Chairman of the Klamath Tribes in Support of S.2379, the Klamath Basin Water Recovery and Economic Restoration Act of 2014," Subcommittee on Water and Power, Committee on Energy and Natural Resources, US Senate.

9   Haynal, "Termination and Tribal Survival."

10   Gentry, "Opening Statement of Chairman of the Klamath Tribes," n.p.

11   US Fish and Wildlife Service, "Determination of Endangered Status for the Shortnose Sucker and Lost River Sucker," Fed. Reg. 53, 27130–27134 (1988).

12   Baker, "Amid Historic Drought, a New Water War in the West."

13   Klamath Tribes, "Klamath Tribes Historic Treaty Right Water Call," June 10, 2013, http://klamathtribes.org/news/press-release/.

14   US Department of Interior, "Two New Klamath Basin Agreements Carve Out Path."

15   Wear, "Historic Dam Removal Project Takes Another Step Forward."

16   Deur, "The Klamath Tribes," 151.

17   Hereford et al., "Survival, Movement, and Health of Hatchery-Raised Juvenile."

18   In the midst of all the tensions in the Klamath Basin, one constructive effort in the region is the Tribal Youth Ecological Forestry Training Program, a collaboration between the Klamath Tribes, the US Forest Service, and the nonprofit Lomakatsi Restoration Project of Ashland, Oregon. Tribal youth receive paid training while engaged in work that seeks to reduce wildfire risk and enhance wildlife habitat on their ancestral homelands. See Feller, "Tribal Youth Reduce Fire Fuels."

19   This section is adapted from portions of Dobkins, "Life Stories for New Generations."

20   *The Old Ox Yoke* is an undated pamphlet of twenty-three pages, written by Dr. Andrew Albert Soulé as "A Preview of Books in the Making—A Hobby" and published by Soulé Printing Company (operated by Andrew R. Soulé, in Klamath Falls) at some time in the 1940s. The pamphlet is archived in the libraries of the University of Oregon, Southern Oregon University, and Oregon Health and Science University.

21   This account of David Chocktoot's life is based on the information provided by Perry Chocktoot and Gerald Skelton, the pamphlet published by Soulé, and the accessions records of the Klamath County Museums. Another way Chocktoot served as a cultural mediator was through his service as an interpreter for anthropologist Cora Du Bois between 1932 and 1934 in interviews she conducted with Northern Paiute speakers in Beatty, Oregon, for research related to her account of the 1870 Ghost Dance (Du Bois, *1870 Ghost Dance*), originally published in 1939.

22   Soulé offers a "thumb nail sketch" of David Chocktoot on pages 19–21 of *The Old Ox Yoke*, along with the photograph of Chocktoot in the elk-hide shirt. In the text Soulé refers to Chocktoot's background and role as an Indian policeman and rancher.

23   This interpretation is based on documents authored by the Soulé children found in the Klamath County Museums accessions records for objects once owned by Dr. Soulé. They were made available to me by curator Lynn Jeche in February 2008.

24   Du Bois, *1870 Ghost Dance*.

25   "Chiefs Damn Scottish Power."

7. THE CONFEDERATED TRIBES OF SILETZ INDIANS

1   The Siletz Agency was added to the National Register of Historic Places in 1976, for its significance in Oregon tribal history. Established in 1857 and closed in 1925, the agency had multiple buildings, including a school, a hospital, a blockhouse, and residences for employees; see Hartwig and Olson, "National Register of Historic Places Inventory—Nomination Form: Siletz Agency Site." Today the community center and powwow grounds are the center for the Tribe's social and cultural activities.

2   Wilkinson, *People Are Dancing Again*.

3   Buckley, "Renewal as Discourse and Discourse as Renewal in Native Northwestern California"; and Kroeber and Gifford, "World Renewal."

4   Robert Kentta wrote this and other statements quoted in this chapter in personal e-mail communications to me in 2015.

5   Alfred "Bud" Lane Jr., interview with the author, 2015.

6   Wilkinson, *People Are Dancing Again*, 89–137.

7   Wilkinson, *People Are Dancing Again*, 149–70.

8   Currently the Nee Dosh is also practiced by the Coquille Tribe and the Tolowa Dee-ni' Nation of the Smith River Rancheria in California, both of which, like Siletz, are Tribes with Athabaskan language–group heritage.

9   Wilkinson, *People Are Dancing Again*, 198–200.

10   Wilkinson, *People Are Dancing Again*, 198–200.

11   Robert Kentta, interview with the author, 2015.

12   Bud Lane interview.

13   Bud Lane interview.

14   Alissa Lane, interview with the author, 2015.

15   The Southwest Oregon Research Project (SWORP) also contributed to the cultural revitalization of the 1990s by making available a wide range of archival documents related to Oregon Tribes, including those of Siletz. Robert Kentta participated as a SWORP researcher. See chapter 3, "Potlatch as a Way of Life: The Coquille Indian Tribe," for a discussion of SWORP and its origins as a collaboration between the Coquille Tribe and the University of Oregon.

16   Rosoff, "Integrating Native Views into Museum Procedures," 38.

17   Cheryl Lane, interview with the author, 2015.

18   Cheryl Lane interview.

19   Kentta, personal communication with the author, 2015.

20 Bud Lane interview.

21 Kentta, personal communication with the author, 2015.

22 Bud Lane interview.

23 Buckley, "Renewal as Discourse," 50–51.

24 Buckley, "Renewal as Discourse," 41.

25 Bud Lane interview.

8. THE CONFEDERATED TRIBES OF THE UMATILLA INDIAN RESERVATION

1 The conversations with Toby Patrick and with those listed below were recorded at Tamástslikt Cultural Institute on January 13, January 14, and February 22, 2016. On January 13, Roberta "Bobbie" Conner and Malissa Minthorn Winks of Tamástslikt and I first had a conversation, and then I spoke with Marjorie Waheneka and John Bevis individually. Toby Patrick and I met on January 14 and were joined by Malissa toward the end of our conversation. On February 22 elders Les Minthorn, Alphonse Halfmoon, and Dr. Ronald Pond, and Ron's daughter Lona Pond gathered with us for discussion; later that day, Malissa and I met with Linda Jones and then were joined by Ramona Yeager. All quotations in this chapter are from these conversations, the recordings and transcriptions of which have been placed in the Tamástslikt Cultural Institute collection. In addition, Malissa Minthorn Winks corresponded with tribal member and linguist Phillip Cash Cash (Cayuse and Nez Perce), whom we honor in the title for this chapter. "Chasing smoke" is a reservation idiom he remembers from his younger days, when the phrase was used to tease those (including himself!) who always seemed to be searching for a sweat to join, "relying upon the goodwill of others," rather than making sweat for themselves. Cash Cash wrote about this phrase in a posting about the Nez Perce language (Cash Cash, personal communication to Malissa Minthorn Winks, 2015).

2 See Lacey, "New Age Guru Guilty in Sweat Lodge Deaths," A16.

3 Karson, ed., *As Days Go By*. The story of how the CTUIR escaped termination, in large part by organizing their own constitution in 1949 and in so doing, creating a mechanism for self-determination, offers another account of how the termination era of the 1950s was experienced in Oregon. For an overview of CTUIR history from the tribal perspective, see the website of the CTUIR, "A Brief History of CTUIR," https://ctuir.org/about/brief -history-of-ctuir/ (accessed March 29, 2021).

4 Dr. Ronald Pond, Alphonse Halfmoon, and Ramona Yeager all remember earth lodges in use during their childhoods.

5 The traditional lands of the Cayuse, Umatilla, and Walla Walla Tribes are described in linguistic, topographical, and visual detail in the richly illustrated and extensively documented Sahaptian place-names atlas published by the Tamástslikt Cultural Institute; see Hunn et al., *Čáw Pawá Láakni*.

6 As the opening creation story suggests, the sweat is a widely practiced tradition in Native America, and the details of the sweat significantly differ between tribes and regions. For instance, the Plains tribes generally sweat in larger lodges with the rock pit in the center, while from northwestern California up through the Northwest Coast Tribes have cedar-plank sweathouses; see Bruchac, *Native American Sweat Lodge*. In the twentieth and twenty-first centuries, versions of the sweat lodge have been incorporated into the Native sobriety and recovery movement, prisons, the American Indian Movement, and other intertribal settings such as boarding schools.

9. CONFEDERATED TRIBES OF WARM SPRINGS

1 Unless otherwise noted, all quotations in this chapter are taken from a recording of a conversation on August 4, 2015, at The Museum at Warm Springs, Warm Springs, Oregon, with tribal members Brigette McConville, Rosalind (Rosie)

Johnson, Rayann Katchia Satanus, and Natalie Moody. The recording is now in the collection of The Museum at Warm Springs.

2 Hunn and Selam, *Nch'i-wána, "The Big River,"* 189–93.

3 Aguilar, *When the River Ran Wild*, 173.

4 Woody, "Confederated Tribes of the Warm Springs Tribes of Oregon," 192–207.

5 Aguilar, *When the River Ran Wild*, 1–22; and Woody, "Confederated Tribes of the Warm Springs Tribes of Oregon."

6 Woody, "Confederated Tribes of the Warm Springs Tribes of Oregon," 198–200.

7 Aguilar, *When the River Ran Wild*, 144–52.

8 Pendleton Woolen Mills, based in Pendleton, Oregon, has long been a major source of blankets for tribal gift-giving. Eighth Generation, a Seattle-based company now owned by the Snoqualmie Tribe of Washington State and founded by Nooksak artist Louie Gong in 2008, is the first Native-owned company making blankets designed by Indigenous artists.

CONCLUSION

1 The name of this movement, Indigenous Futurisms, was coined by Anishinaabe scholar Grace Dillon in her edited volume, *Walking the Clouds*. Dillon gave a name to creative impulses that have long been associated with Indigenous worldviews, including in precontact times; in recent decades many scholars and artists associate the work of Gerald Vizenor and his notion of survivance—the creative ways Indigenous peoples have survived in the face of change and destruction—with the contemporary fluorescence of Indigenous futurist art and thought. See Vizenor, *Manifest Manners*. A 2020 exhibition organized by the Institute of American Indian Arts Museum of Contemporary Native Arts, *Indigenous Futurisms*, offers a vital assessment of this arena.

2 NoiseCat, "How to Survive an Apocalypse and Keep Dreaming." Many other Indigenous authors have asserted this insight well before the Covid-19 pandemic. See Baldy, "Why I Teach *The Walking Dead* in My Native Studies Classes"; and Nick Estes as interviewed by Nick Serpe, "Indigenous Resistance Is Post-Apocalyptic with Nick Estes."

3 NoiseCat, "How to Survive an Apocalypse and Keep Dreaming."

4 Scholarship by twenty-first-century Indigenous authors has been deeply influential to my own thinking and underpins many of the interpretations I offer in this conclusion and throughout the book. In particular, the work of Michelle Jacob (Yakama) and Cutcha Risling Baldy (Hupa), both of whom seek to understand the intersections of cultural revitalization and Indigenous feminisms, has been vital. See Jacob, *Yakama Rising*; and Baldy, *We Are Dancing for You*.

5 Jacob uses this phrase in *Yakama Rising*, 11, as does Baldy in *We Are Dancing for You*, 7.

6 Jacob, *Yakama Rising*, 11–12.

7 Baldy, *We Are Dancing for You*, 17.

8 Baldy, *We Are Dancing for You*, 132.

9 Jacobs, *Yakama Rising*, 5.

10 For an exploration of the meaning of Tamán-wit and contemporary examples of its expression, see Whittle, "Reciprocity of Tradition."

11 Jacobs, *Yakama Rising*, 16.

12 For an assessment of the first three decades of NAGPRA, its limits and possible futures, see Nash and Colwell, "NAGPRA at 30."

13 For a description of the NAGPRA experience at Willamette as well as an assessment of the first decade of the law, see Nafziger and Dobkins, "Native American Graves Protection and Repatriation Act in Its First Decade."

14 Burke Museum, "The Ancient One, Kennewick Man," February 20, 2017, www.burkemuseum.org/news/ancient-one-kennewick-man.

15 For more information, see "Toi Māori Aotearoa (Māori Arts New Zealand)," www.maoriart.org.nz/about-toi-maori.html (accessed June 21, 2021). Two of these gatherings (in 2001 and 2017) have been held at the Longhouse at The Evergreen State College in Olympia, Washington. See Longhouse

Education and Cultural Center, *Tears of Duk'Wi-bahL: International Gathering of Indigenous Visual Artists of the Pacific Rim* (Olympia, WA: House of Welcome Publishing, 2017).

16 My colleague heather ahtone (Choctaw Nation/Chickasaw) has articulated an Indigenous-centered curatorial methodology, which she puts into practice at the First Americans Museum in Oklahoma City. In the keynote for a 2021 symposium called "We Have Words For Art: Writing about Art by Indigenous Peoples of the Americas," ahtone described the 4 Rs of Indigenous methodologies: respect, reciprocity, relationships, and responsibility. She uses the term *kincentricity* to describe her approach to developing ongoing relationships between curators, communities, and objects. See ahtone, "Shifting the Paradigm: A Love Story," February 27, 2021, www.youtube.com/watch?v=LdhbQVvkq2k&t=1274s.

17 Baldy, "Why We Gather."

18 Results of this research can be found in Dobkins et al., *Cultural Plant Harvests on Federal Lands;* and Dobkins et al., "Tribes of the Oregon Country."

19 See Goodman, "Protecting Habitat for Off-Reservation Tribal Hunting and Fishing Rights."

20 Goodman, "Protecting Habitat for Off-Reservation Tribal Hunting and Fishing Rights," 281–82.

21 Teresa G. Jacobs and Santi Alston, in an unpublished 2011 paper titled "Legal Consider-ations for Climate Change Impacts on Tribes' Off-Reservation Resources" prepared in association with the University of Oregon's Tribal Climate Change Project, discuss legal avenues for the prevention of what the authors refer to as the possibility of "ecological removal." See https://cpb-us-e1.wpmucdn.com/blogs.uoregon.edu/dist/c/389/files/2010/11/Legal_briefing_Tribal_CC_April_2011.pdf (accessed June 21, 2021).

22 For an account and analysis of how the coalition was built and the legislation passed, see Sabzalian, Morrill, and Edmo, "Deep Organizing and Indigenous Studies Legislation in Oregon." The Oregon legislation followed similar mandates in Montana (Indian Education for All, passed 1999, funded 2005) and Washington (Since Time Immemorial: Tribal Sovereignty in Washington State, passed 2005, mandated 2015). See Sabzalian, Morrill, and Edmo, "Deep Organizing and Indigenous Studies Legislation in Oregon," 52. Also see Jacob et al., "Gift of Education." An appendix in the latter article refers to additional state initiatives in South Dakota, North Dakota, and Wyoming.

23 US Department of Interior, "Secretary Haaland Announces Federal Indian Boarding School Initiative," June 22, 2021, www.doi.gov/pressreleases/secretary-haaland-announces-federal-indian-boarding-school-initiative.

Aguilar, George. *When the River Ran Wild! Indian Traditions on the Mid-Columbia and the Warm Springs Reservation.* Portland: Oregon Historical Society Press; Seattle: University of Washington Press, 2005.

ahtone, heather. "Shifting the Paradigm: A Love Story." February 27, 2021. www.youtube.com/watch?v=LdhbQVvkq2k&t=1274s.

Alaimo, Michelle. "Grand Ronde Canoe Journey." *Smoke Signals.* August 15, 2011. http://oregonnews.uoregon.edu/lccn/sn93050714/2011–08–15/ed-1/seq-8/.

Allen, Cain. "Malheur Indian Reservation." *Oregon History Project*, 2013. https://oregonhistoryproject.org/articles/historical-records/malheur-indian-reservation/#.XbIjUEF7k2w. Accessed October 24, 2019.

Anderson, Kat. *Tending the Wild: Native American Knowledge and the Management of California's Natural Resources.* Berkeley: University of California Press, 2005.

Appadurai, Arjun, ed. *The Social Life of Things: Commodities in Cultural Perspective.* Cambridge, UK: University of Cambridge Press, 1986.

Baker, Mike. "Amid Historic Drought, a New Water War in the West," *New York Times.* June 1, 2021 (updated June 8, 2021). www.nytimes.com/2021/06/01/us/klamath-oregon-water-drought-bundy.html.

Baldy, Cutcha Risling. *We Are Dancing for You: Native Feminisms and the Revitalization of Women's Coming-of-Age Ceremonies.* Seattle: University of Washington Press, 2018.

———. "Why I Teach *The Walking Dead* in My Native Studies Classes." *Nerds of Color.* April 24, 2014. https://thenerdsofcolor.org/2014/04/24/why-i-teach-the-walking-dead-in-my-native-studies-classes/.

———. "Why We Gather: Traditional Gathering in Native Northwest California and the Future of Bio-Cultural Sovereignty." *Ecological Processes* 2, no. 17 (2013). https://doi.org/10.1186/2192–709–2-17.

Beck, David R. M. *Seeking Recognition: The Termination and Restoration of the Coos, Lower Umpqua, and Siuslaw Indians, 1855–1984.* Lincoln: University of Nebraska Press, 2009.

Beckham, Stephen Dow. "History of Western Oregon since 1846." In *Handbook of North American Indians, Volume 7, Northwest Coast,* edited by Wayne Suttles, 180–88. Washington, DC: Smithsonian Institution Press, 1990.

———, ed. *Oregon Indians: Voices from Two Centuries.* Corvallis: Oregon State University Press, 2006.

Berg, Laura, ed. *The First Oregonians,* 2nd ed. Portland: Oregon Council for the Humanities, 2007.

Boas, Franz. "The Social Organization and the Secret Societies of the Kwakiutl Indians." *Report of the United States National Museum for the Year Ending June 30, 1895,* 309–736. Washington, DC: Government Printing Office, 1897.

Boyd, Robert T., Kenneth M. Ames, and Tony A. Johnson, eds. *Chinookan Peoples of the Lower Columbia.* Seattle: University of Washington Press, 2013.

Briggs, Kara. "Tribes Weave the Past into a Stronger Future." *Oregonian* (December 12, 1999).

Brown, David E., Greg Beatty, J. Elaine Brown, and Andrew Smith. "History Status and Population Trends of the Cottontail Rabbits and Jack Rabbits in the Western United States." *Western Wildlife* 5 (2018): 16–42.

Bruchac, Joseph. *The Native American Sweat Lodge: History and Legends.* Freedom, California: Crossing Press, 1993.

Bruner, Edward M. "Experience and Its Expressions." In *The Anthropology of Experience,* edited by Victor W. Turner and Edward M. Bruner, 3–30. Champaign: University of Illinois Press, 1986.

Buckley, Thomas. "Renewal as Discourse and Discourse as Renewal in Native Northwestern California." In *Native Religions and Cultures of North America: Anthropology of the Sacred,* edited by Lawrence E. Sullivan, 33–52. New York: Continuum, 2000.

Burke Museum. "The Ancient One, Kennewick Man." February 20, 2017. www.burkemuseum.org/news/ancient-one-kennewick-man.

Carroll, Alex K., M. Nieves Zedeño, and Richard W. Stoffle. "Landscapes of the Ghost Dance: A Cartography of Numic Ritual." *Journal of Archaeological Method and Theory* 11, no. 2 (2004): 127–56.

"Chiefs Damn Scottish Power." *London Telegraph.* June 20, 2004. www.telegraph.co.uk/finance/2888344/Chiefs-damn-Scottish-Power.html.

Cowie, Sarah E., Diane L. Teeman, and Christopher C. LeBlanc, eds. *Collaborative Archaeology at Stewart Indian School.* Reno: University of Nevada Press, 2019.

Daehnke, Jon Darin. *Chinook Resilience : Heritage and Cultural Revitalization on the Lower Columbia River.* Seattle: University of Washington Press, 2017.

Dangeli, Mique'l. "Dancing Chiax, Dancing Sovereignty: Performing Protocol in Unceded Territories." *Dance Research Journal* 48, no. 1 (2016): 74–90.

———. "Dancing Our Archive: Bringing to Life B. A. Haldane's Photography." In *Native Art Now! Developments in Contemporary Native American Art Since 1992*, edited by Veronica Passalacqua and Kate Morris, 262–83. Indianapolis, Indiana: Eiteljorg Museum of American Indians and Western Art, 2017.

Deur, Douglas. *Huckleberry Mountain Traditional-Use Study: Final Report.* Seattle: National Park Service, 2002.

———. "The Klamath Tribes: Restoring Peoples, Restoring Ties to the Land." In Berg, *The First Oregonians*, 146–59.

———. "A Most Sacred Place: The Significance of Crater Lake among the Indians of Southern Oregon." *Oregon Historical Quarterly* 103, no. 1 (2002): 18–49.

Dillon, Grace, ed. *Walking the Clouds: An Anthology of Indigenous Science Fiction.* Tucson: University of Arizona, 2012.

Dobkins, Rebecca. "Life Stories for New Generations: The Living Art of Oregon Tribal Regalia." *Oregon Historical Quarterly* 110, no. 3 (2009): 420–39.

Dobkins, Rebecca, Ceara Lewis, Susan Hummel, and Emily Dickey. *Cultural Plant Harvests on Federal Lands: Perspectives from Members of the Northwest Native American Basketweavers Association.* Portland, OR: US Department of Agriculture, Forest Service, Pacific Northwest Research Station, 2016.

Dobkins, Rebecca, Susan Stevens Hummel, Ceara Lewis, Grace Pochis, and Emily Dickey. "Tribes of the Oregon Country: Cultural Plant Harvests and Indigenous Relationships with Ancestral Lands in the Twenty-First Century." *Oregon Historical Quarterly* 118, no. 4 (2017): 488–517.

Donovan, Dennis M., Lisa Rey Thomas, Robin Little Wing Sigo, Laura Price, Heather Lonczak, Nigel Lawrence, Katie Ahvakana, Lisette Austin, Albie Lawrence, Joseph Price, Abby Purser, and Lenora Bagley. "Healing of the Canoe: Preliminary Results of a Culturally Grounded Intervention to Prevent Substance Abuse and Promote Tribal Identity for Native Youth in Two Pacific Northwest Tribes." *American Indian & Alaska Native Mental Health Research: The Journal of the National Center* 22, no. 1 (2015): 42–76.

Du Bois, Cora. *The 1870 Ghost Dance.* 1939; Lincoln: University of Nebraska Press, 2007.

Feller, Alexandra. "Tribal Youth Reduce Fire Fuels." *Herald and News* (Klamath Falls, OR). June 19, 2021. www.heraldandnews.com/news/local_news/klamath-tribal youth reduce-fire-fuels/article_dd128d0c-0e55–504d-8db1–47f9a99dfc92.html.

Fisher, Andrew, and Melinda Marie Jette. "Now You See Them, Now You Don't." In Boyd, Ames, and Johnson, *Chinookan Peoples of the Lower Columbia*, 288–306.

Folwell, Jody, Terrol Dew Johnson, Anne E. Marshall, Diane F. Pardue, Tristan Reader, and Diza Sauers. *Hold Everything: Masterworks of Basketry and Pottery.* Phoenix, Arizona: Heard Museum, 2001.

Goodman, Ed. "Protecting Habitat for Off-Reservation Tribal Hunting and Fishing Rights: Tribal Comanagement as a Reserved Right." *Environmental Law* 30, no. 2 (Spring 2000): 279–361.

Gross, Joan, ed. *Teaching Oregon Native Languages*. Corvallis: Oregon State University Press, 2007.

Hansen, Terri. "Coquille Tribe Regains 3,200 Acres Forested Ancestral Homeland in Oregon." *Indian Country Today*. June 5, 2015. http://indiancountrytodaymedia network.com/2015/06/05/coquille-tribe-regains-3200-acres-forested-ancestral -homeland-oregon-160621.

Hartwig, Paul B., and Gregg Olson. "National Register of Historic Places Inventory—Nomination Form: Siletz Agency Site." August 8, 1975. http://focus.nps.gov/pdf-host/docs/NRHP/Text/76001582.pdf.

Hawkins, Elizabeth H., and C. June La Marr. "Pulling for Native Communities: Alan Marlatt and the Journeys of the Circle." *Addiction Research and Theory* 20, no. 3 (2012): 236–42.

Haynal, Patrick. "Termination and Tribal Survival: The Klamath Tribes of Oregon." *Oregon Historical Quarterly* 101, no. 3 (2000): 270–301.

Hereford, D. M., S. M. Burdick, D. G. Elliott, Amari Dolan-Caret, C. M. Conway, and A. C. Harris. "Survival, Movement, and Health of Hatchery-Raised Juvenile Lost River Suckers within a Mesocosm in Upper Klamath Lake." US Geological Survey Open-File Report 2016–1012. https://doi.org/10.3133/ofr20161012. Accessed August 16, 2016.

Hunn, Eugene S., and James Selam. *Nch'i-wána, "The Big River": Mid-Columbia Indians and Their Land*. Seattle: University of Washington Press, 1990.

Hunn, Eugene S., Thomas Morning Owl, Philip E. Cash Cash, and Jennifer Karson Engum. *Caw Pawa Laakni: They Are Not Forgotten: Sahaptian Place Names Atlas of the Cayuse, Umatilla and Walla Walla*. Pendleton, OR: Tamástslikt Cultural Institute, 2015.

Institute of American Indian Arts Museum of Contemporary Native Arts. *Indigenous Futurisms: Transcending Past/Present/Future*. Santa Fe, NM: Institute of American Indian Arts, 2020.

Ivy, Donald B., and Robert S. Byram, eds. *Changing Landscapes: Sustaining Traditions: Proceedings of the 5th and 6th Annual Coquille Cultural Preservation Conferences*. North Bend, OR: Coquille Tribe of Oregon, 2002.

Jacob, Michelle M. *Yakama Rising: Indigenous Cultural Revitalization, Activism, and Healing*. Tucson: University of Arizona Press, 2013.

Jacob, Michelle M., Leilani Sabzalian, Joana Jansen, Tary J. Tobin, Claudia G. Vincent, and Kelly LaChance. "The Gift of Education: How Indigenous Knowledges Can Transform the Future of Public Education." *International Journal of Multicultural Education* 20, no. 1 (2018): 157–85.

Jacobs, Melville. *Clackamas Chinook Texts*. Bloomington: Indiana University Press, 1958–59.

Johansen, Bruce E. "Canoe Journeys and Cultural Revival." *American Indian Culture and Research Journal* 36, no. 2 (2012): 131–41.

Juillerat, Lee. "Chiloquin Dam Removed." *Herald and News* (Klamath Falls, OR). August 30, 2008.

Karson, Jennifer, ed. *As Days Go By: Our History, Our Land, and Our People. The Cayuse, Umatilla and Walla Walla*. Pendleton, OR: Tamástslikt Cultural Institute, 2006.

Kelly, Isabel T. "Ethnography of the Surprise Valley Paiute." *University of California Publications in American Archaeology and Ethnology* 31, no. 3 (1932): 67–210.

Krmpotich, Cara Ann, and Laura L. Peers, eds. *This Is Our Life: Haida Material Heritage and Changing Museum Practice*. Vancouver, BC: University of British Columbia Press, 2013.

Kroeber, A. L., and Edward Winslow Gifford. *World Renewal: A Cult System of Native Northwest California*. Anthropological Records, vol. 13, no. 1. Berkeley: University of California Press, 1949.

Lacey, Marc. "New Age Guru Guilty in Sweat Lodge Deaths." *New York Times*. June 22, 2011, A16.

Lewis, David. "Shawash Iliʔi Kənim Ikanum (Grand Ronde Canoe Story)." *Oregon Historical Quarterly* 112, no. 3 (2011): 376–79.

Lewis, David, Eirik Thorsgard, and Chuck Williams. "Honoring Our *tilixam*: Chinookan People of Grand Ronde." In Boyd, Ames, and Johnson, *Chinookan Peoples of the Lower Columbia*, 307–25.

Lewis, David G., and Robert Kentta. "Western Oregon Reservations: Two Perspectives on Place." *Oregon Historical Quarterly* 111, no. 4 (2010): 476–85.

Losey, Robert, ed. *Changing Landscapes: Proceedings of the Third Annual Coquille Cultural Preservation Conference*. North Bend, OR: Coquille Tribe of Oregon, 1999.

Mauss, Marcel. *The Gift: Forms and Functions of Exchange in Archaic Societies*. London: Cohen and West, 1969.

Maxwell, Meta L. "Suckerfish and the Klamath Tribe." *Indian Country Today Media Network*, February 14, 2011. http://indiancountrytodaymedianetwork.com/2011/02/14/suckerfish-and-klamath-tribe-16763.

McCarthy, Conal. *Museums and Māori : Heritage Professionals, Indigenous Collections, Current Practice*. Wellington, New Zealand: Te Papa, 2011.

Merrill, Brent, and Yvonne Hajda. "The Confederated Tribes of the Grand Ronde Community of Oregon." In Berg, *First Oregonians*, 121–45.

Miller, Jay. "Basin Religion and Theology: A Comparative Study of Power (*Puha*)." *Journal of California and Great Basin Anthropology* 5, no. 1 (1983): 66–86.

Miller, Robert, and Reg Pullen with the Bandon Historical Society. *Bandon*. Charleston, SC: Arcadia Publishing, 2013.

Nafziger, James A. R., and Rebecca J. Dobkins. "The Native American Graves Protection and Repatriation Act in Its First Decade." *International Journal of Cultural Property* 8, no. 1 (1999): 77–107.

Nash, Stephen E., and Chip Colwell. "NAGPRA at 30: The Effects of Repatriation." *Annual Review of Anthropology* 49 (January 2020): 225–39.

Neel, David. *The Great Canoes: Reviving a Northwest Coast Tradition*. Seattle: University of Washington Press, 1995.

NoiseCat, Julian Brave. "How to Survive an Apocalypse and Keep Dreaming." *The Nation.* June 2, 2020. www.thenation.com/article/society/native-american-postapocalypse/.

Olson, Sue Perry. "Artist Statement." *The Art of Ceremony: Regalia of Native Oregon.* Exhibition catalog. Salem, OR: Hallie Ford Museum of Art, 2008.

Oregon Blue Book. Oregon Secretary of State. https://sos.oregon.gov/blue-book/Pages/default.aspx. Accessed November 23, 2021.

Parker, Patricia L., and Thomas F. King. "Guidelines for Documenting and Evaluating Traditional Cultural Properties." National Park Service. *National Register Bulletin* 38 (1992). www.nps.gov/subjects/nationalregister/upload/NRB38-Completeweb.pdf.

Phillips, Patricia Whereat. *Ethnobotany of the Coos, Lower Umpqua, and Siuslaw Indians.* Corvallis: Oregon State University Press, 2016.

"Rena Adams Beers, 1918–2018." *Burns (OR) Times-Herald.* January 31, 2018. https://btimesherald.com/2018/01/31/rena-adams-beers-1918–2018/.

Rosoff, Nancy. "Integrating Native Views into Museum Procedures: Hope and Practice at the National Museum of the American Indian." *Museum Anthropology* 22, no. 1 (1998): 33–42.

Sabzalian, Leilani, Angie Morrill, and Se-Ah-Dom Edmo. "Deep Organizing and Indigenous Studies Legislation in Oregon." *Journal of American Indian Education* 58, no. 3 (2019): 34–57.

Serpe, Nick. "Indigenous Resistance Is Post-Apocalyptic with Nick Estes." *Dissent Magazine.* July 31, 2019. www.dissentmagazine.org/online_articles/booked-indigenous-resistance-is-post-apocalyptic-with-nick-estes.

Smith, Landis, Cynthia Chavez Lamar, and Brian Vallo. *Guidelines for Collaboration.* Santa Fe, NM: School for Advanced Research, 2019. https://guidelinesforcollaboration.info/.

Smith, Linda Tuhiwai. *Decolonizing Methodologies: Research and Indigenous Peoples.* London: Zed; Dunedin, New Zealand: University of Otago, 1999.

Soucie, Minerva T. "Burns Paiute Tribe." In *The Art of Ceremony: Regalia of Native Oregon.* Exhibition catalog. Salem, OR: Hallie Ford Museum of Art, 2008.

Soulé, Andrew Albert. *The Old Ox Yoke.* Klamath Falls, OR: Soulé Printing Company, ca. 1940s.

Stevens, Stan, ed. *Indigenous Peoples, National Parks, and Protected Areas: A New Paradigm Linking Conversation, Culture, and Rights.* Tucson: University of Arizona Press, 2014.

Strathman, Nicole Dawn. *Through a Native Lens: American Indian Photography.* Norman: University of Oklahoma Press, 2020.

Strong, Pauline Turner. *American Indians and the American Imaginary: Cultural Representation across the Centuries.* Boulder, CO: Paradigm Publishers, 2013.

Tamástslikt Cultural Institute. *Čáw Pawá Láakni; They Are Not Forgotten.* Pendleton, OR: Tamástslikt Cultural Institute, 2015.

Teeman, Diane L. "Cultural Resource Management and the Protection of Valued Tribal Spaces: A View from the Western United States." In *Handbook of Landscape*

Archaeology, edited by David Bruno and Julian Thomas. Walnut Creek, CA: Left Coast Press, 2008.

———. "Issues in Great Basin Historic Preservation: One Practitioner's Considerations." Great Basin Anthropological Conference, October 5–8, 2016, Reno, Nevada. Unpublished paper.

Thornes, Tim. "Wadadɨka'a (Burns Paiute Reservation, Oregon)." *International Journal of American Linguistics* 86 (April 2, 2020): S51–89. doi:10.1086/707227.

Thornes, Tim, and Maziar Toosarvandani. "Northern Paiute Texts: Introduction." *International Journal of American Linguistics* 86 (April 2, 2020): S1–11. doi:10.1086/707224.

Tsinhnahjinnie, Hulleah, and Veronica Passalacqua, *Our People, Our Land, Our Images: International Indigenous Photographers.* C. N. Gorman Museum, University of California, Davis. Berkeley, CA: Heyday Books, 2006.

US Department of Interior. "Two New Klamath Basin Agreements Carve Out Path for Dam Removal and Provide Key Benefits to Irrigators." April 6, 2016. www.doi.gov/pressreleases/two-new-klamath-basin-agreements-carve-out-path-dam-removal-and-provide-key-benefits.

Varese, Stefano, and A. Chirif. *Witness to Sovereignty: Essays on the Indian Movement in Latin America.* Copenhagen: International Work Group for Indigenous Affairs, 2006.

Vizenor, Gerald. *Manifest Manners: Narratives on Postindian Survivance.* Lincoln: University of Nebraska, 1999.

———, ed. *Survivance : Narratives of Native Presence.* Lincoln: University of Nebraska Press, 2008.

Walker, Peter. *Sagebrush Collaboration: How Harney County Defeated the Takeover of the Malheur Wildlife Refuge.* Corvallis: Oregon State University Press, 2018.

Wear, Kimberly. "Historic Dam Removal Project Takes Another Step Forward." *North Coast Journal.* June 17, 2021. www.northcoastjournal.com/NewsBlog/archives/2021/06/17/historic-klamath-dam-removal-project-takes-another-step-forward.

Wells, Gail. "Native American Forestry Combines Traditional Wisdom with Modern Science." *Solutions: For a Sustainable & Desirable Future* 2, no. 6 (2011): 107–14.

Whittle, Joel. "Reciprocity of Tradition." *Oregon Humanities.* April 27, 2020. www.oregonhumanities.org/rll/magazine/union-spring-2020/reciprocity-of-tradition/.

Wilkinson, Charles. *The People Are Dancing Again: The History of the Siletz Tribe of Western Oregon.* Seattle: University of Washington Press, 2010.

Wilner, Isaiah Lorado. "A Global Potlach: Identifying the Indigenous Influence on Western Thought." *American Indian Culture and Research Journal* 37, no. 2 (2013): 87–114.

Woody, Elizabeth. "The Confederated Tribes of the Warm Springs Tribes of Oregon: The Relationship between Peoples, Good Government, and Sovereignty." In Berg, *First Oregonians*, 192–207.

Younker, Jason. "The Southwest Oregon Research Project: Strengthening Coquille Sovereignty with Archival Research and Gift Giving." *American Indian Culture and Research Journal* 29, no. 2 (2005): 1–14.

Younker, Jason, Mark Tveskov, and David Lewis, eds. *Changing Landscapes: Telling Our Stories: Proceedings of the Fourth Annual Coquille Cultural Preservation Conference.* North Bend, OR: Coquille Tribe, 2001.

Zenk, Henry. "Bringing 'Good Jargon' to Light: The New Chinuk Wawa Dictionary of the Confederated Tribes of Grand Ronde, Oregon." *Oregon Historical Quarterly* 113, no. 4 (2012): 561–69.

INDEX

Page numbers in *italic* refer to illustrations.

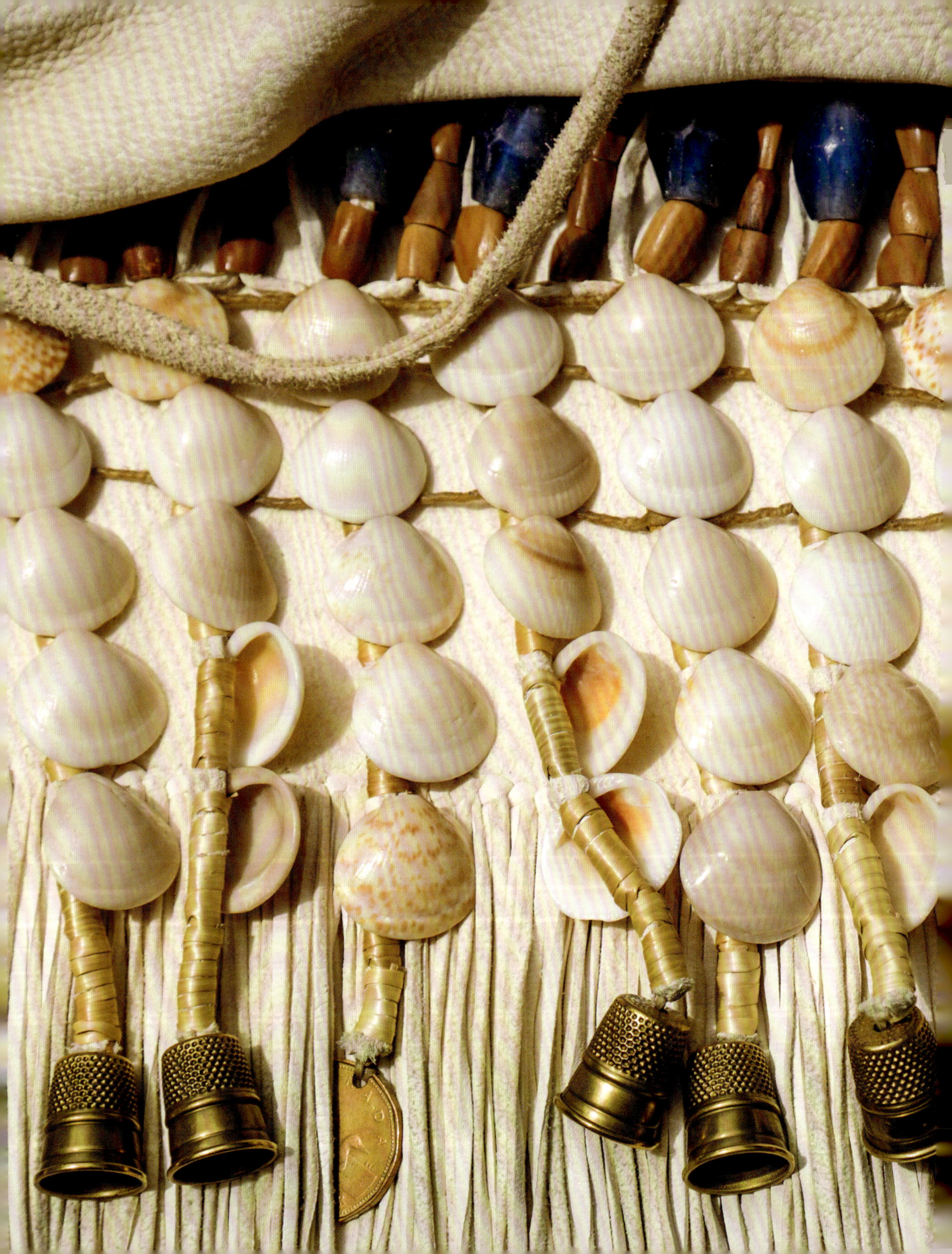

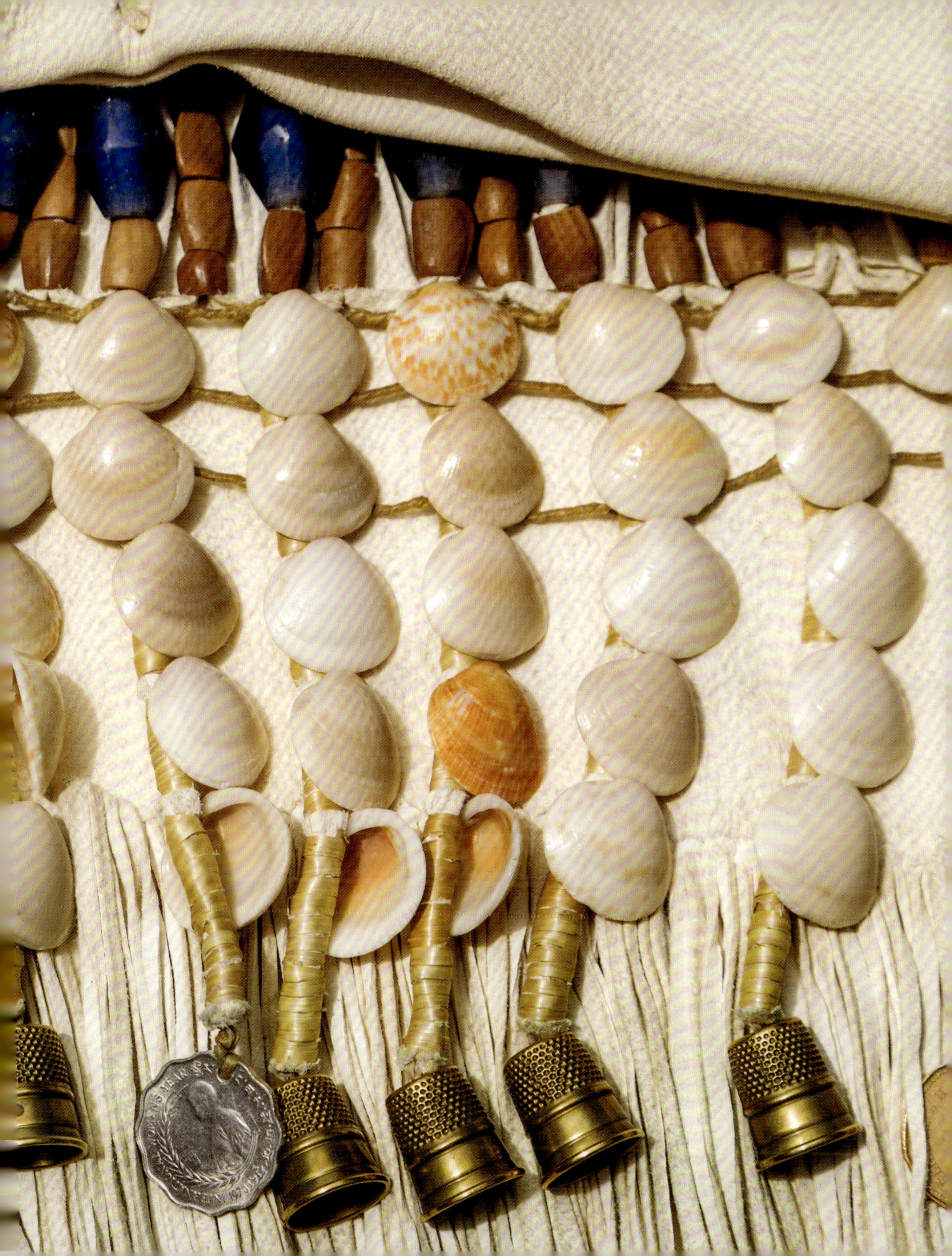

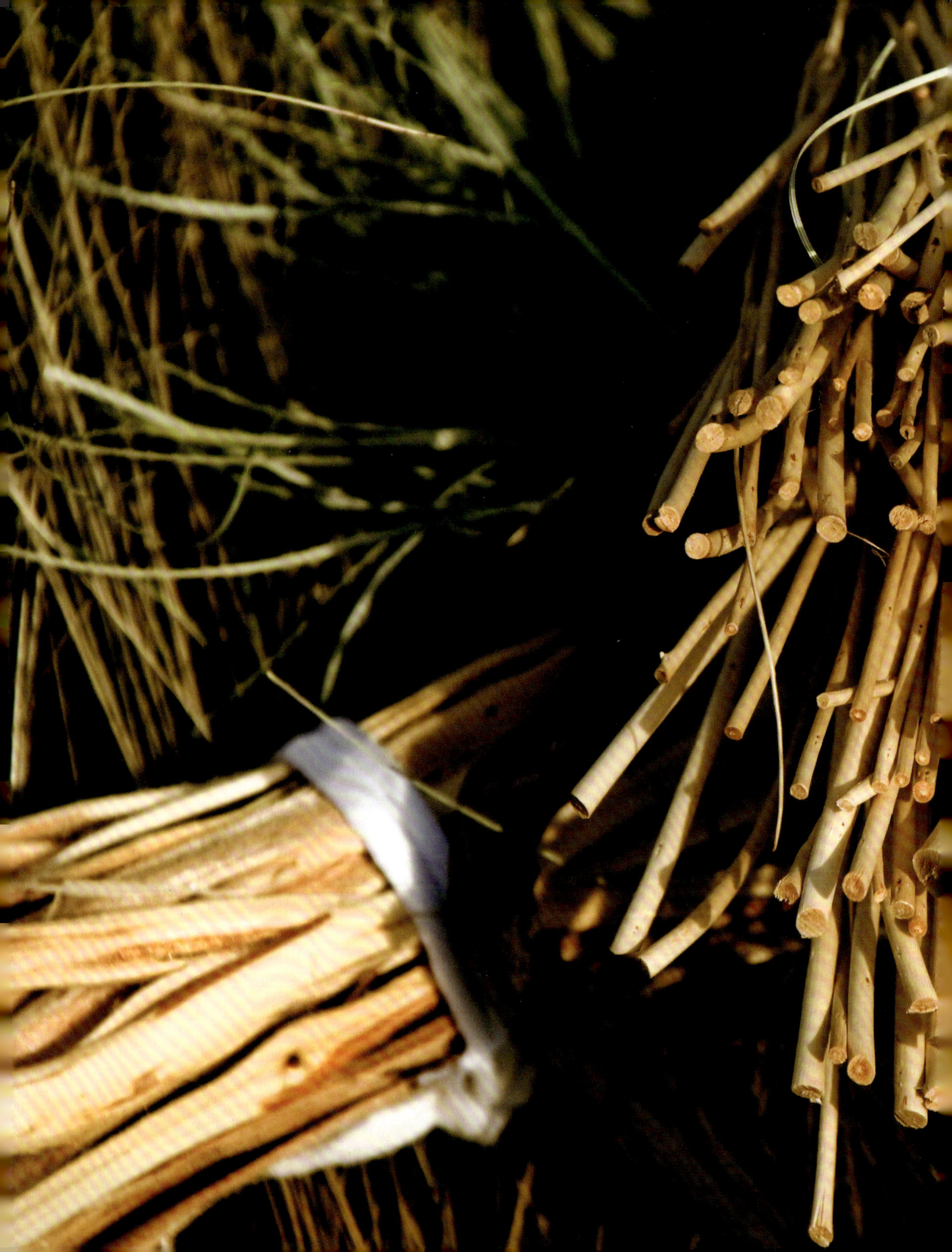

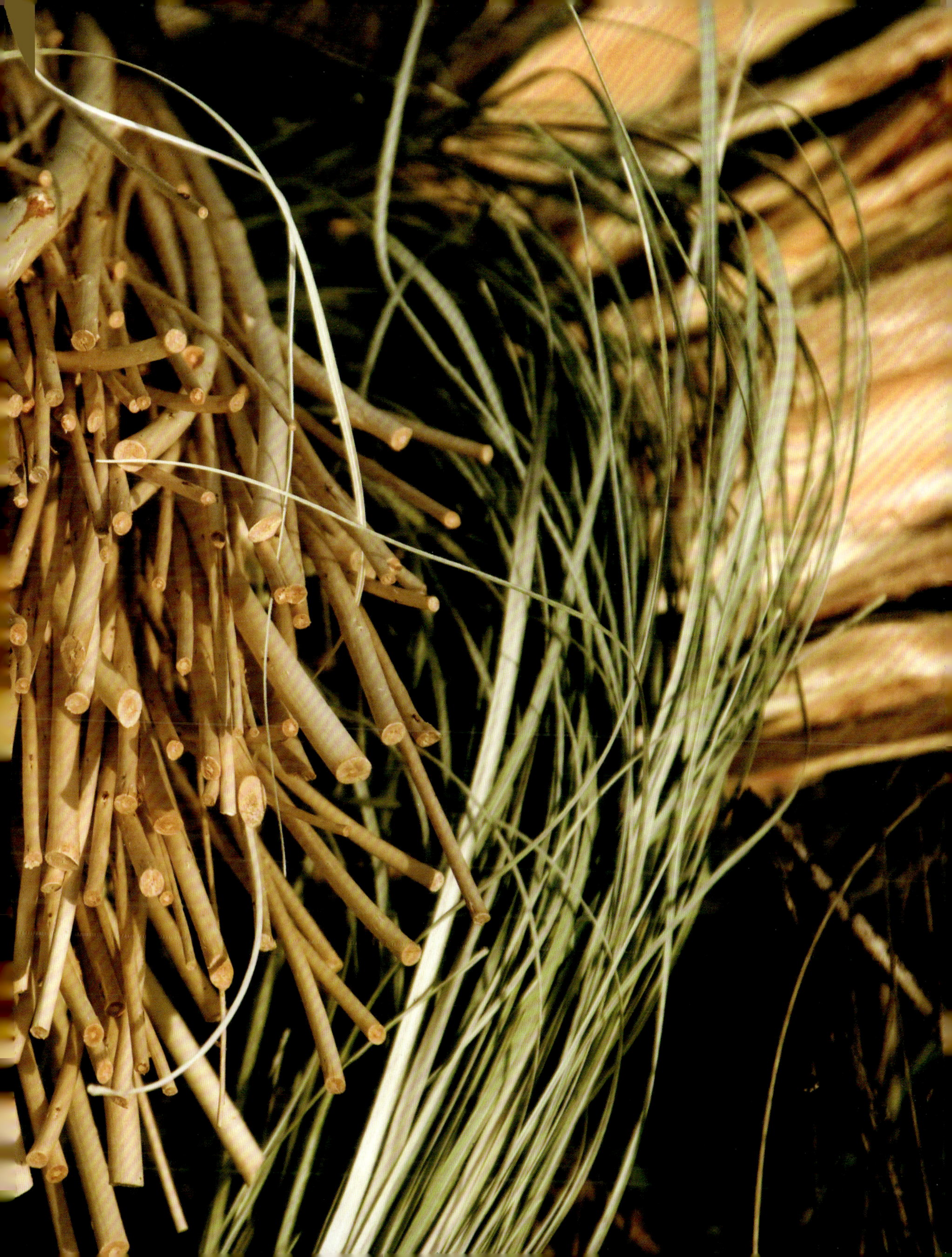